scotland

TRAVELER

scotland

by Robin & Jenny McKelvie

National Geographic
Washington, D.C.

CONTENTS

Pages 2–3: Eilean Donan Castle, Loch Duich
Left: Edinburgh–city of culture and a dash of tartan

TRAVELING WITH EYES OPEN

Alert travelers go with a purpose and leave with a benefit. If you travel responsibly, you can help support wildlife conservation, historic preservation, and cultural enrichment in the places you visit. You can enrich your own travel experience as well.

To be a geo-savvy traveler:

- Recognize that your presence has an impact on the places you visit.

- Spend your time and money in ways that sustain local character. (Besides, it's more interesting that way.)

- Value the destination's natural and cultural heritage.

- Respect the local customs and traditions.

- Express appreciation to local people about things you find interesting and unique to the place: its nature and scenery, music and food, historic villages and buildings.

- Vote with your wallet: Support the people who support the place, patronizing businesses that make an effort to celebrate and protect what's special there. Seek out shops, local restaurants, inns, and tour operators who love their home—who love taking care of it and showing it off. Avoid businesses that detract from the character of the place.

- Enrich yourself, taking home memories and stories to tell, knowing that you have contributed to the preservation and enhancement of the destination.

That is the type of travel now called geotourism, defined as "tourism that sustains or enhances the geographical character of a place—its environment, culture, aesthetics, heritage, and the well-being of its residents." To learn more, visit National Geographic's Center for Sustainable Destinations at *www.nationalgeographic.com/travel/sustainable.*

scotland

ABOUT THE AUTHORS

Robin McKelvie (*www.robinmckelvie.com*) is a native Scot with a master's degree in English literature and a passion for traveling that has taken him to more than 80 countries. In over a decade as a professional travel writer, Robin has written more than 30 travel books, had articles and photographs published in more than 50 magazines and newspapers across five continents, and also worked in radio and TV. His travel adventures have included taking the train from Edinburgh to Hong Kong, swimming with sharks in Belize, and canoeing with crocodiles in Australia. An active member of the British Guild of Travel Writers, Robin makes more than 30 trips a year, at least half of them around his favorite country in the world, which, with his hand on his proud heart, he can honestly say is Scotland.

Jenny McKelvie (*www.jennymckelvie.com*) is an adopted Scot who has been a travel writer and photographer for over a decade, visiting more than 50 countries on the way and living in three of them—Scotland, England, and Australia. Jenny has co-authored more than 20 travel guidebooks with her husband, Robin, and written travel articles for more than 20 magazines and newspapers in the United Kingdom. She also writes travel intelligence reports on global trends and weaves being a full-time mother into her busy travel schedule. Jenny's number one country remains, of course, the country she married into: Scotland.

Charting Your Trip

One of the world's most spectacular countries is blessed with thousands of rugged hills and mountains, hundreds of Atlantic islands, and myriad lochs and rivers, all brimming with bountiful wildlife. Dramatically interwoven into the natural drama are rich layers of history and culture in a country that overflows with world-class cities, ancient castles, and historic towns and villages.

How to Get Around

Getting around Scotland is all part of the fun, but journey times should not be underestimated. This is a nation, after all, with a heavily indented coastline almost three times as long as those of both France and Spain. Take Glasgow to Campbeltown—it takes just over 20 minutes to fly between them but well over three hours to drive by car! Car is, though, by far the best way to get around, as it offers the chance to really see the scenery unfold and stop off wherever you like. Visiting Scotland is as much about discovering little back lanes and hidden spots as it is seeing its famous cities. But you will still need a hand from the ferries *(tel 0800/066 5000, www.calmac.co.uk)* to get your car to the islands. Scotland's rail routes *(tel 0845/601 5929, www.scotrail.co.uk)*, meanwhile, are among the most spectacular on the planet, though they are seldom quicker than traveling by road, so are best enjoyed as an experience in themselves. The more remote Scottish islands, such as the Outer Hebrides or the Shetland Islands, are most easily reached by air *(tel 01392/268 529, www.flybe.co.uk)*. Flying can also be an efficient way of reaching more distant parts of the mainland if you're short on time.

A Week-Long Visit

If this is your first visit to Scotland, you will want to start in its picturesque, historic capital, Edinburgh, and then make a foray into the scenic Highlands, before returning to the central region and its largest city, Glasgow, another historic and deeply cultural hub. All direct flights from North America land into one or other of these two cities, which also have great air links to London and elsewhere in Europe.

Starting out in Edinburgh on **Day 1,** make sure to visit Edinburgh Castle and enjoy a long lazy stroll down the Royal Mile, through the centuries, to the Palace of Holyroodhouse. Don't miss the city's string of national galleries and, in the evening, its lively pubs.

Using Edinburgh as the base for **Day 2,** drive half an hour south out of town to Rosslin and its fascinating

Encounters with Highland cattle are always possible.

Rosslyn Chapel, thought by some to be the home of the holy grail. Enjoy lunch by the water's edge in the relaxed and picturesque suburb of South Queensferry before visiting its grand Hopetoun House. In the afternoon drive a further 7 miles (11 km) west to Linlithgow Palace to swirl in the ghosts of Scotland's most romanticized monarch, Mary Queen of Scots. Return to the UNESCO World Heritage charms of Edinburgh and either take an eerie ghost tour on the Royal Mile or dip into its rich performing arts scene.

Day 3 starts with a two-hour drive north to Perth, passing over the dramatic Forth Road Bridge shortly after leaving Edinburgh. A stroll around the graceful town of Perth is followed by lunch before a short drive north to Scone Palace, where Scotland once crowned its kings. Rejoin the A9 north and you are soon engulfed in the majesty of the Highlands, with mountains crowding all around on the approach to the resort of Aviemore two hours farther north. If it is still light when you arrive, head up the Cairngorm Mountain Railway, which takes you high into the rugged wildscape for a sundowner.

On **Day 4,** easing farther north just over an hour by car, you'll come to the only city in the Highlands, Inverness. Detour to Culloden en route, where a catastrophic defeat for the Jacobite Highlanders in 1746 led to the destruction of the Highland clan way of life. Inverness offers cultural attractions and riverside strolls.

NOT TO BE MISSED:

The panoramic views of Edinburgh from Arthur's Seat 64

Rekindling the passions of William Wallace and Robert the Bruce at Stirling 129

A feast of world-class Scottish seafood at Oban 137

A cruise on Loch Ness in search of Nessie 187

Hiking up Ben Nevis to the highest point in the United Kingdom 188–189

Sampling your favorite wee dram in the distillery where it is conjured up 222–223

Sifting through the ghosts of Neolithic man on Orkney 260–261

Visitor Information

The place to go for information is Visit Scotland (tel 0845/225 5121, www.visitscotland.com), **the country's national tourist office. Here you'll find all kinds of information about accommodations, sightseeing, and activities through Scotland. Most cities and towns also have walk-in tourist information offices, where you can pick up brochures and maps; learn about local tours; and book accommodations. See Travelwise p. 274 for tourist office information in some of the major cities, including Edinburgh and Glasgow.**

Day 5 begins with a hunt for the Loch Ness monster. Enjoy a scenic drive along the famous shores of Loch Ness keeping an eye out for Nessie. Head out on to the water with a boat tour from the trim little town of Fort Augustus, which will also allow you time to ramble around the romantic ruins of Castle Urquhart. The final 1.5-hour drive will take you across to the Atlantic coast and the former garrison town of Fort William, with great views and plenty of facilities.

The fit, brave, and well equipped can kick off **Day 6** by embarking on a full-day hike up the United Kingdom's highest mountain, Ben Nevis. More sedentary souls can still enjoy the high altitude by taking the Nevis Range Gondola and then mountain biking,

The Scottish mountains offer everything from great skill-testing challenges, such as reaching Aonach Mor's summit, a stone's throw from Ben Nevis, to gentle excursions.

embarking on a short walk, or just taking in the views from the café/restaurant.

On **Day 7** take the narrow, twisting A82 road south from Fort William. This road, while not the fastest route, provides spectacular views of some of Scotland's finest scenery, passing though Glen Coe and along the western shore of the beautiful Loch Lomond. Once you have descended from the Highlands, Glasgow awaits with an easy-to-navigate city center replete with grand Georgian and Victorian buildings and a flurry of world-class cultural attractions.

When to Visit

You can visit Scotland at any time of year, but be aware that many visitor attractions close or operate restricted opening times from late October to Easter. The snows of winter give the Scottish landscape even more appeal and Christmas and Hogmanay (New Year) are great times to be in Scotland's cities. The favorite month among Scots is May, which is often the sunniest and the driest. July and August can be afflicted by the harmless, but annoying, biting midge insect, especially in the Highlands and islands.

If You Have More Time

You could spend months in Scotland and still not see all of it. If you do have more time, you should take two or three days to explore south of Edinburgh and Glasgow. Southern Scotland boasts rolling hills, a rugged coastline, a string of ruined abbeys (including the majestic Border abbeys of Melrose, Dryburgh, and Jedburgh), and quintessential towns like Portpatrick, Melrose, and Kirkcudbright. Here you can revel in the writings of Sir Walter Scott and Robert Burns, the two men who have most romantically captured Scotland in prose and poetry, respectively, better than anyone.

The Kingdom of Fife, just north of Edinburgh, is a region that boasts the "home of golf," St. Andrews, as well as cute fishing villages and historic sites. Aberdeen, on the east coast about 120 miles (193 km) north of Edinburgh, is worth a visit. The "oil capital of Europe," with grand granite buildings and easy access to Royal Deeside, was once a favorite mountainous playground of Queen Victoria. North and west of Glasgow is the indented and island-strewn coast of Argyll. Often ignored by tourists, this region is home to numerous sea lochs, hills, and historic attractions, as well as trim towns such as Inveraray (about 1.5 hours drive northwest of Glasgow) and Oban (on the west coast, 2 hours north of Glasgow), the latter having reinvented itself as the "seafood capital of Scotland."

> ### Tipping
>
> **Tipping is not so straightforward in Scotland. In cases where paying for service is optional, locals simply add a little extra onto the bill, while others add an additional 10 percent. As a general guide, add 10 to 15 percent for good service in a café or restaurant. Tipping is not expected in a bar. You may, however, hear the bar person being told to buy one for themselves; when this happens, they will usually add the price of a drink to the bill and take this as a tip. For taxi fares, round up the fare to the nearest pound or add on a couple of pounds.**

The ancient city of Stirling, located about an hour's drive north of Glasgow, is a must for history buffs, as the key battle between the Scots and the English took place here. It is also a gateway to the famous Highlands, which, beyond Inverness and Avemore, stretch from the North Sea to the Atlantic Ocean. The Highlands are sparsely populated but have tremendous natural beauty and intoxicating stories of grand historic causes won and, more often than not, tragically lost.

With more than 800 islands, almost 100 of them populated, there is plenty beyond the mainland. The best plan is to focus on one island or a group of neighboring islands. The biggest, Skye, is ideal for those short on time, as it can be reached by road from Glasgow in about 4 hours. Arran is easier to get to, and can be reached within 2 hours by car and ferry. The little-visited Outer Hebrides, located 50 miles (80 km) off the northwest coast of Scotland, offers an end-of-the-world feel and stunning scenery. The Orkney and Shetland Islands, north of the Scottish mainland, offer whole archipelagos with as much Norse as Scottish history. All of these islands can be reached by short flights from Edinburgh or Glasgow.

More Outdoor Possibilities

Wherever you go in Scotland, the scenery is universally remarkable. Lovers of the great outdoors will be in heaven, and even if you are not normally an active type there will be something for you. Choose from myriad walking opportunities, from skill-testing dangerous ridges, to coast-to-coast trails, to gentle lochside strolls. Then there is mountain biking, with Scotland recently named the world's number one destination. The country has both well-organized mountain-bike centers and wild rural trails where you see more deer than people. Throw in river rafting, kayaking, canyoning, surfing, windsurfing, sailing, and skiing, and Scotland offers a diversity of things to do as varied as the histories of its clans. Wherever you go and whatever you do, it will all come wrapped in that famously infectious Scottish hospitality and friendliness. Enjoy Scotland, *sláinte*–"health." ∎

History & Culture

This Celtic cross at Iona Abbey, on the isle of Iona, Argyll, is one of many throughout Scotland that symbolize the country's unique religious and cultural traditions.

Scotland Today

Scotland is a land of stunning natural beauty—a cultural oasis with a complex history steeped in tradition. The Scots are justifiably proud of their land, which has branded itself onto the global map through its whiskies, fine food, tartan, and so much more. The newly devolved Scotland is bursting with confidence, and there has never been a better time to visit.

Scotland's story is long and complex, to say the least. This is perhaps not surprising given that within its genetic makeup runs the blood of fierce Pictish warriors, Celtic kings, Roman legionnaires, marauding Vikings, and the Germanic Angles. Scotland was first an independent nation more than a millennium ago. The country is today part of the United Kingdom—a political and economic union (with a shared monarchy) with England, Wales, and Northern Ireland. But don't make the mistake of confusing Scotland with England (more about that later).

Old & New

Modern Scotland is a fascinating place to visit and continues to offer a complex web of old and new. The Scots wear their history firmly on their sleeves, and often you almost forget which century you are in as tales of old battles and ancient rivalries simmer in the fissures of the rocks. If you want to revel in this Scotland of heart-stirring clichés, the world of Mel Gibson's *Braveheart* (1995) is still out there and is thoroughly enjoyable.

> **The Scots wear their history firmly on their sleeves, and often you almost forget which century you are in.**

Your visit will be far richer if you make the effort to also delve beyond the tartan-draped clichés. Modern Scotland embraces new technologies, has an economy based firmly on the service sectors, and a people with a passion for succeeding in the high-tech world of the 21st century. Scotland's cities still have those gorgeous castles, cobbled old towns, and all the traditional tourist trimmings, but look farther than the view from an open-top bus tour and you will see that they also have funky modern art galleries, dynamic glass-and-steel architecture, and a plethora of more stimulating and cerebral tourist attractions.

The annual event of the ceilidh is where modern and historic Scotland most happily join hands. This thoroughly fun Celtic celebration has its roots in the mists of clan history, when the tribespeople would party with music and dancing. The tradition continues, and you will find a real mix of creeds and clashing personalities at a modern ceilidh, dancing as a group to traditional fiddle music.

The Scotland that you will discover with your eyes, as well as your heart and mind, is as multifaceted as it has ever been. After a day or two in Scotland, you will realize that you have been lucky enough to discover a place truly unique. A land that may lie on England's doorstep but will never be content to be anything less than an equal

Scotland's vibrant culture is an exciting mix of the traditional and the new.

Life in the Highlands retains its traditional pace and simplicity.

partner, and in a corner of Europe where geopolitical fault lines are as shifting as any of the tectonic plates that have so spectacularly formed this beautiful nation.

The Scots & the English

Scotland's relationship with England is a defining one. Its larger neighbor has been a constant source of torment through the centuries with a series of wars and periods when the "Auld Enemy" (the English) tried to occupy Scotland. Even when they were not engaged in open warfare, the Borders were alive with skirmishes and power struggles, and the next bout of saber rattling was never far away. Today, a large part of the Scottish national identity is formed by "not being English," something the Scots feel they have to actively proclaim, as they are often grouped with their southern neighbors by international visitors unsure of the relationship between the two countries and, worst still, ignorant inhabitants of England. Referring to the country as England will instantly lose you Scottish friends. It is, regardless, rare to find Scots who express genuine hostility toward the English—for many the centuries-old conflict has become little more than a good-natured rivalry.

The issue of Scottish independence has occupied a great deal of Scottish political discussion since the Act of Union joined Scotland with England in 1707, but it is not a straightforward one. Not all Scots wholeheartedly embrace independence and some

Scots today proclaim themselves pro-Union, cherishing their joint British heritage. Others broadly support independence—or at least more power than the current devolved political setup allows—but are fearful of changing the only status quo they have ever known. Having an interest and at least a basic knowledge of the independence issues will both inform your trip, enhance your experiences, and also win you new friends wherever you go in this proud nation.

Highlands & Lowlands

Every country has its internal rivalries; the biggest in Scotland is the seismic rift between the Highlands, generally in the north of the country, and the Lowlands, generally in the south. The country is actually split into three different geographic zones (the Southern Uplands, the Lowlands, and the Highlands), and then into 32 administrative areas (local councils).

The divisions in Scotland are not only physical. Highlanders tend to see themselves as more rugged—people of the earth—and this is where the remnants of traditional Gaelic culture survive and where the Celtic language is still spoken. The Highlands was the region that was decimated after the tragic defeat at Culloden in 1746 (see p. 44). In many ways, the people and the economy of the Highlands have never fully recovered. Romantic tales of the old clans are still immortalized in poignant songs and poetry.

Inhabitants of the Lowlands (or Lallans in Scots, its own rival language to English) take on many hues, but their world is generally a more urban, connected place with cities, highways, and all the trimmings of modern living. The two worlds coexist and inevitably intertwine continuously, but it is a useful division to note, one that will help your understanding of the country's rich history and culture.

EXPERIENCE: Celebrate Hogmanay

It will probably be when you have been hugged by a stranger for the 100th time, with your body warmed by the whisky, that you decide that no matter how many times you have celebrated New Year you have never before savored anything quite like "Hogmanay."

Hogmanay swirls in bizarre traditions. On the isle of Skye, a bull's hide was once burned, with every guest having to sniff the smoke to ward off evil spirits. If the hide went out as you sniffed it, this was meant to bring bad luck. An equally wacky tradition is "first footing"—where it was considered good luck for the "first footer" to step into your house to be a dark-haired male stranger carrying a lump of coal, which symbolizes warmth and fuel. This "first foot" spirit of friendliness is still alive in all of Scotland's cities, with visitors from all over the world welcome to join the party.

Edinburgh (www.edinburghshogmanay .org) offers the biggest of all the nation's Hogmanay parties. Its fierce rival, **Glasgow** (www.winterfestglasgow.com), Scotland's largest city, is not content to play second fiddle with a party that bashes on through the city center. Just along the road in **Stirling,** it is mostly the locals who turn out for the seriously fun festivities in the dramatic setting of Stirling Castle. "Stirling's Hogmanay: Party at the Castle" (www.stirlinghogmanay.co.uk) sees the ramparts come alive with the sound of the massed bagpipes and drums, as well as homegrown pop stars. It's an experience you will never forget!

Scotland's Political & Economic Profile

Scotland rushed into the new millennium flushed with the success of having won devolution (increased political powers being transferred to Scotland from Westminster in London) and having its first parliament in 300 years open its doors in its capital city. However, crucial political decisions, such as defense, foreign affairs, and the economy, stayed in London.

> Queen Victoria . . . was so deeply moved . . . by the wild beauty of [Scotland's] brooding hills and tumbling glens that she bought an estate, Balmoral.

But there is no underestimating the boost to Scottish confidence that devolution engendered. A flush of new legislation driven by a more Scottish viewpoint soon emerged, including the establishment of the nation's first two national parks and the landmark Land Reform Act in 2003. This act laid to rest the lingering embers of the Highland Clearances (one of the darkest periods in the nation's story; see p. 44) and solidified in law the people's right to walk or cycle on the vast estates that emerged during feudalism and still occupy large swaths of Scotland today.

In 2007, the Scottish National Party (SNP) won a landmark victory in the national elections and emerged as the minority government. The main aim of the party has always been to gain outright independence for Scotland. The charismatic leader of the SNP and Scotland's current First Minister, Alex Salmond, has put Scottish issues to the fore. He is a thorn in the side of the U.K. government (who at best has a frosty relationship with his government) and has raised Scottish issues on the European and global stages. His push for independence seemed to be gaining momentum, but some of this was lost in the late part of the last decade as the global recession bankrupted the country's two major banks—the Royal Bank of Scotland and the Bank of Scotland, making people think twice about going it alone during a time of worldwide economic strife.

Other economic and social problems remain in 21st-century Scotland. The decline of traditional heavy industries has left some communities bereft of jobs and, in some cases, devoid of hope, too. There is serious deprivation especially in and around parts of Glasgow, the hub of Scotland's once booming heavy industries, and in areas of Fife, where the mining industry has suffered a collapse. Bright sparks remain in service industries, and Edinburgh is still one of Europe's leading financial centers.

Becoming a Tourist Destination

Scotland as a tourist destination was once an unlikely prospect, even after the grand tour of Europe's cities toward the end of the 17th century really kicked off tourism. Who would want to spend an arduous, uncomfortable trip battling the elements on bumpy tracks, negotiating threatening mountains in a country notorious for its rebellious people? Indeed the whole idea of mountains being somewhere you would actually want to spend time did not really exist until relatively recently. In 1773, English writer Samuel Johnson concluded after his rugged three-month tour that "Seeing Scotland . . . is only seeing a worse England. It is seeing the flower gradually fade away to the naked stalk."

The love of British monarch Queen Victoria for the Highlands is a convenient starting point for the emergence of tourism within Scotland. She first visited in 1842 and was so deeply moved and impressed by the wild beauty of the brooding hills and tumbling glens that she bought an estate, Balmoral. She spent many a happy holiday wrapped in the charms of Balmoral Castle and exploring her beloved Deeside (today known as Royal Deeside in her honor) and beyond. She swathed the Highlands in platitudes and virtually single-handedly made them a fashionable escape.

Tourism developed through the 19th century, but getting around the extremities was still a problem—although perhaps not as difficult as it was in 1773, when Johnson reported that there were no roads on the isle of Skye and so had to travel everywhere on horseback. With the improvement of the railroads, which made it possible to travel deep into the Highlands in a modicum of comfort, more and more people from south of the border discovered the country's natural beauty. Scots concentrated in the central belt started to escape to the wilderness—many in the west heading "doon the watter" to the isles and resorts of the Firth of Clyde, seeking refuge from the nation's increasingly industrialized cities.

Through the 20th century, Scottish tourism continued to grow. However, the advent of cheap jet travel in the 1960s sounded the death knell for the great boom of the Clydeside resorts, as Scots of all social classes headed for the Spanish Costas instead. In recent decades the growth in demand for city breaks has helped Scottish tourism—now a multimillion-dollar industry employing thousands of people, with Edinburgh and Glasgow particularly popular destinations for both domestic and international visitors.

Tourism in Scotland today is a multifaceted beast. Some people come for the traditional castle-and-shortbread bus tour, while others prefer to get away from it all on a romantic Hebridean isle. Still others come to Scotland to test their mountain-bike skills or tackle the mountains. In a country that has never been better set up to meet the needs of tourism, there really is something for everyone.

Scottish Sporting Profile

Perhaps it is because Scotland is not an independent nation that its people constantly strive to raise their country's global profile across myriad fields of endeavor. This is keenly displayed within the sporting arena, where supporters usually wave Scottish and not British flags. This even happens during the Olympics, where their countrymen can only compete under the Great Britain and Northern Ireland banner.

The two main team sports of soccer and rugby are passionately followed. Fittingly for a nation that historically has often seemed to snatch defeat from the jaws of victory, its teams tend to do the same. Scotland's national soccer team spectacularly qualified for five World Cup finals in a row from 1974 through to 1990 but then failed to make it to

Soccer: A National Obsession

If you want to take route one into the Scottish psyche then go to a football (as soccer is called in Scotland) match or just talk "footie" in any pub. The sport is used as a way of demonstrating traditional rivalries along regional and even religious grounds, but it is also a crucial way of venting tensions that might otherwise be expressed in more dangerous places than a football stadium. The greatest rivalry is between Glasgow Celtic and Glasgow Rangers, with even many less firm fans having a preference between the two, as well as supporting their own "lesser" teams.

the group stages in any, losing out only on goal difference in three competitions.

Individual sports stars tend to have been more successful. Scotland invented golf, and in recent years the country's golfers have made their mark with the likes of Sam Torrance, Colin Montgomerie, and Sandy Lyle. Then there is seven-time world snooker champion Stephen Hendry, who has won titles since he was a teenager and continues to challenge in tournaments around the world.

The current Scottish sporting success story is tennis player Andrew Murray. He has won a flurry of tournaments and has managed to make three Grand Slam finals. He has even been adopted by Wimbledon fans after a tricky start when he was pilloried for not publicly endorsing the English football team. Multi-Olympic gold medalist Sir Chris Hoy is another Scottish sporting hero in the field of track cycling. He suffered a horrendous crash in 2009 that could have ended his career. He bravely battled back and after, incredibly, suffering another chilling crash in the qualifying rounds, went on to win another world title in 2010.

> **Lesser-known [Scottish] inventors . . . include William Murdoch, who invented gas lighting, and Robert Watson-Watt, who invented radar.**

Scotland's Gifts to the World

Within the United Kingdom, Scotland has a reputation for being a nation of inventors and creative thinkers. The achievements are less well known farther afield, which is strange as this nation of more than five million people has given the world a lot. In fact, Scotland has handed the world perhaps more inventions per capita than any other country. If that sounds like a bold statement, and you think you could do without Scottish inventions, you had better switch off your TV, not make any calls, not drive on a road (you couldn't anyway without tires), and not use your bike. All of these were Scottish inventions, and the list goes on and on.

Scotland's emergence as a creative cerebral force came during the Scottish Enlightenment of the 18th century. Two of its main luminaries were Adam Smith (1723–1790), whose *Wealth of Nations* remains a seminal economic tome today, and empiricist philosopher David Hume (1711–1776). Then there was John Logie Baird (1888–1946), the man who first gave the world the TV, while his contemporary Alexander Graham Bell (1847–1922) first set tongues wagging on the telephone. It was John Boyd Dunlop (1840–1921) who gave us pneumatic rubber tires to drive on. Many of us owe our dry clothes at work to Charles Macintosh (1766–1843) and his handy waterproof coats. And next time you take a pleasant stroll in the park, spare a thought for John Muir (1838–1914), whose love of nature stirred him to advocate

the preservation of wilderness areas and the creation of U.S. national parks, including Yosemite and Sequoia.

Where would medicine be without James Young Simpson (1811–1870), who invented chloroform, and Alexander Fleming (1181–1955), who has saved millions of lives through his discovery of the antibiotic penicillin? And that is not even mentioning the Scot who invented insulin, or his countryman who created the hypodermic needle, or the Scotsman who first proved the link between malaria and mosquitoes.

Lesser-known inventors, even to many Scots, include William Murdoch (1754–1839), who invented gas lighting, and Robert Watson-Watt (1892–1973), who invented radar, without which the Allied success in World War II (1939–1945) would have been far more tricky and protracted—and by no means guaranteed. Then, of course, there was the creation of one of Scotland's most famous inhabitants, the hugely innovative and controversial "Dolly the sheep"—the first cloned mammal, with the Midlothian-based Roslin Institute the pioneering force behind this particular science. ■

Off the tourist trail at Elgol, with the isle of Skye looming beyond

Highland Games

The Highland Games, or the Highland Gathering, is integral to Scottish culture, celebrating and also harking back to layers of intoxicating history and tradition. These events have their origins in the days of King Malcolm III, when the Scottish monarch used the games as a way of finding the bravest and most skilled warriors.

The Highland Games took on another practical role when the occupying English banned Scottish men from military training for fear of rebellion. The Scots simply traded their swords and daggers for cabers and weighty stones as a way of developing their stamina, physical strength, and, of course, preparing for conflict.

Today, Highland Games take place annually at various venues throughout Scotland. The earliest events take place in May and carry on right through to September, which makes them accessible to many people visiting Scotland. The games are massively popular events that, despite their name, are not limited to the Highlands. In fact, they stretch from the Borders right up to the top of Scotland, with the isles of Arran, Bute, Lewis, Mull, and Skye among those hosting their own games.

Perhaps equally surprising is the fact that the largest Highland Games in Scotland is the Cowal Gathering in Dunoon. This extravaganza ripples through Dunoon during the last weekend in August and attracts more than 3,000 competitors and 20,000 spectators. Other major gatherings take place at Braemar (see p. 163)—an event traditionally attended by members of the British royal family—Grantown-on-Spey, and Crieff, but there are countless other events, and each has charms of its own.

Traditional Events

Perhaps the most famous Highland Games event is the caber toss. This sees a variety of pine logs being lifted by burly men, who then run with them before hurling them through the air. Other events include the hammer throw, a variety of weight throwing events, and hurling a weight over a bar.

The traditional sports are often accompanied by athletics events, such as running various lengths on a track or up (and back down) the nearest steep hill. There are also traditional music performances, with the highlight usually a Highland band that consists of traditional pipers and drummers.

Each Highland Games has its own traditions and events. Some include cattle shows, while

---

EXPERIENCE: Try Your Hand at Highland Dancing

Highland dancing is an expertly choreographed and thoroughly athletic performance, which is always performed solo and usually undertaken in traditional Highland dress to the accompaniment of bagpipes. It is a far cry from the rough and tumble of the games' sports, with more in common with ballet than warfare. On your visit you have the best chance of catching a performance at a Highland Games, but regular competitions are also held across the country during the summer. Key dances to watch for include the Highland Fling, Sword Dance, Shean Truibhais, Reel and Sailor's Hornpipe, and the Highland Laddie. If you are staying longer in Scotland you can sign up for lessons with one of the dance groups. For more information contact the **Scottish Official Highland Dancing Association** (*www.sohda.org.uk*)—the governing body for this national tradition.

The stone put event—a traditional test of strength—at the Highland Games in Dunoon

others have sheepdog trials. There is also the spectacular sight of dancers performing traditional Highland dancing, mimicking the movements of the stag on the Highland hillsides.

At many games there are also plenty of modern distractions to entertain children, which vary from venue to venue but may include funfair rides and games, police dog demonstrations, children's entertainers, spectacular shows featuring birds of prey, children's races, gig tents with live music, and even pet dog shows. For the adults, the food stalls and beer tents often prove an added attraction.

Whichever Highland Games you choose to attend you will get a glimpse of the traditional Scottish way of life and the events that once kept these traditions alive. For more information about any of the Highland Games in Scotland visit the Scottish Highland Games Association (*www.shga.co.uk*) or call in at the local tourist information center to ask about the nearest events.

Food & Drink

Despite boasting some of the world's finest seafood and red meat—in the form of Aberdeen Angus beef—Scottish cuisine has not always enjoyed the best of reputations. All that has changed over the last decade, with a slew of Michelin-starred restaurants being backed up by much better use of the local ingredients throughout the country at all levels.

Traditional Food

For centuries, Scottish food was based around the needs of its largely poor population. Easy to grow and filling staples such as the potato emerged as popular favorites, and there was also the widespread use of oatmeal. This is, after all, the home of porridge, which remains the most popular way to start the day in 21st-century Scotland. To really fit in, have it made with water and seasoned with a little salt.

> The . . . national dish, haggis . . . [is] much maligned and misunderstood, [but] its ingredients are really no worse than most sausages.

The most famous (or perhaps infamous) food is the national dish, haggis. Much maligned and misunderstood, its ingredients are really no worse than most sausages, with sheep's offal mash bulked up by oatmeal and then seasoned with various spices and onion, giving it an extremely pleasant flavor. These days, it is increasingly rare to find haggis served as it used to be—inside the lining of the sheep's stomach. Haggis is traditionally eaten with neeps (turnips to the Scots, swedes to the English, and rutabaga to Americans) and tatties (potatoes); the most renowned producer, Macsween (www.macsween.co.uk), also produces an excellent vegetarian version.

Another staple is, of course, shortbread. This sweet buttery treat originated in Scotland, and it is as popular today as it has always been with both locals and tourists, making for an ideal souvenir—especially when it comes packaged in a cheesy tin adorned with a dramatic Highland landscape or a heroic figure from Scottish history.

Scottish Soups

Another Scottish staple is soup. Scotch broth is a filling soup made up of barley; root vegetables such as carrots, turnips, and rutabaga; and cheap cuts of meat—traditionally mutton but sometimes lamb and (rarely) beef. This popular winter warmer has been around for hundreds of years. Traditionally, the meat was removed after cooking and served as a main course, but today it is retained and eaten as one delicious meal.

Cullen skink might be the soup of choice for more adventurous foodies. This thick, creamy soup is made up of smoked haddock, potatoes, and onions and is thought to originate from the fishing village of Cullen on the northeast coast. Another traditional Scottish soup, cock-a-leekie, dates back to the 16th century and is a popular starter

A selection of Scotland's internationally renowned seafood

The Loch Fyne
Oyster Company Ltd
* * *
OYSTER BARS

to a Burns Night supper (see sidebar below). This nutritious soup is made by boiling fowl such as chicken in a stock with vegetables such as leeks. In the past, chefs added prunes to improve the flavor of the soup. Prunes are rarely added today since they are not to everyone's taste, and even traditional chefs who cook the soup with prunes will remove them before serving.

World-Class Seafood

Scotland's rich seafood larder is often underrated, even within the country, perhaps because most of the freshest produce is spirited off to the fine dining tables of London, Paris, and Madrid, where it fetches a far higher price.

The west coast is the real star, especially when it comes to shellfish. Here the cold, nutrient-rich, and unpolluted waters are ideal for plump wild lobsters and langoustines, the latter known confusingly as prawns in some parts of Wester Ross. Scallops are also excellent—both king scallops and the smaller queenies—with some of the biggest king scallops the size of tennis balls. The most prized are hand-dived king scallops, which are best served simply seared to really let the full flavor speak for itself. Regionally, Orkney crab is excellent and Shetland is generally considered the best source of large, plump, and flavorsome mussels. The best places to try cheap seafood are around the ports themselves, with Oban (see sidebar p. 137), establishing itself as the "seafood capital of Scotland," a good bet. Many of the best Scottish restaurants now have plenty of west coast seafood on their menus, as demand has increased and the prices the fishermen can get locally have risen.

Over on the east coast the specialty is whitefish, caught farther afield in the North Sea, although Eyemouth in the Borders is an excellent shellfish port, too. The main whitefish ports are Peterhead and Fraserburgh in Aberdeenshire (see p. 168), Arbroath in Angus (see p. 157), and the

litter of smaller ports on the southern flank of Fife. Species to look for are haddock (the most common staple in the fish and chips sold up and down the east coast) and the increasingly rare cod.

Scottish salmon is world famous. The majority of it is farmed in sea lochs. Much has been made of the poor conditions in some fish farms, and the situation has certainly improved in recent years. One

Burns Night

Burns Night, on January 25, is one of the biggest nights of the year, when the birth date of national bard Robert Burns is celebrated. He was a legend with an eye for both booze and the ladies and certainly knew how to party; after all, he was the seminal poet and songwriter who penned the world's number one end of party anthem "Auld Lang Syne." Scots traditionally mark Burns Night by eating the national dish of haggis, served with neeps and tatties—a surprisingly tasty treat, especially when accompanied by a liberal serving of culture and traditional dancing.

A traditional haggis ceremony—piping in the bearer

highly regarded fish farm operator is on Loch Duart (*www.lochduart.com*), where environmentally friendly methods reap rewards on the flavor and texture front. Wild salmon, mainly caught in salmon-rich rivers such as the Tweed and the Spey, are highly prized, but you will usually have to catch one for yourself.

Scottish Red Meat & Game

Scottish beef is universally excellent. The most famous breed is the Aberdeen Angus, which produces a consistently good flavor no matter what the cut. In recent years, the Highland breed (the furry beasts with the big horns) has been appearing on more menus, though the slightly richer flavor does not suit all palates. Many Scots hail Buccleuch beef, and Buccleuch fillets and rib-eye are indeed hard to beat.

Scottish lamb is also usually very good, with lamb from the Borders particularly highly prized. Venison—the lean and healthier red meat from deer—is growing in popularity, although its gamey richness can be too much for some and is best offset with a tangy berry-based sauce. Many Scottish butchers also produce excellent homemade sausages, and the famous "Square," or "Lorne," sausage is a favorite hangover cure.

Game is more of a niche market, but during the shooting season it appears on

Talisker Distillery, isle of Skye, the Highlands

menus in more expensive hotels and restaurants. You will usually find grouse and pheasant on offer, with the wild, rich, and often overpowering taste too much for some. When fresh and cooked properly, however, game meat can be excellent.

Regional Specialties

Scotland boasts many regional specialties. One of the most famous are Arbroath smokies, which are a brand of locally caught and smoked haddock. In Aberdeen-shire, look for butteries—a highly calorific pastry treat.

In recent years, Scotland has also been producing some award-winning cheese. The highlights among blues are the Lanark, Dunsyre, and Strathdon blue varieties, while the finest cheddar is the isle of Mull cheddar, which is usually unpasteurized. Traditional cheeses have become immensely popular in recent years, including Caboc (which dates back to the 15th century) from the Highlands and Grimbister from the Orkney Islands.

Today's Dining

You can still "savor" the various deep-fried abominations served up in Scottish fish-and-chips restaurants, or "chippies." Examples include deep-fried pizza and even deep-fried chocolate bars. Standards have improved across the board, however, helped in part by the rise of the celebrity TV chef and a determination of the government to promote a healthy lifestyle. With this has come greater sophistication. Edinburgh leads the way, with no fewer than five Michelin-starred restaurants. Glasgow's eateries are more egalitarian, but there are still many great places to eat. All major towns and cities now boast good, and often great, restaurants. Smaller operators have also opened in the likes of Kinlochleven and Kishorn to offer boat-fresh seafood in informal surroundings. So you can savor the same seafood you would pay a fortune for at the finest dining tables of London or Paris.

Drinks

For Scots, whisky is known as *Uisge Beatha* (water of life; see sidebar below) and little excuse is needed to persuade one of the locals to enjoy a wee dram. Beer is also popular, with the deliciously creamy and full flavor "heavy" similar, but often better, than warmer English beer. Independent microbreweries have also blossomed lately. Brews to look for include those from the excellent Black Isle Brewery (*www .blackislebrewery.com*), the award-winning BrewDog range (*www.brewdog.com*), and the Orkney Brewery, whose Dark Island is a world-class tipple. Of the soft drinks, the ultrasweet Irn Bru is an indigenous fizzy drink that rivals Coca-Cola and Pepsi in national sales and is rated much higher in the country's affections. ■

Whisky—the Quintessential Highland Tipple

Scottish whisky has never been more popular around the world than it is today. However, how many people enjoying a wee dram in Singapore or New York, for example, are really aware of the story behind whisky's early illicit days, or that there are three types of "Scotch"?

The production of whisky—whose recipe of malted barley, yeast, and water is wonderfully simple—had been going on in Scotland centuries before it became fashionable elsewhere in the world. Uisge Beatha, the Gaelic name for whisky, which translates as "water of life," was a lifeblood of the Highland clans who used to roam the wild mist-shrouded glens.

After the 1707 Act of Union, the British government turned its attention to whisky, which was then produced in small stills across the country. This drove production underground, and the Scots started to play a whisky-drenched cat-and-mouse game with the tax collectors.

These days whisky is big business.

There are hundreds of distilleries dotted throughout Scotland, with each region offering different flavors and incarnations. Many of the distilleries are open to the public, offering free or cheap tours with, of course, the chance to sample the hallowed amber spirit.

There are three types of Scotch whisky: grain, malt, and blended. Single malts are the purest of whiskies and are the product of a single distillery, with the fresh water going in one end and whisky coming out the other. Grain malts are similar but usually rougher in taste and these are rarely available for purchase. Blended whisky is made up of at least two different whiskeys, usually a single malt that is mixed with a grain whisky. Some blended whiskeys have more than two blends mixed into them, including whisky that comes from other distilleries located in totally different parts of the country. A blend that has only single malt whiskeys and no grain whisky is called a vatted malt. Most whiskeys are blends.

Land & Environment

The geography of Scotland is one of the most remarkable in the world. Slightly smaller than South Carolina, Scotland boasts an unparalleled natural diversity for its size. It has a coastline twice as long as that of either France or Spain and is alive with mighty mountains, voluminous sea cliffs, and silvery lochs that handily fall into three main geographical areas.

Scotland is split between the Southern Uplands, the Lowlands, and the Highlands, with each region having its own unique natural attractions and features—although all three exhibit the classic effects of glaciation. The country stretches for 274 miles (441 km) from north to south and is between 154 miles (248 km) and 24 miles (39 km) wide, with a total land mass of more than 31,000 square miles (80,290 sq km). The natural stories of the trio of geographical regions and their landscapes dovetail with the human history; in Scotland the imprint of man has always been firmly dictated by the environment. Indeed, some Scots joke that it was the Highlands, and not the Highlanders, that kept the ancient Romans at bay. The country is one of Europe's top wildlife viewing destinations. Any trip is enhanced by both the flora and fauna of this dramatically scenic corner of Europe.

> **[Scotland] has a coastline three times longer than that of either France or Spain and is alive with mighty mountains, voluminous sea cliffs, and silvery lochs.**

Southern Uplands

Scotland's most southerly geographic zone borders England and then runs north along the line of the Southern Uplands Fault, which stretches from Girvan on the west coast across to Dunbar on the North Sea coast. It is a highly attractive area replete with mile upon mile of rolling hills, with a large spine of barren peaks (the actual Southern Uplands) that stretch around 120 miles (190 km) from west to east, although there are no Munros (mountains more than 3,000 feet/914 m). The highest peak is Merrick (2,766 feet/843 m). The region's western and eastern fringes are more fertile, with sweeping glens (valleys) dropping down toward the coastal plains. On the coast lie sea cliffs and sandy beaches awash with birdlife. The Southern Uplands region is also home to large forest areas, including Mabie Forest and Galloway Forest.

The Lowlands

The Lowlands are the area of rift valley that stretches north from the Southern Uplands toward the Highlands. Geologically, the area runs up to the Highland Boundary Fault—roughly from Helensburgh (or Arran if you include the islands) in the west across to Stonehaven (much farther north) in the east. It is rich in sedimentary rocks and hence rich in minerals, which has brought it riches through the mining of coal and iron deposits. It is also the flattest geographic region of

The wild cliffs of Orkney are home to many species of seabirds.

Scotland and the most fertile, which means that it has also become the most agriculturally significant and the most populated, with around 80 percent of the country's population and five out of its six biggest cities (Inverness is in the Highlands).

The main hill ranges in the Lowlands are the Pentlands and Lammermuirs in the east and the Campsie Fells in the west. The region is also home to a number of extinct volcanoes—most significantly Arthur's Seat and Castle Hill in Edinburgh. Of the smaller groups of hills of note, the Bathgate Hills are particularly lovely; they run between the country's two main cities of Edinburgh and Glasgow and offer views across the Forth and Clyde Valleys.

The central Lowlands are indented with a series of river estuaries, known locally as firths. In the west, the Firth of Clyde opens up after the River Clyde passes through Glasgow to end in a wide sweep replete with isles such as Arran and Bute. The River Forth runs east through Stirling before widening out into a firth of its own, and meets the sea east of Edinburgh. Meanwhile, the Firth of Tay merges with the North Sea just east of Dundee.

The Highlands

For most visitors, the north and west of Scotland is the most scenic part of the country. The Highlands is one big dramatic geography lesson on glaciation, as you can see and feel the effects of the mighty glaciers that, during the last ice age,

The bleak beauty of the isle of Lewis highlights the ancient ruin of Dun Carloway broch.

rumbled seaward from the high mountains, carving out the glens and scything deep cuts into the ground, which today are the country's myriad lochs (lakes).

Mountains formed from ancient rock abound in the Highlands. Both Torridonian sandstone and Lewisian gneiss are thought to be among the oldest rocks in the world, with the latter dated to more than three billion years ago. The region overflows with towering peaks and is home to the massive Munro mountains, which attract climbers and walkers from all over the world. The Munros come in all shapes and sizes. Some stand alone—real monarchs of the glen like 3,169-foot (966 m) Ben More, the most northerly—while others are more unassuming, forming part of a chunky range of mountains, such as the Cairngorms.

The scenery in the Highlands is unremittingly staggering. At every turn another mountain looms into view or a gushing burn (stream) rushes past. At its heart is the Great Glen. This fault line runs from the Atlantic town of Fort William in the west across to the Moray Firth and the city of Inverness in the east in a swirl of glens and lochs, all dwarfed by the massive mountains that rear up spectacularly on both sides.

> The scenery in the Highlands is . . . staggering. At every turn another mountain looms into view or a gushing burn (stream) rushes past.

Inland Waterways

Scotland is richly veined with burns and rivers across all its regions, all either running into the North Sea or the Atlantic Ocean. The longest three rivers are the Tay (120 miles / 193 km), which meets the sea at Dundee; the Spey (107 miles / 172 km), which runs into the North Sea at the Moray Firth; and the Clyde—Scotland's most industrial river, which runs through Glasgow (106 miles / 171 km). These three are also the largest rivers in terms of catchment. Other major rivers include the salmon rich Tweed in the Southern Uplands and the Forth, which runs through the central Lowlands and widens its firth into the North Sea, east of Edinburgh.

Climate

Much is made of Scotland's supposedly terrible weather, but for its northerly locale (Aberdeen is on the same line of latitude as Juneau, Alaska) the country's climate is actually surprisingly temperate and, of course, maritime. The chilly northerly winds and the influence of the Arctic are tempered by the warming influence of the Gulf Stream, which flows across the Atlantic from the Gulf of Mexico. The Gulf Stream helps to make the west coast particularly mild, with visitors often being surprised by palm trees growing happily in villages such as Plockton in the Highlands. Even when the weather is extreme, it just adds to the natural drama.

Of course, there are many regional variations. To generalize, the east tends be cooler and drier, while the west is the first place the tempestuous Atlantic weather systems hit, meaning that the west coast is considerably wetter. The Scottish summer—generally considered to be June, July, and August—can be an unpredictable affair; however, the temperatures are generally mild. Both spring and the fall are good times to visit, as temperatures are still mild, with May usually the driest month. In contrast, winters can be harsh, with frequent snowfall affecting transportation, particularly in the

Highlands. The islands can be a law unto themselves, with westerly isles such as Tiree and Coll reporting comparatively tiny amounts of rainfall, while Skye often earns its Gaelic moniker of the "isle of mist."

Flora & Fauna

Scotland is not only the most important part of the United Kingdom for wildlife, but it is also one of Europe's most valuable wild havens. There is a wide range of wildlife to spot, from a species of field mouse that lives only on two of the islands in St. Kilda through to soaring ospreys (sea hawks) and giant killer whales (orcas).

Scotland is free of large predatory wild animals; the native wolves died out in the 18th century at the hands of game hunters and farmers who wanted to protect their livestock. The largest wild land animal is the deer, with the red deer being the most ubiquitous species. Deer are found all over Scotland, but prosper most in the Highlands and islands. The unspoiled isle of Jura is named for the Gaelic word for deer and is one of the finest places in the land to spot them, with deer vastly outnumbering the tiny human population (see p. 221).

The famous Highland cow is unmistakable and is now a common sight, even outside the Highlands. Its shaggy red coat and impressive horns combine with its laid-back nature to make it a favorite with camera-toting tourists. These cattle roam semiwild on large Highland estates. It can be quite an experience having to dive into a ditch to avoid an oncoming herd of Highland cows heading down a narrow track.

Other fauna to spot include the elusive otter, which is found sneaking around Scotland's coast, and the pine marten—another predator that lives in forested areas. Birdlife generally thrives in Scotland. Large birds of prey include the common buzzard (now even found in and around Scotland's urban areas) and the less seen, but deeply impressive, golden eagle—a majestic sight soaring above a Highland glen. Lucky hill walkers will come across a symbol of the nation: grouse. These chiefly ground-dwelling birds, including the rare capercaillie and the ptarmigan, shed their brown camouflage in winter to adopt a white snow-colored sheen.

Out at sea, the elusive sea eagle is a rare but enthralling attraction in the isles, while the cute puffin is a more ubiquitous and fun vision with its awkward flying technique, splash landings, and brightly colored beak. St. Kilda and the Shetland Islands are fantastic places to spot storm petrels (see sidebar on p. 266) and puffins (see p. 267),

First Marine Reserve

When the Scottish government announced plans in 2005 to set up the first protected marine reserve in the United Kingdom, it was met with widespread acclaim among the environmental lobby and the general public alike. Finally, something was officially being done to protect Scotland's massive littoral. However, to date the location of the reserve and the necessary legislation involved from both the Scottish government and U.K. government have not been confirmed. The locals on Arran have pushed things along by having their own small "no fishing" zone declared, working with the Scottish government and local fishermen, with high hopes it can lead the way forward for large-scale protection.

Otters are an enthralling but rare sight on Scottish waterways.

although they can also be found within sight of Edinburgh Castle on the islands of the Firth of Forth (see pp. 78–79).

In the water, you can watch for everything from small porpoises to large bottlenose dolphins (Scotland lays claims to having the world's largest bottlenose dolphins), as well as a range of whales and sharks, including basking sharks, minke whales, and the predatory killer whale (orca). In recent years, the isle of Mull has emerged as something of a hub for marine wildlife-watching trips, although any boat trip off the Scottish coastline can reap rich rewards.

Conservation

Scotland is very serious about conservation. Devolution in 1999 gave the newly formed Scottish Parliament increased political powers, and it wasted no time in swinging them into action when it came to the conservation effort. Unusually, Scotland had no national parks when the SNP came to power, so the new government quickly declared Loch Lomond and the Trossachs National Park and Cairngorms National Park the first two in the country. Various nature reserves and protected areas exist around Scotland, and real attempts are also being made to atone for the natural cost of land mismanagement and the Clearances by replanting swathes of the Caledonian forest that once used to cover the nation in a rich, green cloak.

Direct interventions are also being made to control particular species. The native red squirrel (more than 75 percent of the U.K.'s dwindling population reside north of the border) has been under serious threat from the gray squirrel. A concentrated effort has been made to control the latter's numbers. Recent attempts have also been made to reintroduce the beaver, although the success of the project is far from assured. More success has already been secured with the nation's birdlife, with the rare osprey (or fish hawk) now thriving. ■

History

Scotland's history is a complex, romantic, and controversial tale of heroes, battling peoples, and deadly power struggles. The story begins around 7,000 years ago, when Neolithic settlers eked out a rudimentary existence, and continues through to 1999, when the first parliament in 300 years returned to Edinburgh, and beyond.

The Earliest Peoples

The earliest remaining imprints of humans in Scotland are to be found on the Orkney Islands. Indeed, the well-preserved sites at Skara Brae, Knap of Howar, and Maeshowe are actually the oldest preserved Neolithic dwellings in Europe. Archaeological evidence from the sites suggests that people from mainland Europe drifted into the region around 7,000 years ago and then settled. These people eked out a simple life, but as their settlements became more secure, and their grip on the land became stronger, they cemented their world with the building of large burial cairns and the stone circles that today still stand shrouded in mystery on the Orkney Islands and the Outer Hebrides. The finest is at Callanish on the isle of Lewis, whose stones date back as far as 2000 B.C.

> Archaeological evidence from the sites suggests that people from mainland Europe drifted into the region around 7,000 years ago.

The coming of the Bronze Age brought new tools that made farming far more productive but also gave people the ability to kill others. Struggles for land and food spilled into violence and necessitated the building of defensive crannogs (dwellings built out on lochs with access through one retractable wooden walkway) and more extensive hill forts. Added to the immigration from the Continent came a new wave of arrivals from the south—the Celtic Britons. As competition between the warring tribes escalated, and new threats developed from the sea, a string of brochs (hollow fortified stone towers), where richer families could hunker down and withstand a siege, mushroomed along the coast. The best preserved of these are Dun Carloway on the isle of Lewis and the remarkable Mousa Broch on the eponymous island in the Shetland Islands, which is part of a network of more than 500 brochs that once stood guard around Scotland's coastline.

Romans & Picts

It was the Romans who first coined the term *Picts* (from the Latin *pictus,* which means "painted") to describe the tribes of face-painted warriors that they encountered on their forays into the northern reaches of the British landmass—a region that the Romans named Caledonia. The Romans had dabbled with incursions into southern Britain before, and their fully fledged occupation kicked off in A.D. 43 under the leadership of Emperor Claudius. They soon pacified what is now England

Skara Brae on Mainland, the largest of the Orkney Islands

and Wales and began their efforts to homogenize the local culture and transform the territory by building infrastructure and their own cities. They did not have such an easy time with the northern tribes in what is now Scotland.

The Romans made repeated attempts to quell and then subjugate the Picts but lost legions of men and valuable resources as they were beaten back by both stiff resistance and the wild Highland landscape. So troublesome did the mighty Romans find the battling northern tribes that they built not one but two defensive walls to keep them at bay. They started building the stone Hadrian's Wall in northern England in A.D. 122 and then the turf Antonine Wall in A.D. 142 farther to the north across Scotland's central belt, from the large fort at Cramond on the outskirts of Edinburgh in the east across to Old Kilpatrick in the west. The Romans eventually left Britain around A.D. 500 after half a millennium of occupation. They left without having pacified Scotland, a rare blot on an otherwise unblemished record of military victories across Europe in those centuries. The resistance is something that many Scots are still proud of today.

The Coming of Christianity

The geographical area of Scotland that the Romans left was made up of three main tribes. The Celtic Britons held what is now southern Scotland, while the Picts held vast swaths of the north and east. Added to the mix were the Scotti (Celts from Ireland), who began to arrive on the isles and Scotland's western coast in the latter stages of the Roman occupation and were unwittingly to give the country their name. They spoke Q-Celtic, similar to Gaelic and Irish, while the Celtic Britons and (less conclusively) the Picts are thought to have spoken varying versions of P-Celtic (akin to Welsh and Cornish). Some historians think the Scotti may have been given their name by the Romans.

While the Scotti and the Celts followed the Christian faith, the Picts were a pagan people. As a result, missionary work began to convert the Picts to Christianity. The most famous of these missionaries were St. Ninian in the fourth century and then the Scotti St. Columba, who was more successful in his quest. St. Columba was a saint who fled Ireland in the sixth century and set up a monastery on Iona—a rebuilt version of the same monastery still stands today. According to legend, St. Columba was also responsible for getting rid of the original Loch Ness Monster, who lived in the River Ness.

Forming a Scottish Nation

In a land riddled with rival tribes, the formation of a nation was never going to be an easy task, although by sharing a common enemy of the Romans and facing the emerging threat from the Norse Vikings helped to bring all sides together. Thanks to the efforts of the missionaries, the tribes also increasingly shared a religion. Until recently, the accepted historical wisdom was that the first Scottish king was

Statue of Robert the Bruce at Stirling Castle

the Scotti Kenneth MacAlpine (800–858), leader of the Scotti kingdom of Dalriada, who moved to unite his lands with the Picts in 843 to create the nation of Alba, latterly Scotland.

Alba did not include Strathclyde, the Lothians, and southern Scotland, and some historians argue that you cannot even speak of a "Scotland" until as late as 1468, when Shetland and Orkney came under control. Yet MacAlpine did form a nation that encompassed much of what Scotland is today, paving the way for further consolidation by setting his capital at Scone, as well as giving Scotland what is still its most sacred artifact—the Stone of Destiny—where the fledgling nation's kings were to be crowned.

MacAlpine and the line of succession he established brought some stability to Scotland. One of his family's royal line, Malcolm II (954–1034), went on to defeat the Northumberland Angles at the Battle of Carham in 1018, which secured the land south of the Firth of Forth, including Edinburgh. As the kingdom expanded, so the country became more sophisticated. David I (1083–1153) oversaw the establishment of royal burghs and the foundation of the Borders abbeys, and the cultural and religious dimensions that came with them. Feudalism, at least in the southern and central regions, started to replace the traditional clan system, although the Highlands remained as wild as ever. To the north and northwest, the Norse kings held sway over Shetland and Orkney and also harried many other isles, as well as coastal areas.

The Wars of Independence

The Battle of Largs in 1263 saw a scrambled victory over the Vikings, and the Norse invaders never posed the same threat again. Instead, an even more ruthless threat was brewing south of the border. England watched her neighbor with envious eyes. Skirmishes in the Borders badlands were common, but these broke out into outright invasion in 1296 when King Edward I (1239–1307), the "hammer of the Scots," butchered his way north with a 30,000-strong professional army.

The Scots were never keen on being subsumed into England, and unrest simmered throughout the land. This unrest bubbled to the surface in the unlikely form of man-of-the-people William Wallace (1272–1305), a character portrayed famously by Mel Gibson in the film *Braveheart* (1995). Wallace was not a royal, or even of noble

Scottish Time Line

5000 B.C.	Neolithic man builds structures on the Orkney Islands.
A.D. 43–500	Romans fail to conquer Caledonia.
843	Kenneth MacAlpine, first king of Alba, unifies the Picts and the Scotti.
1314	Robert the Bruce defeats the English at Bannockburn.
1371–1714	Stuart monarchy.
1707	Act of Union passes with England.
1715–1745	Jacobite rebellions attempt to restore the Stuarts and independence.
1746	Battle of Culloden ends traditional clan system.
1746–1886	Highland Clearances.
1887–1945	Scotland's cities prosper as part of the British Empire.
1945–1970s	Heavy industries decline; postwar economic strife.
1970s	Oil and gas boom in the North Sea rekindles calls for independence.
1999	First Scottish parliament in three centuries.

blood, but he showed what could be done by a determined "inferior" force using his knowledge of the landscape to the full with a stunning victory over the English at the Battle of Stirling Bridge in 1297. The feudal nobles, more keen to make deals and garner additional land, were never truly behind Wallace, and he was infamously betrayed after the Scots' defeat at the Battle of Falkirk the following year. Wallace met a horrific death—"hung, drawn, and quartered" by the English in 1305.

Another man, who was both popular with the people and more palatable to the nobles, had learned the lessons of Wallace's victories. Initially, Robert the Bruce (1274–1329) suffered many defeats, but he persevered in his quest to protect the country and won the Scots their most famous triumph over the English in 1314. On the field of Bannockburn, in the shadow of Stirling Castle, Robert the Bruce led the massively outnumbered Scots to an incredible victory. This not only secured his crown but brought Scotland another four centuries of liberty, and the English were "sent hame tae think again," as the words of the unofficial national anthem, *Flower of Scotland,* famously proclaim. The acceptance of the Declaration of Arbroath by the pope in 1320 put the seal on the independent Scottish nation with a defiant and rousing certainty that many Scots still proudly feel today: "For as long as but a hundred of us remain alive, never will we on any conditions be brought under English rule. It is in truth not for glory, nor riches, nor honors that we are fighting, but for freedom—for that alone, which no honest man gives up but with life itself."

Scotland's independence was officially recognized by English king Edward III (1312–1377) in 1328, ending the 30-year War of Independence. Robert the Bruce and then his son, David II (1324–1371), ruled Scotland until 1371, when the House of Stuart came to power with Robert II (1316–1390), David II's nephew on his mother's side. But the fight for freedom was by no means over—the next 200 years were smattered with bloody skirmishes between the two countries and English oppression.

Two Flags

Scotland has two flags—the Saltire (or St. Andrews Cross) and the Royal Standard (or Lion Rampant). The St. Andrews Cross flag, with its distinctive white diagonal cross on a blue background, is the one you will see most often. The "Saltire" is actually only the white cross associated with St. Andrew that apparently once appeared in the sky before a Scottish victory on the battlefield. Today, the name is given to the whole flag. Meanwhile, the Lion Rampant, a fiery red lion on a bright yellow background, is only officially meant to be flown by representatives of the royals or as homage to them in Scotland. Any other usage would once have brought trouble—not that it stops the Scots today.

Religious Strife & Mary Queen of Scots

More storm clouds emerged on the horizon in the 1500s with the immense passions, intrigue, and upheaval generated by the Protestant Reformation. The effects of the Reformation, a backlash against what was seen as the extravagance of the Catholic Church (deemed to have lost its way in its worship and its relationship to God), were felt throughout Europe, but they lashed into Scotland like a tornado.

At the helm of the Scottish Reformation was the firebrand cleric John Knox (1514–1572). In 1561, Knox was granted an audience with the Stuart monarch Mary Queen of Scots (1542–1587). She could not have mistaken the passion for Protestant reform that spat from this impassioned soul. Mary, perhaps the most fondly remembered and romanticized of all the Scottish monarchs, had to play a delicate and increasingly desperate game of cat and mouse to placate her Catholic supporters, the reformers, and the fledgling Protestant Church.

Mary was a monarch draped in controversy. Born at Linlithgow Palace in 1542, she was proclaimed Queen of Scotland when her father James V died less than a week earlier. Her colorful childhood saw her spirited off to France and at one point she was crowned Queen of France, with aspirations for the English and Spanish thrones, too. Perennially embroiled in scandal, her first husband, Lord Darnley, had her supposed lover David Rizzio murdered in front of a pregnant Mary. Many historians attribute Darnley's subsequent murder to Mary herself.

Mary Queen of Scots, painted by Sir James I around 1580

Mary eventually fled Scotland in 1567, seeking refuge with her cousin Elizabeth I in England, who was so distrustful of her scheming relative that she had her imprisoned. After being accused of numerous plots, and never tasting freedom again, Mary was executed on Elizabeth's orders in 1587.

As Scotland lurched between a Catholic monarchy and—thanks to John Knox's tireless work—demands for Protestantism, the nation was in turmoil. In 1610, James VI (1566–1625), also by now James I of England and Wales, restored the bishops, which only added further fuel to the fire. His son, Charles I (1600–1649), tipped the situation over the edge in 1637, imposing a new prayer book on the Scottish Church. In response, the reformers organized a National Covenant to outline their views on the division of the church and the monarchy. Charles I could not stop the movement exploding across the country, with Covenanters raising an army and taking control of the country. Their stint lasted until 1650, when Charles II (1630–1685) was persuaded to sign the Covenant. His rule was a short one. Oliver Cromwell's parliamentarian army pushed north and took Scotland, ruling until the 1660 Restoration under Charles II.

In 1689, James VII of Scotland (1633–1701), James II of England, was forced into exile, partly as his Catholic views clashed with the English Church. His Protestant daughter, Mary, took up the reigns with her Dutch husband, William of Orange. The couple failed to produce an heir, and her sister lost all her children, so the English parliament seized the opportunity to replace the House of Stuart with a new dynasty—the Hanoverians—who took the reigns in 1714 and started a lineage that stretches all the way to the modern British Royal Family.

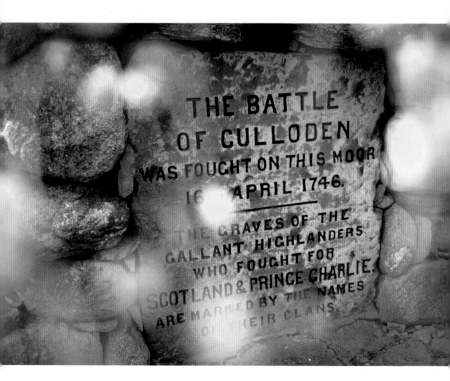

The Scots' devastating defeat at the Battle of Culloden marked the end of the Jacobite rebellions.

Union with England

Controversy still surrounds the run up to, and the reasons behind, Scotland's union with England. The Act of Union was passed in Scotland in January 1707. It remains a dark day for many Scots—the day that independence was officially surrendered.

The signatories insisted that the decision was good for the economy, because it would open up new trade routes for Scotland through England and make the country's future safer and more secure. Others felt that England's economic bullying should not be rewarded with Scotland being subjugated into an unequal union with England. National bard Robert Burns later proclaimed, "We're bought and sold for English gold, Such a parcel of rogues in a nation!" He was referring to the nobles and schemers who had accepted bribes to smooth the passage of the Act of Union—an act that was greeted with rioting and unrest in many parts of Scotland when it was made public.

Jacobite Rebellions

The supposed economic benefits that were promised when the Act of Union was signed did not materialize quickly, which fueled popular unrest and the desire for independence. Bound up within these calls were demands to bring back the pre-1714 Stuart monarchy. In particular, the Highlands were struggling economically, and there was a real sense that bringing back the Old Pretender, James VII, was the way forward—an act it was felt would give Scotland her independence back. The

Jacobites (named after the Latin for *James*) kicked off their first major rebellion at Braemar Castle on September 1, 1715, and were soon on their way.

The British government was wrong-footed by the speed of the uprising. Initially, the Jacobites made some progress, and James himself returned triumphant, with hopes high in many Jacobite hearts both in Scotland and England. However, the pivotal Battle of Sheriffmuir in November of the same year had no clear victor and left the Jacobites weakened and unfocused, with the rebellion petering out as quickly as it had begun. James was soon on his way back across the North Sea to remain the "king over the water," a moniker that survives today in romantic Jacobite songs and dreams.

Desires for independence and for a Stuart monarch to be put back on the throne did not dissipate, however, and the cause was taken up by James VII's son, Charles Edward Stuart (1720–1788), who became popularly known as the Young Pretender, or Bonnie Prince Charlie. The latter moniker hints at his good looks and the manners he had learned in his upbringing in French royal circles. He was an unlikely leader for the 10,000

EXPERIENCE: Visit the Battlefields

Bannockburn

Bannockburn (see p. 129) is the most celebrated of Scotland's victories over England. Mention this victory to any red-blooded Scot and expect his or her patriotic fires to instantly burn. It can be hard to get as passionate about it as a visitor, but a trip to the excellent visitor center is a great way to help you understand the history.

Once you have the background, head for the enormous statue of Robert the Bruce and imagine him standing in 1314, wondering just how his heavily outnumbered and previously defeated forces were going to beat King Edward II's well-drilled army.

But win they did. Robert the Bruce's skillful tactics, and innovative use of the local terrain, turned the unwieldy English army's strengths into weaknesses in what became a bloodbath that famously turned the Bannock Burn red. The English fled in chaos, with only one sizable force making it back across the border. Edward scrambled to escape by sea from Dunbar.

You can visit Bannockburn most weekends in the summer. Actors play some of the roles of the warriors on that day, further enhancing the experience and giving you a clearer insight into the famous victory that paved the way for the next 400 years of independence.

Culloden

While the new visitor center is an excellent addition to the Culloden battlefield, you need to stand on the bleak moor itself to really experience it. Look for the fluttering red flags that line up near the parking lot and mark government lines. Cast your eyes west to the blue flags, which is where the Jacobites massed in 1746 and took shattering rounds of cannon fire while their leader, Bonnie Prince Charlie, dithered. Try hauling yourself across this unforgiving ground, and you will see how difficult it must have been for the men who were laden down with weapons and being blasted with grapeshot as they struggled on. Those who did make it to the government lines were quickly dispatched, as "Butcher" Cumberland had drilled his men in new techniques for fighting at close quarters with the Highlanders. After your trip to the battlefield, enjoy a well-earned pit stop in the visitor center café (see p. 177).

or so rugged clansmen who joined the "45," as the rebellion of 1745 became known.

This time the success of the Jacobites was quick and impressive. After taking Edinburgh and defeating the British Army at Prestonpans, the Jacobite army battled confidently south, with Bonnie Prince Charlie's claims that the English Jacobites were waiting to rise up in support and that the French military invasion was imminent, echoing in their ears. After crossing the border the army reached Derby, and even London was panicked as its population feared an impending and decisive attack. However, the English Jacobites did not rise in significant numbers, nor did the promised French attack materialize, leaving the Jacobites divided over what to do next. Reluctantly, Bonnie Prince Charlie led his troops on a thoroughly morale-sapping retreat north, with the eager Duke of Cumberland, son of the Hanoverian George II, and his professional army (now free from battling the French on the Continent) in hot pursuit.

In 1746, after a draining winter, the unde-feated Bonnie Prince Charlie resolved to take on Cumberland and his British Hanoverian army. An ambitious attempt to surprise the British government forces by marching over-night to catch the duke on his birthday failed. Instead, the shattered Jacobites were dragged into battle the next morning, immediately after their exhausting night march. To date their infamous "Highland Charge" had seen them outmaneuver the organized British army, but this time the prince chose his battlefield poorly—the boggy moor at Culloden—which made their blood-curdling charge almost impossible. Badly led and demoralized, the Jacobite army was decimated in a horrendous carnage that saw more than 1,500 men slain for the loss of a couple hundred British troops.

The Clan System

Under the clan system that existed up until the Highland Clearances, the local men pledged to take up arms for their chief in return for land and their place in society. Under the new feudal system, the British government banned many traditional Scottish activities, including wearing tartan and playing bagpipes, and it prohibited the clan chiefs from having their own armies. The clan chiefs who supported the Jacobite uprising lost their lands.

The Highland Clearances

The defeat at Culloden was cataclysmic for the Highland way of life. The Highlands were hammered by "Butcher" Cumberland and his men, with wounded or captured clansmen slaughtered where they lay on and around Culloden. Months of systematic murders, beatings, and rapes ensued as Cumberland's army—a "British" army—sought revenge throughout the Highlands on ostensibly British citizens.

The new regime that took over the Highlands following the defeat at Culloden was the feudal one that had developed around most of Europe by this time—the same social model that already operated in the Scottish Lowlands to some extent. The new breed of landowner, or laird, backed by the British government, set about pacifying the Highlands and making the land more economically viable. The Highlanders were forced from their homes to make way for sheep and other more profitable uses, in a human tragedy that has become known as the Highland Clearances.

The more enlightened landowners tried to give the clanspeople new livelihoods in industries such as fishing. But many of the lairds forced the Highlanders on to unsustainable crofts (small infertile plots of land over which they had no security of tenure and that could not sustain a decent way of life). Soon, thousands of Scots were leaving the Highlands for new lives in far-flung corners of the world. Families were torn apart, with those too frail to make the long journey abroad often left behind to die. The Clearances continued until the Crofters' Holdings Act of 1886, which finally granted security of tenure as well as other essential guarantees and reforms.

Industrial Revolution & Scotland in the Empire

The Act of Union had been slow to boost the Scottish economy. But the start of the industrial revolution and Scotland's role both in it and in the establishment of the British Empire soon brought the nation and its people the possibility of fame and fortune. As a western port crucially offering easier access to the Americas, Glasgow was at the spearhead of this surge in trade.

With rich natural resources, particularly coal and iron, Scotland was well placed to grow during the industrial revolution. The River Clyde soon became the birthplace of many of the world's ships. This economic transformation brought with it social change, too, as the country's population increasingly flocked to the central belt, and particularly Glasgow, looking for work. The Scots were in a unique position, being both keen colonists in the British Empire and a colonized nation within the United Kingdom, but the bureaucrats in London still called the shots.

Scotland in the 20th and 21st Centuries

World War I (1914–1918) brought massive suffering to Scotland. It is estimated that 20 percent of British deaths during the Great War were Scots soldiers, despite Scots only making up 10 percent of the British population. Scotland had still not fully recovered when the economic depressions of the 1930s hit. Systemic problems in Scotland's heavy industries and cheaper competitors started to bite—a trend that World War II (1939–1945) merely delayed. The war helped prop up Scotland's failing heavy industries, such as shipbuilding, and other factories were turned to munitions supply, keeping workers not off to the battlefields employed. But in the postwar years, a slump hit as domestic demand died away and foreign markets offered cheaper alternatives.

On May 12, 1999, the first Scottish parliament in three centuries sat in Edinburgh, and the nation once again wrested some control back from its "Auld Enemy."

One of the darkest periods in modern Scottish history followed as the nation endured almost two decades ruled by a Conservative government that was repeatedly voted in by the English, but not the Scots, who chose the Labour Party. The main focus of wrath was the "Iron Lady," Margaret Thatcher, who was seen as dismissing the Scots and any desire they had for devolution or independence.

Then, in 1997, the new Labour government honored their promise of a fair referendum. The Scots responded with a resounding 75 percent in support of devolution. On May 12, 1999, the first Scottish parliament in three centuries sat in Edinburgh, and the nation once again wrested some control back from its "Auld Enemy." The thrust for greater independence has continued with the Scottish National Party's success in the 2007 elections, who are committed to achieving total independence from England. ■

The Arts

Scotland's rich cultural heritage harks back to the days of oral clan culture, where the storytelling ballad was king in what scholars now believe was a far more developed and sophisticated culture than previously thought. Over the centuries, this has evolved to create some world-famous names in the fields of art, architecture, literature, film, music, and the performing arts, with a vibrant arts scene integral to the psyche of the modern nation.

Painting & Sculpture

Scotland's earliest art was created by its prehistoric people, but little remains. Unfortunately, the same can be said of its clans, who for centuries relied more on oral storytelling than more fixed art mediums. In the 18th century, however, some famous painters emerged, such as Sir Henry Raeburn (1756–1823) and Allan Ramsay (1713–1840). Raeburn's most enduring work is perhaps "The Reverend Robert Walker Skating on Duddingston Loch" (1795), while Ramsay was most famous for his portraits, many of which are now on show in the National Portrait Gallery in Edinburgh.

Scotland's most famous living painter of the 21st century is undoubtedly the controversial Jack Vettriano (1954–).

From the 1870s, the Glasgow Boys emerged with a Scottish take on impressionism, usings its styles to reinvent the city and the surrounding countryside. Chief among them were Joseph Crawhall (1861–1913), Sir James Guthrie (1859–1930), and George Henry (1858–1943).

Taking their cues from the Glasgow Boys, as well as directly from their experiences with the French Impressionists, the artistic movement of the Scottish Colourists emerged in the early 20th century. Perhaps the best known was John Duncan Fergusson (1874–1961), who spent time with Picasso and became influenced by the Fauvists.

On the east coast, the Edinburgh School emerged in the 1930s. William Gillies (1898–1978) and Anne Redpath (1895–1965) stand out, as does Sir Eduardo Paolozzi (1924–2005), whose best sculpture is on show at the Modern Art Gallery in Edinburgh, along with a re-creation of his former studio.

Scotland's most famous living painter of the 21st century is undoubtedly the controversial Jack Vettriano (1954–). This self-taught artist has been embroiled in accusations of being too commercial, but his paintings are as appealing in art galleries as they are on the walls of homes around the country. Interestingly, no art gallery in Scotland outside his native Fife has yet exhibited his work. His supporters attribute this to an elitist Scottish artistic establishment. At the time of writing there were suggestions that the National Galleries of Scotland were considering exhibiting some of his work. An even more controversial contemporary Scottish painter is Peter Howson (1958–), who brutally captures the urban landscapes of Glasgow, as well as directly tackles a range of themes as extreme as rape and painting nudes of pop star Madonna.

"The Reverend Robert Walker Skating on Duddingston Loch" (1795) by Sir Henry Raeburn

Literature

Much of Scotland's earliest literature has been lost because it was focused around the oral traditions—stories passed down through the centuries by the tribes who lived in the Highlands and islands. In 1919, the English writer T. S. Eliot, when quizzed on what he thought about Scottish literature, famously retorted, "Was there a Scottish literature?" There was then, and there still is. Scotland boasts a rich canon of work that is becoming increasingly recognized as the devolved nation grows in confidence.

Scotland's writers only really came to global attention in the age of Romantic literature. Sir Walter Scott (1771–1832) penned perhaps the first ever historical novel with *Waverley* (1814) and went on to weave a succession of romanticized historical novels, eulogizing folk heroes such as Scotland's own Robin Hood, in *Rob Roy* (1817). Scott also delved back through the centuries and collated some of the traditional Borders ballads. Scotland's national bard, Robert Burns (1759–1796), also collated traditional ballads, but he was most renowned for his colorful poems in the Scots language and, of course, for writing one of the world's most famous songs, "Auld Lang Syne." Every bit the tragic romantic poet, his all too short life was peppered with love affairs, illegitimate children, and all sorts of scandal, further endearing him to a nation deeply fond of flawed heroes.

In the 19th century, the great figure was Robert Louis Stevenson (1850–1894), a novelist whose *Strange Case of Dr. Jekyll and Mr. Hyde* (1886) may have been set in London, but only so that Stevenson could safely satirize the duality of Edinburgh and the Scottish psyche. His famous novels *Kidnapped* (1886) and *Treasure Island* (1883) perfectly bridge the divide between thriller and children's literature. Stevenson's contemporary, Arthur Conan Doyle (1859–1930), studied medicine at the University of Edinburgh before going on to create the famous detective Sherlock Holmes—a character based on the Edinburgh physician and pioneering forensic scientist Joseph Bell.

By the start of the 20th century, Scottish novelists were taking a keen interest in the social conditions around them. The *Scots Quair* trilogy by Lewis Grassic Gibbon (1901–1935) is not only a great work of art but also a lucid insight into life in Aberdeenshire in the years swirling around World War I; *The Silver Darlings* by Neil M. Gunn (1891–1973) does the same with the aftermath of the Highland Clearances. Emerging female writers included modernist Muriel Spark (1918–2006), whose seminal *Prime of Miss Jean Brodie* perfectly captures 1930s Edinburgh; this prodigious talent wrote 20 other novels as well.

In the field of poetry, Hugh McDiarmid (1892–1978) emerged as a true giant of language and thought, celebrating the use of Scots and vehemently defending its increasing usage and written form. By contrast, Edwin Muir (1910–1996) showed what could still

UNESCO City of Literature

As a city that is founded on centuries of books, and which still revels in literature of all kinds, it was no surprise that UNESCO chose Edinburgh to be its first City of Literature in 2004. Since then it has been joined by Melbourne and Iowa City. Every year, a range of events—from poetry readings to lectures—are held, with more than 60 events staged between 2007 and 2010. More direct action includes handing out free books and, in 2010, encouraging people in the city to "Carry a Poem." See www.cityofliterature.com for more information.

be done writing about Scottish themes in English, while Sorley MacLean (1911–1996) did the same for the threatened Gaelic language.

In recent decades, Scottish writers have also embraced modernist as well as postmodernist styles. Alistair Gray (1934) wove a magical realism and fantasy into the Scottish urban experience in a groundbreaking novel, *Lanark* (1981)—a literary experience that have led some scholars to dub it "Scotland's *Ulysses.*"

Irvine Welsh (1961–) has violently committed Scots, and even more extreme dialects, to the novel format with a series of shocking novels, the most famous of which, *Trainspotting* (1993), became a successful movie. The more cerebral Booker Prize–winning (for *How Late It Was How Late*) James Kelman (1946–) has consistently flung himself into defiant use of the vernacular—not just weaving it around the standard English novel form but declaring war on traditional narrative with his beautifully brutal flowing prose style and frequent use of the sort of swear words that his characters would indeed pepper their everyday speech with.

> **Scotland boasts a rich canon of work that is becoming increasingly recognized as the devolved nation grows in confidence.**

Ian Rankin (1960–) stuck more to traditional English narrative forms in his gritty Rebus detective novels, painting as vivid a picture of Edinburgh as has ever been painted. Meanwhile, Iain Banks (1954–) perfectly conveys the dualism and confused identities at the heart of much Scottish literature and culture as he pens beautifully perceptive novels such as the disturbing and powerful *The Wasp Factory* (1984) and the unorthodox Scottish family saga *The Crow Road* (1992) under his own name; under his alter ego, Iain M. Banks, he conjures up science fiction. His excellent *Raw Spirit: In Search of a Perfect Dram* (2003) is an ideal whisky travelog for timid whisky drinkers and connoisseurs alike. In recent years, Scottish women novelists have started to muscle into what has been a male-dominated literary canon. Chief among them are Al Kennedy (1965–) and Janice Galloway (1955–), whose award-winning debut, *The Trick Is to Keep Breathing* (1989), is an excellent read.

Film

With its landscapes and breathtaking drama, the Highlands could have been designed with the movie industry in mind. However, Scottish moviemaking has suffered under the dominance of the Union with England. It took the recent advent of Scottish Screen (*www.scottishscreen.com*) to kickstart the domestic industry. Hollywood has always had a love affair with Scotland, however, with blockbusters such as *Local Hero* (1983), starring Peter Riegert as a cynical oilman being won over by the local community; *Braveheart* (1995), which told the story of William Wallace and Robert the Bruce (taking a few historical shortcuts on the way to hype up the drama); and *Rob Roy* (1995), a depiction of one of Scotland's most romanticized outlaws.

At the other end of the spectrum, Danny Boyle (1956–) did not so much burst onto the world's cinema screens as explode in a pile of gritty realism that shocked as much as it impressed global cinema audiences with *Trainspotting* (1996)—the perfect antidote for some to the saccharine romanticism of *Braveheart* and *Rob Roy*. Danny Boyle has emerged as Scotland's greatest living director, with further global successes such as the

Academy Award–winning *Slumdog Millionaire* (2008). Another contemporary Scottish director to keep an eye on is Kevin McDonald (1967–), whose *Last King of Scotland* (2006) was a global hit that focused not on any Scottish king but notorious African leader Idi Amin.

Today, the most famous Scottish actor is, of course, Sean Connery (1930–). This gravel-voiced screen lothario was the ideal James Bond, but he has also starred in countless other hits including *Highlander* (1986), set in his homeland, and *The Hunt for Red October* (1990). In recent years, a new generation of male leads has emerged, with Ewan McGregor (1971–) using his inspired performances in *Trainspotting* to become both a serious arthouse actor as well as earning big bucks in Hollywood. The cerebral Robert Carlyle (1961–) also used *Trainspotting* to launch a more considered career that has included a litany of interesting roles, in films such as *The Full Monty* (1997) and *Stone of Destiny* (2008), which tells the story of the audacious theft in 1950 from Westminster Abbey of the Stone of Scone and its return to Arbroath Abbey in 1951.

Architecture

Scotland's treasure trove of prehistoric architecture stands among the finest in Europe—particularly the well-preserved sights at Skara Brae and the Knap of Howar in the Orkney Islands. The Romans also left their mark with a higher density of marching camps—estimated to have been built by their invading and occupying armies—than anywhere else in Europe, with most sites yet to be excavated. Sturdier remnants are the rugged stone brochs built around the coastline to fend off seaborne intruders, especially from the north.

For buildings created in the days of a united nation, David I goes down in architectural history for commissioning the remarkable Borders abbeys, whose romantic ruins are graced with a variety of styles. Meanwhile, Dunfermline Abbey is a classic example of Romanesque and early Gothic styles, as are the ruins of Holyrood Abbey in Edinburgh. Linlithgow Palace shows the Stuart monarchs' taste for the Renaissance, which they also demonstrated at the sibling Falkland Palace.

By the 1990s, a new wave of glass and steel was being interwoven with solid sandstone, marrying the new and the old architectural styles.

Following the 1707 Act of Union and the increasing concentration of Scottish society into her cities came the refined era of Georgian architecture. This period saw Edinburgh's graceful New Town emerge in a sophisticated revolt against the medieval Old Town. Seminal Scottish architects at this time included William Henry Playfair (1790–1857), William Adam (1684–1748), and his son Robert Adam (1728–1792). Neoclassical styles ruled the day and were adopted in Glasgow, too. Grand country houses, such as Hopetoun House in South Queensferry, and even those found in far-flung corners such as the coastal town of Inveraray, demonstrate this love affair with the neoclassical style.

As part of the British Empire, Scotland's cities prospered during the reign of Queen Victoria (1837–1901). The prosperity brought more graceful stone town houses to Edinburgh and Glasgow, but also to Aberdeen and Dundee. It was perhaps fitting that it was Scotland's greatest Victorian-era writer, Sir Walter Scott, who

The strikingly modern Clyde Auditorium, Glasgow, is known locally as "the armadillo."

created one of the most outlandish Victorian temples, with his Abbotsford retreat in the Borders.

The 20th century started well. Charles Rennie Mackintosh (1868–1928) brought his unique brand of art nouveau to the city, with his remarkable Glasgow School of Art and a whole host of other remarkable buildings. During the 20th century, more and more people flocked to Scotland's cities in search of work, and the economically difficult decades following World War II brought a new architectural functionalism that saw the ubiquitous use of concrete and cheaper materials.

This unlovable functional style of architecture, typified by office buildings and soaring tower blocks that quickly became urban ghettos, continued on through the 1960s and 1970s. However, there were some more positive creations. By the 1990s, a new wave of glass and steel was being interwoven with solid sandstone, marrying the new and the old Georgian and Victorian styles in Scotland's cities. Probably the most dramatic—and certainly the most contentious—building of the 21st century has been the new Scottish Parliament building in Edinburgh, which again weaves in old and new styles and very much reflects the zeitgeist of modern Scottish architecture.

Music

Music was integral to life under the old clan system. Mournful ballads drifted through the glens centuries ago as the oral culture both celebrated and recorded the history of the day. This tradition has carried on into modern times, with much Scottish music atmospherically harking back to the themes of lost kinship and struggles for independence.

The key proponents of traditional folk music once included the Battlefield Band, The Corries, and Alba. But Scotland's music, like the country around it, has constantly evolved. Gaelic rock band Runrig brought Celtic rock into the mainstream in the 1980s. Karen Matheson, lead singer of the excellent Capercaillie, both in her solo and group work, has shown how Scottish music relies on its rich heritage, but also constantly evolves, exploring styles such as blues. Exciting talents on the current folk music scene include the Blazin' Fiddles, Salsa Celtica, and Shooglenifty.

The bagpipe, the accordion, and the fiddle are key instruments in Scottish folk music, but the more recent addition of the acoustic guitar, and then the more powerful electric guitar, opened doors that global rock success stories such as Big Country (with guitars sounding like bagpipes) and Simple Minds were keen to explore with their stadium-filling hits. During the 1990s, influential Glasweigan indie pop band Belle and Sebastian achieved international cult success with their breakthrough 1998 album, *Boy with the Arab Strap.*

Scottish Music in the 21st century: Increasingly, Scottish music in the 21st century is entwining traditional forms into modern media—or at least demonstrating the same type of pioneering innovation, rather than harping after American or English

Students rehearse at the Royal Scottish Academy of Music and Drama.

styles, as was sometimes the case in the past. Kilsyth's dark alternative rockers the Twilight Sad and Selkirk's mournful but jaunty alternative popsters Frightened Rabbit have both incorporated enigmatic storytelling in their work with dramatic results. In recent years, well-known acts on the pop front have included Franz Ferdinand, which has broken through on both sides of the Atlantic, while fellow west coasters Glasvegas have hit heady heights in the United Kingdom. Calvin Harris from Dumfries has enjoyed considerable success in the dance music charts.

These Scottish pop acts are not afraid to use their own accents, which isn't the issue it once was and is a sign of a nation brimming with musical confidence. In Scotland, bashing along to a powerful alternative rock band is as much part of the musical landscape as taking in an informal folk session in a traditional pub. Both share a musical legacy in which telling a story laced with melancholy and longing in an innovative and appealing way is at the forefront of the mix.

Other Performing Arts

The performing arts are crucial to Scottish culture, with the massive Edinburgh International Festival in August (*www.eif.co.uk*; see pp. 68–69)–the world's biggest arts extravaganza–a sign of how Scotland views the performing arts. Indeed, there are five national performing arts bodies. On the classical music front, the Royal Scottish National Orchestra (*73 Claremont St., Glasgow, tel 0141/226 3868, www.rsno.org.uk*), formed way back in 1891, is one of Europe's leading symphony orchestras and symbolically performed at the opening of the Scottish Parliament building in 1999. The Scottish Chamber Orchestra (*4 Royal Terrace, Edinburgh, tel 0131/557 6800, www.sco.org.uk*) may have only been founded in 1974, but it is also highly regarded.

The largest performing arts organization in the country is Scottish Opera (see Travelwise p. 308), with a base at the Theatre Royal in Glasgow–the oldest theater in the country. Meanwhile, Scottish Ballet (see Travelwise p. 306) moved into a dramatic new base at the Tramway, Glasgow, in 2009, which has given a new backbone to their work. The company continually tours, however, having covered much of the country since their foundation in 1974.

A newcomer since devolution has been the National Theatre of Scotland (*www .nationaltheatrescotland.com*). A sign of both a renewed interest in the arts and also of the Parliament's desire to foster Scottish culture, the National Theatre of Scotland's remit is to take the arts to the people, which they do by performing around the country and nurturing budding local talent.

While these official organizations are the most renowned, they are backed up by a plethora of groups, companies, and performers of all shapes and sizes. They appear at a multitude of venues—from world-class performance spaces in Scotland's cities to more modest village halls and schools. Take in any manner of performance and your visit will be the richer for it, and even better if you can make it to the Edinburgh International Festival in August. ∎

> **The performing arts are crucial to Scottish culture, with the massive Edinburgh International Festival in August—the world's biggest arts extravaganza.**

Steeped in culture and history, a vibrant and cosmopolitan capital standing proudly on rocky crags overlooking the Lothians

Edinburgh & the Lothians

The spectacular Edinburgh Military Tattoo under the gaze of Edinburgh Castle

Edinburgh & the Lothians

Scotland's capital city does not so much wear its history on its sleeve as overflow with intoxicating tales of feuding warlords, medieval villains, and royal and religious intrigue. This sense of history spills into the surrounding region of the Lothians, which offers premier golf courses, picturesque villages, and areas of stellar natural beauty.

Edinburgh has always been at the heart of Scotland's turbulent history—whether it was when the city's castle held out against Bonnie Prince Charlie during his ill-fated quest to reclaim the British throne or when it was at the epicenter of the seminal Scottish Enlightenment.

Today, a new Edinburgh has emerged—a city of boutique-style shopping and stylish hotels. Scotland's capital has once and for all established a modern identity at the head of

the devolved nation. Edinburgh has ruled over a country that now has its first parliament in 300 years. With this role has come a new sense of confidence, which has spiced up the city's traditional charms.

Edinburgh has earned plaudits such as "the Athens of the North" with its combination of stunning natural setting and well-preserved architecture. More importantly, the city recently won recognition from UNESCO with both the medieval Old Town and Georgian

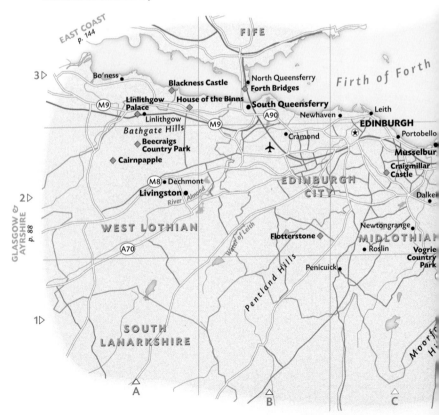

EAST COAST p. 144

FIFE

3▷ Bo'ness

Blackness Castle

North Queensferry
Forth Bridges

Firth of Forth

Linlithgow
M9 Palace   House of the Binns

South Queensferry

A90   Newhaven   Leith

Linlithgow

Bathgate Hills

M9

EDINBURGH

Cramond   Portobello

★   Musselbur

Beecraigs
Country Park

Cairnpapple

EDINBURGH
CITY

Craigmillar
Castle

M8 Dechmont

Livingston

River Almond

GLASGOW & AYRSHIRE p. 88

2▷

Dalke

WEST LOTHIAN

Water of Leith

A70

Flotterstone

Newtongrange

MIDLOTHIAN

Roslin   Vogrie
Country
Park

Penicuik

1▷

Pentland Hills

SOUTH
LANARKSHIRE

Moorfo
Hi

A   B   C

New Town commended on the World Heritage List. And its grand location, graced with peaks of volcanic rock, rugged hills, and the mighty River Forth estuary has always given the city a certain air.

Further charms await outside the city center in the old port of Leith, now reinvented as a gastronomic hub, and the charming suburb of South Queensferry, which is home to two of the world's greatest bridges. With so much to offer, it is easy to see why Edinburgh is Scotland's most visited city.

The three regions surrounding Edinburgh— East Lothian, Midlothian, and West Lothian, collectively known as the Lothians—have their own treats to offer, from the resort towns and top golf courses of East Lothian, the rolling hills and historic churches of Midlothian, and the royal castles and palaces of West Lothian. ■

NOT TO BE MISSED:

**Edinburgh Castle, dominating the
  Scottish capital 60–64**

**Taking a walk at Arthur's
  Seat, the remnants of an
  extinct volcano 64**

**The National Museum of Scotland,
  cultural oasis at the heart of
  historic Scotland 65**

**Strolling through the beautiful
  Royal Botanic Garden,
  with hot houses and a top
  restaurant 72–73**

**South Queensferry's world-famous
  bridges, cozy restaurants, and
  grand country houses 76–77**

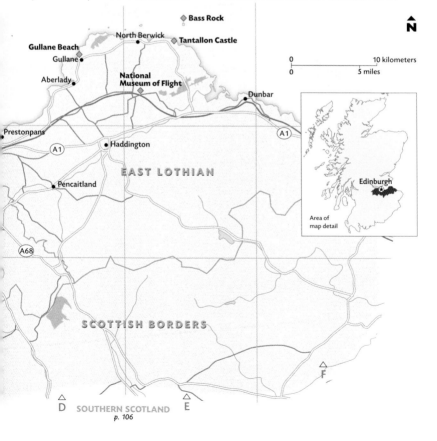

SOUTHERN SCOTLAND
p. 106

Edinburgh

With a stunning castle perched atop the remains of an extinct volcano and a distinctly medieval Old Town set against the well-heeled New Town to the north, which is itself more than 200 years old, Edinburgh does not just impress on first sight, but blows away your senses and steals your heart.

Edinburgh
- 56 C2, 59, 62–63

Visitor Information
- 3 Princes St.
- (0845) 225 5121
- **www.edinburgh.org**

Greyfriars Kirkyard
- Greyfriars Place
- (0131) 226 5429
- $ $
- **www.greyfriarskirk.com**

Edinburgh's History

The story starts at Castle Rock, the imposing volcanic plug that lies at the very heart of modern Edinburgh. The city's original Gaelic name, Dunedin, comes from "Eidyn's Fort," which is a name given by the Celtic tribes who once held sway in these wild lands. Historians think that Northumbrian invaders first anglicized the name to its current Edinburgh.

Greyfriars Bobby

The story of the world's most famous dog after Snoopy is more alluring given that the dog was real and the story draped in tragic romance. "Greyfriars Bobby" is the name given to the faithful pooch that became a resident of Greyfriars Kirkyard when his master died in 1858. Bobby spent the rest of his 14 years in a vigil by the grave. The dog became a local celebrity and, when he died, a statue was erected just outside Greyfriars Graveyard. Disney made a film out of the story (The True Story of a Dog), and his story lives on in the hearts of generations of tourists.

Further English incursions followed as various Scottish kings tried to establish their authority over what had become a deeply strategic fortress. A small settlement grew up around the ridge that climbed to the castle (today's Royal Mile), and by the 12th century Edinburgh had its own mint and was emerging as a serious national player. By the 14th century, Scottish king Robert the Bruce had bestowed a new charter on Edinburgh and brought the port of Leith within its bounds.

In 1707, Edinburgh's status as the capital of an independent nation was snatched away as the Act of Union joined Scotland and England. London would always be Britain's capital. Yet the loss of political power was mitigated by the advent of the British Empire. Edinburgh benefited from the increased prosperity and emerged as a center for finance, invention, learning, and philosophy as luminaries such as David Hume and Adam Smith came to the fore.

As Edinburgh expanded, the new wealthy citizens turned their back on the medieval squalor of the Old Town, building a perfectly planned city to the north, just across the drained Nor Loch. Wide boulevards, a neat gridlike street plan, leafy squares, and elegant sandstone town houses

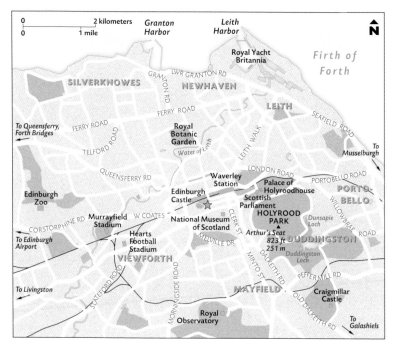

graced the New Town—the brainchild of architects James Craig (1739–1795), Robert Adam (1728–1792), and William Henry Playfair (1790–1857). The Georgian order and style of the New Town was the complete antithesis of the nefarious and ramshackle Old Town. This helped to add to the sense of duality that has pervaded Edinburgh's heart and soul through the centuries.

Two World Wars depleted Edinburgh's population, but its lack of industrial development compared to other Scottish cities spared it the worst of the World War II air raids. In the years following, the city found an outlet to promote its charms on the global stage with the founding of the Edinburgh Festival in 1947.

As Scottish oil generated billions of dollars for the British economy in the 20th century, this new source of wealth helped fuel a desire for independence that had lain dormant, like Arthur's Seat (the extinct volcano in the

Holyrood Park

🅰 59

✉ Holyrood Park Road

☎ (0131) 652 8150

$ $

**www.historic
-scotland.gov.uk**

Edinburgh Castle

🏔 59

✉ Castlehill

☎ (0131) 225 9846

💲 $$$

**www.edinburgh
castle.gov.uk**

National War Museum

🏔 62

✉ Edinburgh Castle, Castlehill

☎ (0131) 247 4413

💲 $$$

**www.nms.ac.uk/
war/home/index.asp**

heart of Edinburgh), but by no means expired. This desire culminated in a 1997 referendum that solidly backed the establishment of a devolved parliament. The new parliament first sat in 1999 and moved to a striking purpose-built home in Holyrood in 2004.

Like other cities, Edinburgh has struggled economically recently. Never before has tourism played such a crucial role, and people from all over the world continue to flock to this unique city.

Edinburgh's Old Town

Edinburgh's Old Town is a deeply evocative warren of medieval streets, where ghosts of the past swirl around the cobbles and seep into every pore of the narrow wynds (lanes) and closes (alleyways). The streets are awash with cafés, pubs, and restaurants and the Old Town is very much the tourist epicenter.

Edinburgh Castle: The castle hangs omnipresent over the city on its volcanic perch and must be visited for its rich history and dramatic views over the city. Once home to Mary Queen of Scots, the castle is remarkably well preserved. Its unique structure encompasses the military innovations of various eras, while the many exhibits shed further light on the

Edinburgh Castle is the capital's iconic landmark and offers sweeping views over the city center.

nation's history. For most of its existence, however, Scotland's most visited tourist attraction has had little time for tourists, standing resolute against various foes. The best way to get a real feel for the fortress is on a guided tour or on one of the new self-guided audio tours.

Key features to look for include the expanse of the **Esplanade** as you enter, home to the Military Tattoo (see sidebar right). Inside the castle, the **National War Museum** covers Scottish soldiers after the Act of Union with a cornucopia of arms, medals, and well-preserved uniforms. A poignant recent addition includes portraits of Scottish troops serving in Afghanistan.

In the **Crown House** you can view Scotland's Crown Jewels—the Honours of Scotland—and the deeply symbolic Stone of Destiny, over which Scottish kings were once crowned. This important relic was repatriated from Westminster Abbey in London in 1996.

The **Great Hall** was once the venue for lavish banquets and all sorts of regal revelry. It was built during the reign of James IV and once served as the seat of the Scottish Parliament; it has been more prosaically a hospital and barracks. Its most recent, and somewhat ostentatious, makeover came in the 19th century.

St. Margaret's Chapel is the oldest surviving part of the castle, dating back to the 12th century and the reign of King David I.

If you have a taste for the darker side of life, you can delve

Military Matters

The Edinburgh Military Tattoo at Edinburgh Castle (see pp. 60–61 & 69), held every August, is one of the wonders of the modern military world. The sight of the massed pipes and drums of the Scottish regiments parading proudly beneath the floodlit castle ramparts is unforgettable. The tattoo is sold out well in advance (for tickets: *tel 0131/225 1188* or *www.edintattoo.co.uk/ tickets $$$$–$$$$$*) as 200,000 people flock to watch the bands perform. In recent years, camels and elephants have joined the show, along with eclectic performers who light up the pageantry with dancing and flag-waving. Expect the unexpected.

into the bowels of the castle and explore its vaults, which served as a military prison. Watch for the graffiti etched into the walls by the poor souls once condemned to eke out their days here.

Palace of Holyroodhouse: This palace, at the foot of the Royal Mile, is the British Royal Family's pad in town. Built next to the dramatic ruins of **Holyrood Abbey,** it is today a rambling but charming ruin. In the 12th century, during the reign of David I, the abbey was a mighty religious icon but was sacked by rampaging English armies.

The palace dates back to the days of James I and, despite its role as a regal residence, you can visit when the royals are not around. The interior is awash with fine fabrics, delicate oil paintings, and period furniture, but the highlight for many is the bed of Mary Queen of Scots. On this spot, Mary almost miscarried her

(continued on p. 64)

Palace of Holyroodhouse

⚑ 59

✉ End of Royal Mile

☎ (0131) 556 5100

$ $$$

www.royal.gov .uk/TheRoyal Residences

A Walk Down the Royal Mile

English writer Daniel Defoe once described the Royal Mile as the "finest street in the world." Despite the blight of a number of tacky souvenir shops, the majestic regal thoroughfare remains breathtaking. The Royal Mile originates in the craggy heights of Edinburgh Castle and descends in a tumble of cobbles—and three name changes—to the green expanse of Holyrood Park, where awaits the Edinburgh residence of the queen, the Palace of Holyroodhouse.

Descending from **Edinburgh Castle ❶** (see pp. 60–61), the Royal Mile starts at Castlehill, with sweeping views of the city at its western extremity, before stopping at the **Camera Obscura ❷** *(549 Castlehill, tel 0131/226 3709)*, home to more breathtaking views. These views are projected onto a disk in its distinctive tower using an archaic system of mirrors to the delights of young and old alike. The other floors are crammed full of weird and wonderful optical illusions and hands-on exhibits.

Across the road, **The Scotch Whisky Experience** *(354 Castlehill, tel 0131/220 0441, www.whisky-heritage.co.uk)* is next up. This thoughtfully laid out attraction is essential for lovers of a wee dram and starts with a cute whisky barrel ride. You can find out about all aspects of whisky and its production, and there is also a very well stocked whisky bar and a highly regarded Scottish restaurant on-site for a drink and a bite to eat before continuing on your walk.

The Royal Mile then rushes through two name changes, the Lawnmarket and then High Street. As you cross at the junction that marks the end of Lawnmarket you will see the old headquarters of the once mighty **Bank of Scotland ❸** *(The Mound)*, which nearly collapsed and lost its independence following the

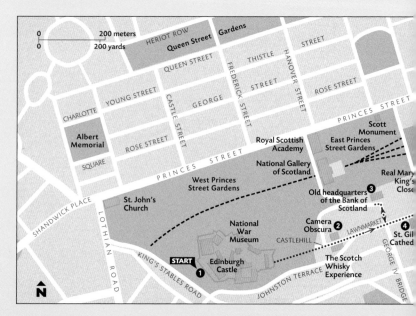

global recession of 2008. **St. Giles' Cathedral** ❹ *(High Street, tel 0131/225 9442)* proudly welcomes you to High Street. A religious edifice has stood on this site since 854. The oldest sections date from 1120, and Charles I designated it a cathedral back in 1633.

If you are brave, you can meet the city's famous ghosts close up at the **Real Mary King's Close** ❺ *(2 Warriston's Close, tel 0845/070 6244, www.realmarykingsclose.com).* As the grand Georgian Edinburgh took shape, some of its poorer plague-ridden inhabitants were quarantined to die here, and the foundations of the City Chambers (which still stands) were built over them. Sections of their former quarters can be explored on distinctly eerie tours—definitely not for the faint-hearted.

As you leave High Street, glance to the south and you can see the **Tron Church** ❻ *(122 High Street).* Sadly, this church is now closed, but it used to be the hub of the city's Hogmanay street party before the New Year celebrations took on a more corporate air and moved to a ticketed event on Princes Street. If you are in need of refreshments, the **Bank Hotel** *(1–3 South Bridge, tel 0131/556 9940, www.bankhoteledinburgh.co.uk)* is on hand with its friendly bar, which demonstrates how the city has constantly reinvented its buildings while retaining their grandeur. You won't enjoy such frivolous revelry at the **John Knox House** ❼ *(43 High Street, tel 0131/556 9579),* farther down High Street, which provides insight into the strict firebrand religious campaigner who led the Protestant Reformation of Scotland in the 16th century.

The penultimate stop on this lively city walk is the new **Scottish Parliament** ❽ *(Holyrood, tel 0800/092 7600 for guided tours, by arrangement only).* There are guided tours around the ultramodern Parliament building, which opened in 2004. Eyesore or inspirational, decide for yourself and engage in lively debate, a favorite Edinburgh pastime since time immemorial. Fittingly, you have now traveled from the old seat of power—the castle—to the new Scottish one. At the end of the Royal Mile, the British Royal Family keeps an eye on proceedings from the **Palace of Holyroodhouse** ❾ *(Holyrood, tel 0131/556 5100; see p. 61).*

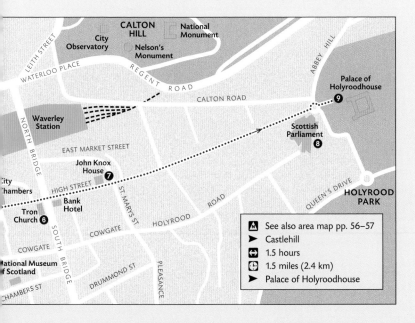

baby (the future King James VI), later born in Edinburgh Castle, after she witnessed her alleged lover being murdered at the hands of henchmen under the instructions of her husband, Lord Darnley.

South of the Royal Mile:

This is a wonderful place to come to grips with the Old Town and evoke its medieval character. Delving down **Victoria Street** is like leafing through the pages of a dusty old history book. The cobbled crescent descends in a curl of antique shops, bookshops, custom-made clothes stores, and some characterful pubs and restaurants. Look above to see a second tier leading up to the castle.

Victoria Street spills on to the **Grassmarket,** a scenic cobbled square that was once home to a popular market and, more gruesomely, where the city dwellers

INSIDER TIP:

Take a tour of the Real Mary King's Close [see p. 63]. This step back into 16th-century city life allows you to experience firsthand the difficult living conditions of these crowded alleyways.

—NICOLE ENGDAHL
*National Geographic
Development Office*

used to gather to witness public hangings. **The Last Drop** *(74–78 Grassmarket, tel 0131/225 4851)* is a pub based around the macabre theme as is its neighbor, **Maggie Dickson's Pub** *(92 Grassmarket, tel 0131/225 6601),* named for a woman said to have been hanged as a witch who was bumped back to life as the undertaker's cart thundered over the cobbled streets. Maggie won a reprieve that had more people believing she was a witch than ever before. Scotland's Shakespeare—the poet Robert Burns—wrote some of his most memorable verse a few doors along at the **White Hart Inn** *(34 Grassmarket, tel 0131/226 2806).*

At the end of Grassmarket, across the dramatic sweep of George IV Bridge on Chambers Street, is the building formerly known as the Museum of Scotland—a grand swish of modern architecture that somehow manages to blend seamlessly with the older Royal Museum building. Following a massive renovation

---

EXPERIENCE:
Climbing Arthur's Seat

Join the locals who like to hike up this 820-foot (251 m) dormant volcano in the heart of the city center. The best place to start is the steep trail that leads off St. Margaret's Loch, but there are numerous ways to the summit. Just take care and avoid the west face, which has been the site of a few fatal accidents. The rocky summit offers the best possible views of Edinburgh, with the entire city and its suburbs unfurling below as you chat with the equally breathless locals. Now descend to the south and the village-like suburb of **Duddingston,** where the famous **Sheep Heid Inn** and its traditional skittles alley awaits.

Old pubs along Grassmarket in the Old Town area

project, the two museums have now merged into one, known as the **National Museum of Scotland**. An exhibition in the modern building brilliantly tells Scotland's story from the arrival of primitive man to the wild years when the people fought to forge their nation in the face of English dominion, through to Scotland's pivotal role in the rise and fall of the British Empire, finally ending with an interesting exhibit on "Modern Scotland."

Particularly evocative items on display in the museum include the Cramond Lioness—a Roman sculpture left behind in Edinburgh when the Romans decamped back to the Eternal City—and 11 of the Lewis Chessmen (a group of 78 12th-century chess pieces found in 1831 on the isle of Lewis, the rest of which are still housed in the British Museum in London) that shine resplendent in their exquisite ivory glory.

More modern highlights include the homemade bicycle of "Flying Scot" Graeme Obree, a very Scottish hero who famously set the world hour record in a velodrome. Obree's record is all the more amazing given that he saw off his competitors on a contraption fashioned with parts from an old washing machine. There are also antiquated mounted animals and intricate scale models of once glorious steamships and railroad engines. The voluminous **Great Hall** is an airy marvel and a work of art in itself. Also check out the collage of ancient Greek and Roman pieces, the ghoulish Egyptian mummies, and the rather incongruous looking totem pole.

After you have exhausted the

Arthur's Seat

59

walking.visitscotland
.com/walks/central
scotland/holyrood_
parkarthurs_seat

**National Museum
of Scotland**

59

Chambers Street

(0131) 225 7534

www.nms.ac.uk/our
_museums/national
_museum.aspx

Princes Street in New Town Edinburgh

look at the story of Scotland in a striking sail-like avant-garde building that nestles in the shadow of Arthur's Seat (see sidebar p. 64). This is the city center's premier family attraction. Its amazing array of interactive exhibits thrills the senses in an exciting and energetic experience that allows you to face the dangers of a volcanic eruption, dive beneath the waves and explore a coral reef, take flight over the glaciers of Norway and Sweden, and wander through a tropical rain forest. Those without children in tow may want to give it a miss, but a call to all parents— don't even think about missing this attraction if you are visiting Edinburgh for any great length of time.

New Town

Edinburgh's New Town is not so new anymore. The area dates back more than two centuries to the days when the city's rich and prosperous citizens employed visionary architects and town planners to create an idyllic new abode away from the maelstrom of the Old Town. The New Town retains its dignified neoclassical air, with green spaces, arrow-straight streets laid out largely on a neat grid, grand town houses, and some of the finest art galleries in Britain.

The most dramatic way into the New Town is descending from the Royal Mile down **The Mound,** so named as it is literally the pile of earth that built up when the Nor Loch was drained to connect the newer quarter with the Old Town. Today, the castle

Our Dynamic Earth

✉ 116–118 Holyrood Road

☎ (0131) 550 7800

💲 $$$

www.dynamicearth .co.uk

exhibits at the museum you can linger in its café, take in views of the city from the roof garden, or enjoy lunch in the buzzy bistro-style Scottish restaurant. Be sure to book a window table for the panoramic Old Town views.

Farther east back toward Holyrood Park, **Our Dynamic Earth** takes a more scientific, geological

lies proudly to the west while the grand facades of the New Town greet to the south. In between lie Princes Street Gardens.

Princes Street Gardens:

Both parts of the gardens are replete with benches and grassy areas ideal for a picnic. **West Princes Street Gardens** is also home to the Ross Bandstand (venue for the city's famous Hogmanay concerts, see sidebar p. 17), the striking gold Ross Fountain, and **St. John's Church,** a religious edifice as renowned for the views from its terrace as its splendid interior. Look, too, for the **Scottish-American War Memorial,** which was commissioned by the Scottish-American War Memorial Committee to commemorate those Scots who fought in World War I. Sculpted by Scottish-Canadian R. Tait McKenzie (1867–1938), the memorial was unveiled in 1927 by then U.S. ambassador to Britain, Alanson B. Houghton.

The **East Princes Street Gardens** are less grand, but things brighten up during the Christmas period, when an ice rink and Ferris wheel are assembled, and a German Christmas market helps locals and visitors alike get in the festive mood. This is a great time for families to visit.

Crowning The Mound itself are the **National Gallery of Scotland** and the **Royal Scottish Academy.** William Henry Playfair (1790–1857) designed these two Georgian temples—the academy in classical Doric style and the gallery in Ionic style. The two buildings are connected by an underground walkway extension, the **Weston Link** (opened in 2004), which is an architectural marvel in itself. Make sure you relax with a drink or enjoy a meal in the Weston Link to appreciate the views out across East Princes Street Gardens to the landmark Balmoral Hotel and Princes Street.

The more time you can afford in the galleries the better. They are a real treasure trove of domestic and international art displayed in an environment that brings out the best in the paintings. Must-see works include "The Reverend

INSIDER TIP:

Ramsay's B&B will give you an authentic, personalized visit while staying in the heart of the city. Sharon Ramsay treated me like a dear friend.

—JENNIFER SEGAL
National Geographic Development Office

Robert Walker Skating on Duddingston Loch" by Scottish artist Sir Henry Raeburn (1756–1823; see p. 47), "The Feast of Herod" by Peter Paul Rubens (1577–1640), "The Virgin and Child" by Raphael (1483–1520), and "The Three Tahitians" by Paul Gauguin (1848–1903).

East of the galleries, East

(continued on p. 70)

St. John's Church

⚑ 62

✉ West Princes Street Gardens, Princes Street

☎ (0131) 229 7565

www.stjohns-edinburgh.org.uk

National Gallery of Scotland

⚑ 62

✉ The Mound

☎ (0131) 624 6200

www.national galleries.org

Royal Scottish Academy

⚑ 62

✉ The Mound

☎ (0131) 225 6671

www.royal scottishacademy.org

Ramsay's Bed & Breakfast

✉ 25 East London St.

☎ (0131) 557 5917

💲 $

www.ramsaysbed andbreakfastedin burgh.com

Edinburgh Summer Festivals

Every summer, Scotland's capital explodes with myriad festivals, including the largest arts event in the world—the Edinburgh Festival. There is an amazing vibe in the city as celebrities, performers, and festival-goers flock to its concert halls, theaters, and pubs to soak up the many various forms of entertainment on offer.

Acrobats perform street theater near Princes Street during the Edinburgh Festival Fringe.

Every year an increasing number of European cities tout their arts festivals as the biggest and best. Edinburgh doesn't need to make such idle boasts, as its festival is undeniably the biggest and, as most festival regulars would confirm, the best. Since its inception in 1947, this global mega-event has transformed into a cocktail of overlapping and constantly evolving festivals that keep the city buzzing from late July through to early September.

The **Edinburgh International Festival** (mid- Aug.–early Sept., www.eif.co.uk) is the "official festival"–the traditional linchpin of the Edinburgh summer–with classical music, theater,

and dance gracing venues such as the Festival Theatre and Usher Hall. Past highlights include innovative performances by the Scottish Ballet and the Budapest Festival Orchestra. For many, the fantastic firework finale and concert, held in Princes Street Gardens, is its crowning glory.

An Alternative Approach

The **Edinburgh Festival Fringe** (Aug., www.edfringe.com) has been going strong for more than 60 years. This colossal event (well over a million tickets are sold each year and the number of shows in every kind of venue imaginable is mind-boggling) delivers everything from famous stand-up comedy acts such as Englishman Ricky Gervais through to risqué amateur productions. Randomly picking a show, rooting out an obscure venue, and learning that you are the only spectator is all part of the fun and captures the true essence of the Fringe.

The **Edinburgh Military Tattoo** *(Aug., www.edintattoo.co.uk; see sidebar p. 61)* is another hugely popular part of the festival, staged at Edinburgh Castle. Thousands of spectators converge to watch bekilted Scottish regiments and military bands from around the globe parade and perform in this deeply atmospheric arena.

Meanwhile, fans of pop music can enjoy the **Edge Festival** *(Aug., www.theedgefestival.com)*, which has recently seen big-name acts such as Faith No More and Kanye West, as well as local talent, perform at venues across the capital.

The **Edinburgh International Book Festival** *(Aug., www.edbookfest.co.uk)*—the largest of its kind in the world—first graced Charlotte Square Gardens in 1983. Today, more than 200,000 visitors pour through its gates for an audience with authors, poets, journalists, and scholars from around the globe. Previous book festival favorites include the likes of Ian Rankin and J. K. Rowling.

Another record breaker, the **Edinburgh Jazz & Blues Festival** *(late July–early Aug., www.edinburghjazzfestival.co.uk)* is the longest running event of its kind in Britain. A colorful Mardi Gras and a three-hour jam in the Grassmarket set the pace for this jamboree. Another highlight is the open-air "Jazz on a Summer's Day," which takes place in Princes Street Gardens. The **Edinburgh Mela** *(Aug., www.edinburgh-mela.co.uk)* is another extravaganza of dance, theater, and music, which celebrates Scotland's ethnic and cultural diversity.

World-class visual art arrives in the city's galleries and museums via the **Art Festival** *(late July–early Aug., www.edinburghartfestival.com)*. A relatively recent addition to the "Festival"—the first event took place in 2004—it has quickly established itself as Scotland's largest annual festival of visual art. As well as works

Street entertainer at the Edinburgh Festival Fringe

from masters such as Picasso and Warhol, the many exhibitions also showcase local artists.

Tasting the Delights

Another relative newcomer is the **Foodies at Edinburgh Festival Park** *(Aug., www.foodiesfestival.com)*, which brings an epicurean extravaganza to the city's Holyrood Park. This three-day event displays the talents of the country's celebrity chefs, with demonstrations given by the likes of Tom Kitchin and Jeff Bland—both Michelin-starred chefs. Ticket holders can also participate in cookery classes, sample and buy the finest Scottish produce, and take advantage of the free live entertainment on the main stage.

Edinburgh's summer festivals may boast enough scheduled entertainment to captivate visitors, but much of the action is out on the streets. Buskers liven up the city center with everything from daredevil fire-eating and acrobatics to Charlie Chaplin–style mime and spontaneous performances from inebriated revelers. Grab a prized seat in a Royal Mile café, sit back, and watch the street life bustle past. No doubt you will soon agree that Edinburgh's festivals really are the best in the world.

Scott Monument

🄰 62

✉ East Princes Street Gardens

☎ (0131) 529 4068

💲 $

www.edinburgh.gov.uk

Waverley Station

🄰 62–63

☎ (08457) 114 141

www.networkrail.co.uk/aspx/807.aspx

National Monument

🄰 63

✉ Calton Hill

☎ (0131) 556 9536

www.edinburgh.gov.uk

Princes Street Gardens leads on to the controversial **Scott Monument.** This tribute to Scotland's greatest historical novelist, Sir Walter Scott (1771–1832), was completed in 1840 by George Meikle Kemp (1795–1844). Today it divides local opinion: Some see it as a fittingly towering tribute to the great man, others as a prime example of Victorian pomposity. Whatever you think, don't miss the chance to climb the hefty steps to the top of the rocket-like 200-foot-tall (61 m) tower offering great views over the city center.

More sweeping views await at the east end of Princes Street on the other side of the **Balmoral Hotel** (see Travelwise p. 277), the city's finest hotel and an impressive piece of Victorian architecture.

The hotel was originally built to serve the needs of **Waverley Station,** a 19th-century station with an elaborately decorated dome, during the golden age of the railroads. A few hundred yards beyond the hotel lies the access to Calton Hill. Take the steps on the north side of Waterloo Place.

Calton Hill: Scottish writer Robert Louis Stevenson (1850–1894) thought this modest hill offered the finest views of the city, and he had a point. You can see both the castle and Arthur's Seat, as well as right down the Firth of Forth, out to the open sea, with the Ochil Hills in the distance to the northwest. Calton Hill is also home to the **National Monument,** which was to be Scotland's very own

A walk up Calton Hill offers a spectacular view across the city center.

Parthenon. However, the project ran out of steam and all that was ever built were the slightly bereft looking Doric columns of the facade. Also up here is **Nelson's Monument** and the **City Observatory,** as well as a chunky Portuguese cannon, which is a great spot to have your photo taken staring down

INSIDER TIP:

The Beltane Fire Festival is an incredible spectacle, with hundreds of drummers and torch bearers on Calton Hill at midnight on April 30, escorting the May Queen on her ancient pagan pilgrimage of rebirth.

—JIM RICHARDSON
National Geographic photographer

the barrel of Princes Street. **George Street:** Back down from Calton Hill, two blocks north of Princes Street and separated by narrow and largely pedestrianized **Rose Street**—a great place to stop off in one of the many pubs and restaurants—is **George Street.** Once the seat of many wealthy banks and financial institutions, George Street lost much of its luster until recently. Its grand Georgian buildings have been reinvented as trendy bars, chic restaurants, and designer stores.

Two charming squares lie at either end of George Street. On the eastern end is **St. Andrew Square.** Its seating and coffee stall are popular with locals and visitors alike, who are watched over by the **statue of Lord Melville** (1742–1811), the naval secretary to the British Prime Minister William Pitt the Younger (1759–1806), surveying the scene from his perch.

Some of the homogeneity of this Georgian square was lost to 1960s and 1970s functionalism, but more successful modern architecture is on show in the shape of the **Harvey Nichols** *(30–31 St. Andrew Sq.)* department store—the first branch to open outside London. Retail addicts will also want to make a trip along **Multress Walk,** Edinburgh's newest street, which runs east from the north side of Harvey Nichols and is home to a flurry of designer stores.

One block north of St. Andrew Square is the **Scottish National Portrait Gallery.** In contrast to the austere Georgian architecture elsewhere in the New Town, this gallery is an ostentatious riot of Gothic architecture made all the more dramatic by its striking red sandstone hue. The portrait gallery is as much a historical gem as an artistic one, since it is made up of portraits of celebrated Scots through the ages. Highlights include seminal figures such as Mary Queen of Scots and Bonnie Prince Charlie, right through to more contemporary notables such as Sir Sean Connery. Note the gallery is going through a

Nelson's Monument

- 🅰 63
- ✉ 32 Calton Hill
- ☎ (0131) 529 3993
- 🕐 Closed Sun.
- 💲 $

www.edinburgh.gov .uk

City Observatory

- 🅰 63
- ✉ Calton Hill

www.astronomy edinburgh.org

Scottish National Portrait Gallery

- ✉ 1 Queen St.
- ☎ (0131) 624 6200
- 🕐 Closed until Nov. 2011

www.national galleries.org

Georgian House

✉ 7 Charlotte Sq.
☎ (0131) 226 3318
$ $
www.nts.org.uk/
property/56/

Scottish National Gallery of Modern Art

✉ 75 Belford Rd.
☎ (0131) 624 6200
www.national
galleries.org

Dean Gallery

✉ 3 Belford Rd.
☎ (0131) 624 6200
www.national
galleries.org

Royal Botanic Garden

🚶 59
✉ Inverleith Row
☎ (0131) 552 7171
$ Grounds: free; Hothouses $
www.rbge.org
.uk/the-gardens/
edinburgh

major renovation and is slated to reopen by the end of 2011.

At George Street's western end awaits exclusive **Charlotte Square.** Designed by Robert Adam (1728–1792; see sidebar p. 105) a year before his death, it's now a focus of the city—Scotland's First Minister resides at number six, **Bute House.** His house sits on the northern flank, while neighboring **Georgian House** is open to the public. Owned by the National Trust for Scotland, this grand building retains the dignified air of Edinburgh life in the first half of the 19th century. Keep an eye out for paintings by Sir Henry Raeburn and Allan Ramsay (1713–1784).

Across the Dean Bridge: On the opposite side of Edinburgh's modest river, the Water of Leith, lie more regal Georgian town houses, interspersed with hotels. This area is home to a world-class art gallery in a plush and spacious wooded setting, the **Scottish National Gallery of Modern Art,** which is partnered by the equally dramatic and also neoclassical

Dean Gallery. Before you even enter the national gallery, take in the sculptures dotting the grounds—the highlights are works by Henry Moore (1898–1986) and Barbara Hepworth (1903–1975). Inside, avant-garde legends such as American Andy Warhol (1928–1987) and native Brit Damien Hirst (1965–) are celebrated alongside less well-known local talent.

The Dean Gallery is most renowned for its collection of sculptures by Sir Eduardo Paolozzi (see sidebar below). He left the gallery thousands of pieces when he died, including some of his finest work, and a re-creation of his studio sheds light on the work of this homegrown genius. On the ground floor, the Roland Penrose Gallery and Gabrielle Keiller Library have a collection of dada and surrealist art featuring Pablo Picasso (1881–1973), Joan Miró (1893–1983), and Salvador Dalí (1904–1989).

Royal Botanic Garden: South of the New Town is the world-

Edinburgh's Scrap Metal Sculptor

Sir Eduardo Paolozzi was born in 1924 into Edinburgh's large Italian community. His parents ran an ice-cream shop in Leith until World War II broke out, and he and his family were interned as enemy aliens. He was released after three months, but his father, grandfather, and uncle drowned when a ship transporting prisoners to Canada was sunk by a German U-boat. In 1943, after maintaining the family

business for several years, Paolozzi left the city to study sculpture in London.

Paolozzi went on to become a successful sculptor, creating many high-profile works of public art, and his art and ideas were major influences on the pop art movement of the 1960s. He is most famous for his sculptures made from machine parts, scrap metal, and other discarded items.

Revelers enjoy themselves in an Edinburgh bar.

class **Royal Botanic Garden.** Its stunning views back toward the New Town and Old Town skyline, with the castle clearly visible overlooking the scene and seemingly within touching distance, are not to be missed. The grounds have an eclectic mix of trees and shrubs from all over the world. Late spring is the best time to visit, when the flowers all come into bloom.

It is worth paying the modest admission fee to visit the ten huge hothouses, which are heated to different temperatures to house flora from around the world. Pools laden with carp and little bridges ideal for strolling also emerge from the lush greenery. The **Chinese Garden** is the best place to ponder. You can also ponder art at **Inverleith House,** which is home to an ever changing array of exhibitions.

A glorious new addition to the botanic garden is the multi-million-dollar **John Hope Gateway** at the West Gate. It has information on the gardens, interactive displays, a plant sales section, a gift store, and the **Gateway Restaurant** *(John Hope Gateway Centre, Arboretum Place, tel 0131/552 2674, www.gateway restaurant.net),* offering garden views and a large terrace for summer dining. ■

Leith & the Docks

Leith was once a separate town from Edinburgh, and some of the residents of this waterfront district continue to proclaim their independence. Visitors often ignore this charismatic quarter, but Leith and its docks boasts a rich history. In recent years, the area has reinvented itself as a culinary and nightlife oasis.

Barges and trendy bars and restaurants line the Shore where the Water of Leith widens into the port.

Leith

🅰 56 C3

Visitor Information

✉ Leith Mills,
70–74 Bangor
Rd., Edinburgh

☎ (0131) 555 5225

www.edinburgh.org

Although it lies beyond the city center, the lively medieval port of Leith has played a major role in the history of the capital. In the 15th century, Mary of Guise (1515–1560) presided from here on behalf of her young daughter, Mary Queen of Scots (1542–1587). When Oliver Cromwell's (1599–1658) men were in town, they chose Leith as their base. Right up until World War II, Leith was a major port, with a bustling hinterland. More recent luminaries born in Leith include Sir Sean Connery and the writer Irvine Welsh.

After World War II, Leith's port slumped into major decline. By the 1980s, it was a rundown area with serious drug problems and an active "red-light" district, as described by Irvine Welsh in his novel *Trainspotting* (1993).

Since 2000, investment by both public and private sectors has rejuvenated the area with large-scale developments, including tourist attractions, shopping malls, and upmarket waterfront housing. The renaissance will be crowned by 2012 when Leith will be connected to the airport by Edinburgh's new tram system.

Visiting Leith

The best way to get to Leith is to wander down the lengthy **Leith Walk**—a wide thorough-fare that is also the route of the tram. "The Walk" has also seen a lot of redevelopment, with many new stores, pubs, and restaurants opening up. The recent smoking ban has made its characterful pubs more appealing, and its popular Chinese cafés and Polish delis show the area's changing demographics.

Just as Leith Walk reaches its northern denouement, the **Leith Links** appears to the east. This modest parkland does not look like much, but the locals insist that it has a stronger claim than St. Andrews to being the "home of golf." Documents suggest that King James IV of Scotland (1473–1513) banned his men from playing golf on the links and that the rules were codified here a full decade before they were committed to paper in St. Andrews.

The cobbled harbor area of **The Shore** is a charming sendoff as the Water of Leith widens into the port area (now off limits and slated for closure). Until recently, the once grand merchant and seafarer houses had seen better days. Today, new pubs, restaurants (both on shore and floating), and the Michelin-starred Restaurant Martin Wishart (see Travelwise p. 278) have turned this area into a hip evening haunt.

Running west from The Shore is **Commercial Quay.** Once a bustling network of warehouses, alive with boats and cranes, it is now home to more restaurants, including The Kitchin (see Travelwise p. 278)—another Michelin-starred establishment. Look toward the water and the massive utilitarian building you see

is the administrative home of the **Scottish Government.**

Also visible to the west is **Ocean Terminal** *(Ocean Drive, tel 0131/555 8888, www.oceanterminal.com).* This giant shopping mall and multistory leisure oasis boasts more than 70 stores, plenty of places to eat and drink, a cinema, spa, indoor skate park, and panoramic views out over the waterfront and the Firth of Forth. If that isn't enough, Leith's most famous tourist attraction, the **Royal Yacht** *Britannia* (see sidebar below), is moored below.

Royal Yacht
Britannia

✉ Ocean Terminal, Leith

☎ (0131) 555 5566

💲 $$$

www.royalyacht britannia.co.uk

Britannia **Rules the Waves**

The Royal Yacht *Britannia* is a permanent addition on the Leith waterfront. Edinburgh demonstrated its drive and ambition by fighting off Glasgow, where the ship was launched from John Brown's Shipyard in Clydebank back in 1953, to become the resting place of this slice of floating history. You can explore the lavish and stately rooms where the British Royal Family entertained foreign royalty and dignitaries, as well as sneak little insights into the royal way of life on board the ship. Make sure to enjoy the quintessentially British tradition of tea in the café.

To some extent, the global recession has delayed the massive transformation of Edinburgh's larger waterfront area. However, it is fairly clear that the local authorities and private developers are keen to continue the development, having invested heavily in transportation links to the area. For now, Leith remains the shining example of what can be done with a rundown waterfront district. Watch this space. ∎

Outside the Center

Edinburgh is not a very big city by global standards, but in its outskirts you'll find a brace of charming waterfront communities—including Cramond, South Queensferry, and Portobello—as well as a sweep of hills that offer great views over the city.

Brave souls brace the icy waters of the Firth of Forth, South Queensferry, during the "Loony Dook."

Cramond
🅰 56 B2

South Queensferry
🅰 56 B3

Queensferry Museum
✉ 53 High St., South Queensferry
☎ (0131) 331 5545
🕐 Closed Tues.–Wed.

www.gnws.co.uk/ edinburgh/ queensferry.htm

Cramond

Cramond lies on the western fringe of Edinburgh and has a charmingly forgotten feel. This seaside suburb was once a Roman stronghold, and the sparse ruins of the fortress can still be made out. The village itself is a pretty affair, with a row of whitewashed houses lining the banks of the River Almond, a small sailing club making the most of the widening Forth estuary, and both a pub and a cozy little restaurant.

It is also possible to walk over to **Cramond Island,** but check the tides in advance, which are usually posted on a sign at the start of the tidal causeway to the island. The island is a bird-watcher's dream, but the tides are frighteningly quick here, so don't take any risks. Every year, visitors and locals alike get stranded as the causeway disappears.

South Queensferry

South Queensferry is quite simply one of the prettiest coastal settlements in Scotland. Although it lies within the official city boundaries, it feels a world away from Edinburgh, surrounded by protected countryside on three flanks and the Firth of Forth on the other. These days, South Queensferry is most famous for its mighty bridges—the Forth Bridge (which carries trains) and the Forth Road Bridge (see pp. 78–79).

South Queensferry takes its name from Queen Margaret (1045–1093), the monarch who first commissioned the ferries across the river. Some pedantic locals may insist that you are in the Royal Burgh of Queensferry, but most still call it South Queensferry to distinguish it from North Queensferry across the Forth.

South Queensferry's charming cobbled High Street is lined with well-preserved stone buildings, some painted in pastel hues. The oldest, the **Black Castle,** dates back as far as 1626. Pop into the **Queensferry Museum** to learn about the suburb's rich history, from its pagan Burry Man Festival through to the "Loony Dook," when the locals, and any visitors daft enough to join them, welcome in the New Year with a chilly dip in the Forth.

South Queensferry is surrounded on three sides by private estates, each home to a grand country house. Dundas Castle is not open to the public, but **Dalmeny House** allows limited public access to its impressive art gallery. The star attraction is **Hopetoun,** which has been dubbed "Scotland's Versailles" and is one of the finest houses in the land. The grounds are also impressive, with views of the Forth and a selection of flora to enjoy as

well as the chance to spy deer. The on-site café serves teas and cakes and even offers a suitably grand champagne afternoon tea.

Portobello

The name hints at the romance of the Mediterranean, and Portobello, 3 miles (5 km) east of the city center, does have a dash of seaside romance. Before the days of cheap jet travel, the city's residents flocked to the beach on sunny days. Today, the suburb is a little down at heel, but the views across the Firth of Forth are superb, the sands are still wide and welcoming, and the walks are always refreshingly bracing— the sense of better times having slipped through its sands giving it an extra layer of romance. ∎

Dalmeny House

✉ 2 miles (3.2 km) from Dalmeny train station; follow signs off the A90 Forth Bridge Rd.

☎ (0131) 331 1888

🕐 Closed Aug.–May

💲 $$

www.dalmeny.co.uk

Hopetoun

✉ 12 miles (16 km) W of Edinburgh via the A904

☎ (0131) 331 2451

🕐 Closed Oct.–Easter

💲 House & grounds: $$; Grounds only: $

www.hopetoun.co.uk

EXPERIENCE:
A Walk on the Wild Side

This lovely 7.5-mile (12 km) walk is something of a local secret. The best plan is to take a train from Edinburgh northwest to Dalmeny, South Queensferry's nearest train station, and walk north down to the Forth Bridge. Follow the track that leads into the Dalmeny Estate to the east. Highlights include grand **Dalmeny House** (see this page), superb views of the Forth Bridge and Edinburgh, the **Eagle Rock** where a Roman legionnaire once carved graffiti, and the sealife scattered along the sandy coastline. The ferry across to Cramond is currently closed, but this allows a scenic detour up to **Cramond Brig** and a walk back down a marked walkway along the **River Almond** into the village. For further information visit: *walking.visitscotland.com/walks/centralscotland/south_queensferry_dalmeny.*

Forth Bridges

No one forgets their first sight of the Forth Bridges—the twin thoroughfares that connect the banks of the Firth of Forth. Each stands as a testament to the finest engineering of its time. Hop on a train over the Forth Bridge, cycle, drive, or walk over the Forth Road Bridge, or simply sit in the charming seaside suburb of South Queensferry and marvel as the two bridges rear up and dominate the skyline.

The Forth Bridges are a wonderful spectacle at night.

The River Forth estuary has been a natural obstacle for people for as long as history has been written. As early as the 11th century, Queen Margaret of Scotland had commissioned the first ferry service to transport pilgrims from the capital to the abbeys in Dunfermline and St. Andrews. Ferries continued to run until 1964, when the road bridge finally opened.

Forth Bridge

The Forth Bridge (the railroad bridge) first opened in 1890 and is almost everyone's favorite. As one of the finest examples of Victorian engineering in the world, this rich red monster of steel proudly stretches 1.5 miles (2.5 km) across the estuary, crossing the river in a unique triple cantilever design. The Forth Bridge was the work of railroad engineers Sir John Fowler (1817–1898) and Sir Benjamin Baker (1840–1907), who had learned well from the earlier tragic collapse of the Tay Bridge farther north.

The sheer amount of materials involved in its construction was staggering—55,000 tons (60,000 tonnes) of steel, 635,700 cubic feet

(18,000 cubic m) of granite, and more than eight million rivets. The human effort was equally breathtaking, with a whole community of workers billeted in South Queensferry—98 of them paid the ultimate price with their lives. The bridge has also crossed over into popular culture, appearing in Hitchcock's movie version of *The 39 Steps* (1935).

In recent years, there have been calls to petition UNESCO to have the Forth Bridge placed on its coveted World Heritage List, and preservation has become a key issue. A recent study shows that the steel used in the construction was of a high and consistent quality, which bodes well for its longevity. A popular local refrain describes a repetitive task as being "like painting the Forth Bridge," which even many locals believe must be done continuously. In fact, that has never been the case, and the most recent coat is set to last for another quarter century.

Forth Road Bridge

If the Forth Road Bridge sat next to any other bridge it would get far more attention, but it pales in comparison to its older and more famous sibling. However, this grand suspension bridge actually bears a strong resemblance to its relative in San Francisco and was the largest of its kind in Europe when it opened in 1964. It has also been immortalized as the focus of Iain Banks' critically acclaimed novel *The Bridge* (1986).

Today, the Forth Road Bridge carries far more traffic than it was ever designed for, and some studies have suggested that it is deteriorating much faster than had originally been envisaged. The Scottish government has recently brought forward plans for a new road crossing, but many questions remain to be answered—not least of which who will pay for the expensive structure.

Planned New Forth Bridge

During the early years of the new millennium, FETA (the body that oversees the

On the southern flank of the bridges, South Queensferry is surrounded by greenbelt on three sides with some seriously good walking, so put aside time for discovering the hinterland after viewing the bridges.

—SALLY McFALL
National Geographic contributor

running of the Forth Road Bridge) decided that deterioration in the existing bridge meant a new crossing was essential. Following fierce debate over whether it was really necessary, the site for a new bridge was chosen, just west of the existing structure. The planned bridge would vault 1.4 miles (2.2 km) across the Forth, with the main span of the cable-stayed bridge stretching 4,500 feet (1,375 m), making it among the ten longest spans in the world.

Travel Information

Scotrail (*www.scotrail.co.uk*) runs many different services across the Forth Bridge, from Dalmeny in South Queensferry and from North Queensferry. The Maid of the Forth (*www.maidoftheforth.co.uk*) and the Forth Belle (*www.forthtours.com*) operate a range of unique cruises that pass under the bridges. However, anyone can walk or cycle across the Forth Road Bridge and enjoy the spectacular views. There is access from both South and North Queensferry.

In South Queensferry, both Orocco Pier (*www.oroccopier.co.uk*) and the Boat House (*www.theboathouse-sq.co.uk*) are excellent restaurant/bars with stunning views of both bridges. The Railbridge Bistro (*www.therailbridgebistro.com*) is dedicated to the eponymous bridge, displaying memorabilia and information boards as well as a scale model, and serves fresh contemporary Scottish food in cozy surroundings.

The Lothians

Many visitors to Edinburgh never bother to venture beyond the city limits to sample the rest of the Lothians. Those who do can look forward to a scenic region kissed by hills, the Firth of Forth, and the North Sea. The area is alive with ancient palaces and mysterious churches, as well as the little-known town that claims to be the site of the world's first oil production.

Bass Rock, home to a colony of around 80,000 gannet nests, near North Berwick, East Lothian

East Lothian

🄼 57 D2–D3,
E2–E3, F2–F3

Visitor Information

✉ 31 Court St.,
Haddington

☎ (01620) 827 422

www.edinburgh.org

North Berwick

🄼 57 E3

Visitor Information

✉ 1 Quality St.,
North Berwick

☎ (01620) 892 197

www.edinburgh.org

East Lothian

East of Edinburgh, **Musselburgh,** with its famous racecourse, is worth a visit for horse-racing fans. Fans of ice cream should stop off at the home of the legendary **Luca's** (32–38 High St., tel 0131/665 2237, www.s-luca.co.uk). A must for golfers is **Musselburgh Links** (Balcarres Road, tel 0131/653 5200, www.musselburgholdlinks.co.uk; see p. 166), the world's oldest golf course; it's been documented that golf was first played here in 1672, and some say that Mary Queen of Scots played here in 1567.

After the rather brutal sight of Cockenzie power station, East Lothian becomes less urban with a string of sandy beaches lining the littoral. The finest is perhaps **Gullane Beach,** a generous oasis of clean sands that rise up to meet unspoiled dunes. In the summer, people flock here from the city, but off season, you will have it largely to yourself. Keen golfers will take more interest in the superb **Muirfield Golf Course** (Duncur Road, Muirfield, tel 01620/842 123, www.muirfield.org.uk; see p. 166), which has previously hosted the British Open.

The most charming of the coastal settlements is undoubtedly **North Berwick.** This grand resort town experienced a golden age in the Victorian era, when trains ran direct from London to service stressed city types looking for fresh air and a healthy dip in the waters. To get an idea of the layout of the town head just south of town and take a one-hour hike up to the top of **North Berwick Law.** The distinctive craggy hill offers tremendous views over the town and East Lothian in general.

North Berwick's main attractions are its beautiful sandy beach, a trio of fabulous golf courses, and the excellent **Scottish Seabird Centre**—a modern attraction constructed to open up the remarkable Bass Rock just offshore. **Bass Rock** is a volcanic rock stack that looms out of the Firth of Forth's icy waters like a giant submarine beginning to surface. This towering 350-foot (107 m) monster looks impregnable, and largely is, except to its huge population of seabirds. Greedy gannets and cute puffins are among its colorful and noisy residents. Members of the public are not allowed to land on the protected island, but the mainland center reveals the rock's daily life story through a system of well-placed cameras. In summer, boat tours take you much closer. The sheer variety of birds that flock here make Bass Rock a key scientific research station.

East Lothian's Hinterland

Farther east, the coastline becomes wilder and rockier. A dramatic imprint of man is at the rugged ruin of **Tantallon Castle** (2 miles/3.2 km E of North Berwick, tel 01620/892 727, www .historic-scotland.gov.uk, $), with its spectacular views overlooking the sea. This stunning 14th-century castle was once the refuge of one of Scotland's most famous historical families, the Douglas Earls of Angus.

Dunbar is a last flourish as East Lothian turns south toward the Borders. This honest and attractive fishing town is replete with some sturdy sandstone architecture and a busy little port.

Farther inland, the world-class attraction is the **National Museum of Flight** at the old military airfield at East Fortune. On show are scores of well-preserved aircraft from over the ages, either displayed in hangars or even more atmospherically out on the aprons. The trusty old Spitfire, which played a crucial role in World War II during the Battle of Britain, as well as the Vulcan bomber that caused a political storm when it made an emergency landing in Brazil during Britain's Falklands War with Argentina, are the highlights. You can also board a British Airways Concorde and learn all

Scottish Seabird Centre

- ✉ The Harbour, North Berwick
- ☎ (01620) 890 202
- 💲 $$

www.seabird.org

Dunbar

- 🅰 57 E3

Visitor Information

- ✉ 143 High St., Dunbar
- ☎ (01368) 863 353
- 🕐 Closed Nov.–March

National Museum of Flight

- 🅰 57 E3
- ✉ East Fortune Airfield, East Lothian
- ☎ (0131) 247 4238
- 💲 $$

www.nms.ac.uk/ flight/our_ museums/ museum_of_flight .aspx

Flying on the Concorde

These days, you cannot experience the full joy of flying on the supersonic airliner Concorde, but the **National Museum of Flight** (see above) lets you enjoy a touch of the high life on the excellent "Concorde Experience." You are given a "boarding pass." The journey begins with an audio tour that takes you around main parts of the aircraft, with the thoughts of its flight attendants and pilots offering their insights into life aboard this amazing passenger airliner, and ends with a glimpse into the surprisingly cozy cockpit.

Hiking in Pentland Hills, near Edinburgh in Midlothian

Lennoxlove House

✉ Lennoxlove Estate, Haddington

☎ (01620) 828 614

💲 $$

www.lennoxlove .com

Glenkinchie Distillery

✉ Pencaitland, Tranent, East Lothian

☎ (01875) 342 004

💲 $$

www.discovering -distilleries. com/ glenkinchie

Midlothian Snow Sports Centre

✉ Biggar Road, Hillend

☎ (0131) 445 4433

💲 $$

www.midlothian .gov.uk

glenkinchiemid lothian.gov.uk

about the world's only supersonic passenger plane, which was retired in 2003 (see sidebar p. 81).

A few miles from the museum is the neat inland market town of **Haddington,** which was first recognized by Kind David I back in the 12th century. Haddington is a relaxed place for a stroll and café stop. The most visually appealing part of town is **Church Street,** with its well-preserved 18th- and 19th-century architecture. The most alluring building is **Lennoxlove House,** 0.5 mile (1 km) south of the town, which dates back to the 14th century and boasts a sprinkling of remnants from one of its most famous guests, Mary Queen of Scots, including a death mask. The best way to explore the Lennoxlove House is on one of the excellent guided tours.

This may not strike you as whisky country, but East Lothian boasts its very own **Glenkinchie Distillery,** which the locals are keen to point out does not produce "Edinburgh's Malt" but their very own—a mild, easygoing malt, which is best enjoyed as a gentle aperitif. The distillery runs excellent tours that explain how they mercurially turn the local water into this hallowed dram.

Midlothian

The **Pentland Hills** are a chunky necklace of rolling hills that form a natural border along the western side of the old county of Midlothian, or "Edinburghshire." Most of the Pentland area is protected but open to the public. Just off the Edinburgh Bypass road lies Hillend at the east of the range, which is home to the **Midlothian Snow Sports Centre**—the longest dry ski slope in Europe, offering daytime and floodlit nighttime skiing. Farther into the Pentlands, the land turns more rugged, and the hustle and bustle of modern life quickly eases away. **Flotterstone** is the best access point for a hike, with a free parking lot, information center, walking trails marked on maps, and an inn for sustenance after the walk. The highest point is only 1,900 feet (579 m), which makes the Pentlands an appealing and safer winter alternative to Scotland's more serious mountains. Further hiking awaits in the **Moorfoot Hills,** south of Midlothian on its boundary with the Borders.

Midlothian's star attraction is undoubtedly **Rosslyn Chapel** at **Roslin,** which has recently been made world famous by Dan Brown's bestselling 2003 novel *The Da Vinci Code* (see sidebar opposite) and the 2006

Hollywood blockbuster. Sir William St. Clair (1404–1482) was the man who realized his dream in seeing the chapel completed in 1446. Its newfound fame has helped finance essential ongoing renovation work. Tom Hanks, lead actor in the film version of Brown's novel, made a donation. However, the increase in visitors has caused problems of its own.

The exterior of this atmospheric building is a collage of flying buttresses and scary-looking gargoyles, but the intricacies inside the church are what really excite. The genius of the master stonemason, with all manner of symbols and allegorical images, speaks through the centuries. The walls of the 69-by-42-foot (21-by-13 m) church are covered almost entirely with hundreds of carvings, depicting everything from knights on horseback and the pagan Green Man through to a nativity scene and Lucifer bound, gagged, and hanging upside down.

Rosslyn Chapel is a special place, and it is no surprise that its Freemasonry and Knights Templar connections add further fuel to fire the imaginations of its many visitors. Adding to the intrigue are the carvings of North American plants that date back to before the apparent discovery of the Americas by Christopher Columbus (1451–1506) in 1492. Recent research found an underground chamber, adding to the speculation in some quarters that the holy grail lies buried beneath the chapel. Conspiracy theorists and those with vivid imaginations might like the fact that "Dolly the Sheep" was genetically engineered nearby at the Roslin Institute.

Midlothian was once a major coal producer and provided the fuel to power Scotland's thriving capital during the industrial age. The demise of industrialization has cast an economic shadow over the area; however, the excellent **Scottish Mining Museum** commemorates the once booming industry. Located in one of the best-preserved Victorian-era collieries in Europe, the museum features two exhibitions—the "Story of Coal" and "A Race Apart." Audio tours re-create the mining experience with the aid of helmets fitted with audio gear, which go down well with young visitors, as does the play area.

Roslin itself is not all about world-famous churches. **Roslin Glen** is a bucolic escape, with walking trails and a ruined castle—both attractions come without the crowds that can hamper a visit to the chapel itself. Another green oasis is **Vogrie Country Park,**

The Da Vinci Code

Rosslyn Chapel plays a central role in Dan Brown's novel *The Da Vinci Code,* when the author suggests that it was once the resting place of the holy grail. The book's central characters, Robert Langdon and Sophie Neveu, visit the chapel to seek out the holy grail but find out that it has been moved to France by the shadowy Priory of Sion. During the visit to Scotland, Neveu speaks to her grandmother and finds out more about her own ancestry, which links her directly back to the supposed lineage of Jesus and Mary Magdalene.

Rosslyn Chapel

✉ Chapel Loan, Roslin
☎ (0131) 440 2159
www.rosslynchapel .org.uk

Scottish Mining Museum

✉ Lady Victoria Colliery, Newtongrange
☎ (0131) 663 7519
💲 $$
www.scottishmining museum.com

Roslin Glen Country Park

✉ Between Roslin village and Rosewell via the B7003
☎ (01875) 821 990

Vogrie Country Park

▲ 56 C1–C2

✉ 12 miles (19 km) from Edinburgh; S on the A68, right on the B6372 for 1.2 miles (2 km) to park entrance

☎ (01875) 821 990

⑤ $

www.midlothian .gov.uk

Almond Valley Heritage Trust

✉ Millfield, Livingston

☎ (01506) 414 957

⑤ $$$

www.almondvalley .co.uk

which is a short drive away. At the center of the park is the eponymous house, which includes a café with soft-play area, a scenic golf course, some interesting public sculpture, and some walking trails.

West Lothian

West Lothian is perhaps the most underrated corner of central Scotland and is largely off the beaten tourist track. Its claim to fame is that it is the "home of oil," and it lays a decent claim—it was here that the Scottish chemist James "Paraffin" Young (1811–1883) first produced oil from shale.

At one point, more than 13,000 people worked in the local oil industry that Young established in West Lothian. His legacy is a landscape underpinned by mine workings and the very visible slag heaps, known locally as "bings," that resemble miniature versions of Uluru (Ayers Rock) at sunset.

Visitors can explore the days of shale mining at the **Almond Valley Heritage Trust** in the planned New Town of **Livingston.** One section re-creates a mineshaft with pitch-black tunnels and mine trucks. Large maps show the extent to which the mining spread

its tentacles out over West Lothian. There is also a children's farm at the trust, which is guaranteed to keep younger visitors happy for at least half a day. The farm area slopes down the hillside toward the **River Almond,** with a series of enclosures and buildings housing a cornucopia of animals. As well as learning about the animals, you can take a ride on the narrow-gauge rail track or on a trailer pulled by a tractor.

On the fringe of the Livingston green belt is the village of **Dechmont**—the unlikely setting of one of the world's most famous UFO incidents. In 1982, a local man and his dog were knocked unconscious and suffered burns at the hands of what he described as a floating spherical-type object. Scientists and the media descended on the area from all over the world, but the only legacy today is a small plaque at the landing site near Dechmont Hill, between Dechmont and Livingston.

Many of West Lothian's towns are rather scruffy affairs, but one shining star, north across the **Bathgate Hills** from Dechmont, is **Linlithgow.** The birthplace of Mary Queen of Scots is a richly historic town, and it is handily

Visiting Beecraigs Country Park

The Bathgate Hills offer a bucolic escape, but you'll need a car or bike to get to its highlight—Beecraigs Country Park *(The Park Centre, near Linlithgow, tel 01505/844 516, www.beecraigs.com).* Head south from Linlithgow into the heavily forested park, home to a deer farm, a restaurant, and a fishing reservoir where you can rent boats and tackle. You can camp overnight in a forest clearing or limber up on the fitness course. People from all over the region flock here in summer, so you will meet a complete cross-section of West Lothian society.

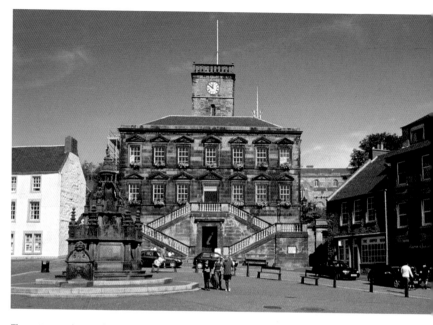

The austere sandstone of Linlithgow Town Hall

located on the main Edinburgh–Glasgow railroad line. The cobbled High Street is awash with cafés and stores, making it the perfect location for a relaxed stroll and lunch stop. A good day to visit is on the fourth Saturday of every month, when a lively farmers' market descends on the town. Delve through the grand stone arch by the tourist office (now temporarily closed, so check at the time of your visit), where you can pick up a useful leaflet that outlines a "Linlithgow Heritage Trail," and be instantly transported through several centuries of Scottish history. On the right-hand wall of the arch the kings and queens of Scotland are listed through the ages until you come to **Linlithgow Palace** itself.

The palace is a breathtaking 15th-century building that rises robustly from a grassy knoll overlooking the waters of **Linlithgow Loch.** Mary Queen of Scots was born in Linlithgow Palace in 1542. The building is now a ruin, but there is still plenty worth exploring, not least the views from six stories up over the town and loch. Unlike many castles in Scotland, Linlithgow is not bedecked with hordes of memorabilia. Indeed, much of the charm of the place is imagining what it might have looked like in its day. Legend has it that the fountain in the courtyard, built during the reign of James I (1566–1625), flowed with wine when Charles I (1600–1649) visited in 1633.

The centerpiece of the palace is the magnificent and voluminous **Great Hall,** where you can let

Linlithgow
🅰 56 A3
Visitor Information
✉ County Buildings, High Street, Linlithgow
☎ (01506) 775 320

Linlithgow Palace
🅰 56 A3
✉ Boghall, Linlithgow
☎ (01506) 842 896
💲 $$
www.historic -scotland.gov.uk

St. Michael's Church

✉ Cross House, The Cross, Linlithgow

☎ (01506) 842 188

💲 $

www.stmichaels parish.org.uk

Linlithgow Canal Centre

✉ Canal Basin, Manse Road, Linlithgow

☎ (01506) 671 215

🕐 Closed Oct.–March

💲 $

www.lucs.org.uk

your imagination wander back to the past, when the palace walls echoed to the cries of a baby girl who was to have a monumental effect on the nation into which she had just been born.

If you visit the castle, make sure you also have a look at **St. Michael's Church** next door. The church itself dates back to the 13th century, but the structure is topped by a spiky aluminum crown that has divided the critics since it was added just after World War II. Back across the High Street and up the hill past the railroad station is another more modern addition, the **Union Canal,** which was built as a transportation link between Edinburgh and Glasgow. The canal basin is home to the **Linlithgow Canal Centre,** which has a modest museum and runs short canal cruises to the Avon

Aqueduct in spring and summer.

If you prefer to explore the area by foot, the walk around **Linlithgow Loch** is an enjoyable experience. This circular adventure is best taken heading west, away from the palace. The first stretch is awash with eager ducks and swans touting for tidbits from passersby. Soon the town center disappears as you ease past some exclusive houses with views back across the waters to the palace. Information boards illuminate the route and both the loch's human and natural history. Look for the site of an old crannog—an island hideout used centuries ago by the local people to live their lives in a modicum of safety. The path rejoins the main road back into the center, but stay on the marked trail to the loch, which provides a thrilling denouement in the approach up to the

A jousting tournament captivates crowds at Linlithgow Palace, birthplace of Mary Queen of Scots.

The Tragic Life of Mary Queen of Scots

The real life of Mary Queen of Scots reads more tragically and unbelievably than any modern-day TV drama. Born in Linlithgow Palace in December 1542, Mary became Queen of Scotland as a six-day-old baby. After spending much of her childhood in France, where she was briefly Queen, Mary returned to Scotland in 1561. As a staunch Catholic, Mary's attempts to undermine the Protestant faith failed, and she was forced to abdicate. She fled to England to seek refuge with her cousin, Elizabeth I, but was jailed and spent the rest of her days under house arrest, implicated in various plots—and executed in 1587.

palace from the lochside.

There are two more historic buildings within easy reach of Linlithgow, both to the west, back toward the city center. They can be savored with a first-rate lunch as part of the experience at the Michelin-starred **Champany Inn** or just a burger in the chop house (see Travelwise p. 279).

The **House of the Binns** has been in the Dalyell family for more than four centuries. Its most famous recent resident is the controversial and outspoken politician Tam Dalyell, former Labour Member of Parliament, who always furrowed his own path and raised tricky questions about the political makeup of Britain.

Often ignored, **Blackness Castle** can be found sturdily guarding the shores of the Firth of Forth. This fortress and its drama was recognized in Mel Gibson's *Hamlet* (1990), when it was used as a location. There is a superb riverside and forest walk east from the castle back to South Queensferry (see pp. 76–77), where you can also take in Hopetoun, dubbed Scotland's Versailles. Allow at least three hours for the strenuous hike, after which you can pick up a taxi back to your car or the bus into the city center or back to Linlithgow.

A marvel of transportation, and a popular family attraction, is the restored stretch of railroad and station at **Bo'ness.** After being mothballed, the project was brought back to life by a team of volunteers. The station houses the **Scottish Railway Museum,** which is the country's largest dedicated railroad exhibition, with sheds full of locomotives, wagons, and other exhibits. In the summer, there are regular train trips on the **Bo'ness and Kinneil Railway** (*www.srps .org.uk/railway*)—many of them atmospherically hauled by steam engines. There is the option to visit an old mine to break up the return journey, with a café and tourist information center at the station, too.

The best view in West Lothian is the one from **Cairnpapple** in the rolling hills, taking the road just south of Linlithgow past **Beecraigs Country Park** (see sidebar p. 84). Cairnpapple offers panoramic views of central Scotland, and there is also a burial cairn you can explore. ∎

House of the Binns

◪ 56 A3
✉ Linlithgow, West Lothian
☎ (01506) 834 255
$ $$

www.nts.org.uk/ Property/33/

Blackness Castle

◪ 56 A3
✉ Blackness
☎ (01506) 834 807
$ $

www.historic -scotland.gov.uk

Bo'ness

◪ 56 A3
Visitor Information
✉ Bo'ness Station, Union Street, Bo'ness
☎ (08452) 255 1996

Scottish Railway Museum

✉ Bo'ness Station, Union Street, Bo'ness
☎ (01506) 822 298
$ $$

www.srps.org .uk/railway

A sprawling cosmopolitan city that occupies the valley
of the River Clyde, below the rolling hills of agricultural Ayrshire

Glasgow
& Ayrshire

Glasgow's busy city center

Glasgow & Ayrshire

Over the past two decades, Scotland's largest urban center has been transformed from a run-down industrial sprawl into one of Europe's most dynamic, culturally savvy, and enticing cities. A string of awards—not least the title of 1990 European City of Culture—has cemented its status. But further attractions await beyond the city center, around the River Clyde and out along the stunning Ayrshire coast.

Glasgow—or the "dear green place" as it poetically translates from its Gaelic moniker—is a bustling city that swirls in layers of history and a vibrant sense of culture. In the decades following World War II, the days when

Glasgow was the booming "second city of the empire" and Clyde-built ships ruled the waves, post-industrial decline set in. But Glaswegians have always been a passionate, spirited people, and they set about turning

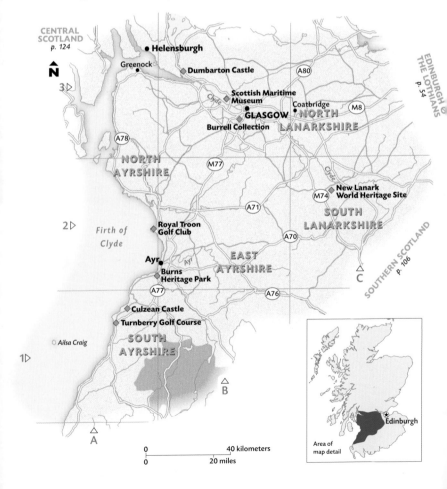

CENTRAL
SCOTLAND
p. 124

EDINBURGH &
THE LOTHIANS
p. 54

Helensburgh
Greenock
Dumbarton Castle
A80
Scottish Maritime
Museum
Clyde
Coatbridge
GLASGOW
NORTH
Burrell Collection
LANARKSHIRE
M8
A78
NORTH
AYRSHIRE
M77
New Lanark
M74
World Heritage Site
A71
SOUTH
LANARKSHIRE
Royal Troon
Firth of
Golf Club
Clyde
A70
Ayr
EAST
Burns
AYRSHIRE
Heritage Park
A77
A76
Culzean Castle
Turnberry Golf Course
SOUTH
Ailsa Craig
AYRSHIRE
SOUTHERN SCOTLAND
p. 106

Ayr

N

3
2
1

A
B
C

0   40 kilometers
0   20 miles

Area of
map detail
Edinburgh

around perceptions of their city in the 1980s. Since then, Glasgow has been awarded the honor of European City of Culture and City of Architecture and Design. This meteoric renaissance will be crowned when Glasgow hosts the Commonwealth Games in 2014.

A City Transformed

In recent years, massive development has transformed the city center. The previously raffish Buchanan Street, now known as the "Style Mile," is laced with designer stores and trendy bars. The city may not boast any Michelin-starred restaurants, but it has plenty of great places to eat and drink, where you are as likely to meet the city's remaining shipbuilders as you are local pop stars and its hallowed soccer players.

And Glasgow may not have the immediate visual appeal of Scotland's celebrated capital, but the more effort you put in, the deeper the rewards. Who cannot be charmed by a city that was once home to the seminal architect and designer Charles Rennie Mackintosh (1868–1928), who created some of Glasgow's finest buildings and who made

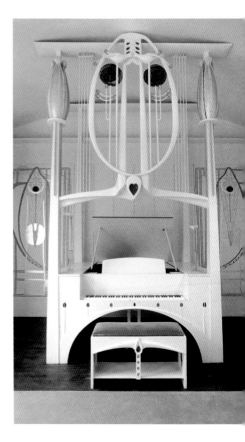

The piano in the music room, House for an Art Lover in Bellahouston Park, southwest Glasgow

NOT TO BE MISSED:

such an impression on the world stage with his creative—yet practical—designs, which are unmistakably Glaswegian?

Beyond the city center, the Clyde Valley is well off the beaten track, but the immaculately preserved New Lanark Heritage Centre is a world-class attraction that has been recognized by UNESCO. To the south are the rolling hills of Ayrshire—farming country—once the haunt of Scotland's most romantic poet, Robert Burns, who also had the ability to speak to and live the life of the common people, fitting in perfectly with what is still very much the Glaswegian zeitgeist. ■

Central Glasgow

Glasgow's city center is easy to navigate—the uniform grid layout makes sightseeing simple, and all the main attractions are within walking distance. Much of the city center has been redeveloped, so the area is also alive with lively bars, cafés, restaurants, and smart stores.

A beautiful stained-glass window in Glasgow Cathedral

Glasgow

[A] 90 B3

Visitor Information

[✉] City Marketing
Bureau, 11
George Square,
Glasgow G2
1DY

[☎] (0141) 566 0800

**www.seeglasgow
.com**

City Center

In such a sprawling city, it can be hard to pinpoint Glasgow's exact center, but **George Square** is a good starting point. The square is handily sandwiched between the two main railway stations—**Central Station** and **Queen St. Station**—and lies in the middle of the urban grid of Georgian and Victorian architecture, a legacy of the city's industrial heyday. Take a seat on a bench and admire the grandiose **City Chambers** *(George Square, tel 0141/287 2000, www.glasgow .gov.uk),* which appeared in a lavish swirl of Victorian pomposity in 1888 (and were inaugurated by the Queen Victoria herself). Take a guided tour and walk through time to the days when the British Empire dominated the globe. Friezes of all the countries in the empire at that time cement the sense of Union swagger. Before leaving the square, pop into the tourist information office on the southwestern corner. There you can buy tickets for the excellent open-top bus tours of the city *(www.city sightseeingglasgow.co.uk),* as well as pick up a range of maps and leaflets, including an excellent one on the Merchant City, which is your next stop.

Merchant City spreads its refined tentacles across a neat grid of stately streets immediately southeast of George Square. The elegant sandstone buildings were erected in the 19th century by ostentatious cotton and tobacco traders, as well as businessmen who grew rich from the blossoming shipyards. They now house residences, shops, bars, and restaurants.

**Steer clear of too
many discussions
about the relative
merits of Glasgow's
Rangers and Celtic
soccer teams. The religious underpinnings
can evoke deeply emotional reactions.**

—LARRY PORGES
National Geographic editor

One of the most impressive
redevelopments here is the **City
Halls** *(Candleriggs, tel 0141/353
8000, www.glasgowconcerthalls.com)*,
which reopened as a concert hall
in 2006 following a multimillion-
dollar renovation. Luminaries as
diverse as writer Charles Dickens
(1812–1870) and comedian Billy
Connolly have performed here.
Free tours also now run at the
Trades Hall—Robert Adam's finest
contribution to the city, which was
built as a meeting place.

One block to the west of
George Square lies **Buchanan
Street**—Glasgow's "Style Mile."
Much of Buchanan Street has
been pedestrianized, making
Glasgow one of the finest British
shopping cities outside London.
At the southern end of Buchanan
Street is the sparkling redevelop-
ment of the **St. Enoch Shopping
Centre**—a telling symbol of new
Glasgow. On the other side lies
the entrance to **Princes Square.**
This stylish shopping mall is home
to a flurry of designer stores,
niche shops, and restaurants.

The retail frenzy continues as
you head north. When you notice
the grand **Buchanan Galleries**,
yet another stylish shopping mall,
look to your right for a statue
of a rather unimpressive-looking
bespectacled man. Donald
Dewar (1937–2000) was the
inaugural First Minister of the
first Scottish Parliament, which
sat in Edinburgh in 1999—the
first time in more than 300 years.
Dewar sported a deep sense of
intellect and patriotism, and he
was a popular political leader.

The northern end of Buch-
anan Street ends with the **Royal
Concert Hall** *(2 Sauchiehall St., tel
0141/353 8000, www.glasgowcon
certhalls.com)*, home of the lively
Celtic Connections music festival in January, as well as a string
(continued on p. 96)

Trades Hall
✉ 85 Glassford St.
☎ (0141) 552 2418
**www.tradeshall
glasgow.co.uk**

**St. Enoch
Shopping Centre**
✉ St. Enoch Square
☎ (0141) 204 3900
www.st-enoch.co.uk

Princes Square
✉ Buchanan Street
☎ (0141) 221 0324
**www.princessquare
.co.uk**

**Buchanan
Galleries**
✉ 220 Buchanan St.
☎ (0141) 333 9898
**www.buchanan
galleries.co.uk**

EXPERIENCE:
Under the Skin
of Mackintosh

The unique architecture and design of
Charles Rennie Mackintosh (1868–1928)
is inexorably woven into the fabric of Glasgow. You can follow his trail, picking
up a free guide at the tourist office on
George Square. In the city center, there is
the **Glasgow School of Art** *(168 Renfrew
St.)*, **Willow Tea Rooms** *(217 Sauchiehall
St.)*, and the **Daily Record Building** *(Mitch-
ell St.)*. In the West End, the highlight is the
Hunterian Gallery *(University Ave.)*. On
the city fringes watch for the **Scotland
Street School Museum** *(225 Scotland St.)*,
Ruchill Church Hall *(15–17 Shakespeare St.)*,
and the **Mackintosh Church** *(870 Garscube
Rd.)*. Visit *www.glasgowmackintosh.com* for
more information.

Walk Around Glasgow

With so many modern shopping malls and new building works, Glasgow city center may appear rather uninspiring on first impression. Take a closer look and you will see many interesting sights and sounds. Georgian- and Victorian-era buildings are all around—the legacy of the city as a major player in the expanding British Empire.

Rainswept George Square in the center of Glasgow

Leaving **George Square** on North Hanover Street, cut east along Cathedral Street to the landmark **Glasgow Cathedral** ❶ *(Cathedral Square, tel 0141/552 8198, www .glasgowcathedral.org.uk)*. A church has stood here since the 12th century, but today's incarnation dates back to the 15th century. Some find the haunting cathedral a touch oppressive, but that perhaps misses the point—the building was meant to instill rectitude in its worshippers.

Just beside the cathedral, **St. Mungo's Museum** ❷ *(2 Castle St., tel 0141/276 1625)* is an ambitious attempt to portray the world's six major religions across a three-story town house. For sheer uniqueness of vision, it is worth visiting. The museum also organizes guided tours of the sprawling **Necropolis** ❸, which lies just across Wishart

NOT TO BE MISSED:

Glasgow Cathedral • Necropolis • People's Palace • Gallery of Modern Art

Street to the east. Here the great and good of Glasgow (in all 50,000 people) are buried in one giant ornate city of the dead.

Cutting south down High Street takes you to the unmistakable hulk of the **Tolbooth** ❹. This used to be Glasgow's center, home to both the town hall and a prison. Now the center has moved farther west; all that remains is this mighty 126-foot (38.5 m) tower topped with a clock that watches over the traffic below.

Proceed south down the Saltmarket, and the city's favorite green lung, **Glasgow Green,** opens up to your left. The highlight is the **People's Palace ❺** (*Glasgow Green, tel 0141/276 0788*), which tells an informal story of the city and its lively citizens.

Head back up the Saltmarket, and this time turn left at the Tolbooth so you are traveling west along Trongate to the **Tron Theatre ❻** (*63 Trongate, tel 0141/552 4267, www.tron.co.uk*). Originally an old church, topped with a 16th-century steeple, the Tron was revamped in the late 1990s as a contemporary arts venue. Pop into the bar/restaurant and take the artistic pulse of this booming cultural city.

Pushing west, Trongate turns into Argyle Street, and you will pass under the massive Victorian expanse of **Central Station ❼**. To find the station's grand main entrance, turn right up Hope Street and right again on Gordon Street. Step inside and look up

at the colossal roof, which once filled with steam billowing out from the old engines. Some of that glamour can still be felt as today's trains romantically set off in search of the old Clyde piers.

From the station, cut two blocks east to Buchanan Street and continue into **Merchant City** (see p. 92) through Royal Exchange Square to the **Gallery of Modern Art ❽** (*Royal Exchange Sq., tel 0141/287 3050*). Opened in 1996, it is the second-most visited art gallery in Britain, after London's Tate Modern. The gallery puts on a range of exhibitions, and there is a children's creative area and a café.

ℕ See also area map p. 90
▶ George Square
↔ 4 miles/6.4 km
⊘ A half day
▶ George Square

EXPERIENCE: Soccer in the City

Glasgow's two main soccer teams—Rangers and Celtic—together known as the "Old Firm," possibly garner as much support around the world as the national team does from their fun-loving and friendly "Tartan Army." Snaring a ticket for an Old Firm derby is tricky given the fierce rivalry between the two teams, but you can often find tickets for games with less demand online or by visiting their box offices in person. The same applies for friendly internationals. It's well worth the price of a ticket, since hearing the Tartan Army in full voice is a moving experience, not least for the weight of history that echoes around through their patriotic songs. **Rangers** (*www.rangers .co.uk*) offer guided tours of Ibrox Stadium as do **Celtic** (*www.celticfc.co.uk*) at Celtic Park, while the **National Museum of Football** is housed at Hampden Stadium (*www.scottishfootballmuseum.org.uk*).

Kelvingrove Art Gallery & Museum

✉ Argyle Street
☎ (0141) 276 9599
**www.glasgow
museums.com**

of cultural events throughout the year. To the west is **Sauchiehall Street**—a much less salubrious shopping street and very much "old Glasgow."

Glasgow won yet another accolade in 2008 when it was named a UNESCO City of Music. The award was given in recognition of the litany of classical, folk, and pop musicians who have emerged from Glasgow over the years. The award also recognizes the fact that the city actively promotes music in all its forms. Famous Glaswegian musicians include Lulu and the late Lonnie Donnegan, as well as modern stars Franz Ferdinand and Glasvegas. The highlight of Glasgow's musical calendar is the Celtic Connections concert in January at the Royal Concert Hall (see p. 93), but there are also regular concerts at the Barrowlands (*www.glasgow-barrow land.com*) and the O$_2$ Academy (*www.o2academyglasgow.co.uk*).

West End

Glasgow's West End is far less hurried and much greener than the city center, which is more in keeping with the city's "dear green place" origins. The West End was built later in the 19th century, however, when the city's wealthy looked for space and clean air. The West End is also a place of learning and culture—the home of Glasgow University and a collection of first-rate galleries and museums.

Kelvingrove Park: The large green lung of Kelvingrove Park is the star of the West End, and at its heart is the **Kelvingrove Art Gallery & Museum.** To call this recently refurbished museum/gallery just a museum or an art gallery is selling it way short. Within its palatial Victorian walls, you can see a Spitfire fighter plane soaring above, get up close and personal with an elephant, take in one of the most famous works of Salvador Dalí (1904–1989), "The Christ of St. John of the Cross," and then explore some of the mysteries of Egyptian mummies.

In all, more than 8,000 exhibits are on display. Much thought has gone into the multimillion-dollar refurbishment, and the exhibits make use of the excellent natural light and drama afforded by this massive building. For those with an interest in history, an exhibition that explores how the nation's view of itself has evolved through its art is particularly compelling. So, too, is the exhibit about the remote Scottish islands of St. Kilda—handy for those unable to get out there. Of course, the city's most famous artistic son, Charles Rennie Mackintosh (1868–1928; see sidebar p. 93), has a room to himself, displaying some fine examples of his trademark furniture. Younger visitors are catered to as well, with plenty of interactive displays to keep them busy.

Just across from the Kelvingrove, on Argyle Street, is the **Transport Museum.** There are plans to move all of its exhibits to a striking new Transport Museum down on the banks of the Clyde before the end of 2011. The current location boasts one striking central space, **Kelvin Hall,** which is crammed with all manner of buses, steam trains, and trams that were once the city's transportation lifeline. The most charming section is a re-creation of the old Victorian-era underground network, complete with a platform and vintage underground trains. The collection of old automobiles and motorbikes also offers a trip down memory lane.

Glasgow University: North though Kelvingrove Park along Kelvin Way, the greenery spreads out in all directions as you

(continued on p. 100)

Transport Museum
✉ 1 Bunhouse Rd.
☎ (0141) 287 2720
**www.glasgow
museums.com**

Glasgow University
☎ (0141) 330 2000
**www.gla.ac.uk/
visitors**

Ry Cooder performs on stage with the Chieftains as part of the 2010 Celtic Connections festival at Glasgow Royal Concert Hall.

Shipbuilding on the Clyde

The River Clyde was once the shipbuilding center of the world, making Glasgow one of the most important cities of the British Empire. Today, it is hard to imagine the time when more than half of the world's ships were "Clyde-built." This narrow, shallow waterway is a shadow of its former glory. Busy shipyards and congested waterways have been replaced with abandoned warehouses and crumbling docks.

The harbor tunnel entrance and the giant Finnieston Crane, built to lift locomotives onto ships

In many ways, the River Clyde made Glasgow what it is today. Shortly after the 1707 Act of Union merged Scotland and England to form the Kingdom of Great Britain, Glasgow found itself a central trading post with emerging markets around the world. Merchants were trading cotton, tobacco, and cash with countries in Africa, India, and the West Indies, and the city started to expand as new money poured in.

Local demand for new ships grew rapidly, but shipyard owners in England also realized the potential of a city with a cheap supply of skilled labor, plenty of iron and coal, and easy access to the Atlantic Ocean. The Scottish spirit of pioneering and ingenuity also came to the fore, as new technologies started to emerge in the west of Scotland. One of the most important inventions, the steam engine, was developed by Scottish engineer James

Watt (1736–1819), and his idea revolutionized ship production. Between 1812 and 1820, Glasgow's shipyards produced no less than 42 wooden-hulled steamships.

Cranes soon sprang up from Rutherglen in the east right through the city center and on to the wide mouth of the Clyde at Greenock in the west. Massive dry docks, myriad quays, millions of tons of iron and coal, as well as the huge workforce, poured into the "second city of the empire." Developments in steel production provided the opportunity to deliver bigger and more powerful ships, and Glasgow was well placed to cash in on another new wave of shipbuilding. The boom years between 1860 and 1920 made Glasgow the shipbuilding center of the world, with the peak production—a staggering 838,000 tons (760,000 tonnes)—occurring in 1913.

A dramatic social realist mural tells its own emotive story at the Scottish Maritime Museum in Braehead.

serious decline. The *Queen Elizabeth 2* was the last major vessel to roll off the production lines in 1967.

An Industry Revived

Fast forward to the present day, and the Clyde's surviving shipyards have had to make themselves more efficient and flexible than ever before in the face of a new economic downturn. Fortunately, globalization has also provided some opportunities, helping to win new markets and lucrative contracts from governments at home and abroad. Once again, you can see working cranes west of the city center as work starts on a new wave of warships.

If you want to explore Glasgow's shipbuilding history or get under the social fabric of a city whose rise was inexorably bound up with shipbuilding (100,000 citizens were employed in 39 shipyards in 1930), head to the "Clydebuilt" exhibition at the Scottish Maritime Museum (*Kings Inch Road, Braehead, tel 0141/886 1013, www.scottishmaritime museum.org, $*) on the south banks of the River Clyde. This innovative museum exhibit is spread across multiple levels, and life-size model shipyard workers and naval architects tell you their stories.

INSIDER TIP:

Conjure up the days when Clyde-built ships sailed the world's seas by cruising past the old shipyards "doon the watter" on the P.S.S. Waverley [www.waverley excursions.co.uk], a romantic old paddle steamer.

—LEON GRAY
National Geographic contributor

The launch of the *Queen Mary* in 1934 was perhaps the Clyde's final triumph, but even that could not paper over the cracks that had started to appear in Glasgow's shipbuilding industry. The combined effects of global economic depression during the 1930s, increased competition from foreign shipyards following World War II, and the advent of affordable air travel plunged the Clyde shipyards into

Hunterian Museum & Art Gallery

✉ University Avenue

☎ (0141) 330 5431

www.hunterian.gla.ac.uk

Armadillo

✉ Scottish Exhibition and Conference Center, Exhibition Way

☎ (0141) 248 3000

www.secc.co.uk

approach Glasgow University. Grand sandstone buildings make this quarter feel more like a historic castle than a university, but you will still see students strolling around as they have done since 1870. The university has a visitor center if you want to learn more about the various buildings and statues. It can also organize tours up the university's voluminous tower, which offers sweeping views out across the city.

Just across the road is the **Hunterian Museum and Art Gallery.** The main attraction is the largest collection of paintings outside of Washington, D.C., by James Abbott McNeill Whistler (1834–1903). The collection consists of 80 oil paintings, a range of drawings and watercolors, and over 2,000 prints. The gallery also houses works by the renowned group of painters known as the Glasgow Boys, represented by Sir James Guthrie (1859–1930) and Edward Hornel (1864–1933), as

well as a small collection of work by the Scottish Colorists, including the movement's leading figure, John Duncan Fergusson (1874–1961). The work of Glasgow's celebrated creative genius, Charles Rennie Mackintosh (see sidebar p. 93), includes an interior of his home—the pieces of his work that he deemed good enough to live with everyday.

Just a five-minute walk from the gallery, off University Avenue, is one of the loveliest little lanes in the city and something of a local secret. **Aston Lane** is a cobbled gem lined with graceful stone buildings that house a sprinkling of bars, cafés, and restaurants. At the end of this exquisite lane is the city's most bohemian thoroughfare—**Byres Road**—which is also replete with eating and drinking venues, as well as stylish boutiques.

Around the Clyde

The River Clyde was neglected for decades before its recent reinvention. In place of hulking shipyards (see pp. 98–99), the Clyde now sports a string of visitor attractions, as well as modern architecture. Today, tour boats and seaplanes (see sidebar left) fly its deeply historic waters.

The North Bank: The most impressively revamped stretch of the river lies west of the **Clyde Arc,** which is itself a striking new structure known affectionately as the "Squinty Bridge" due to the unusual angle at which it straddles the Clyde. On the north bank is the sprawling **Scottish Exhibition and Conference**

EXPERIENCE:
Seaplane Splash Down

The Clyde has always been a main transport route through the city, and now there is a new way to experience traveling on the river. **Loch Lomond Seaplanes** *(50 Pacific Quay, next to Glasgow Science Center, tel 01436/675 030, www.lochlomondseaplanes.com)* has started up a service that splashes down near the Glasgow Science Centre. It is a stunning way to experience the city, and you can also push farther afield, with services to Loch Lomond and Oban. Private charters also available.

Centre (SECC)—two massive but purely functional spaces that house music concerts and other events. The SECC also houses the **Armadillo** performance venue—the 1995 addition by Lord Norman Foster (1935–). A new 12,500-capacity concert venue, designed by Lord Foster, is currently under construction, as is the new Transport Museum (see p. 97), designed by award-winning Iraqi-born architect Zaha Hadid (1950–). The **Finnieston Crane,** preserved for shipbuilding heritage reasons, overlooks the new developments.

Another historic legacy on the North Bank lies father west. The **Tall Ship at Glasgow Harbour** (*100 Stobcross Rd., tel 0141/222 2513, www.glenlee.co.uk*) is a huge square-rigger called *Glenlee,* one of the last surviving Clyde-built sailing ships. Launched in 1896, *Glenlee* is a remarkable testament to the last wave of steel-hulled sailing ships before steam took over, having circumnavigated the globe four times and rounded Cape Horn on 15 voyages. The restored vessel is slated to be moved to the Scottish Maritime Museum at Braehead (see p. 99) by the end of 2011.

The South Bank: Across a pedestrian bridge, facing the SECC on the opposite bank of the river, lies a brace of glass and steel structures that house the British Broadcasting Corporation (BBC) and Scottish Television (STV) broadcasting companies, as well as the popular **Glasgow Science Centre.** The main building—the giant titanium and glass **Science**

Mall—holds an innovative visitor attraction spread across three stories. The museum emphasizes interactive displays and gadgets, which appeal to younger visitors. Here you can meet Madagascan hissing cockroaches, make your own hot-air balloon, conjure up a rocket to launch, and visit the museum planetarium.

The Scottish Exhibition and Conference Centre, designed by architect Lord Norman Foster

Part of the same complex is the **Glasgow Tower,** which is Scotland's tallest freestanding building at 417 feet (127 m). Engineers used more than 3,300 tons (3,000 tonnes) of concrete to establish the 65-foot-deep (20 m) foundations of this unique tower. In good weather, you can ride a lift up to a viewing platform for unparalleled views of the city. This riverside complex also contains an **IMAX Cinema** (*tel 0141/420 5000*), probably the finest of its kind in Scotland. ∎

Glasgow Science Centre
✉ 50 Pacific Quay
☎ (0141) 420 5000
$ $$$
www.glasgow
sciencecentre.org

Glasgow Tower
✉ 50 Pacific Quay
☎ (0141) 420 5000
$ $$
www.glasgow
sciencecentre.org

Beyond the City Center

Glasgow is Scotland's largest city, and its suburbs radiate into the surrounding countryside. The suburbs eventually trail off into satellite towns that lie on the banks of the Clyde and south into Lanarkshire, which is home to one of Scotland's top attractions, New Lanark.

An 18th-century cotton mill on the banks of the River Clyde in New Lanark

Dumbarton

Visitor Information

- ✉ Information Centre, 7 Alexandra Parade, Milton
- ☎ (08452) 255 121

Dumbarton Castle

- ⚠ 90 B3
- ✉ Castle Road, Dumbarton
- ☎ (01389) 732 167
- 💲 $$

Helensburgh

- ⚠ 90 A3

Visitor Information

- ✉ Information Centre, The Clock Tower, East Clyde St.
- ☎ (01436) 672 642

One of the most interesting Glasgow overspill towns is **Dumbarton.** While depressing postwar housing character-izes most of the town, shining through the gloom is the mighty **Dumbarton Castle,** which sits atop a volcanic crag and stares out across the Clyde, guard-ing Glasgow from the threat of marine invasion. Indeed, Dumbarton has been the stag-ing post for its own invasion in 1548—that of Mary Queen of Scots, when she set sail for France in her quest to become queen of the country.

If you have caught the ship-building bug during your travels in Glasgow, you may want to check out the **Denny Tank** (*Castle Street, Dumbarton, tel 01389/763 444,*

www.scottishmaritimemuseum .org/dumbarton, $), part of the Scottish Maritime Museum. Denny Tank is the site of the world's oldest testing tank, which has launched a thousand ships.

A little farther north, on the train line from Glasgow, is elegant **Helensburgh**—famous as the birthplace of John Logie Baird (1888–1946), the engineer who invented the first working televi-sion. Helensburgh may no longer be a popular seaside resort for holidaying Glaswegians, but an air of nostalgic romance still hangs over the town.

You can sample some of the history of Helensburgh at **The Hill House,** whose interior was immaculately and inspira-tionally crafted by another of

INSIDER TIP:

Glasgow and the Clyde Valley have the most extensive railway network in Scotland, and it can be fun to skip around on it.

—LARRY PORGES
National Geographic editor

Helensburgh's most famous sons, Charles Rennie Mackintosh (see sidebar p. 93).

New Lanark

As you head in a southeasterly direction, the Clyde narrows and starts to meander across the bottom of a large valley gripped by new developments. Beyond the pleasant town of Lanark itself is the shining light of the **New Lanark World Heritage Site.**

This 18th-century cotton mill is so valuable, both historically and socially, that UNESCO has given it a place on its protected World Heritage List. To get the most out of your visit to the site, the first port of call should be to the visitor center, where you can learn all about the enlightened industrialists David Dale (1739–1806), who, in partnership with Richard Arkwright (1733–1792), founded the village in 1785 to make cotton on a grand scale, using the River Clyde as a source of power. However, it was mill manager Robert Owen (1771–1858) who grabbed the opportunity to do something special. He provided his workers with the world's first day nursery, as well as schooling for children to the age of 12. Owen realized that culture and education were as important as work if improved production and quality were to be achieved.

Highlights of the site include the "Annie McLeod Experience," where the ghost of a mill girl takes you on an unorthodox tour of life in the 1820s. Then there is the well-made film in Robert Owen's School, which takes you on a trip back through time. If the weather allows, you should follow the riverside walkway to the impressive **Falls of Clyde,** a trio of attractive waterfalls. ∎

The Hill House
- Upper Colquhoun Street, Helensburgh
- ☎ (0844) 493 2208
- $ $$$

www.nts.org.uk/
Property/58

New Lanark World Heritage Site
- 🔺 90 C2
- New Lanark Road, Lanark
- ☎ (01555) 661 345
- $ $$$

www.newlanark.org

Falls of Clyde
- ☎ (01555) 665 262

www.newlanark
.org/fallsofclyde
.shtml

The Burrell Collection

The Burrell Collection *(Pollock Country Park, 2060 Pollockshaw Rd., tel 0141/287 2550, www.glasgowmuseums.com; see map 90 B3)* is an art gallery and museum that offers a huge volume of work—the personal collection of shipping magnate William Burrell (1861–1958). Highlights among the 8,000-strong collection include iconic works such as "The Thinker" by Auguste Rodin (1840–1917), as well as the collection of oil paintings on the upper story, which includes works by Édouard Manet (1832–1883), Eugène Boudin (1824–1898), and Alfred Sisley (1839–1899), as well as the remarkable "Le Château de Medan" by Paul Cézanne (1839–1906). For some visitors, the Burrell Collection, which is 3 miles (5 km) southwest of the city center, is one of the main reasons to come to Glasgow, such is the importance of the work on display. The on-site café/restaurant is superb.

Ayrshire

Ayrshire extends south from the last of the Clydeside shipyards on the Firth of Clyde down to the Irish Sea, which impresses with sweeping, sandy beaches and world-famous golf courses. County town Ayr is most famous as the birthplace of Robert Burns, Scotland's Shakespeare.

Attractive gardens surround the imposing Culzean Castle.

Turnberry Golf Course

🏔 90 A1

✉ Maidens Road, Turnberry

☎ (01655) 334 032

www.turnberry .co.uk

Royal Troon Golf Club

🏔 90 A2

✉ Craigend Road, Troon

☎ (01292) 311 555

www.royaltroon .co.uk

Golf

Ayrshire is prime farming country, but the area is best known as the home of two of the biggest hitters in the world of golf—Turnberry and Royal Troon. **Turnberry** sports three separate courses—Ailsa, Kintyre, and Arran—all of which overlook the iconic lighthouse that has featured on TV coverage of previous British Open Championships.

Just to the north, **Royal Troon**—the "Royal" addition was awarded in 1978—also boasts a trio of courses, in the form of Royal Troon, Portland, and Craigend. The back nine on the signature Royal Troon course may justly lay claim to be the most challenging in the world. Ayrshire is home to countless other courses, both public and private, which share gorgeous views out over sandy beaches toward Arran and Ailsa Craig.

Alloway

First and foremost, Ayrshire is Burns Country. Scotland's Shakespeare is venerated as a king in Alloway, the sleepy village sandwiched between Turnberry and Royal Troon, where he was born in 1759. It is fitting that the **Burns Heritage Park** is located here. The park comprises the Burns Cottage, Burns Memorial, Tam O'Shanter Experience, and a Burns museum.

Make the **Burns Cottage** your first stop. It was here, as the bitter winter winds swirled all around, that one of the world's great romantics and lyricists burst into the world—the man who gave the world "Auld Lang Syne," among myriad other classics. The cottage now provides insight into his early years in the house his father so splendidly built.

The **museum** is adjacent to the cottage, and other highlights within a short stroll include the large **Burns Memorial,** a large stone edifice built between 1820 and 1823, and the **Tam O'Shanter Experience,** which is named for one of Burns' most famous poems. This audiovisual experience uses modern technology to bring Burns back to life, and the attraction also stages a regular roster of special events, with Burns center stage.

Culzean Castle

By far the most dramatic buildings in all of Ayrshire, and one of Scotland's most impressive castles, is Culzean Castle, located 12 miles (19 km) south of Ayr on the south Ayrshire coast. Once the residence of the Marquess of Ailsa, parts of this mighty structure date back to the 15th century. Constant additions and embellishments,

however, have made it more grand country house than serious fortified castle. The first port of call is the visitor center, where you can watch an excellent audiovisual presentation that sheds light on the castle's eclectic history.

The castle's exterior may be dramatic, but inside lie further treasures, such as a huge collection of armaments that were bought from the Royal Family and shipped up from the Tower of London back in 1812. Look for the Oval Staircase—the work of seminal Scottish architect Robert Adam (see sidebar below)—who revamped much of the original medieval interior in his unique style between 1772 and 1790. You can see his table and chair designs. Then take a stroll in the vast castle grounds. ∎

Adam's Style

Robert Adam (1728–1792) was born in Fife, Scotland, the son of an architect. He traveled to Italy, where he studied the classical style, and returned to Britain with new ideas. Adam rebelled against the then-dominant Palladian style. While still drawing on classical influences, his innovative light, elegant lines refused to follow slavishly classical proportion and decoration. His final project was Culzean Castle, which he remodeled in stages between 1772 and 1790 to make the most of its outlook over the sea.

Alloway

🗺 90 A2

Burns Heritage Park

🗺 90 A2
✉ Murdoch's Lane, Alloway
☎ (01292) 443 700
💲 Cottage: $$; Tam O'Shanter Experience: $; Museum & Monument: free

www.burnsheritage park.com

Culzean Castle

🗺 90 A1
✉ Near Maybole, Ayrshire
☎ (0844) 493 2149
💲 $$

www.culzean experience.org

The rolling hills of Dumfries, Galloway's dramatic coastline, and the green fields and heather-clad hills of the Borders region

Southern Scotland

Galloway Forest Park is famous for its stunning natural beauty.

Southern Scotland

Although southern Scotland is often overlooked by visitors heading north to Edinburgh and Glasgow, or farther afield to the Highlands, the area has much to offer. The district of Dumfries and Galloway boasts lush forests and a rugged coastline, while the Borders' crumbling abbeys speak of the region's turbulent history.

NOT TO BE MISSED:

Sampling fresh seafood in the charming coastal resort of Portpatrick **111, 112**

Hiking or biking in Galloway Forest Park's forested hills **115**

Glimpsing the legacy of the monastic orders that once lived at the Border abbeys **118–119**

The charming town of Melrose, set between the River Tweed and the surrounding rolling hills **117**

Enjoying some of the freshest fish with your chips in the working seaport of Eyemouth **123**

Dumfries & Galloway

Created when the historic counties of Dumfriesshire and Galloway were merged in 1975, the district of Dumfries and Galloway has a range of attractions from the beautiful coastal towns of Kirkcudbright and Portpatrick to the trail of Rabbie Burns in bustling Dumfries. The many picturesque villages and castles

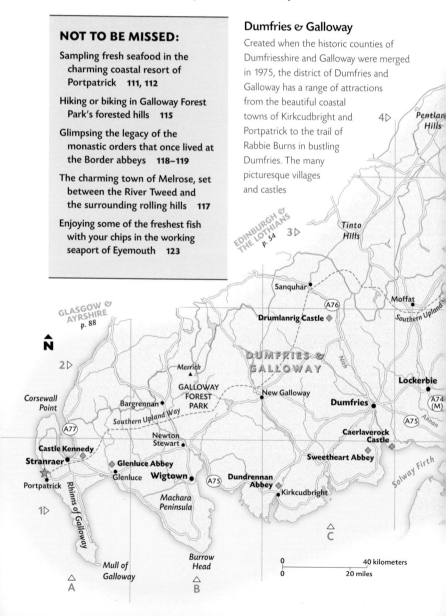

scattered across the Dumfries and Galloway countryside reward curious explorers. Castles to keep an eye out for include Kennedy and Caerlaverock, while the abbeys of Dumfries and Galloway are less well known than those of the Borders but equally charming.

Natural attractions include the spectacular coastline dubbed "Scotland's riviera," which unfolds along the Solway Firth in the south; the beautifully windswept Rhinns of Galloway on the edge of the Irish Sea to the west; and the Galloway Forest Park, which includes part of the Southern Upland Way. This popular walking route cuts through the heart of Dumfries and Galloway and on across the Borders.

The Borders

Scotland and England have battled for control of the region known as the Borders for centuries. Spreading across 1,800 square miles (4,600 sq km), the Borders stretch from the rolling hills and moorland in the west, through gentler valleys and high agricultural plains, to the rocky east coastline. Add pretty market towns, dramatic ruined abbeys, and some of the most attractive country houses in Britain, and it is easy to understand why people fall deeply in love with the region.

The star attractions are undoubtedly the Border abbeys, home to Cistercian and Augustinian monks in the 12th to 16th centuries, but now in ruins. The rolling hills and snaking River Tweed also have plenty to offer. Melrose is the epitome of what is so appealing about the Borders, with its impressive abbey, independent shops, affordable hotels and restaurants, and rich literary history—this is Sir Walter Scott country, after all. The Borders are great for active types, too, with some of the best hiking and biking Scotland has to offer.

The Borders are awash with country houses and castles given the region's rich history and strategic importance. The pick of the bunch are Floors Castle near Kelso, Traquair House near Peebles, and the astonishing Abbotsford—Sir Walter Scott's own home. ■

Dumfries & Galloway

From the warm beaches of "Scotland's riviera" to the rolling hills of Dumfriesshire, Scotland's most southwesterly region is a far cry from the rugged mountains of the Highlands. Its historic towns, once home to the poet Robert Burns, have much to offer lovers of art and literature.

The pedestrianized heart of Dumfries, a traditional market town

Dumfries

108 C2

Visitor Information

✉ 64 Whitesands, Dumfries

☎ (01387) 245 555

www.visitdumfries andgalloway.co.uk

Burns House

✉ Burns Street, Dumfries

☎ (01387) 255 297

🕐 Closed Sun.–Mon.

www.burns scotland.com

Dumfries

Ayrshire may have been the birthplace of Robert Burns (1759–1796; see p. 48), but the market town of Dumfries also claims a strong link to Scotland's national poet—he spent the last five years of his life here and is immortalized in a magnificent marble statue on the High Street. Burns was very much a man of the people, however, and much preferred the busy company of an inn to being put on a pedestal. The **Globe Inn** (*56 High St., tel 01387/252 355,*

www.globeinndumfries.co.uk) was his favorite local drinking den. Burns had one of his notorious affairs with a barmaid at the Globe, and she bore him a child. **Burns House,** where the poet tragically died at the age of 37, is a more conventional memorial. His widow, Jean Armour, lived here until her death more than 30 years later. The most interesting exhibits are his personal letters and handwritten notes. On the same bank of the River Nith lies the neoclassical **Mausoleum,** where his body lies.

INSIDER TIP:

Threave Castle sits on a wee island in the middle of a river. Ring the bell and a boatman will come to take you over for a tour.

—JIM RICHARDSON
National Geographic photographer

Across the River Nith lies the **Robert Burns Centre.** This popular attraction is well worth a visit as it illuminates Burns's connections with Dumfries in the charming setting of an old mill. The highlight is the audiovisual presentation, which takes place in the center's cinema—itself open to the public for screenings outside museum opening times.

Galloway

Kirkcudbright, located 23 miles (37 km) southwest of Dumfries, is the star of the "Scottish riviera"; this relaxed waterfront oasis comes complete with a working fishing harbor. Today,

Kirkcudbright has become more popular with artists than fisherfolk, with an active local community attracted by the quality of the light. Other attractions include the sturdy **MacLennan's Castle** and **Broughton House,** which is a gorgeous 18th-century town house now open as a museum that offers insight into the town's literary connections. Also worth visiting is the dramatic ruin of **Threave Castle,** which stands on an island in the River Dee around 10 miles (16 km) north of Kirkcudbright.

Portpatrick, on Galloway's west coast, is a glorious last flourish before the Irish Sea takes over. With its sheltered bay, this attractive seaside village curls around a sweeping hill and boasts many attractive whitewashed and pastel-painted houses; some open these days as hotels and excellent seafood restaurants. No longer a major port for ships heading for Northern Ireland, Portpatrick is now basking in a tranquil retirement. It is the western terminus

(continued on p. 114)

Robert Burns Centre
- ✉ Mill Rd., Dumfries
- ☎ (01387) 264 808
- 🕐 Closed Sun.
- 💲 $

www.rbcft.co.uk

Kirkcudbright
- 🅰 108 C1

MacLennan's Castle
- ✉ Castle Street, Kirkcudbright
- ☎ (01557) 331 856
- 💲 $$

Broughton House
- ✉ 12 High St., Kirkcudbright
- ☎ (01557) 330 437
- 💲 $$

Threave Castle
- ✉ Threave Castle, Castle Douglas
- ☎ (07711) 223 101
- 💲 $

Portpatrick
- 🅰 108 A1

Gretna Green Weddings

The town of Gretna Green in southern Dumfriesshire is a place long associated with secret marriages and romance. This tradition dates back to 1753, when a law was passed in England that prevented those under 21 from marrying without their parents' consent. As this law did not apply to Scotland, Gretna Green, just across the border on the main road to Glasgow, became a favorite spot for young English couples who wanted to marry. Scottish law allowed pretty much anyone to carry out marriages, and Gretna Green's blacksmiths performed so many ceremonies that impulsive marriages became known as "anvil weddings." Although the legal loophole was closed in 1853, the town's romantic history still draws thousands of couples every year to marry or renew their vows.

Walk: The Galloway Coast

On the high cliffs north of Portpatrick, with the wind whipping up from the Mull of Galloway, it's hard not to feel that you have traveled far into the wild, empty country of the Highlands. This walk on a portion of the Southern Upland Way quickly whisks you into spectacular Rhinns of Galloway, only a few miles from civilization.

Looking north to Killantringan Lighthouse near Portpatrick

With its clutch of excellent hotels, pubs, and restaurants, the charming seaside town of **Portpatrick** is a popular base for those who wish to explore the dramatic coastline of the Rhinns of Galloway. The town is the western terminus of the Southern Upland Way, a 212-mile (340 km) hiking route that goes all the way to the North Sea coast. You don't have to travel great distances, however, for an invigorating and rewarding hike, nor do you have to forsake the comforts of a Portpatrick hotel in the evening.

The starting point for this walk is the parking lot at **Portpatrick harbor ❶**, where an information board provides a primer on the Southern Upland Way. The path rises steeply away from the town on a staircase cut through the layered rock of the cliffs. If you look back toward the town as the steps kink their way up the steep slope, you will see the desolate ruin

NOT TO BE MISSED:

Portpatrick • Sandeel Bay • Killantringan Lighthouse

of **Dunskey Castle,** a 14th-century tower-house that stands high on the cliffs south of Portpatrick. This walk only takes you on the first few miles of the Southern Upland Way, so don't be daunted by the waymarkers that say there are more than 200 miles to go.

From the top of the stairs, the path runs along the cliff top beside Portpatrick golf course. After about a mile (1.5 km), you will reach the picturesque **Sandeel Bay ❷**. This beach was once popular with bathers, but there are few around today who would be willing to dive into its cold waters. Instead, visitors admire the caves and waterfalls at the edges of the beach. Continue north from the beach, up another staircase cut into the cliff. This one is a little narrower and rougher, so be careful where you step. The same advice applies to the path beyond, which hugs the cliff edge for a few minutes as it makes its way around to the next bay, **Port Kale ❸**. Here two peculiar hexagonal huts are the only remains of the first telegraph connection between Scotland and Ireland. The steps up from this bay are steeper than the previous ones, but there is a railing for support as you climb.

For the next 1.5 miles (2.4 km) the route takes you across the open headland above the cliffs to Killantringan Lighthouse. From the high points of this path you will get your first glimpses of the lighthouse, and on a clear day this is a good vantage point to watch the ferries making trips between Stranraer and Belfast. When the tide is low, it is possible to see the wreck of the *Craigantlet*, a cargo ship that ran aground in 1982.

The attractive white and yellow **Killantringan Lighthouse ❹** is still operational, so it is not open to the public, but the outcrop of Black Head on which it stands provides excellent views along the coast, including the broad sandy beaches of Knock Bay to the north.

From here you can either retrace your steps along the coast, or, if you prefer to take a circular walk, follow the single-track road inland. After 1.3 miles (2 km) this road will meet with the B738 road to Portpatrick. Turn right at the junction and follow the road south. The B738 sees slightly more traffic than the track from the lighthouse, but has broad verges for pedestrians to walk on. Follow this road for about 2 miles (3.2 km) before turning right when it joins the A77 on the outskirts of Portpatrick. From here follow the road around 0.5 mile (1 km) into town, passing the village's war memorial and church before turning right again onto Dinvin Street, which takes you the short distance back to the harbor and your starting point in the parking lot.

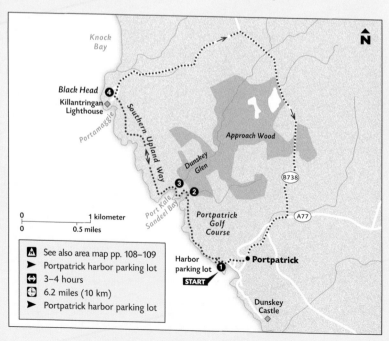

Knock Bay

Black Head ❹
Killantringan Lighthouse

Portamaggie

Southern Upland Way

Approach Wood

B738

Dunskey Glen

❸ ❷

Port Kale
Sandeel Bay

Portpatrick Golf Course

A77

N

0 ———— 1 kilometer
0 ———— 0.5 miles

Harbor parking lot
❶
START

● **Portpatrick**

Dunskey Castle

🅰 See also area map pp. 108–109
▶ Portpatrick harbor parking lot
↔ 3–4 hours
🕐 6.2 miles (10 km)
▶ Portpatrick harbor parking lot

"Scotland's Bard" Robert Burns spent the last three years of his life at what is now called the Burns' House in Dumfries.

Drumlanrig Castle

◪ 108 C2

☎ (01848) 331 555

⑤ Castle: $$; Gardens & estate: $$

www.drumlanrig.com

Caerlaverock Castle

◪ 108 C1

✉ Church Street, Glencaple

☎ (01387) 770 244

⑤ $$

www.historic-scotland.co.uk

Sweetheart Abbey

◪ 108 C1

✉ New Abbey, Dumfries

☎ (01387) 850 397

⑤ $

www.historic-scotland.co.uk

of the **Southern Upland Way,** a 212-mile (340 km) coast-to-coast hiking trail (see pp. 112–113), as well as a good base for exploring the western flank of the region on local walks.

Castles & Abbeys

A number of abbeys, castles, and country houses tempt many visitors heading out of Dumfries. North of the town lies a chunky Renaissance gem, **Drumlanrig Castle,** which was built in 1691 by the first Duke of Queensberry, himself an architect, using pink sandstone. The 80,000-acre (32,000 ha) estate also boasts a country park and a Victorian garden. Guided tours of the castle offer access to one of the finest private art collections in Scotland—the Buccleuch Collection, which includes works by Thomas Gainsborough (1727–1788), Rembrandt van Rijn (1606–1669), and Aert van der Neer (1603–1677). The lavish reception rooms are the architectural highlight of the

interior and offer a glimpse into the lifestyles of the dukes and duchesses who have called Drumlanrig home through the centuries.

The deeply romantic ruin of **Caerlaverock Castle** lies 7 miles (11 km) south of Dumfries in Glencaple. Dating from the 15th century, the castle sports a unique triangular design and a double moat. Walk around the outside and you can see right inside the very skeleton of the castle, thanks to a battering by invading armies. Cross into the castle itself, and you will have to use your imagination as the castle now lies in ruins. A modest visitor center looks at its history and the bitter sieges its inhabitants once endured. Take time to explore the grounds on the network of walking trails, including one that reveals the foundations of an earlier fortification.

Farther west from Caerlaverock Castle you'll find a trio of ruined Cisterian abbeys. The well-preserved **Sweetheart Abbey** lies just 5 miles (8 km) south of Dumfries. It was commissioned and later named by Lady Devorgilla in the 13th century as an enduring tribute to her late husband. About a mile (1.5 km) inland from the Solway Firth, to the west, is **Dundrennan Abbey,** which took English monks about 50 years to build in the 12th century. One important historical claim to fame is that Mary Queen of Scots spent her last night at Dundrennan before being boated off to England, never to see her beloved Scotland again.

Built in the 12th century, **Glenluce Abbey** lies much farther west. Most of the abbey is now a ruin, but the chapter house survives intact and is well worth a visit to gaze over the grotesque characters that adorn the corbels and ceiling bosses. You can look at artifacts, including decorated floor tiles and pottery items, in the modest visitor center.

Just as the land narrows into the scenic peninsula known as the Rhinns of Galloway, 55 miles (88 km) west of Dumfries, you'll find the last grand castle, **Castle Kennedy.** In fact, you get two castles for the price of one. The original castle was destroyed by fire in 1716 but its ruins can still be seen around the more recent **Lochinch Castle,** which overlooks the White Loch.

Natural Attractions

The wide sweep of the Solway Firth is the main attraction in the south of Dumfries and Galloway. It is dotted with coves and sandy bays, perfect for cycling or driving around. There are plenty of places to stay and camp on "**Scotland's riviera,"** a mild holiday oasis popular with Scots but little known farther afield.

The **Southern Upland Way** (see pp. 112–113) runs through the heart of Dumfries and Galloway, and the best place to appreciate its beauty is the **Galloway Forest Park**—Britain's largest forest park (see sidebar right). This bucolic oasis stretches its tentacles over 300 square miles (776 sq km) of brooding hills and silvery lochs, considered to be one of the world's best star-gazing spots. The land is rich in myths and legends,

most poignantly that the Scottish king Robert the Bruce, hid away here before uniting his country in victory against the "Auld Enemy," England. If you are short on time, focus on **Glentrool**—home to the impossibly pretty Loch Trool. There are plenty of trails for cyclists and walkers.

The scenic **Rhinns of Galloway** peninsula, at the southeasternmost point of the region, is surrounded on three sides by the Irish Sea. To appreciate the views, head to its southern extremity—and Scotland's most southerly point—the **Mull of Galloway.** Here it will often just be you, the wildlife, and the lonely lighthouse blinking out a warning to ships to avoid this treacherous stretch of coast. ■

Dundrennan Abbey
- 108 C1
- ☎ (01557) 500 262
- $ $

Glenluce Abbey
- 108 A1
- ✉ Glenluce
- ☎ (01581) 300 541
- $ $
- www.historic-scotland.gov.uk

Castle Kennedy
- 108 A1
- ✉ Stair Estate, Rephad
- ☎ (01776) 702 024
- $ $$
- castlekennedygardens.co.uk

EXPERIENCE:
Cycling in Galloway Forest Park

A number of excellent trails open up the unspoiled scenery in and around Galloway Forest Park (tel 01776/ 702 024, www .forestry.gov.uk/gallowayforestpark, $$). **"Round the Loch"** takes in an easy 14-mile (22.5 km) route around Clatteringshaws Loch. Perhaps the most popular trail, the **"Palgowan,"** leaves from Glentrool Visitor Centre and makes an 8-mile (12.9 km) circuit along forest roads, quiet backroads, and small hills. Bikes are available for rent at **HDI Ltd.** (80 Victoria St., tel 01671/ 404 002, www.hdi-online.biz/bike-sales.asp) in Newton Stewart, which is within easy biking distance of the forest park. There are three park visitor centers: **Kirroughtree** (tel 01671/402 165) and **Glentrool** (tel 01671/840 302), both near Newton Stewart; and **Clatteringshaws** near New Galloway.

Borders

The Borders are no longer the disputed "Badlands" between warring Scotland and England, but there is a rich legacy of those troubled days, with ruined abbeys, castles, and grand country houses complementing attractive market towns and excellent hotels and restaurants.

Picturesque Kelso on the banks of the River Tweed

Peebles

109 D3

Visitor Information

✉ Peebles Visitor Information Centre, 23 High Street, Peebles

☎ (01721) 723 159

www.peebles.info

Kailzie Gardens

✉ Kailzie, Peebles

☎ (01721) 720 007

$ $$

www.kailzie gardens.com

Peebles

Less than an hour's drive south of Edinburgh is Peebles, one of the most attractive towns in the region. Flanked on three sides by rolling hills, and on the other by the wide sweep of the mighty River Tweed, this prosperous little oasis is an excellent base. The busy **High Street** speaks of a Victorian golden age, with a sprinkling of little delis and specialist shops making a pleasant break from the ubiquitous shopping mall.

Just a few minutes' walk upstream from the town center the landscape becomes much more wild. Here the River Tweed is lined by parks and open land, and a footpath takes you along the pebble-fringed banks of the river toward the imposing bulk of **Neidpath Castle.** The castle is not open to the public, but it is still worth walking upriver to see. Looking at this 14th-century tower-house from the river, you can still see the damage inflicted when it was attacked by Oliver Cromwell's army during the English Civil War (1642–1651).

In the opposite direction, around 3 miles (4.8 km) east of Peebles on the B7062 to Cardrona, lie **Kailzie Gardens—** an attractive country estate on the site of a long-since vanished

INSIDER TIP:

During the Hawick and Selkirk Common Ridings [see sidebar p. 122], which date back five centuries, hundreds of riders set out to ride a circuit of the common land held by each village.

—JIM RICHARDSON
National Geographic photographer

12th- century castle. These beautiful walled gardens are the result of many decades of work finding plants that can tolerate the brutally harsh winters this exposed site experiences.

Farther along the road from Kailzie, 5 miles (8 km) south of Kelso, is the ancient **Traquair House.** According to some, this is Scotland's oldest inhabited house. The current occupants trace their

family line back to the 15th century. Built in the style of a fortified mansion, its facade is exquisite in its whitewashed simplicity. You can explore the stately rooms (watch for the bed said to have been slept in by Mary Queen of Scots) and vaulted cellars and explore the grounds, with wandering peacocks a range of short walks to enjoy.

Tweed Valley

The River Tweed is one of the defining features of the Borders landscape, marking the eastern half of the border between England and Scotland. It flows from the hills around Peebles to the English border town of Berwick-upon-Tweed.

Melrose: A neat and charmingly attractive old market town, Melrose sits in a scenic fold of hills on the banks of the Tweed. The well-preserved town center is awash with cobbles and sturdy stone buildings, with a deep

(continued on p. 120)

Traquair House

✉ Innerleithen
☎ (01896) 830 323
🕐 Open daily April–Oct., weekends only Nov.; closed Dec.–March
💲 House & grounds: $$; Grounds only: $

www.traquair.co.uk

Melrose

🔼 109 E3
Visitor Information
✉ Melrose Visitor Information Centre, Abbey House, Abbey Street, Melrose
☎ (01896) 822 283
www.melrose.bordernet.co.uk

EXPERIENCE: Cycling in Glentress Forest

Glentress Forest, located about 2 miles (3 km) east of Peebles on the A72, offers world-class mountain biking, showcasing some 50 miles (80 km) of trails. Rent equipment and get some advice at **The Hub in the Forest** *(tel 01721/721 736, www.thehubintheforest.co.uk)*, a bike shop at the entrance to the forest owned by two former professional mountain bikers. Although the well-stocked rental shop usually has spare bikes, it's best to book a bike ahead.

The sweeping forested hillsides that fall down toward the River Tweed are perfect mountain-biking territory, and you have your choice of forest roads, single tracks, and obstacle courses to tackle. The green route is suitable for families and less experienced riders, while there is a tougher, 13-mile (19 km) red route and a near-suicidal, 18-mile (30 km) black single track, complete with huge berms and severe drop-offs. And if you want to practice your double jumps, there's also a free-ride area.

Note that the forest is also popular among hikers and trail runners. For more information: *tel 01750/721 120, www.glentressforest.com or www.forestry.gov.uk/glentressforest.*

Border Abbeys

The Scottish Borders have always been home to passions, struggles, and strife. The region has always been a spiritual place, too, as its great abbeys attest. Today the Border Abbeys are a necklace of ruins, which have lain in various states of disrepair since they were sacked by English invaders centuries ago. But while only hinting at their former glory, the ruins have lost nothing of their charm and romance.

The majestic Abbey Church dominates the pink- and red-tinted stone ruins of Melrose Abbey.

The Border Abbeys were founded during the reign of King David I of Scotland, who invited a quartet of monastic orders to build their abbeys in the Borders in the 12th century. King David wanted to demonstrate that his power extended even to the southern fringes of his kingdom. Over the years, the orders grew wealthy in their own right and started to wield their own power.

Once the grandest of structures, the magnificent **Kelso Abbey** (*Abbey Row, Kelso, www.historic-scotland.gov.uk*), was devastated as the land disputes between Scotland and England raged on. However, the striking Romanesque design still reveals itself in the ruins, and you can conjure up some of what life would have been like for the Benedictine monks who lived here. You can see the towers and transepts that were part of the unusual double-cross design.

Jedburgh Abbey (*Abbey Bridge End, Jedburgh, tel 01835/863 925, www.historic-scotland .gov.uk, $$*) also endured centuries of attack, yet even today its majesty is a reminder of King

David I of Scotland's message to England. In commissioning such a grand design, he wanted to prove that his country held sway over the Borders. The abbey was built on the site of a much earlier church, dating back to the 700s. At one stage, the abbey was heavily fortified, but it was eventually destroyed by the Scots to keep it from falling into English hands. The remains of the abbey still cast an unmistakable presence on the local skyline and dominate the approach to the town. Jedburgh Abbey is the best one to visit on a rainy day since it has a good visitor center, where you can take in a short audiovisual show. The center is also home to the abbey's greatest treasure, the priceless Jedburgh Comb. This beautiful artifact, carved from fine ivory, dates back over a millennium.

The crumbling remains of Kelso Abbey

INSIDER TIP:

Visit Melrose Abbey on an afternoon in fall, when the pink stonework of its walls positively glows as the sun sinks in the west.

—TIM HARRIS
National Geographic contributor

Hidden among the trees on a horseshoe bend in the River Tweed about 10 miles (16 km) west of Kelso are the striking ruins of the medieval **Dryburgh Abbey** *(tel 01835/822 381, www.historic-scotland.gov.uk, $$).* Although not as well preserved as the other abbeys, it still provides insight into the cloistered lives of the resident monks. The church has long since fallen, but large parts of the monastic quarters survive. Dryburgh Abbey is a place of pilgrimage for visitors who admire the work of the great Sir Walter Scott, whose grave lies in the chapel of the abbey—an understated granite monument unlike the overblown "rocket" that bears his name in Edinburgh. Long after its destruction in 1544, the abbey was acquired by the Earl of Buchan. At the end of the 18th century he worked to preserve the ruins and had formal gardens planted in the grounds.

Perhaps the most romantic of all the abbey ruins are those of **Melrose Abbey** *(Abbey Street, Melrose, tel 01896/822 562, www.historic-scotland.gov.uk, $$).* According to some, the ghost of Scotland's greatest warrior king lives on at Melrose Abbey—Robert the Bruce's heart is believed to have been laid to rest here. The Scottish monarch is said to have wanted his heart to be taken on a crusade to the Holy Land—to atone for his brutal murder of a political rival years earlier—but this request was not carried out. Extra weight was given to the idea that it lies at Melrose Abbey when a casket with a heart was discovered in 1997.

Take the stairs up the abbey's tower for sweeping views across Melrose and the surrounding hills. Melrose Abbey's elaborate design incorporates dramatic Gothic touches to spice up the original Cistercian designs. The intricacy and creativity of the stone carvings is remarkable—gargoyles of pigs playing bagpipes being particularly memorable. Delve into the museum if you want to learn more about the expert stonemasonry.

EXPERIENCE:
Fishing in the Tweed

The Tweed offers excellent fishing with well-organized sport for visitors. The easiest way is to organize a trip through your hotel, but you can also seek out a permit to fish from a tackle store. Good tackle stores include Tweedside Tackle (*36–38 Bridge St., Kelso, tel 01573/225 306, www.tweedsidetackle.co.uk*) **and Orvis** (*11 The Square, Kelso, tel 01573/225 810, www.orvis.co.uk*). **The Tweed is one of the top salmon fishing rivers in the world, so the highlight is the chance to catch wild salmon as they make their journey upstream in the autumn. The Tweed boasts a bounty of trout, too. Some hotels, including Burt's in Melrose** (*www.burtshotel.co.uk; see p. 283*), **not only organize fishing but can also cook your catch for supper.**

Abbotsford

- ✉ 2 miles (3 km) W of Melrose
- ☎ (01896) 752 043
- 🕐 Closed Nov.– mid-March
- 💲 House & grounds: $$; Grounds only: $

www.scotts abbotsford.co.uk

sense of continuity and tradition that is apparent in the town's active cultural life. Its history is dramatic, as for centuries this was serious "Border Country," with tensions between England and Scotland often boiling over into skirmishes and battles. The windswept landscape around Melrose has long been associated with the quasi-mythical "Border Reivers"—bands of raiders who stole livestock and took part in inter-tribal warfare during medieval times.

Melrose is proud of its traditional stores—first-rate butchers, a fishmonger, a wine merchant, and a well-stocked deli. A sprinkling of cafés, tearooms, and restaurants serve up the local produce.

When it comes to sport, forget soccer—this is rugby country. Melrose has a rich rugby history,

and this tiny town is the proud birthplace of Rugby Sevens, a version of the game now played all around the world. It is fairly easy to pick up tickets for a full rugby match between Melrose and a string of other Scottish sides. For a real treat, come in April and experience the Sevens tournament for yourself—a buzzing event when the atmosphere in Melrose is electric.

A Trail to England: Melrose Abbey (see p. 119) in the center of town is the starting point for **St. Cuthbert's Way** (*www.stcuthbertsway.fsnet.co.uk*), which is one of many excellent walking trails that run in and around Melrose. St. Cuthbert's Way is a 62-mile (100 km) trail that continues across the border to Lindisfarne monastery in England. Follow the trail south out of town, and you will find yourself among the Eildon Hills. It is relatively easy to climb up and enjoy a panorama that encompasses the Tweed Valley and a huge swath of the Borders, with England visible in the distance. Enjoy a sandwich at the top, and you might find that your only company is a family of grouse.

Abbotsford: Seminal Scottish writer Sir Walter Scott built this mansion, about 2 miles (3 km) to the west of Melrose. Born in Edinburgh's Old Town in 1771, Scott grew to become Scotland's most celebrated and prolific novelist (see p. 49). In his final years, the building of the grand Abbotsford retreat came back to haunt Scott as the writer struggled financially, working himself into an early grave in 1832.

The great writer lived in Abbotsford for two decades, from 1812 onward, although building work continued for almost half that time. The exterior of this grand stately mansion borrows from a variety of architectural styles—Scottish baronial is perhaps the most striking. Half a dozen rooms are now open to the public, offering unique insight into the life and times of the novelist. The eclectic displays include a lock of Rob Roy's hair and the cross Mary Queen of Scots took to her execution. As you might expect, Scott's collection of books is voluminous. Work is currently under way on a new visitor's center adjacent to the main house. Perhaps the most quintessential. If you are blazing the Scott trail, you should also visit **Scott's View,** which is 3 miles (4.5 km) to the east of the town. This was the writer's favorite view—the **Eildon Hills** rising up above a broad bend in the River Tweed, with thick forests and lush greenery filling in the rest of the picture-postcard view to the west. So enamored was Scott by the view that it is said that his horses used to stop here unprompted. His funeral cortège passed by here, too, as he waved his last farewell to the landscape he loved so much.

Kelso: The historic town of Kelso lies 15 miles (24 km) to the east of Melrose. **Floors Castle** is an unmissable attraction on the approach to the town center. Despite the name, Floors is not a castle but a grand country house set in a vast estate on the banks of the River Tweed. Although there may once have been a medieval tower-house on the site, nothing of that remains today. For centuries it has been the lavish country seat of the powerful dukes of Roxburghe.

Kelso
🔺 109 E3

Visitor Information
✉ Kelso Visitor Information Centre, Town Hall, The Square, Kelso
☎ (01573) 228 055
www.kelso .bordernet.co.uk

Floors Castle
✉ Roxburghe Estates, Kelso
☎ (01573) 223 333
💲 Castle & grounds: $$; Grounds only: $
www.roxburghe.net

Traquair House is believed to be the oldest inhabited house in Scotland.

Mellerstain House

✉ Gordon, Berwickshire

☎ (01573) 410 225

🕐 Open p.m. only. Open Sun., Wed., & bank holidays May, June, Sept.; Sun.–Mon. & Wed.–Thurs. July–Aug.; & Sun. only Oct. Closed Nov.–Good Friday

💲 House & gardens: $$; Gardens only: $

www.mellerstain .com

It was John Ker (1680–1741), the first Duke of Roxburghe, who commissioned renowned Scottish architect William Playfair (1790–1857) to design the castle, which was completed in 1721.

Floors Castle is steeped in history and romance. In the early 20th century, Henry John Innes-Ker (1876–1932), the eighth Duke of Roxburghe, married a beautiful young American, Mary Goelet, who was not only an heiress, but arrived complete with her own superb collection of fine art and tapestries. Many are still on display and make a pleasant distraction from the family portraits. Between the two World Wars, the ballroom underwent a revamp, and it now evocatively conjures up the spirit of the 1930s.

Acres of scenic grounds surround the castle. The formal gardens were the work of William Adam (1689–1748) in the 18th century. The woodland garden

and the perfectly planned walled garden are must-sees. Here, too, you'll find a children's adventure playground, restaurant, coffee shop, garden center, and even a championship golf course. There are also stores in which you can

INSIDER TIP:

The coffee shop at St. Abbs Head National Nature Reserve serves up excellent takeout lunches to fuel your walk along the rugged Borders coastline.

—SALLY McFALL
National Geographic contributor

buy produce that comes from the grounds of the estate.

Kelso itself unfurls in Georgian grandeur around the confluence of the Tweed and Teviot Rivers, which are spanned by a trio of bridges. It has always been a strategic town, sacked and rebuilt on numerous occasions. The grand main square is the place to start a walk. The **Town Hall** is a large building with the clock that towers over the cobbled plaza below. You can also follow a riverside walk from the main square, which starts down Roxburghe Street and leads off to Floors Castle.

Mellerstain House is another outstanding country house, located 5 miles (8 km) northeast of Kelso. It is particularly noteworthy as it involved the work of the architect William Adam (1689–1748) and his gifted son

Common Ridings

Today, the turbulent history of the Borders is commemorated in the annual **Common Ridings**, or Marches, that take place across the region early in the summer (*www .returntotheridings.co.uk*). There are 11 festivals in all, which hark back to the 13th and 14th centuries, when townsfolk were forced to patrol the town's boundaries on horseback to ensure their rivals were not encroaching on the common land. One of these, Kelso Civic Week, involves the "Kelsae Laddie" and his followers visiting neighboring villages on horseback *(www .kelso.bordernet.co.uk)*, and in Selkirk every June the highlight is a cavalcade of hundreds of horses and riders.

Wild waters on the rocky coast of St. Abbs Head National Nature Reserve

Robert Adam (1728–1792; see sidebar p. 105), who oversaw the completion of the project after his father's death.

The Borders Coastline

The Borders region boasts some fine beaches along its small stretch of coastline. The pick of the coastal settlements are Eyemouth and St. Abbs. Eyemouth is a busy fishing village and a great place to sit with a steaming "poke" of fish and chips as gulls call overhead and trawlers ease out of the harbor.

The **Eyemouth Maritime Centre** has given the old fish market a new role, shedding light on the town's rich fishing history. A number of old boats are the highlight of the exhibition. The **Eyemouth Museum,** housed in an old church, is worth a visit to see the Eyemouth Tapestry, which depicts the disaster in 1881 when a wild storm wiped out the fleet, killing more than 100 fishermen

and crippling the town. It took the skills of 20 local women to complete this remarkable piece of social art in the 1980s.

The pretty old fishing village of **St. Abbs** lies about 4 miles (6.4 km) north of Eyemouth, where you can take a scenic cliff-top walk between the two towns.

Nearby, the rocky headlands of the **St. Abbs Head National Nature Reserve** (*tel 0844/493 2256, www.nnr-scotland.org.uk*) harbor a large seabird colony— thousands of guillemots, razorbills, and kittiwakes nest on the cliffs in spring and early summer, while shearwaters and skuas arrive in late summer. Check in at the visitor center for the best walk for the time of year. The imposing **Stevensons' Lighthouse** here, built by David and Thomas Stevenson and located at the end of a waymarked trail, is a fabulous place to take in a broad sweep of coastal scenery. ■

Eyemouth Maritime Centre
✉ Harbour Road, Eyemouth
☎ (01890) 751 020
$ Visitor center: $; Museum: free
www.worldof boats.org

Eyemouth Museum & Visitor Information Centre
✉ Auld Kirk, Market Place, Eyemouth
☎ (01890) 750 678
$ Museum: $; Visitor center: free
www.eyemouth museum.org.uk

The very heart of rural Scotland, the gateway between the southern lowlands and the mountainous Highlands

Central Scotland

Sailing ships moored on the banks of the Crinan Canal in Argyll

Central Scotland

An easily accessible wonderland of attractive lochs and rugged mountain backdrops, central Scotland has an equally epic history to match. With heather-clad mountains, brooding lochs, and romantic castles, it is Scotland in microcosm.

The center of Inveraray on the western shore of Loch Fyne

Central Scotland is swathed in history—the heartland of William Wallace, the real life "Braveheart," and heroes such as Robert the Bruce and Rob Roy, who stamped a permanent mark on the nation. It is also blessed with wonderfully scenic landscapes: silvery sea lochs, an attractive coastline, and a backdrop of rugged mountains.

The city of Stirling is home to Scotland's most strategic castle, which proudly stands on guard at the gateway north to the Highlands. The castle is steeped in history—and it's home to the ghosts of William Wallace and Robert the Bruce. Nearby at Bannockburn, Scotland scored its most famous victory over the "Auld Enemy" in 1314. A memorial and a visitor center tell the story, while the Wallace Monument stands as a proud and defiant testament to the Scots' enduring love of the country's greatest patriot and martyr.

Central Scotland is also home to what became Scotland's first national park in 2002. Loch Lomond and the Trossachs National Park spreads across a vast swath of Scotland. The loch is the largest body of freshwater in Britain and a real leisure oasis. The Trossachs, meanwhile, are a smaller-scale version of the Highlands' peaks, whose slopes are much more accessible to walkers and cyclists. This, combined with the first-rate tourist facilities, makes the Trossachs ideal for visitors short on time.

Oban & the West

To the west, Argyll and the Cowal Peninsula shimmer around the Irish Sea. Despite its many attractions, and the fact that it is easily accessible from Glasgow, the area remains off the main tourist routes. Scotland's busiest ferry port, Oban, lies on the west coast

NOT TO BE MISSED:

Immersing yourself in history at Stirling Castle, Scotland's most impressive **128**

The rugged hills and spectacular lochs of the Trossachs **130–132**

Taking a walk around the mountain-fringed expanse of Loch Lomond **132–133**

A short stay in Inveraray, a historic town on the banks of Loch Fyne **134–135**

Paying a visit to Scone Palace, where Scottish kings were once crowned **142**

and tempts visitors with graceful stone buildings, a distillery, and world-class seafood. Just inland, Loch Awe remains a local secret and a much less touristy escape than Loch Lomond and Loch Ness.

The Kintyre Peninsula is a romantic, end-of-the-world type of place that juts out into the sea toward Ireland in a forgotten stretch of quiet roads, half-abandoned towns, and sweeping sandy beaches. Part of the same finger of land—but not actually part of the Kintyre Peninsula—is the trim town of Inveraray. Sitting on the shore of Loch Fyne, Inveraray is as historic and welcoming a town as any in Scotland and a great base for exploring this remarkable region.

Perthshire

Moving back east toward a slew of sinewy lochs, you will meet Perthshire. The capital, Perth, is an unsung urban star with lively restaurants and cultural scenes. The rest of this affluent county is alive with Munro mountains (peaks more than 3,000 feet/914 m high), sweeping lochs, and historic castles. It is also home to Scone Palace—once the crowning place of the Scottish kings and home of the Stone of Destiny. With so much history, drama, and beautiful scenery, central Scotland is a must-see for any visitor to the country—a visit that is made much easier by the excellent transport links. ■

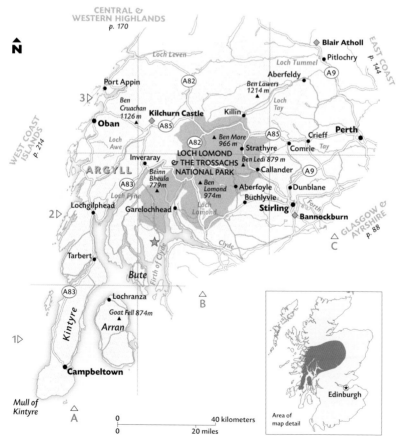

Stirling

Stirling may be something of a newcomer as a city, but it is one of the most deeply historic places in Scotland. Tucked between the waterways of the Clyde and Forth—and guarded by the surrounding hills—Stirling overflows with attractions and is worth the visit.

Surrounded by cliffs on three sides, Stirling's castle has long been an important fortification.

Stirling

⚠ 127 C2

Visitor Information

✉ Castle Esplanade, Stirling

☎ (01786) 479 901

www.instirling.com/
sight/visitor.htm

Stirling Castle

✉ Castle Wynd, Stirling

☎ (01786) 450 000

💲 $$$

www.stirlingcastle
.gov.uk

Everyone from the Scots and the English, right back to the Romans, have fought for control of Stirling, such is the city's strategic importance. And they have all left their indelible marks.

Stirling Castle

The historic legacy is most obvious at Stirling Castle, used by James IV (r. 1488–1513), James V (r. 1513–1542), and Mary Queen of Scots (r. 1542–1567). In the palace you'll find some impressive Renaissance sculptures and the recently renovated Great Hall, where Scottish monarchs of old once wined and dined their

guests. The Castle Exhibition gives you the necessary historical background.

The views from the castle are sublime, with one flank staring back down the throat of the River Forth to the east, while the Trossachs, Ochils, and even the Pentland Hills vie for attention to the west. Look for **Stirling Bridge,** where William Wallace's heavily outnumbered men crushed the previously untouchable English in 1297.

Old Town

The castle is without doubt Stirling's main attraction, but

spare a couple of hours for the fascinating **Old Town Jail,** which you see as you descend toward the town. There you can meet "Stirling's nastiest prison warden" and learn about the experience of being locked up under the harsh regime of a Victorian jail. Younger visitors will enjoy the specially designed audio tour. The attractions don't end there, though, and on the same route into town there is also the well-preserved **Argyll's Lodging**—a graceful 17th-century town house—as well as the **Church of the Holy Rude** *(St. John Street, tel 01786/475 275, www.holyrude.org)* with one of the last surviving medieval timber roofs in the country. Call ahead if you plan to visit as you will need to book the guided tour.

A little farther east you come to the attractive and historic Old Town. The ambience is reminiscent of Edinburgh's Old Town, particularly the Royal Mile. Many buildings date back to the 16th and 17th centuries and Stirling's golden age as a royal burgh. The Old Town is magical at night. Go for a moonlit walk and you pretty much get it all to yourself.

Bannockburn

The famous battlefield of Bannockburn lies 2 miles (3 km) south of Stirling. This is the site of the famous Scottish victory over the English in 1314—where King Robert the Bruce led his brave but seriously outnumbered warriors into a fight to the death with the professional English army that had marched north to crush Scotland's desire for independence. Not only did Bruce's men win, but they annihilated "proud Edward's army" and "sent them back tae think again," as Scotland's unofficial national anthem, "Flower of Scotland," famously celebrates.

The mighty equestrian statue of a somber but defiant-looking Bruce shows the esteem in which he is still held, and the excellent visitor center provides Robert the Bruce's full story and that of the nation he so spectacularly led. In

Wallace Monument

One sight you cannot miss from Stirling Castle is the imposing stone skyscraper of the **Wallace Monument** *(Hillfoots Rd., just outside Stirling, tel 01786/472 140, www .nationalwallacemonument.com, $$).* It is worth the short trip east of Stirling to see this grand Victorian statement and enjoy the sense of history. Be warned: The 246 steps rise up some 220 feet (67 m) to the top. You end up surveying a scene that overflows with history, enjoying a view William Wallace literally would have killed for. Pick up an audio tour before you start.

addition to various displays, there is the chance to try on a heavy chainmail helmet, which will give you some insight into how difficult it must have been to fight in the full armor of the day.

Two great days to be in Bannockburn are June 23 and 24, when volunteers dress in period costume and reenact Scotland's most famous battle against the "Auld Enemy." ∎

The Trossachs & Loch Lomond

For those short on time, or who are confining their trip to Scotland's Central Belt, the Trossachs are the perfect "Highlands in Miniature" experience, with rugged hills, pristine lochs, and attractive towns.

Ben Ledi rises up above the waters of Loch Lubnaig near Callander.

**Loch Lomond &
the Trossachs
National Park**

 127 B2–B3

✉ National Park
Gateway Centre,
Loch Lomond
Shores, Balloch

☎ (0845) 345 4878

**www.lochlomond
trossachs.org**

Loosely speaking, the Trossachs is the area of wooded glens and braes that unfurls west of the twin towns of Callander and Aberfoyle and sweeps off in search of the famously "bonny bonny banks" of Loch Lomond (see pp. 132–133). In fact, Loch Lomond forms the western boundary of the area and is usually grouped with it as the **Loch Lomond and the Trossachs National Park.** An enjoyable way into the Trossachs is along the scenic route west from

Stirling to Aberfoyle, which takes you over the flat Carse of Stirling and past the **Lake of Menteith.** One of the few bodies of water known as a "lake" in Scotland, this is a lovely spot on a sunny day, where you can enjoy a boat ride out to the 13th-century ruins of **Inchmahome Priory** before having lunch at the **Lake of Menteith Hotel** (*Port of Menteith, Perthshire, tel 01877/385 258, www.lake-hotel.com, $$$*), which reclines right on the water's edge.

Exploring the Area

To delve deeper into the Trossachs, drive, cycle, or take a bus up the vertiginous road that heads north from Aberfoyle and traverses the Duke's Pass to Callander. This winding trail takes you into a hilly wonderland blessed with mighty forests that occasionally give way to reveal stunning views of glacial lochs. Check that the road is open before planning a trip during the winter months, when the snow and ice often close it.

Of all the hills in this area there are two that deserve special attention. **Ben A'an** (1,488 feet/454 m) is less than an hour's walk from the parking lot on the A821 at the west end of Loch Achray and offers one of the best effort-to-view ratios of all the hills in Scotland. A more challenging hike takes you up nearby **Ben Ledi** (2,884 feet/879 m), a brooding monster that lies above the attractive Loch Lubnaig. The walk takes you through thick forest and out onto a bare ridge that makes its way across to the summit and a panorama that you won't forget.

Sedentary souls may want to take a trip on Loch Katrine on the historic steamer **SS Sir Walter Scott.** A minor road heads west from the Ben A'an parking lot to a small pier where this charming old steamship awaits to transport her passengers back in time as they slowly make their way down Loch Katrine and back.

Head back east to **Callander,** the other popular gateway to the Trossachs. This small town enjoys more visitors than Aberfoyle and

INSIDER TIP:

The Trossachs offer some of the best walking of any small area in Scotland. Its appeal is greater because—unlike other ranges—it isn't bursting with walkers.

—SALLY McFALL
National Geographic contributor

boasts a busy main street, outdoor clothing shops, a few hotels, and some great walks. Close to Callander is the exceptional **Mona chyle Mhor Hotel** *(Balquhidder, Lochearnhead, tel 01877/ 384 622, www.mhor.net, $$$$),* which also operates a number of businesses in town including a superb bakery, **Mhor Bread** *(8 Main St., tel 01877/339 518),* and a first-class "chipper"/informal seafood restaurant, **Mhor Fish** *(75–77 Main St., tel 01877/330 213).*

Inchmahome Priory

- ✉ Island in Lake of Menteith, reached by boat from pier at Port of Menteith
- ☎ (01877) 385 294
- 💲 $$

www.historic-scotland.gov.uk

Callander

- 🄰 127 B2

Visitor Information

- ✉ 10 Ancaster Square, Callander
- ☎ (08452) 255 121

www.incallander.co.uk

SS Sir Walter Scott

- ✉ Trossachs Pier, Loch Katrine, near Callander
- ☎ (01877) 332 000
- 🕒 Closed Sun.
- 💲 $$$

www.lochkatrine.com

EXPERIENCE:
Bike the Trossachs

One of the best ways to experience the Trossachs is on two wheels, because one of the most stunning stretches of the National Cycle Network runs through the region, from Loch Lomond to Killin. **Wheels Cycling Centre** *(Invertrossachs Road, Callander, tel 01877/331 100, www .scottish-cycling.com)* is the best cycle store, with a range of mountain bikes. **Trossachs Cycles** *(Trossachs Holiday Park, Aberfoyle, tel 01877/382 614)* is another option, 2 miles (3 km) south of Aberfoyle on the A81.

Loch Lomond

127 B2

The restaurant at Monachyle Mhor enjoys a stunning location just north of the Trossachs, surrounded by a remote loch and hills near Balquhidder, a few miles north of Callander. Fans of Rob Roy should head here anyway as it is the site of the grave of the infamous outlaw.

Scaling Ben Lomond is a real test of stamina. Loch Lomond is visible in the far distance.

Loch Lomond

At 23 miles (37 km) long and up to 5 miles (8 km) across, Loch Lomond is by far the largest body of fresh water in Britain. Dotted with 37 islands, this tranquil oasis is one of the most stunning lochs in Scotland and remains a popular natural attraction.

Since 2002, the loch has been protected within the **Loch Lomond and the Trossachs National Park** (see pp. 130–131)—a stunning wilderness area packed with hills, many more lochs, and a dizzying array of things to see and do. Loch Lomond itself is within easy striking distance of Glasgow, and many Glaswegians know it as "Glasgow's loch," which it certainly feels like on busy summer weekends when half the city's population seems to be there.

A good starting point is at **Loch Lomond Shores** in Balloch—a large visitor complex that includes the Gateway Centre, where you can find out about the loch, its heritage, and its role today. You can also take the kids to **Loch Lomond Aquarium,** go for a paddle in a canoe, have a bite to eat, or even indulge in some souvenir shopping. The more energetic can hire mountain bikes to explore farther afield.

The western shore is Loch Lomond's most developed side, which is also home to the busy A82 road. The most charming village here is **Luss**—an idyllic escape that once starred in the popular Scottish TV show *Take the High Road.* This refers to the ballad "Loch Lomond," which touches

EXPERIENCE: Tackling Ben Lomond

Mountains in Australia, New Zealand, and the United States have all been named for Ben Lomond. At 3,200 feet (974 m) in altitude, this majestic Munro (the name for a Scottish peak above 3,000 feet/914 m) casts an unmistakable shadow across Loch Lomond and beyond. It is the most southerly of the Munros and one of the most famous. Given its easy accessibility from the Central Belt, it offers an ideal introduction to Scottish mountaineering for visitors with the right equipment and an up-to-date weather forecast in hand.

You will need to travel to **Rowardennan,** on the shore of Loch Lomond, to start the ascent. Here, the main (or "tourist") trail is signed from the parking lot. Make sure you pick up a map of the area (Ordnance Survey Explorer Map nos. 347 and 364), because the route is a bit of a slog. After escaping the attractive wooded foothills, much of the time spent is on a long, featureless ridge. The trail is easy to follow since it is rough-paved.

The view from the top is staggering. Loch Lomond stretches below like a rippling blue carpet dotted with her necklace of islands. All around, hills and mountains vie for attention. If you catch "the Ben" on a good day, this is a truly wonderful climb and it may whet your appetite for another. The walk is about 7 miles (11 km) and should take 3 to 4 hours. For information about guided walks, contact **C-N-Do Scotland** (33 Stirling Enterprise Park, Stirling, tel 01786/445 703, www.cndoscotland.com).

on the ill-fated Jacobite cause with the refrain: "You take the high road and I'll take the low road and I'll be in Scotland before you."

The loch's eastern side is less developed than the western shores. As you travel north from the pleasant town of **Drymen,** the large caravan parks soon give way to a narrow lochside road, which is dotted with little bays and quiet stretches of beach.

Most of Loch Lomond's forested islands are privately owned, but a few are still open to the public. The best bet is to head to the island of **Inchcailloch** from the relaxed village of **Balmaha** on the eastern shore. Scottish Natural Heritage owns the island, but anyone can cross without a permit in groups of less than 12 by using the on-demand ferry (The Boatyard, tel 01360/870 214,

www.balmahaboatyard.co.uk, $$).

Once on the picturesque island you'll find two walking trails—the Low Path and the Summit Path. As its name suggests, the latter is the more strenuous option, but it really opens up the surrounding scenery. There is also a small picnic area and a modest campsite for anyone who has fallen instantly in love with Inchcailloch and wants to spend the night.

Balmaha is an attractive place in its own right. Within easy walking distance along the loch, to the north, lies Millarochy Bay, which is a great place to relax and take in the beauty of Loch Lomond. The road eventually peters out at Rowardennan, and the only way farther north is on the **West Highland Way** walking route (www.west-highland-way.co.uk). ∎

Loch Lomond Shores

✉ Ben Lomond Way, Balloch

☎ (01389) 751 035

www.lochlomond shores.com

Loch Lomond Aquarium

✉ Loch Lomond Shores, Balloch

☎ (0871) 423 2110

💲 $$$

www.sealifeeurope .com

Argyll

Argyll, which extends from the tip of the Mull of Kintyre in the south to Oban in the north, is another part of the country that Scots hold dear to their hearts, but the region has not found a place on the tourist trail. Visitors will discover a region steeped in history and a landscape blessed with a dramatic Atlantic coastline, scenic lochs, and plenty of tempting towns.

The rugged Kintyre coastline is home to an abundance of wildlife.

Argyll

 127 A1–A3,
B2–B3

Inveraray

 126 B2

Visitor Information

✉ Front Street,
Inveraray

☎ (08707) 200 616

**www.visitscottish
heartlands.omscottish
heartlands.com.uk/
index.php**

Loch Fyne & Kintyre

The most spectacular approach to Argyll is west from Loch Lomond, up and over the legendary "Rest and Be Thankful" on a vertiginous route that follows an old military road. What opens up is an impressively rugged landscape of steep-sided mountains, tumbling waterfalls, and dense forests. The route pushes on through the **Argyll Forest Park,** past the fjord-like Loch Goil, and underneath the Cobbler which, at 2,891 feet (880 m), is not Argyll's highest peak but is certainly one of its

most distinctive, making for an excellent and relatively easy climb for a reasonably fit hiker.

Loch Fyne is a massive sea loch, with the world-famous **Loch Fyne Restaurant** *(Clachan, Cairndow, tel 01499/600 236, www .lochfyne.com/Restaurants/ Locations/Cairndow, $$$$)* in Cairndow at its northern tip. This seafood eatery has spawned a U.K.-wide chain and is one of the best places in Britain to savor fresh and perfectly cooked seafood.

Inveraray: Just a short drive south is the lochside town of

Inveraray—an unmistakable sight with its church spires and white-washed buildings glinting off the silvery expanse of Loch Fyne. Most of the action is on Main Street, which tumbles down to the loch and is home to a range of stores unashamedly geared to the tourists. However, there is quality among the souvenir stores, with an excellent deli, a choice of decent cafés, an old-fashioned candy store, and the highlight for whisky connoisseurs, **Loch Fyne Whiskies.**

This delightful liquor store offers generous tastings and some very rare malts, the most expensive of which comes in at more than $75,000 a bottle. The store also caters to professed whisky objectors by offering their own liqueur—a sweet orange and chocolate concoction that might just manage to make whisky palatable to the unconverted.

On wet weather days, Main Street has plenty to keep visitors occupied, but there is also **Inveraray Jail.** Here you'll obtain unique insight into the life and times of prisoners in years gone by, including the poor children who were once holed up here. Waxworks and actors in period costume help bring the harsh realities to life.

The town's number one attraction is **Inveraray Castle.** Enjoying a prime position overlooking the town and Loch Fyne, Inveraray Castle as it stands dates back to 1789. The castle is the ancestral home of the Duke of Argyll—a progressive figure who is very popular among the local population. He is a man intent on working with the local community to push Inveraray forward, rather than shutting himself away on his sprawling estate. You can take a tour of the castle and explore the lavish function rooms, and there is a café in the basement that serves light lunches and great cakes.

Kintyre Peninsula: If you head south down Loch Fyne, the Kintyre Peninsula awaits. The most appealing settlement is **Tarbert** in the north of the peninsula. This pretty little fishing village boasts some colorful houses, and it is a characterful place to spend a few hours. Check out the art gallery by the yacht club, and stop at the café for a tea or coffee and home-made cake to accompany the

Loch Fyne Whiskies

✉ Top of Main St., Inveraray
☎ (01499) 302 219
www.lfw.co.uk

Inveraray Jail

✉ Church Square, Inveraray
☎ (01499) 302 381
$ $$
www.inverarayjail.co.uk

Inveraray Castle

✉ Cherrypark, Inveraray
☎ (01499) 302 203
$ $$$
www.inveraray-castle.com

Mull of Kintyre

No fan of ex-Beatle Paul McCartney needs an introduction to the Mull of Kintyre, the most southwesterly section of the Kintyre Peninsula that was eulogized by him in his eponymous ballad. You have to hike out to the Mull on foot, with views opening up all around. Push on to the very edge of Scotland—a symbolic point so far west that it feels like you can touch the emerald isle of Ireland, only 12 miles (20 km) distant. Standing at this lonely spot, it is easy to understand why McCartney felt so compelled to immortalize its beauty. The lighthouse at its tip was remodeled by Robert Stevenson (see sidebar p. 205).

Delicious fresh shellfish gives Oban its moniker, the Seafood Capital of Scotland.

Tarbert
🅐 127 A2

Campbeltown
🅐 127 A1

Kilchurn Castle
🅐 127 B3
✉ Lochawe
☎ (01838) 200 440
💲 $$

**www.historic
-scotland.gov.uk**

impressive landscape paintings.

Kintyre sports some lovely sandy beaches, and one of the most stunning is **Machrihanish.** Stroll along the sands and enjoy the sea views and flocks of wild seabirds that live along the rugged coast. All around Kintyre birds abound, and one of the most impressive sights is to watch the gannets dive-bomb into the water. Like many of the beaches in this part of Scotland, Machrihanish boasts an otherworldly quality, with other islands and even Ireland shimmering in the distance.

As you approach the famous **Mull of Kintyre** (see sidebar p. 135), the last outpost is **Campbeltown.** The town has seen better days, but there are some grand old houses, with palms swaying along the waterfront. Campbeltown is set in an attractive bay, with

the island of **Davaar** just off the coast. Davaar is easily accessible at low tide and by using one of the regular boat trips. The on/off ferry service to Ireland offers hope for Campbeltown, but for now it is a pleasantly run-down place ideal for strolling around dreaming of past glories.

North Toward Oban

The western coastal road that pushes north from Kintyre is a scenic route. Near the village of Crinan it meets the **Crinan Canal,** a short-cut that allows boats to avoid the hours-long passage around the peninsula. The canal is an impressive piece of Scottish engineering. Take a seat by the canal's mouth and watch the modern yachts pass by, as well as the jumble of historic sailing ships that evocatively speak of past times.

Just to the north is **Kilmartin.** Within a 6-mile (9 km) radius of the village are 350 ancient monuments—the largest collection of monuments in Scotland, many of which date back to prehistoric times. A museum and café are on hand in the village, but the atmosphere of this area is as special as any interpretative board.

Pushing north of Kilmartin you have two choices—stick to the largely coastal road or head inland in search of **Loch Awe.** Scotland's longest inland loch may not be as famous as Loch Ness and Loch Lomond, but there is plenty to see and do for visitors of all ages. It's renowned for trout fishing.

The most famous historic site in these parts is **Kilchurn Castle.**

Seafreedom Kayak [*www.seafreedom kayak.co.uk*], based near Oban, offers sea kayaking tours. Paddle between medieval castles and distilleries in one of the world's most spectacular environments.

—ANDREW TODHUNTER
National Geographic writer

Climb the tower to enjoy sweeping views of Loch Awe.

A good wet weather option is **Ben Cruachan,** the "hollow mountain," at the northern end of the loch. A huge hydroelectric project is housed inside. You can take a tour (*Dalmally, tel 01866/822 618, www.visitcruachan .co.uk, $$*) to learn about one

of Scotland's emerging green technologies. An electric bus ride is part of the experience.

Oban

Oban is Scotland's busiest ferry port. Hills sweep around and enclose the town's broad bay, and the town itself boasts some gorgeous grand Victorian guest houses and hotels. The historic **Oban Distillery** is the town's main attraction, but the **Scottish Sealife Sanctuary** is also popular and runs a successful seal pups rescue program. Just north of Oban, but rarely open for visitors, is **Castle Stalker,** best appreciated from a distance. Another worthwhile detour is the quiet village of **Port Appin**—a local secret where Scots come for cozy weekends away.

This is a good spot for a seafood lunch (see sidebar below) before pushing farther north. ∎

Oban
🗺 127 A3
Visitor Information
✉ Argyll Square, Oban
☎ (01631) 563 122
www.oban.org .uk/index.php

Oban Distillery
✉ Stafford Street, Oban
☎ (01631) 572 004
💲 $$$
www.discovering -distilleries.com/ oban

Scottish Sealife Sanctuary
✉ Barcaldine, Oban
☎ (01631) 720 386
💲 $$
www.sealsanctuary .co.uk/oban1.html

EXPERIENCE: Oban Seafood

The coastal town of Oban is developing into something of a seafood oasis. It is not without some justification that a banner now welcomes new arrivals by proclaiming that they have just entered the Seafood Capital of Scotland. The highlight for many visitors are the informal stalls that line the pier, where you can sit on a picnic bench and munch your way through fresh langoustines and delicious squat lobster tails for a fraction of what you would pay in a posh restaurant—and at the same time watch the fishing boats and ferries ease in and out of the beautiful Oban bay.

But the town also boasts posh restaurants. The chefs at **Ee-usk** (Gaelic for fish; *North Pier, tel 01632/565 666, www .eeusk.com*) get a bit more creative with the local seafood. In town, **Coast** (*104 George St., tel 01631/569 900, www .coastoban.co.uk*) is similarly creative with the likes of seared scallops laced with pork belly. A more recent arrival, just out of the town center, the **Seafood Temple** (*Gallanach Road, tel 01631/566 000, www .templeseafood.co.uk*) is perhaps the best place to eat, despite its awkward opening hours. Reservations are essential and are rewarded with perfectly cooked seafood.

Drive Around the Cowal Peninsula

The Cowal Peninsula is a hidden gem definitely off the tourist trail. Relax and enjoy the stunning surroundings—quiet, winding roads and ferry trips are all part of the fun. The drive can be done in a day, but allow three to fully reap the benefits.

Tarbert on the shores of Loch Fyne, near Kintyre

The best way to reach the Cowal Peninsula is by taking a car ferry from the Clyde port of Gourock to Dunoon. Two operators ply the route—Caledonian MacBrayne (*www.calmac .co.uk*) and Western Ferries (*www.western -ferries.co.uk*). The short crossing still allows time to leave the busy city behind.

Dunoon ❶, Argyll's largest town, has seen better days and is no longer a favorite of vacationing Glaswegians. The best time to visit is in August during the **Cowal Highland Gathering**—a thriving and captivating celebration of traditional Scottish music and dancing. **Castle Hill** is the highlight at other times of year. This modest mound has a museum attached (*Castle Gardens, Dunoon, tel 01369/701 422, closed Nov.– Easter*), whose most interesting section looks at the old "steamers" that used to carry those Glaswegians "doon the watter."

Head northwest on the A815; the wide loch to your right is **Holy Loch ❷**. Until the early 1990s, this loch was, controversially, a

NOT TO BE MISSED:

• Tighnabruaich • Ardkinglas • Argyll Forest Park • Benmore Gardens

nuclear submarine base for the U.S. Navy—as famous for its antinuclear protestors as for its submarines. Cut west along the B836 and you leave modern life behind as the scenery grows wilder in Glen Lean.

Keep pushing west on the A836, head up the A886, then turn south on the A8003 to **Tighnabruaich viewpoint ❸**, where you get a supreme view of the **Kyles of Bute**. In Gaelic, the word *kyles* means "narrows," which refers to the narrow waters that separate Cowal from the isle of Bute. This is prime sailing country, but the views are equally stunning from the land, too. Farther south awaits the charming village of **Tighnabruaich ❹**. Tighnabruaich is a Gaelic name meaning "house on the hill," which aptly describes the many houses on the steep hills that rise above the Kyles. A good place to stay overnight, or just stop for some delicious fresh seafood, the town offers a number of excellent guest houses, hotels, and restaurants.

Rounding the peninsula on an unclassified road you come to **Portavadie** ⑤, which is one step below unassuming but handy for those wanting to continue on to Kintyre—you can catch a ferry across to Tarbert. Proceed north up the B8000, rejoin the A886, and you come to tiny **Strachur** ⑥, home to **Creggans Inn** (*www.creggans-inn.co.uk*). This is a great place for a lunch of fresh seafood, with stunning views over Loch Fyne.

Cowal's most unlikely attraction is the **Ardkinglas Woodland Garden** ⑦ (*Cairndow, tel 01499/600 261, www.ardkinglas.com, $*), farther north on the A815. A network of paths snake through this verdant 25-acre (10 ha) oasis, which has seen an eclectic range of trees planted as far back as the 18th century. The high local rainfall and the moderating influence

of the Gulf Stream combine to make this an ideal environment for trees. Indeed, some of the most impressive in the country stand here, including the tallest fir tree in Britain, vaulting skyward more than 200 feet (61 m).

Head back to Strachur, but this time continue inland on the A815 and travel south deeper into Cowal and the **Argyll Forest Park** ⑧ (*tel 01877/382 383, www.forestry.gov.uk*), an oasis for bikers and hikers alike.

Your last stop is **Benmore Botanic Garden** ⑨ (*Benmore, Dunoon, tel 01369/706 261, www.rbge .org.uk/the-gardens/benmore, $$*), where 300 species spread across 120 acres (49 ha), from rhododendron to a spectacular avenue of giant redwoods. From here follow the A815 south into Dunoon, where the ferry back across the Clyde awaits.

🅰	See also area map p. 127
►	Gourock
↔	103 miles (162 km)
⊕	Choice of 1–3 days
►	Gourock

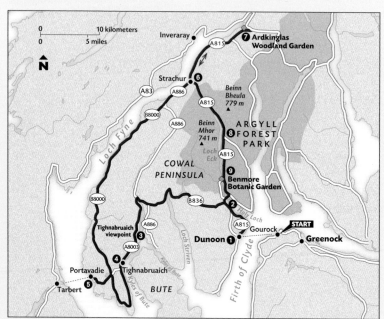

Perthshire

Perthshire is the self-styled "tall tree country" and packs a powerful natural punch with its stunning landscape of thick forests, scenic lochs, and majestic mountain ranges. Then you can explore the trim capital and a bounty of historic attractions.

Blair Castle, ancient seat of the dukes and earls of Atholl, sits in the heart of Highland Perthshire.

Perthshire

Visitor Information

✉ Lower City Mills, West Mill Street, Perth

☎ (01738) 450 600

www.perthshire .co.uk

Loch Tay

▲ 127 B3–C3

Loch Tay to Pitlochry

The reflections of Perthshire's mighty Munros bounce off Loch Tay on calm days, making the loch look like a glacial grand canyon. The highest peak is **Ben Lawers**, which towers a whopping 3,984 feet (1,214 m) over the land. Experienced walkers can make a whole day of it and tackle a flurry of Munros on one arduous ridge walk. At the eastern end of Loch Tay lies the **Scottish Crannog Centre**

(Kenmore, Loch Tay, tel 01887/830 583, www.crannog.co.uk, $$), where you can learn about the old crannogs that people used for shelter and protection more than 2,000 years ago. These simple stilted dwellings were laid out in the water along a retractable walkway, which made them hard to attack. A reconstruction houses a museum that illuminates the lives of the people in those days. Hire a guide to get the most out of your visit.

Aberfeldy is a short drive farther east. This graceful little town sports stately streets laden with grand stone buildings. Scotland boasts hundreds of distilleries, but **Dewar's World of Whisky** (Aberfeldy Distillery, Aberfeldy, tel 01887/822 010, www.scotland whisky.com/distilleries/highlands/ Dewars, $$ for tour) is an excellent visitor center that offers one of

INSIDER TIP:

Perthshire is legendary for its soft fruits. In summer keep an eye out for roadside signs marking the fruit farms where you can pick your own ultra-fresh strawberries and raspberries.

—SALLY McFALL
National Geographic contributor

the most enjoyable experiences, with the highlight, of course, sampling a wee dram.

On roads heading north, the conical bulk of **Schiehallion** is never far away—this mountain helped give maps contour lines as the concept was pioneered on its slopes. You will eventually end up at **Loch Tummel,** hemmed in by hills on all sides. This loch was a favorite of Queen Victoria, so much so that a visitor center now stands at the **Queen's View.**

Along the A9

Heading south down the lifeblood A9, your next stop

is **Blair Atholl.** The village is a sleepy and relaxed affair, and the highlight is the dramatic **Blair Castle** (tel 01796/481 207, www.blair-castle.co.uk, $$). This remarkable building lies at the very heart of a massive 145,000-acre (58,679 ha) estate, which overflows with charming scenery and fine walks. Nearby **Killiecrankie** is a tiny place made famous by one man's great leap. In 1689, when the Jacobites smashed an English force at the Battle of Killiecrankie, one plucky and extremely lucky English soldier escaped by leaping across the gorge—an impressive feat that some skeptics file under the urban-myth category. A visitor center fills you in on the history.

Continue south down the A9 and you come to **Pitlochry,** the Victorian-era resort and popular tourist stop, replete with tacky souvenir shops on the busy High Street. The **Edradour Distillery** is the smallest in the country, but it

Aberfeldy
🅰 127 C3

Queen's View
✉ Strathtummel, Pitlochry
☎ (01350) 727 284

Killiecrankie
✉ 3 miles (5 km) N of Pitlochry
☎ Visitor center: (0844) 493 2194
www.nts.org.uk/ Property/39

Pitlochry
🅰 127 C3

Edradour Distillery
✉ A924, Pitlochry
☎ (01796) 472 095
🕐 Closed Sun.
💲 $$$
www.edradour.co.uk

EXPERIENCE:
Take in T in the Park

T in the Park (www.tinthepark.com) is a huge music festival that started back in 1994 at Strathclyde Country Park. It is now staged in Balado, just off the A9 in Perthshire. Every July, a litany of rock, pop, and alternative acts descend on Balado from all over the world. Many acts insist that T in the Park is their favorite festival, with the Scottish crowd famously appreciative, boisterous, and welcoming. Tickets to this three-day musical extravaganza are famously hard to come by, however, so book yours well in advance.

Perth

◩ 127 C3

Visitor Information

✉ Lower City Mills, West Mill Street, Perth

☎ (01738) 450 600

www.perthshire
.co.uk

Perth Concert Hall

✉ Mill Street, Perth

☎ (01738) 621 031

www.horsecross
.co.uk

Perth Museum & Art Gallery

✉ 78 George Street, Perth

☎ (01738) 632 488

🕐 Closed Sun.

www.pkc.gov.uk/
museums

Comrie

◩ 127 C3

Comrie Croft

✉ Braincroft, Crieff

☎ (01764) 670 140

www.comriecroft
.com

still manages to conjure up a fine dram and lay on fun tours. Also in Pitlochry, the **Scottish Hydro Electric Visitor Centre, Dam and Fish Pass** *(Pitlochry Power Station, tel 01796/473 152, www.aboutbritain .com/HydroElectricVisitorCentre.htm, $,)* is a must for fish fanatics as you can take in the action on the salmon ladder. Wild salmon battle their way up and down the river using this innovative system, built after the dam threatened to stop their journey upstream to spawn.

Perth

A trim town by the River Tay, Perth is often ignored by Scots. Its center is hemmed in by two

---

Scone Palace

With its period furnishings and antiques, Scone Palace *(Perth, tel 01738/552 300, www.scone-palace.co.uk, $$$)* today may be every bit the graceful country house. Centuries ago, however, this bucolic retreat was bathed in drama as the site where the independent Scottish kings were crowned. The legendary Stone of Destiny is long gone, but there is a tangible sense of history. It was here that the first Scottish king, Kenneth McAlpine, was crowned in A.D. 843 on Scotland's most famous stone. Scone House is a ten-minute drive north of Perth on the A93. The pleasant grounds are also worth strolling around.

---

parks to the north and south— the North and South Inch— and then on its eastern flank by the silvery Tay. The broad landscaped walkway is ideal for bracing riverside strolls.

Cultural pursuits are on offer at the funky **Perth Concert Hall.** This modern arts venue plays host to an impressive roster of events. Next door is the **Perth Museum and Art Gallery,** an ideal place to spend an hour or two with the family. The gallery houses an ever changing array of temporary exhibitions, and the natural history section includes a variety of mounted animals.

Comrie & Beyond

Comrie, to the west of Perth, is the epitome of urban, or rather urbane, Perthshire. Its grand Victorian buildings hark back to the days when it was a major player and even had its own railway station. Indeed, a lot of its charm comes from this sense of faded grandeur and the passion for Comrie that lives on in today's proud inhabitants.

Comrie is also famous as the earthquake capital of Scotland, with more recorded seismic activity than anywhere else on the British mainland. Little wonder, since the town lies in the middle of the Highland Boundary Fault.

Comrie is home to the unique **Earthquake House** *(The Ross, Comrie, www.strathearn.com/pl/ earthquake.htm)*. The world's first seismometer was set up here in 1874, and you can see a model of it, as well as some more modern equipment. If you plan to stay

South Inch Park, a lovely green space within Perth town center

in Comrie for the weekend or more, there is more to keep you occupied—a golf course, riverside walks along the River Earn, and various cultural events.

There are two good times to visit Comrie. The first is for the summer festival, called the **Comrie Fortnight,** with a string of cultural events—including dances and a parade—during the last week of August and the first week of September. The highlight of the local calendar, however, is **Hogmanay** (see sidebar p. 17), when the local "Flambeaux" reaches its dramatic denouement. Villagers make their way through the town center and circle its old perimeter with flaming torches in an effort to ward off evil spirits for the year ahead, then the local pipe band kicks off a shindig.

A quick hop by motorway south of Perth is **Loch Leven**—one of Scotland's most historic lochs. The loch sits in a fold of hills, with a castle-topped island in the middle. The castle is, of course, linked to Mary Queen of Scots, who was imprisoned here for almost a year. You can retrace her steps by taking a small boat out to visit the castle.

The loch and its surroundings are part of the **Loch Leven National Nature Reserve,** which is teeming with myriad birdlife. The U.K.'s largest concentration of breeding ducks congregate here, as well as thousands of migratory geese, ducks, and swans every autumn and winter. Viewing hides and a good café are located at **Vane Farm.** ■

Loch Leven Castle
☎ (01577) 862 670
🕐 Closed Nov.–March
$ $
www.historic-scotland.gov.uk

Loch Leven National Nature Reserve
✉ The Pier, Kinross
☎ (01577) 864 439
www.snh.org.uk/scottish/taysclack/nnr.asp

Vane Farm
✉ Kinross
☎ (01577) 862 355
$ $

Wooded glens, impressive mountains, captivating castles, Pictish relics, and a smattering of distilleries to enjoy a wee dram or two

East Coast

A Scottish bagpiper plays in the hills above Braemar.

East Coast

The East Coast may not have the majestic mountains that run down the edge of the West Coast, but the region is steeped in centuries of history and offers its own natural and man-made treasures. It is also home to a much larger population than that found on the West Coast, boasting the two bustling cities of Aberdeen and Dundee.

The natural beauty of Scotland's East Coast has only been enhanced by the addition of dramatic castles, grand country houses, vast abbeys, and a number of lively towns and cities to the landscape. The southern extremity of this region is also home to St. Andrews, known the world over as the "home of golf."

The self-styled "kingdom of Fife" lies to the north of Edinburgh, just across the Firth of Forth. The region was once a power base for the Scottish kings, and the grand Falkland Palace and Dunfermline Abbey are fitting legacies. In the coastal resort town of St. Andrews, the massive ruined cathedral hints at the church's once mighty power. Of course, St. Andrews is now the headquarters for golf and home to Scotland's most famous course, in the shape of the Old Course.

Just across the River Tay lies the region of Angus, which is home to the underrated city of Dundee. Over the last millennium, Dundee has transformed from a humble fishing port into a bustling industrial hub, and it is now home to a string of both historic and cultural attractions—the latter part of an ongoing attempt to regenerate the city and shake off its depressed, postindustrial image.

Outside the city, the historic delights of Glamis Castle—one of Scotland's grandest castles—and the natural beauties of the scenic Angus Glens await. These glens offer everything from simple low-level walks that most people can enjoy through to challenging Munros—mountains in Scotland that are more than 3,000 feet (914 m) high—where having the right gear can make the difference between life and death. On the Angus coast, Arbroath is swathed in history and is also a great place to buy and/or eat fresh seafood, while Broughty Ferry is Dundee's relaxed seaside escape.

The vast Cairngorm mountain range separates Angus from Royal Deeside—the charming area of lush valleys and forested hills where Queen Victoria chose to have her summer retreat, Balmoral, back in the 1840s. This is a land swathed in tartan and tradition, where the Highland Games were born. Today, tourists flock to this archetypal "shortbread tin" image of Scotland to spend time in pretty towns and villages like Braemar and Ballater.

On the coast east of Royal Deeside lies the "granite city" of Aberdeen—Scotland's third largest city. The "oil capital of Europe" is a monument in granite with a grandeur that today is supported by the serious wealth generated by the oil industry. Aberdeen has plenty of history and heritage landmarks, too, along with a sandy city beach and a surprising amount of green space. The port of Aberdeen also serves as a gateway to the islands in the north, with regular ferry services to and from both Orkney and Shetland.

The Aberdeenshire coast is a dramatic one, laced with sweeping sandy beaches, rugged cliffs, and attractive little fishing villages, such as Cullen and Portsoy, that are hidden away in the countless coves and bays. Then there are the busier ports, such as Peterhead and Fraserburgh, which bring home a bountiful deep-sea catch from the North Sea. Seafood lovers can enjoy the highlight on Scotland's East Coast—the world-class white fish—in many of the local restaurants. ■

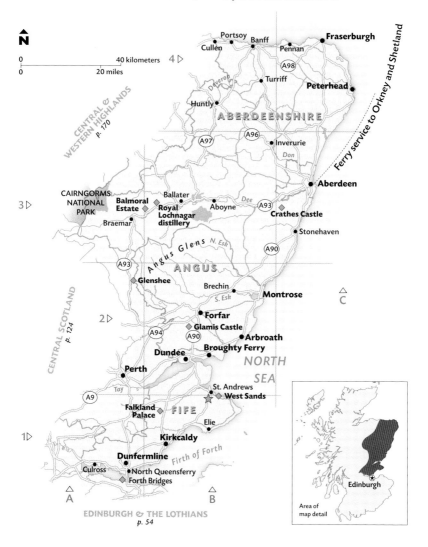

EDINBURGH & THE LOTHIANS
p. 54

Fife

Hemmed in by water on three sides—the Firth of Forth separating it from the Lothians to the south, the North Sea to the east, and the River Tay dividing it from Angus to the north—the "Kingdom of Fife" feels like an island. This impression is reinforced by its strong sense of identity, variety of sights, and collage of landscapes.

An Elie fisherman repairing his net

Fife

⚑ 147 A1, B1

Visitor Information

✉ The Merchant's House, 339 High Street, Kirkcaldy

☎ (01592) 267 775

🕐 Closed Sun.

www.visitfife.com

Forth Bridges

⚑ 147 A1

Visitor Information

www.forthbridges .org.uk

South Coast

The towering twin Forth bridges (see pp. 78–79), monuments to Scottish engineering, are the main routes into Fife from Scotland's capital, Edinburgh, providing a fittingly grand entrance to the "Kingdom of Fife." Lying on the Fife flank of the Forth is former prime minister Gordon Brown's (1951–) hometown of **North Queensferry.** The relaxed village tumbles down to the water, where an old harbor and a sprinkling of pubs and restaurants await.

The main attraction in North Queensferry is **Deep Sea World** (*Battery Quarry, tel 01383/411 880, www.deepseaworld.com, $$$$*), the most impressive aquarium in the land. A must for children—and interesting for adults, too—the highlight is one of the world's longest shark tunnels, complete with huge sharks, billowing rays, and all manner of marine life. The interior boasts myriad tanks laden with tropical fish and exotic species such as piranhas, while outside there are the more familiar seals.

Just north of North Queensferry is the ancient town of **Dunfermline.** It may be blighted by a clog of modern housing and a gaggle of faceless shops at its core, but it is still home to one of Scotland's most important abbeys. **Dunfermline Abbey** *(18 St. Margaret St., tel 01383/724 586, www.dunfermlineabbey.co.uk, closed Nov.–March, $)* was originally commissioned as a priory church by Queen Margaret (1045–1093), who set up a ferry from South Queensferry to help pilgrims across the Forth. It opened in 1072, with her son, King David I (1085–1153), later developing it as an abbey to commemorate her. Today it is still an active place of worship. Seven kings of Scotland are buried in the abbey, including Robert the Bruce (1274–1329).

After visiting the abbey, check out what is very much a local secret, **Pittencrieff Park.** This lovely 76-acre (31 ha) green lung, with its main entrance off Dunfermline High Street, was a gift to the town by its most famous son, Andrew Carnegie (1835–1919)— once the richest man in the world, and one who had such a seminal influence on North America as well as his homeland. You can visit the **Andrew Carnegie Birthplace** *(Moodie Street., tel 01383/724 302, www.carnegiebirthplace.com, closed mid-Dec.–March, $)*, created by his wife in tribute and then over the years revamped to shed light on both his life and 19th-century Fife.

West of Dunfermline, the most interesting settlement is **Culross,** a truly remarkable time capsule. Once a busy port that grew rich on the back of its salt and coal industries, Culross slipped into decline by the 20th century. The National Trust for Scotland seized the opportunity to preserve this perfect piece of 17th-century Scotland and has worked tirelessly to do so. Highlights include the mustard-colored **Culross Palace** (1597), the **Townhouse** (1626), and the **Abbey Church,** parts of which date back to 1217.

East of Dunfermline, interesting coastal towns and villages include **Aberdour** (with its graceful town houses, castle mound, and sandy beach), **Kinghorn** (with

Dunfermline
⚠ 147 A1
Visitor Information
✉ 1 High St., Dunfermline
☎ (01383) 720 999
www.dunfermline .info

Culross Palace
✉ Culross
☎ (0844) 493 2189
🕐 Closed Nov.–March
💲 $$
www.nts.org.uk/ Property/22/

EXPERIENCE: Walk the Fife Coastal Path

The Fife Coastal Path is a long-distance path—the kind that Scots love and which handily opens up the country for visitors, too. The walk stretches for more than 93 miles (150 km), from the shadow of the Forth bridges at North Queensferry, east along the Firth of Forth coast, before turning north at the Fife Ness headland. It then follows the North Sea up past St. Andrews and on to the River Tay, where it reaches its denouement at the Tay Bridge overlooking Dundee. Along the way are pretty working fishing villages, castles and churches, nature reserves, and even the massive military air force base at Leuchars.

The organizers of the walk split it into seven bite-size stretches (see their website, *www.fifecoastalpath.co.uk,* which also details attractions and handy transport information). Some of these can be tackled as day trips—the section from the pretty fishing village of **Pittenweem** to **Fife Ness,** Fife's easternmost point, is ideal. At 8 miles (12.5 km), it skirts the coastline along some rough trails through attractive fishing villages, coves, and beaches, before a dramatic finale at the headland.

Kirkcaldy Museum & Art Gallery

✉ Abbotshall Road, Kirkcaldy

☎ (01592) 412 860

💲 $

www.fife.gov.uk

Falkland Palace

🅰 147 B1

✉ Falkland, Cupar

☎ (0844) 4932 186

💲 $$$

www.nts.org.uk/ Property/93

Scotland's Secret Bunker

✉ Troywood, St. Andrews

☎ (01333) 310 301

🕒 Closed Nov.–Feb.

💲 $$$

www.secretbunker .co.uk

a picturesque fishing harbor), and **Kirkcaldy**—the birthplace of great 18th-century thinker Adam Smith (1723–1790). **Kirkcaldy Museum and Art Gallery** has a fine collection of art, including a large treasure-trove of works by the Glasgow Boys (see p. 100).

Inland Fife

The Fife hinterland is a little explored oasis of neat farmland, gently rolling hills, and quiet villages, dotted with less attractive towns that have suffered in recent years as the traditional heavy industries have flagged. The shining light is the expanse of **Falkland Palace,** 11 miles (18 km) north of Kirkcaldy. Built between 1450 and 1541 in a fold below the rambling walking country of the Lomond Hills, this was a refuge of the Stuart kings and queens in the days when they were genuine rivals to the Hanoverian dynasty Britain still has today. The lavish gardens are worth visiting, and the palace's 17th-century Flemish tapestries and captivating portraits of Stuart monarchs are a poignant throwback to what might have been.

A throwback to a different, but no less compelling, era is **Scotland's Secret Bunker.** This site, located on the B540 south of St. Andrews, is where Scotland would have been governed from 100 feet (30 m) down, in the event of a nuclear war with the former Soviet Union. The size of two soccer fields and spread across two floors, this timepiece perfectly conjures up the suspicion and fear of the Cold War, especially for Scottish visitors, who would have been left to their fate above while their leaders sought sanctuary far below the ground.

Golfers head back to the clubhouse after a round on the Old Course at St. Andrews.

The Spiritual Home of Golf

Although locals in Leith claim to have pioneered the game, St. Andrews proudly proclaims itself to be the "home of golf" and is recognized by most of the world as such. Golfers used to drive balls around the land as far back as the 15th century, though King James II in 1457 famously banned the sport—he reckoned it interfered with his men's archery practice!

The Royal and Ancient (still golf's governing body today) was founded in 1754, when 22 local men met to codify the rules. The R&A (tel 01334/460 000, www.randa.org) still runs the town's most famous courses, including the iconic Old Course, where the British Open came home in 2010. See the sidebar on p. 166 for more information on golf in Scotland.

St. Andrews

If you only visit one town in Fife, make sure it is St. Andrews. The "home of golf" offers far more than just the rich heritage of the game. It is a deeply historic place laden with sights, and with an active student population that helps imbue its old stone streets with a real energy. The setting is sublime, too, with the North Sea wrapped around its old town and stunning beaches spreading out in all directions.

Named for Scotland's patron saint, the site was allegedly founded when the custodian of the saint's relics was shipwrecked here. The **cathedral,** near the town center and dedicated to the saint's legend, is the main attraction. Once the mightiest religious building in the land, natural elements have taken their toll and it's now a ruin scattered about a large site. Here, too, are the ruins of **St. Rule's Church,** whose soaring tower, if it is open, is worth the hike up its 157 steps for sweeping views of the town and the North Sea.

The other essential historical sight is ruined **St. Andrews Castle.** Dating from the 12th century, it is inexorably bound into the history of the cathedral, as it was another power base of the Scottish church. Exhibits shed light on the castle's history and gruesome past, but half the fun is ambling around the walls and conjuring up the days when men clashed swords and the sea rumbled on in the background just as it does today.

The sprawling **University of St. Andrews** owns many of the town's buildings. To get an insight into university life, try striking up a conversation with one of the students (alumni include Prince William, second in line to the British throne).

The dramatic coastline around St. Andrews appeals to both golfers (see sidebar above) and beach lovers. The most famous stretch is **West Sands,** a 15-minute walk from the town center, where the film *Chariots of Fire* was shot. Runners still batter along the firm sands, but the less athletic can try a bracing paddle in the North Sea or a stroll to the end of the beach to view seabirds. Watch the tides, though—the "beach" quickly turns into a sandbar, and then the sea. ∎

St. Andrews

🅰 147 B1, B2

Visitor Information

✉ 70 Market St., St. Andrews

☎ (01334) 472 021

www.visitfife.com

St. Andrews Cathedral

☎ (01334) 472 563

💲 $$

www.historic
-scotland.gov.uk

St. Andrews Castle

✉ North Street, St. Andrews

☎ (01334) 477 196

💲 $$

www.historic
-scotland.gov.uk

University of St. Andrews

✉ College Gate, St. Andrews

☎ (01334) 476 161

💲 $$

www.historic
-scotland.gov.uk

Drive Around the East Neuk of Fife Fishing Villages

The East Neuk of Fife is within easy reach of Edinburgh, Glasgow, and Dundee but could not feel less urban—the pace of life seems to get slower every year as its once mighty fishing fleets dwindle away. Today, the picturesque whitewashed fishing villages house a modest sprinkling of hard-working fishermen with lobster pots sitting prettily by the harbors and an abundance of first-rate fish-and-chips restaurants.

Robust stone and whitewashed cottages line the harbor at St. Monans.

Organizing a Trip

This drive can be done as one long day out from St. Andrews and back. To get the most out of the trip, though, it is better to allow a night, preferably two, to really soak up the flavors of each village, which can seem very similar but reveal their own distinct personalities the more time you devote to them.

It is popular to do much of the Elie to Crail section of this route as a walk, following the **Fife Coastal Path** (see sidebar p. 149), or you can take a few days to cycle the whole route.

NOT TO BE MISSED:

Elie • The Seafood Restaurant in St. Monans • Scottish Fisheries Museum • Crail

Village Hopping

As the major tourist town in Fife, **St. Andrews ❶** (see p. 151) makes for an ideal starting point. Soon the town's beaches are left behind as you ease south on the A915 through the rural hinterland. Take the B941 south after Largoward, and the water quickly reappears, this time the Firth of Forth, with Edinburgh's dramatic skyline looming beyond the southern bank.

As you approach the Firth, take the A917 south to the first of the pretty fishing villages, **Elie ②**. Here, the **Ship Inn** (see Travelwise p. 291) is the heart of the community and great for a seafood meal or a pint of ale while catching up on the local gossip. On summer weekends, watch for their legendary seafood barbecues. Aside from the pretty harbor, lined with distinctive whitewashed houses, with their ocher roof tiles, there are gorgeous beaches to enjoy here.

Farther east along the A917, **St. Monans ③**, the smallest of the East Neuk villages, is something of a local secret and home to one of Scotland's finest seafood restaurants—the aptly named **Seafood Restaurant** (16 West End, tel 01333/730 327, www.theseafoodrestaurant.com), which serves up superb fish and sweeping views.

Another short hop along the A917 brings you to **Anstruther ④**, a working fishing port that really feels authentic, and home to a brace of award-winning fish-and-chips restaurants. The town also boasts the **Scottish Fisheries Museum** (St. Ayles, Harbourhead, tel 01333/310 628, www.scotfishmuseum.org), which reclines in a collage of deeply historic houses on the waterfront and fills visitors in on this coastline's fishing and whaling past. The best "chippies" to look out for are the legendary **Anstruther Fish Bar** (see Travelwise p. 291) and **The Wee Chippy** (see Travelwise p. 291), recently

See also area map p. 147
► St. Andrews
◄► Choice of 1–3 days
⏱ 33 miles (53 km)
► St. Andrews

heralded by the British national newspaper The Observer as serving the "best fish and chips in the world."

The last of the East Neuk villages along the A917 is **Crail ⑤**. It tumbles down the hillside in a gaggle of stone houses, many populated by artists who find inspiration in the architecture, colorful people, and special light. The **Jerdan Gallery** (42 Marketgate South, tel 01333/450 797, www.thejerdangallery.com) is a rewarding place to take the pulse of the local artistic community, while the informal wooden shack down by the water is where you can kick back with some boat-fresh lobster and watch the fishermen at work. Here you can take in a scene that will live long in your memory before turning back north along the trusty A917, which flirts in and out of the coast all the way back to St. Andrews.

Dundee & Angus

Over the last millennium, Dundee has transformed from a humble fishing port into a bustling hub that is now Scotland's fourth largest city. This rise in status is in no small part due to its strategic location on the legendary banks of the River Tay, allowing trade to flourish with all corners of the globe. The surrounding Angus region boasts everything from the bucolic escape of the Angus Glens to a stretch of stunningly attractive coastline.

RSS *Discovery*, docked in Dundee's Discovery Cove, took Capt. Robert Falcon Scott on his tragic Antarctic trip.

Dundee

Dundee's golden age began in the 14th century, when it prospered as a trading center and boasted a burgeoning wool industry that underpinned its economy for more than 200 years. Over time, however, a number of events conspired to undermine Dundee's fortunes. These included a 1548 fire started by the "Auld Enemy," the English; a lethal plague in 1607–1608; and further English attacks.

In 1878, the Tay Railway Bridge opened, linking the city with Fife to the south. Measuring almost 2 miles (3 km) long, it was the largest single-span bridge in the world at the time. Triumph soon turned to tragedy, however, and today's replacement crossing (still Europe's longest railway bridge) is one of Dundee's most poignant symbols.

The remains of the old pier still haunt from the Firth of Tay and are an enduring reminder of the events of December 28, 1879. On that fateful night, the bridge collapsed; 75 passengers plunged to their deaths in the stormy river below. For the best view over the Tay bridges (the road bridge was completed in 1966), as well as the river and the coast beyond, head up to the **Mills Observatory,**

INSIDER TIP:

Dundonian is a rich local dialect that is a mystery even to many Scots, but persevere and it is fascinating to listen to and not as impenetrable as it first sounds.

—LARRY PORGES
National Geographic editor

which hangs 572 feet (174 m) over the city atop an extinct volcano called Law Hill. The observatory has a modest museum and stages regular planetarium shows.

Dundee's largely modern landscape is dotted with architectural gems that bring its colorful history to life, such as **St. Andrews Church** (*2 King St., tel 01382/224 860*), completed in 1722; the early 20th-century **Caird Hall Theatre** (*City Square, tel 01382/434 451, www.cairdhall .co.uk*); the historic town houses on **South Tay Street**; the currently defunct **Tay Hotel**; and Dundee's oldest building, **St. Mary's Tower** (1480), located on Nethergate. Built in the Gothic Revival style of 1867, the striking **McManus,** Dundee's premier art gallery, specializes in art from the 19th and 20th centuries. A recent renovation has seen it really boost the city's cultural profile.

Tourism has become a pillar of Dundee's economy. In 1986, the return of **RRS** *Discovery*— the ship built for Capt. Robert Falcon Scott's 1910–1913 Antarctic voyage, during which he reached the South Pole only to discover that Roald Amundsen had reached it first, and went on to perish during the return journey—brought a new generation of visitors to the city's historic waterfront. Before boarding the elegant tall ship, join Captain Scott (1868–1912) on his ill-fated expedition, detailed at the **Discovery Point Visitor Centre.**

The city's other maritime relic is the **HM Frigate** *Unicorn.* Moored at Victoria Dock, this 1824 classic whisks you back to the days when Britain ruled the waves. Although never seeing action, she is one of the world's oldest surviving warships. The tour's highlights include the graceful unicorn figurehead and the huge cannon on the gundeck.

Dundee Jute

Jute was first spun mechanically in Dundee in 1833. By the 19th century, the city had become the European center for jute production—aptly nicknamed "Juteopolis." This coarse fiber is ideal for a multitude of uses, most obviously in the manufacture of strong and durable sacks, which were much prized during the heyday of the British Empire. Cheaper rival production in India sent the local industry into a nosedive, but you can still explore the days of old at the **Verdant Works Museum** (see p. 156).

Dundee

🗺 147 B2

Visitor Information

✉ Discovery Point, Discovery Quay, Dundee

☎ (01382) 527 527

www.angusand dundee.co.uk

Mills Observatory

✉ Glamis Road, Balgay Park, Dundee

☎ (01382) 435 967

💲 $

www.dundeecity .gov.uk

The McManus

✉ Albert Square, Meadowside, Dundee

☎ (01382) 307 200

💲 $

www.mcmanus.co.uk

RRS *Discovery*

✉ Discovery Point, Discovery Quay, Dundee

☎ (01382) 309 060

💲 $$$

www.rrsdiscovery .com

HM Frigate *Unicorn*

✉ Victoria Dock, Dundee

☎ (01382) 200 900

💲 $$

www.frigateunicorn .org

Verdant Works Museum

✉ West Henderson's Wynd, Dundee

☎ (01382) 309 060

💲 $$$

www.undiscovered scotland.co.uk/ dundee/verdant works

Dundee Rep Theatre

✉ Tay Square, Dundee

☎ (01382) 223 530

www.dundeerep theatre.co.uk

Dundee Contemporary Arts

✉ 152 Nethergate, Dundee

☎ (01382) 909 900

www.dca.org.uk

You can explore another aspect of Dundee's industrial age at the **Verdant Works Museum.** In the 1860s and 1870s when Dundee's jute industry was in its prime, up to 50,000 workers—the total population of the city was around 90,000 at the time—produced the coarse fiber at more than 60 factories. This former mill employed 500 people. You can learn about every aspect of the production of jute and its many uses around the globe, before getting your hands on the more interactive exhibits.

Forward-Thinking City:

While it has been inextricably shaped by its colorful past, Dundee is also a vibrant and forward-thinking city. A swath of investment in everything from the landmark **Overgate Shopping Centre** (bordered by West Marketgait, High St., & Reform St.)

to its lifeblood waterfront are testimony to Dundee's ongoing regeneration. This city is making a real effort to push on from the decades of industrial decline that have blighted it since World War II.

A crucial element of Dundee's renaissance has been the city's artistic reawakening. Immediately west of the city center, High Street becomes Nethergate and passes into the cultural quarter. Here, the **Dundee Rep Theatre** boasts a funky café, a resident group of actors, and a contemporary dance company. Staging a string of daring productions, it has established itself as one of Scotland's premier venues. Here, too, the **Dundee Contemporary Arts** (DCA) is an avant-garde venue that stages everything from modern art exhibitions to art-house movies.

If the pace of sightseeing and

Dundee's pedestrianized City Square—a good place to start for shopping or a tour of the city

EXPERIENCE: Walking in the Angus Glens

The Angus Glens stretch across Glen Esk, Glen Prosen, Glen Clova, Glen Doll, and Glen Lethnot. They are one of Scotland's secret walking treasures—a wild landscape tucked away in the foothills of the mighty Cairngorms. These rugged valleys feature spectacular mountains, fast, twisting rivers, and lush, green forests.

Easily accessible from Dundee, this stunning area is alive with heather, wild deer, and bountiful birdlife. As you watch a burn tumbling through the rocks, a dragonfly may dance in front of you. As you climb to the top of a Munro—a 3,000-foot-plus (914 m) peak—you may see the rare alpine flowers that thrive on the high ground. And if you are very lucky, you may spot a golden eagle soaring above the rocky outcrops where they nest.

The Angus Glens provide an ideal location for many outdoor activities such as fishing and hunting and, for the very

adventurous, canoeing, rappelling, and climbing. The most popular activity is hill walking, with myriad routes to explore on your own (see www.walkingstories.com/original/angus.htm for some recommended routes) or on guided walking or cycling tours, offered by **Glentrek** (*100 East High St., Forfar, Angus, tel 01307/469 536, www.glentrek.com*).

Walkers looking for company should visit during the **Angus Glens Walking Festival** (*www.angusahead.com/walking festival*), which takes place every June. It incorporates more than 20 guided walks, for all ages and abilities, that are led by experienced local mountain leaders, accompanied by countryside rangers and estate managers who share their knowledge of the area. At the end of a day in the Angus countryside, there are various evening activities, including a ceilidh and traditional music concerts.

---

shopping gets too much, go for a relaxing walk at the **University of Dundee Botanic Gardens**—one of the city's enjoyably green lungs. Alternatively, indulge in a treatment at **Yu Spa**—a modern health spa at the APEX Hotel (see Travelwise p. 293).

Beyond Dundee

Dundee is surrounded by lush countryside, where the tranquil **Angus Glens,** sweeping beaches, and historic fortifications number among its myriad attractions. The town of **Broughty Ferry,** 4 miles (6.5 km) east, charms visitors with its ruined castle and windswept beaches. This is also the place to relax with lunch in a traditional

inn or the contemporary waterfront Glass Pavilion.

Arbroath Abbey, 17 miles (27 km) northeast of Dundee, is one of Scotland's most important historic sites. It was here that Robert the Bruce signed the stirring Declaration of Arbroath (see p. 40). After its romantically ruined sandstone abbey, Arbroath's other attraction is its smokies—strongly flavored smoked haddocks. Buy some and enjoy them down by the harbor for a real Angus treat.

The area's must-see attraction is **Glamis Castle,** 12 miles (19 km) north of Dundee. Famous as the setting for the Shakespearean murder of King Duncan by Macbeth, it's said to be the most haunted castle in Britain. ■

University of Dundee Botanic Gardens
⊠ Riverside Drive
☎ (01382) 381 190
💲 $
www.dundee.ac.uk/botanic

Arbroath Abbey
☎ (01241) 878 756
💲 $$
www.historic-scotland.gov.uk

Glamis Castle
⊠ Glamis, Angus
☎ (01307) 840 393
💲 $$$
www.glamis-castle.co.uk

Deeside

Until the 19th century, Deeside—the region named for the River Dee—was a remote and rugged wilderness of craggy mountains, gushing rivers, and quiet villages. All that changed when British monarch Queen Victoria (1819–1901) decided to cement her love of the Scottish Highlands and buy the expansive Balmoral Estate. Her purchase instantly transformed the area into Royal Deeside. The estate is still a popular retreat for British royalty today.

The 17th-century turreted stronghold of Braemar Castle

Glenshee

▲ 147 A2

Glenshee Ski Centre

✉ Cairnwell, Braemar

☎ (01339) 741 320

$ $$$$

www.ski-glenshee.co.uk

The most dramatic approach into Royal Deeside descends from the dizzy heights of **Glenshee.** In winter, this is one of Scotland's busiest ski fields. In the summer, it turns into first-class walking territory. Tumbling down the slopes from rough, wild Glenshee, the first Royal Deeside town of **Braemar** emerges like another world, where nature is tamed with graceful granite buildings, reassuringly old hotels, and cozy tea rooms.

The focus of much of the town's attention is on the rather run-down **Braemar Castle.** The local community is determined to return the castle to its former glory, with much money now being channeled into its revival. Tourism is a slick affair, too, with many stores on hand to outfit you for cycling, skiing, and walking, as well as restaurants and tea rooms to offer refreshment both before or après ski.

INSIDER TIP:

Never assume even in what seems to be a pro-Union area that everyone is a fan of the current U.K. political set-up; treading carefully avoids sticky conversational moments.

—SALLY McFALL
National Geographic contributor

The main annual event is the **Braemar Gathering** (see sidebar p. 163)—the world's most famous Highland Games—which attracts royalty and celebrities in equal measure. If you are a serious hill walker, don't miss the hike up **Morrone** (2,818 feet/859 m), which starts just south of Braemar village center. This remarkable mountain opens up great views of the town, but also out toward the expanse of the Cairngorm Mountains to the north. As you overlook Braemar from this vantage point, close your eyes, then reopen them. Imagine the scene in 1715 when the hillsides echoed with the war cries of the Jacobite clans who gathered here to raise their standard in defiance of the united British government.

Balmoral Castle & Estate

The A93 east from Braemar crisscrosses the gushing **River Dee** all the way to Ballater (see p. 162)—another town that has thrived as a result of the royal connection. Watch for **Balmoral Castle** as it looms out of the stunning countryside. In summer, this holiday retreat for the British royal family allows a few visitors into a limited number of its palatial spaces. If you want to learn more about the castle's estate, dodge the tour buses and embark on an illuminating official Balmoral Estate Safari. These tours by Land Rover start from the formal grounds but soon eke out into the wildly magnificent terrain that so entranced Queen Victoria all those years ago. Pickups in Ballater and Braemar can be arranged.

Whisky Country

Enter Deeside and you are also sneaking into serious whisky country, with the smells of Speyside almost discernible across the mountains. Continuing the royal theme, one of Prince Charles's famous tipples is the malt conjured up at **Royal Lochnagar** in Ballater. However, if you prefer working off calories rather than drinking them, try hiking up the 3,790-foot (1,115 m) Munro of **Lochnagar,** which is said to be Prince Charles's favorite mountain in Scotland.

The locals of **Ballater** love the royals so much that even the bakers and the bus company that have received royal approval brandish their polished royal crests *(continued on p. 162)*

(continued on p. 162)

Braemar
⛰ 147 A3

Visitor Information
✉ The Mews, Mar Road, Braemar
☎ (01339) 741 600

guide.visitscotland.com

Braemar Castle
✉ Braemar
☎ (01339) 741 219
💲 $$

www.braemarcastle.co.uk

Morrone
www.walkhighlands.co.uk/cairngorms/morrone.shtml

Balmoral Castle & Estate
⛰ 147 B3
☎ (01339) 742 534
🕐 Closed Aug.–March
💲 $$; Balmoral Estate Safari: $$$$$$

www.balmoralcastle.com

Royal Lochnagar Distillery
✉ Craithie, Ballater
☎ (01339) 742 700
💲 Tours: $$

www.discovering-distilleries.com/royallochnagar

Lochnagar Munro
www.walkhighlands.co.uk/munros/lochnagar

The Tartan Tradition

To put it simply, tartan is a crisscrossed pattern of horizontal and vertical threads whose various colors are woven together to create a dramatic and unique design. Tartan fabric is made up of colored threads woven at right angles to each other to form alternating bands of similar warp (length) and weft (width). The sequence of lines and squares formed by the weave create a pattern known as the sett.

The first Scottish tartans, thought to have been made in the Highlands as far back as 600–500 B.C., were not as colorful as they are today. The oldest actual sample of a tartan, known as the Falkirk tartan, resides in the National Museum of Scotland in Edinburgh (see p. 65) and dates from A.D. 300.

A tartan kilt being made in a Scottish shop

Some people call tartan "plaid," which to the Scots makes no sense. For them, plaid was originally the traditional name for a large sheet of woven material that men sculpted around their bodies or used as a blanket to keep warm. Only later did the shorter, neater kilt that we now know come into being, with a more elaborate ceremonial version today still being known as plaid.

To many Scots, tartan is more than just a design or fabric. It is a phenomenon that reaches deep into their history and has taken on semimythical status. Although many Scots think of tartan as being inexorably bound up with individual clans (or families), this was not always the case. Traditionally, the colors and patterns came from the country's regions, with the colors determined by the natural dyes that were available to the weavers in each area.

Showing Their True Colors

When the various clans piled into battle in support of Scotland's inspirational leaders, such as William Wallace and Robert the Bruce, they wore a blaze of different tartans, with myriad kilts/plaids. Sometimes a soldier would wear more than one tartan design in his garb. That all changed after the disastrous defeat at Culloden, when the British government butchered the tartan army where they lay and thrust through the heart of the traditional Highland way of life. Tartan and Highland dress were actually banned by the British government in 1746 by way of the Dress Act.

This ban was eventually rescinded in 1782. During the following century, tartan became

EXPERIENCE: Playing Bagpipes

Another iconic Scottish tradition, the Scottish Highland bagpipe is essentially a woodwind instrument with enclosed reeds that are fed from a bag of air the player has to keep inflated. Key components include the chanter, which provides the melody, and the drone, the cylindrical reed-filled tube that sits above the bag. The origins of the bagpipe are hotly disputed—there are similar types of instruments in Ireland and Spain—but there is evidence that the Scottish variant has been around since at least the 1400s. Indeed, one surviving set of bagpipes is said to have been played at the landmark Battle of Bannockburn in 1314. Today, you can hear them played at Highland Games, competitions, and at major sporting events and festivals. If you want to learn how to play the bagpipes, the best way is to start with tunes on the chanter. The **National Piping Centre** in Glasgow (*30–34 McPhater St., tel 0141/353 0220, www.thepipingcentre.co.uk*) sells all the necessary equipment and has a school that offers everything from individual lessons through to extended courses. The center also has a museum that delves into the history and culture surrounding Scotland's national instrument.

popular again, although this time not as a pattern used in everyday dress, but more as a way of displaying traditions, heritage, and clan allegiance. Tartan became the national symbol that it remains very much today. Natural dyes were replaced by brighter, bolder, and more consistent artificial coloring. This trend reached its zenith during George IV's famous visit to Edinburgh in 1822, when Scots were encouraged by Sir Walter Scott to sport their tartan finery to impress the visiting British monarch.

Modern Tartans

Today, there are thought to be more than 7,000 different tartans, with more designs being created every year. Most are linked to the various clans and regions. Others are purely constructed, such as Flower of Scotland or the tartan created for the Tartan Army—the fanatical followers of Scotland's national soccer team. Even then, only a small minority of them sport the "official" tartan, choosing to wear their own clan and regional tartans instead, much as their ancestors would have done centuries ago. Two of the most famous tartans in Scotland are the Black Watch and the Royal Stuart. The "official" British royal tartan is the Balmoral, designed by Prince Consort Albert in 1853 and commissioned by

INSIDER TIP:

Don't be tempted by the cheap "kilts" in some of the tacky tartan tat shops on Edinburgh's Royal Mile and go to a proper kiltmaker, who will measure you and supply a genuine quality garment that will probably outlast you.

—ALASTAIR GOURLAY
National Geographic contributor

his wife, Queen Victoria, the British monarch who had a celebrated love of the Highlands.

Today, tartan is a global phenomenon—a design borrowed by fashion creators and celebrities and adored by Hollywood stars. Everyone from the 1970s punk band Sex Pistols through to Lady Diana (there is now a Lady Diana Memorial tartan) has embraced the traditional Scottish fabric. Tartan is now not limited to kilts and other items of Highland dress, nor confined to its country of origin, popping up throughout the globe in a far cry from its humble beginnings in the wild, windswept glens of the Highlands.

Ballater

⬧ 147 B3

Visitor Information

✉ The Old Railway
Station, Station
Square, Ballater

☎ (01339) 755 306

**www.ballater
scotland.com**

Banchory
Museum

✉ Bridge Street,
Banchory

☎ (01330) 823 367

$ $

**www.aberdeenshire
.gov.uk**

Crathes Castle

⬧ 147 C3

✉ Near Banchory

☎ (0844) 493 2166

$ $$$

**www.nts.org.uk/
Property/20**

with great pride. The main attraction is **Ballater Royal Station** (see sidebar below), but the town center also perfectly portrays what Royal Deeside is all about. Ballater is a neatly polished affair of trim stone houses, tourist-orientated coffee shops, outdoor activity operators, and everything that has a royal connection.

Ballater is also starting to push itself as a base for adventure sports fans. Queen Victoria loved the rugged, bleak mountain landscapes here, but if you prefer your mountain landscapes unadulterated with chairlifts and cozy mountain huts, you will love the cycling and hill walking the region has to offer. Stock up on outdoor gear and hire mountain bikes at one of two rental shops in town—The Bike Shop *(Station Square, tel 01339/754 004, www.bikestationballater.co.uk)* and Cycle Highlands *(The Pavilion, Victoria Rd., tel 01339/755 864, www.cyclehighlands.com)*—to explore the local terrain; trails cater to all levels of biking ability.

Farther east, the A93 follows the River Dee into the lovely town of **Banchory,** which, in

essence, marks the start of the Aberdeen overspill; an unmistakably urban feel creeps into the rural idyll. There are high-street stores and fast-food joints, but also plenty of graceful buildings, green spaces, and fine walks. The **Banchory Museum** interprets this lively little town with, of course, a royal connection in the form of commemorative royal crockery.

Deeside is also replete with grand country houses and castles. You can find your own favorite among them, but if you are short on time, the 16th-century **Crathes Castle** is an ideal introduction. The jeweled ivory Horn of Leys given to the Burnett family to mark the generous gift of land granted in 1323 by King Robert the Bruce, on which the family later built the castle, is prominently displayed in the Great Hall. The grounds include formal gardens and a woodland garden, plus the new **Skytrek,** a tree-top rope assault course whose high wires open up views of Deeside in all its royal glory. ∎

Ballater Royal Station

With one long blast of a whistle, the first passenger train made its steam-shrouded arrival at Ballater station in 1866. Over the next century, one of Britain's most charming Victorian stations blossomed as the terminus of the Deeside Line, which was a favorite of Queen Victoria and traveled through some of Scotland's wild and dramatic scenery. The now defunct Deeside Line and the revamped station at Station Square in Ballater are draped in a swath of intoxicating legends of British royal visits and Russian czars. A museum *(Station Sq., Ballater, tel 01339/755 306, $),* opened as part of the $1.5-million refurbishment, sheds light on the station and its intriguing history. One of the former royal carriages was added in 2008, complete with "Victoria" herself about to make her last departure.

EXPERIENCE: Braemar Royal Highland Gathering

The Highland Games are said to have originated in Royal Deeside during the reign of King Malcolm Canmore, so it is fitting that the most famous Highland Gathering today is held in Braemar. Attending this event offers a fascinating insight into Scottish heritage, class, and pageantry.

The Braemar Royal Highland Society began life as the Braemar Wright Society in 1815, changing its name to the Braemar Highland Society in 1826. In 1866, Queen Victoria, herself a big fan of the Highland Society Gatherings, decided that it needed royal patronage and the "Royal" was added to the society's name; it runs the games in this guise today.

The Braemar Gathering is not the biggest, but that may be because it is so popular that spectator numbers are limited—unusual for Highland Games (see pp. 22–23). Held on the first Saturday of September, this lively event re-creates the Highland spirit in a style that those who turn up each year have become accustomed to. If you only go to one Highland Games, make it Braemar.

The highlight is the massed **drummers and pipers,** who impress the crowd with their sound reverberating around the heather-clad hills. The event's **competitive aspect** is broken into two sections—"heavy" events and "track" events. The latter you may recognize as traditional athletics events, such as running, while the former includes traditional Highland sports, like tossing a long wooden

Scottish dancers twirl to the tune of bagpipes at the Braemar Gathering Royal Highland Games.

pole called the caber. A titanic struggle also sees various branches of the British armed forces doing battle in a fiercely competitive tug-of-war.

More Fun

Other fun events include **Highland dancing,** in which tartan-clad dancers show off their graceful skills to traditional music, and the dramatic long leap. The children's **sack race** is always a laugh for children and spectators alike. The fit can tackle the tough **hill race** that sees the foolish and the brave sprint up and down the rugged mountain Morrore.

Otherwise, the **March of the Lonach Highlanders** (www.lonach.org) in Aberdeenshire is also well recommended.

Tickets

Tickets for the grandstand are near impossible to come by, but visit the website (www.braemargathering .org) in February when they go on sale and you may be able to get tickets for the uncovered stand or the cheapest area—the ringside seats. If not, you can buy a ticket to the beautiful 12-acre (5 ha) grounds, which is much cheaper, but seeing the main events properly from here can be a bit of a lottery.

Aberdeen

Aberdeen is Scotland's third largest city (pop. 210,400). As the self-styled "oil capital of Europe," it is crisscrossed by the Don and Dee Rivers, and its historic center is laden with granite architecture, bustling port, sandy beach—and more green spaces than any other British city.

Aberdeen's world-class port, the heart of its oil and gas industry

Aberdeen

 147 C3

Visitor Information

✉ 23 Union St.

☎ (01224) 288 828

**www.aberdeen
-grampian.com**

Given its strategic location in the middle of Scotland's East Coast, it is no surprise that by the 13th century Aberdeen had become a major trading hub. The 19th century saw its trading role grow, and the city followed suit with the coming of the oil industry, instigating another boom that continues to this day. Aberdeen serves as the base for the massive North Sea oil industry.

Aberdeen is known to Scots as the "granite city," a moniker it well deserves. All of the city's most prominent buildings are built in this solid stone, its main streets forming granite canyons that can

take on an intimidating air when the North Sea storms howl in.

Union Street, the heart of the bustling city center, is one of Scotland's great thoroughfares. Any English visitors who think that the name indicates a warm embrace of the 1707 Union might want to think again. The city's motto, "Bon Accord," comes from the night in 1306 when its citizens ransacked the English garrison and massacred its defenders.

Start your city tour at **Castle-gate,** a square at the east end of Union Street, where the city's majestic castle once stood. Admire the 17th-century **Mercat Cross**

Aberdeen's Oil Industry

The oil and gas industry only emerged after vast reserves were found in the North Sea off Scotland's east coast in the mid-20th century. As the closest city, and a coastal one at that, Aberdeen was perfectly positioned to become the "oil capital of Europe." Today, it boasts the world's busiest heliport and a bustling harbor that caters to the myriad offshore rigs.

All is not entirely rosy, though, as any fluctuation in the demand for oil greatly impacts upon the city. There is also an inherent danger in the oil industry, as evidenced by the 1988 Piper Alpha Disaster, in which 167 men lost their lives in a horrific offshore fire. Aberdeen is currently trying to future-proof itself by becoming a world leader in new, more sustainable energy sources.

INSIDER TIP:

Don't miss the March of the Lonach Highlanders in August, when hundreds, from several clans, march the winding roads of Aberdeenshire, stopping at each country house for a wee dram of hospitality from the local laird.

—LEON GRAY
National Geographic contributor

here, once the focus of the city, with its intricate carvings. Farther west, at the start of Union Street, is the **Town House,** perhaps the city's most dramatic edifice. The lavish 19th-century façade is wonderfully overblown. It conceals the earlier Tolbooth, which is now home to the **Tolbooth Museum,** which explores crime and punishment during its heyday as a jail in the 17th and 18th centuries.

A block north of Union Street is an even more dramatic

creation—the **Marischal College,** which is the second largest granite building in the world. This lavish building looks like someone has dripped granite all over a massive wedding cake. It is owned by Aberdeen University. Take time to explore the spectacular exterior before visiting the modest **Marischal Museum,** with its cornucopia of exhibits brought back by explorers from the Victorian era. Opening hours are erratic due to ongoing renovation work.

Farther west on Union Street, with its entrance to the north on Belmont Street, is **Aberdeen Art Gallery.** This wonderfully eclectic collection boasts an impressive array of 19th- and 20th-century fine art, as well as early archaeological finds from ancient Greek and Roman periods. A maritime collection sheds light on the city's relationship with the North Sea. This creative space also stages many temporary exhibitions and concerts of everything from traditional Scottish ceilidh music through to Indonesian gamelan.

Heading directly south from Castlegate, you will descend into the old **harbor.** There you will

Tolbooth Museum
- ✉ Castle Street
- ☎ (01224) 621 167
- 🕐 Closed Oct.–July
- 💲 $

www.aagm.co.uk

Marischal Museum
- ✉ Marischal College, Broad Street
- ☎ (01224) 274 301
- 💲 $

www.abdn.ac.uk/marischal_museum

Aberdeen Art Gallery
- ✉ Schoolhill
- ☎ (01224) 523 700
- 🕐 Closed Mon.

www.aagm.co.uk

Lonach Highland Gathering & Games
- ✉ Bellabeg Park, Strathdon, Aberdeenshire
- ☎ (01975) 651 297
- 💲 $

www.lonach.org

EXPERIENCE: Play a Round of Golf

With more than 500 golf courses dotted around the nation, Scotland is the world's number one golfing destination. Playing a round or two while you are here is obligatory for golf fanatics, while for less accomplished players the sport is a fascinating way of getting to the heart of the national psyche—not to mention of also experiencing some its most dramatic scenery.

With the Grampian Mountains in the background, golfers tee off at Pitlochry Golf Club—one of Scotland's most scenic courses.

The oldest golf course in the world lies in Musselburgh near Edinburgh (see p. 80). Documents show the game was played here as early as 1672, but there are tales that Mary Queen of Scots enjoyed a round in 1567.

Golf in Scotland is always evolving, with existing courses constantly being improved and perennial plans hatching for new ones, such as Donald Trump's current vision of a massive golf resort north of Aberdeen (see sidebar p. 169).

Scotland is famous for its "links" courses, set along the coastal sand dunes. Most golfers with a reasonable handicap head for the grand courses that have hosted the British Open, such as **Muirfield** in East Lothian (see p. 80), **Royal Troon** and **Turnberry** in Ayrshire (see p. 104), **St. Andrews** in Fife (see p. 151), and **Carnoustie** (tel 01241/802 270, www .carnoustiegolfclub.com) in Angus. Book in advance if you want to play at one of these hallowed courses.

Many inland courses, like **Pitlochry** (tel 01796/472 792, www.pitlochrygolf .co.uk) in Tayside, are just as scenic and prestigious, though. Perhaps the most impressive golf resort does not even lie on the coast. **Gleneagles** (see Travelwise p. 285), with its grand hotel, spreads proudly across 850 acres (344 ha) of stunning Perthshire countryside, surrounded by woodland and hills. There are three courses—the King's Course, the Queen's Course, and the new Jack Nicklaus—designed PGA Centenary Course. The latter is set to be the venue for the Ryder Cup in 2014.

In Scotland, golf is very much the people's game. Many courses are open to the public, ranging from world-class links to modest courses within city boundaries. There are also simple nine-hole courses that are ideal for new players.

How you arrange to play golf in Scotland is up to you. Whether you want to hire one of the many golf tour operators to arrange games on famous courses and fly between them by helicopter or just play a quick game on a municipal course, see golf .visitscotland.com for all the information you will need. However you choose to play, the experience is magnified by knowing that you are enjoying a round in the country where it all began.

find a hive of activity, as well as a tumble of old stone cottages, cobbled streets, and warehouses. Much of the modern working port is off-limits, but you can really feel the buzz of the oil and gas industries here. At the **Aberdeen Maritime Museum** you can learn about the city's long relationship with the sea, from the days when fishing was the main maritime industry right through to today's massive oil and gas industry. The well-constructed exhibits also cover shipbuilding and sailing ships, and the museum incorporates **Provost Ross's House,** which was built back in the late 16th century. The views from here out over the harbor tell their own story.

North of the harbor lies **Aberdeen Beach,** where the whole city seems to flock on sunny days. This long stretch of sand is ideal for families, and there is a promenade that works well for strolls, which can be refreshingly bracing when the wind is coming off the sea. The area has a good selection of cafés and restaurants, as well as arcades and amusement parks, and it is well set up for leisure activities. Chief among these is the **Beach Leisure Centre** *(Beach Promenade, Aberdeen Beach, tel 01224/655 401, $$$),* with its swimming pool, wave machine, flumes, climbing wall, and other sporting activities. This is an ideal attraction for active families on a wet day, which are all too common in this windswept, coastal city.

Aberdeen is a regular winner of "Britain in Bloom"—the competition to find Britain's greenest and most attractive place. It may be laden with gray granite, but real efforts are made to brighten it up with flower beds, which seem to pop up from every available pore.

Of all the city's plentiful parks, the 44-acre (18 ha) **Duthie Park** is the highlight. In summer, the "Rose Mountain" is spectacular, while on colder days you can check out the **Winter Gardens,** where exotic species (including Britain's largest collection of cactuses) thrive in the artificially warm climate. In summer, the boating lake opens so that you can ease around the water and enjoy a slice of the city where the oil boom seems very far away. ■

Aberdeen Maritime Museum

- ✉ 52–56 Shiprow
- ☎ (01224) 337 700
- $ $
- www.aagm.co.uk

Duthie Park

- ✉ Polmuir Road
- ☎ (01224) 585 310
- $ $
- www. aberdeencity .gov.uk

Relaxing in the atmospheric Soul Bar at 333 Union Street

Fishing Villages

The northeast coastline is renowned for its busy fishing ports. Fishing has been on the decline in recent years, but many of these picture-postcard villages still run small fleets. Atmospheric harbors are strewn with lobster pots and pretty stone fishing cottages, with thick walls built around them to protect their inhabitants against the biting North Sea winds.

Traditional whitewashed fishing cottages line the streets in the idyllic village of Pennan.

Stonehaven

🅰 147 C3

Visitor Information

✉ Stonehaven Tourist Information Center, 66 Allardice St.

☎ (01569) 762 806

Tolbooth Museum

✉ The Harbour, Stonehaven

☎ (01771) 622 906

🕐 Closed Nov.–May

💲 $$

A good place to start exploring the fishing villages of this corner of Scotland is **Stonehaven,** south of Aberdeen. Its main attractions are the great local fish and chips, the historic harbor, and its oldest building, the **Tolbooth,** which is now a museum that delves into the local fishing heritage. Boat trips are available in summer, and the best time to visit is during the folk festival in early July.

The landscape is much wilder north of Aberdeen, with stone villages set among sweeping sand dunes and looming sea cliffs.

Peterhead is the biggest whitefish port in Europe and is worth a stop to feel the pulse of Scottish fishing and to try a 10-ounce (283 g) slab of boat-fresh haddock at Zanres (35 Queen St., tel 01779/477 128, www.zanres.co.uk).

Fraserburgh, at the northeastern tip of Aberdeenshire, is worth a stop to visit the **Museum of Scottish Lighthouses.** Here you can learn about the work of the Stevenson family, who designed many of Scotland's impressive lighthouses and gave birth to the literary talent of Robert Louis Stevenson.

INSIDER TIP:

During storm tides, waves in Pennan can wash over parked cars and nearly onto the steps of the little inn and pub. Worth a visit for anyone, but an absolute must for fans of the cult movie classic *Local Hero*, which was set here.

—JIM RICHARDSON
National Geographic photographer

Pennan, west of Fraserburgh, is the area's quintessential village, sitting snug beneath huge cliffs with little more than a few houses set on one waterfront street. So idyllic is it that Hollywood came calling when they were looking for a pretty village to star in the film *Local Hero*. Many of the cottages are now holiday homes and there is little to do in Pennan but relax and while away the time. **The Pennan Inn** has decent lunches and old newspaper clippings from the days when Burt Lancaster came to town.

Just a few miles farther west, the twin settlements of **Crovie** and **Gardenstown,** less than a mile apart, get fewer tourists than Pennan but are also beguilingly pretty. Gardenstown is a great place to enjoy top-quality seafood.

Farther west again, **Portsoy** is one of the most complete fishing villages. Although quiet these days, you can still see the twin harbors and the voluminous old warehouses, while the modest little **Portsoy Maritime Museum** sheds light on its "Golden Age" in the 17th century, as does the local independent tourist information office. **The Shore Inn** is a cozy place to enjoy a pint and the tall tales of the local characters.

The trim little Moray village of **Cullen** is famous for "Cullen skink"—the delicious, creamy smoked haddock soup. The modern part of Cullen sits on a hilltop, with some grand civic buildings, cafés, and an ice-cream store, while down by the sea (under the old railway viaduct that sweeps around the village), the windswept harbor hints at former glories. ∎

Donald Trump Comes to Town

The most controversial planned construction project in Scotland in recent years is the brainchild of American billionaire Donald Trump. His attempt to turn a virginal swath of Aberdeenshire's seaboard north of Aberdeen into an exclusive golf course and luxury residential oasis has met with some objection. The project (*www.trump golfscotland.com*) will spread its tentacles over some 1,500 acres (607 ha) of coastline, and the locals are split between environmental concerns and the lure of massive investment and long-term job prospects.

Peterhead
⚑ 147 C4

Fraserburgh
⚑ 147 C4

Museum of Scottish Lighthouses
✉ Kinnaird Head, Stevenson Rd., Fraserburgh
☎ (01346) 511 022
💲 $$
www.lighthouse museum.org.uk

Pennan
⚑ 147 C4

The Pennan Inn
✉ Pennan
☎ (01346) 561 201
www.thepennaninn .co.uk

Portsoy Maritime Museum
✉ Portsoy Harbour
💲 $

The Shore Inn
✉ 49 Church St., Portsoy
☎ (01261) 842 831

Towering mountains, heather-clad hills, and deep primeval lochs (complete with monsters), plus winter sports and whisky galore

Central & Western Highlands

The tranquil beauty of Loch Insh

Central & Western Highlands

This wildly beautiful region has visitors agog at the sheer scenic splendor of it all, and making hasty plans to return before they have even left. Boasting world famous lochs, the country's highest mountain, and top-notch adventure sports, this richly historic land is every bit as romantic as its legends suggest.

The central and western Highlands are Scotland at its best, a scenic and historic oasis that runs from coast to coast. Hulking mountain peaks rise up all around, while rugged passes slit through the glens, and deep-blue sea lochs spread out like fjords toward the Atlantic Ocean.

The only city in the Highlands and the region's capital, Inverness, on the northeast coast, is developing at a rate that shows the area is finally recovering from the aftermath of the calamitous Battle of Culloden in 1746, an event that shaped the human and natural history of this region as much as any ice age. Currently one of Europe's fastest growing cities, Inverness has become increasingly sophisticated and appealing for visitors, many of whom now often spend a few nights here rather than just passing straight through.

Aviemore, south of Inverness, is Scotland's busiest winter sports resort. It hangs in the shadow of the voluminous Cairngorms, a mountain range boasting some of the United Kingdom's highest peaks, including the mighty Ben Macdui. The region is popular in summer with hikers and climbers who give way in winter to skiers and proponents of that particularly Scottish winter sport, curling.

On the foothills of the range sits the efficiently run Rothiemurchus Estate, a forested sanctuary that has something for everyone, from fishing and mountain biking to wildlife-watching and dog-sledding. Its well-maintained confines provide a neat condensed introduction to the charms of the area.

Just east is Speyside, where some of the world's most famous whiskies are made, including Glenfiddich and Glenlivet. The major distilleries lie close together and can be easily combined into a tour. The region's graceful capital, Grantown-on-Spey, makes

Edinburgh

Area of
map detail

a comfortable base. This rolling, relaxed river valley is also busy throughout the year with walkers, cyclists, and canoeists.

On the opposite coast to Inverness, at the end of a 60-mile-long (100 km) series of glens (valleys) known as the Great Glen, is Fort William. The Great Glen encompasses no less than four lochs, including Loch Ness, home to the world's most famous (and elusive) monster, Nessie. You can walk, cycle, canoe, or even take a boat between the two coasts. The remarkable Caledonian Canal, a wonder of 19th-century Scottish engineering, connects the quartet of lochs to the North Sea and the Atlantic Ocean.

These days, Fort William is emerging as a real adventure hub, offering easy access to the United Kingdom's highest mountain, Ben Nevis, and the great Nevis Range that surrounds it, which is now a hotbed of mountain biking and skiing action. This region of the

---

NOT TO BE MISSED:

Learning about Scotland's most infamous battlefield at Culloden's eco-friendly visitor center 177

Loch Ness, Scotland's largest inland loch and home to the world's most famous monster, Nessie 187–188

Exploring Glen Coe, the most beautiful of the glens and laced with human tragedy 192–193

Glenfinnan, a magical glen blessed with epic scenery and a profound sense of history 194, 196

Highlands is also serious walking country, with trails to suit all levels of ability and experience.

Glen Coe, south of Fort William, may be the most attractive glen in the country, even if its name is inextricably linked with one of the most poignant Scottish tales of tragedy. To the north you can take a train or drive the "Road to the Isles," seeking out the Atlantic Coast. It arrives having passed through a string of spectacular glens and unfurls in a sweep of starched white-sand beaches around the quiet villages of Morar and Arisaig. The fishing port of Mallaig awaits at the end of the line, providing a gateway to the isles themselves, with Skye clearly visible across the water. The mainland north of Mallaig and Knoydart is as wild as anything found on Scotland's islands, and is again steeped in tragedy, resulting from the direct (and indirect) consequences of that defeat at Culloden—a battle that seismically shifted the Highland way of life forever and still fires the imagination and hearts of both locals and visitors today. ■

Inverness

The city of Inverness stands at the northern tip of the Great Glen, where the waters of Loch Ness flow down to Beauly Firth. Inverness stands at the crossroads between the highlands and the lowlands, and has seen many violent clashes over the centuries, from medieval clan warfare to the carnage of Culloden in 1746. Today it is the largest urban area in the Highlands, a dynamic modern city with a population of more than seventy thousand people.

Inverness's suspension footbridge links the busy center with the quieter side of the River Ness.

Inverness

172–173 C2

Visitor Information

✉ Tourist Information Centre Inverness, Castle Wynd, Inverness

☎ (08452) 255 121

www.visithighlands. com

Inverness's population has grown in recent times, and it was formally proclaimed a city in 2000. It has also prospered thanks to its growing tourist industry, styling itself as the "gateway to the Highlands," which in many ways it is. Today more and more travelers are making Inverness an essential stop on their Scottish travels, and more and more Scots are choosing it as a place to live and work.

The main sight is **Inverness Castle** (*Castle St.*). The structure has been flattened on numerous occasions throughout its turbulent history, and the current red-hued sandstone building bears little resemblance to the original. Nonetheless, the ghosts of dead Highlanders, Mary Queen of Scots, and Robert the Bruce are never far away. Now used as a courthouse, it is not open to the public, but you can stroll around the grounds and check out the statue of Flora MacDonald in front of the castle, a tribute to the Scots woman who helped Bonnie Prince Charlie escape after his army's defeat at Culloden.

INSIDER TIP:

For a healthy dose of Highland hospitality and dry Scottish wit, stay with Richard and Jenny at Moyness House, just a few minutes' walk from the city center.

—JENNIFER SEGAL
National Geographic Development Office

The Center

Just a block north of the castle, on Castle Wynd, is the recently revamped **Inverness Museum and Art Gallery.** With free admission it is well worth a visit, and not only covers the history of the city but also delves into the past of the whole Highland region. Exhibits include everything from brutal weapons and bagpipes to modern interactive displays that shed light on the traditional Highland way of life. Many of the paintings in the collection, meanwhile, show local history scenes. The curator's favorite piece is an old penny coin that was sculpted by an air force pilot into the shape of a plane to give to his sweetheart.

Pushing a short distance farther north brings you to the **Town House.** This building dates back to 1878 and is constructed in a Gothic style, which contrasts with much of the city center. The most famous gathering here was in 1921 when the first British cabinet meeting ever held outside

London was rapidly convened as Ireland ceded from British control. Today guided tours are the main way of getting inside, although the building is also used as a concert venue. The city's **Mercat Cross** and the **Stone of Tubs,** where women used to rest their washing tubs en route to and from the river, are just outside. Legend has it that as long as this stone stays in place, Inverness will continue to thrive.

Crossing over Bridge Street to the north, the pedestrianized shopping heart of Inverness spills out to your left. It's a handy retail oasis selling everyday essentials that will come in useful for forays into the wild Highlands. There are also plenty of tourist-oriented "Scottish" shops. If you always wanted to buy a kilt, a furry sporran, or even a set of bagpipes, this is the place to do it. Some of the more specialized retailers offer good deals, although half the fun is hearing all the myths and stories

Moyness House
✉ 6 Bruce Gardens
☎ (01463) 233 836
www.moyness.co.uk

Inverness Museum & Art Gallery
✉ Castle Wynd
☎ (01463) 237 114
🕐 Closed Sun.
inverness.highland .museum

Town House
✉ Castle Wynd
☎ (01463) 702 000
🕐 Closed Nov.–May
💲 $$
www.highland .gov.uk

EXPERIENCE:
The Calm of Ness Islands

A short stroll south of Inverness's busy center you'll find the Ness Islands, a park spread over a number of small river islands. Here the sounds of traffic are replaced by the swish of fresh water and the song of birds. The islands are linked by walkways and, strolling along them on a sunny day, you will meet few other tourists, but will instead mix with locals walking their dogs or merely taking the air. Find the islands at the east end of the Infirmary Bridge; it's the first footbridge upstream from the main roadbridge.

**Scottish
Kiltmaker Centre**
✉ 4–9 Huntly St.
☎ (01463) 222 781
🕐 Closed Sun.
💲 $
**www.highland
houseoffraser.com**

**St. Andrew's
Cathedral**
✉ 15 Ardross St.
☎ (01463) 233 535
💲 $
**www.inverness
cathedral.co.uk**

you will inevitably be told when asking about the merchandise.

Three blocks north, at 71 Church Street, is **Abertaff House.** Reputed to be the oldest building in the whole of Inverness, this protected structure dates back to 1593. Although you cannot go inside, it is still worth visiting. Along with the other buildings on and surrounding Church Street— including the **Steeple** (2 Bridge Street) and the **Old High Church** (corner of Church Street and Friars' Lane)—the house harks back to a very different era.

Across the River

Behind the Old High Church is a footbridge that crosses the River Ness to the quieter east bank.

Turn immediately south and you will come to the **Scottish Kiltmaker Centre.** Here you can learn all you ever wanted to know about tartan and kilt-making, while fans of the movies *Braveheart* and *Rob Roy* can check out some of the costumes worn during the filming. They have been fitting men out for kilts at this establishment for half a century, so you are in good hands. You can read their online guide to buying a kilt before going for a fitting.

Easing south along the river you pass the most graceful of the city's bridges, the **Ness Bridge,** before the bulk of **St. Andrew's Cathedral** looms into view. This unheralded cathedral dates back

The snow-covered battlefield at Culloden

only to the 19th century and, though it may not be highly rated architecturally, makes a great photograph from across the River Ness on a sunny day, and has a relaxed, refined charm.

Near the cathedral, the **Eden Court Theatre** is an impressive new cultural icon befitting a city on the rise. They take a multi-disciplinary approach to their program, laying on an eclectic roster of performances and activities—everything from interactive children's events and plays to classical music concerts.

Three miles (5 km) west of the city center via the A862, **Craig Phadrig Hill,** the former stronghold of the Pictish King Brude, is home to an Iron Age fort and offers great views of the Moray Firth.

Culloden Moor

East of the city is an attraction that anyone with even a passing interest in Scottish history has to visit. Mention Culloden to any Scot and you will always elicit a response, which can range from a recollection of something they have heard about at school to a fiery burn in the eyes that will make you feel like the battle only mangled the Highlands and its traditional way of life yesterday.

The bleak moor occupies a sacred, painful place in Scottish history. It was here, in 1746, that the Jacobite rebels supporting Bonnie Prince Charlie met with the Duke of Cumberland's government army. After only an hour of fierce fighting, thousands of

---

Moray Firth Dolphins

The large bottlenose dolphins that can often be seen flinging themselves out of the Moray Firth—the body of water connecting Inverness with the North Sea—or messing around in the wake of boats, are part of the most northerly pod in the world. They can occasionally be spotted from the shore, along with harbor porpoises and minke whales, but for a close look, you'll need to head out on to the water as part of an organized boat trip. Try **Inverness Dolphin Cruises** (*Shore Street Quay, tel 01463/717 900, www.inverness-dolphin-cruises.co.uk*).

Highlanders lay dead on the boggy ground and the Jacobite rebellions (see p. 42) were crushed once and for all. In the aftermath of the battle the Duke of Cumberland's men marched north through the Highlands, destroying communities and killing thousands, effectively ending the traditional Highland way of life.

For a long time, the battlefield was marked by little more than a small cairn and the musket balls and rusted weapons that were occasionally recovered from the ground. Recently, however, a state-of-the-art **visitor center** has been opened on the moor. It tries to recount the events from both the Jacobite and the government points of view, using historical accounts and archaeological evidence before a "battle immersion" room vividly brings the horrific fighting to life. Pick up the self-guided audio tour as you leave the museum, which really helps you get more from your walk around the battle lines. ■

Eden Court Theatre

✉ Bishops Road
☎ (01463) 234 234
💲 $–$$$$$$

www.eden-court
.co.uk

Culloden Moor

✉ About 4 miles (6.5 km) E of Inverness on the B9006 (Culloden Moor)
☎ (0844) 493 2159
🕐 Visitor center closed Jan.
💲 $$$$

www.nts.org.uk/
culloden

Aviemore & the Cairngorms

Some 30 miles (45 km) southwest from Inverness, perched on the edge of the mighty Cairngorms—and almost a thousand feet up!—is the Scottish ski resort of Aviemore. With long,
snow-filled winters not always guaranteed, this Highland gateway has done much to diversify
its appeal. The slopes and ski lifts are ready for when Scotland gets a decent dump of snow, but
there's now much more, including a golf course, mountain-bike tracks, and a health spa.

The Cairngorms provide skiers with readily accessible slopes—but snow is unpredictable.

Aviemore

⚠ 173 C2

Visitor Information

✉ Unit 7, Grampian
Rd., Aviemore

☎ (0845) 225 121

**www.visithighlands
.com**

**Cairngorm
Mountain
Funicular**

✉ Aviemore

☎ (01479) 861 261

🕒 Closed 10 days
in Nov.

💲 $$$

**www.cairngorm
mountain.co.uk**

Aviemore

Aviemore is clearly serious about
its redevelopment and reposi-
tioning. The recently formed
Aviemore and Cairngorms Desti-
nation Management Organisa-
tion (ACDMO) has set the goal
of transforming Aviemore into
Scotland's very own version of
the Canadian resort of Whistler.
The opening of the Cairngorms
National Park, the United
Kingdom's largest, has also
greatly helped the area, both in
terms of its conservation efforts
and also in its drive to promote
sustainable tourism.

A good way to get a feel for
Aviemore and its surrounds is

on the **Cairngorm Mountain
Funicular,** which spirits you up to
Munro height. There's a café and
restaurant at the top where you
can relax while watching walkers
trudge past on their way to and
from the lofty peaks all around. In
winter the railway is jammed with
skiers and snowboarders coming
up to hit the slopes.

In the center of town,
Aviemore's **Victorian railway sta-
tion** *(Dalfaber Road)* is a charming
old gem; timber-built and redolent
of a bygone era when trains were
not just a way of getting from
A to B. The **Strathspey Steam
Railway** is a wonderful throwback
to the great days of steam travel

and offers some stunning views of the Cairngorms National Park as it rattles off on a route from Aviemore through Boat of Garten to Broomhill. You can travel third class, or treat yourself to first.

Aviemore's **Spey Valley Golf Course,** just to the north of the town, is one of Scotland's most exciting new golf facilities. It is a tough course, laden with thick heather and tight fairways, but, even if your shots are going awry, you can still enjoy views of the famous River Spey and the surrounding hills and mountains. Some of the walks between the holes are quite long, so hiring

a golf cart is a good idea. The course looks set to become one of Scotland's most famous, so book a round on it while you can.

Keen mountain bikers can head farther south to Laggan where awaits the **Wolftrax** mountain bike course *(tel 01463/791 575, www.forestry.gov.uk/wolftrax).* One of the best courses in the United Kingdom, it offers a comprehensive range of blue, red, and black downhills. The reds provide a particularly stern test with scary rock drop-offs and tight single tracks winding through the forests. An easier option is the "wilderness trail,"

(continued on p. 182)

Strathspey Steam Railway

- ✉ Aviemore Station, Dalfaber Road
- ☎ (01479) 810 725
- 💲 $$$
- 🕐 Closed Nov.–March

www.strathspey railway.net

Spey Valley Golf Course

- ✉ Aviemore
- ☎ (0844) 879 9152

www.macdonald hotels.co.uk

EXPERIENCE: Enjoying Winter Sports

Every year thousands of Brits jet off on expensive trips to Europe and farther afield in search of winter sports adventures, even though world-class winter sports are available right here in Scotland. The resorts may not be as glitzy, nor the operations as slick, as the jet-set retreats in the European Alps, but if you are here in winter and love the outdoors, there are a wealth of activities, which really open up the landscape in a way a car journey or bus tour never could.

Perhaps Scotland's most famous winter sport is curling. This Olympic discipline (Scotland has produced Olympic champions numerous times in both the women's and men's events) takes place on an ice rink. The 40-pound (18 kg) granite stones, used by competitors from all over the world, come from just one place—the dramatic rock stack of Ailsa Craig on Scotland's west coast. The four-person team event is highly tactical. One member of the team slides or "curls" the stone along the ice, while the other three use

brushes to speed it up, slow it down, or change its direction. You'll find the game being played throughout Scotland at ice rinks, and occasionally outside during particularly severe winters. Contact the **Royal Caledonian Curling Club** (*tel 0131/333 3003, www.royalcaledoniancurlingclub.org*) for details of curling venues. One of its most famous outdoor events is the **Grand Match,** which is played very infrequently (increasingly warm winters mean it has not been held since 1979) on the Lake of Mentieth (see p. 130).

More conventional winter sports on offer include skiing and snowboarding at Scotland's five ski centers (see p. 313). The snow can be unreliable, but on a good day the skiing is excellent, even if most of the runs are of a beginner or intermediate level. If you don't feel like doing all the hard work yourself, you can always go dog sledding at the **Cairngorm Dog Sledding Centre** (*Moormore Cottage, Rothiemurchus Estate, Aviemore, tel 07767/270 526, www .sled-dogs.co.uk*).

A Cairngorm Walk: Cairn Gorm & Ben Macdui

Until the start of the 20th century, many people thought that Ben Macdui, and not Ben Nevis, was Scotland's highest peak. It's certainly a huge mountain, a 4,296-foot (1,309 m) monster at the heart of the massively wild Cairngorms. Ben Macdui sits on a mountain plateau that provides an unforgiving but truly breathtaking escape from the pressures of the modern world.

Hiking in the Cairngorms near Aviemore

In the spring and summer Aviemore makes a good base for tackling Ben Macdui. The Cairngorm Plateau is not recommended for inexperienced hikers, and it is best avoided altogether in winter unless on an official guided trip. You'll need to be prepared with proper outdoor clothing, plenty of food and drink, a map and compass, and someone in the party who knows how to use both.

Start at the **parking lot 1** at the Cairngorm ski center, where the temptation is to set off to tackle the steep scree-strewn corries (bowl-shaped gullies) that protect the plateau. Don't be tempted—instead follow the much safer and easier-to-follow path that curls off to the southwest.

NOT TO BE MISSED:

Miadan Creag an Leth-Choin • Lochan Buidhe • Ben Macdui • Cairn Gorm

---

Walking far below the mighty rock monsters of the Cairngorms is a humbling and challenging experience. At least you won't have to tackle the mountain burns, as the path has **stepping stones 2** to ford the waterways draining Coire an t-Sneachda and—farther along the walk—Coire an Lochan. Coire an t-Sneachda itself is a stunning place with imposing rock walls.

The long, chunky ridge of **Miadan Creag an Leth-Choin 3** is your access point onto the plateau. Be patient and steady with your movements now, and your thighs and calves will thank you later. Gaze east right down the throat of **Coire an Lochan** to its chill waters, if the clouds part long enough.

The rich forests around Aviemore are now replaced with testing bog. Watch for wild ptarmigans—snow-white in winter and equally well camouflaged in their brown plumage in summer. As you edge deeper across the plateau, conditions become ever harsher with the only sign of life coming in the form of little shrubs on the approach to **Lochan Buidhe.** The summit of **Ben Macdui 4** (4,296 feet/1,309 m) is a rubble of stones with a simple stone shelter where you can enjoy your lunch out of the gales that sweep in with little or no notice.

Retrace your steps back down to **Lochan Buidhe 5**. You can follow the same route back, but a more interesting choice is to cut northeast from the lochan toward Cairn Gorm itself. Avoid getting too close to the sheer edge of the plateau, however, always a risk in poor visibility. The views from the summit of **Cairn Gorm ❻** (4,081 feet/1,244 m) are even more impressive than Ben Macdui. If the **funicular,** just below the summit, is open, you can take the quick way down *($$)*. Alternatively, the ski-slope-scarred **Corrie Cas ❼** awaits, or the longer, more scenic **Fiacaill a Choire Chais.**

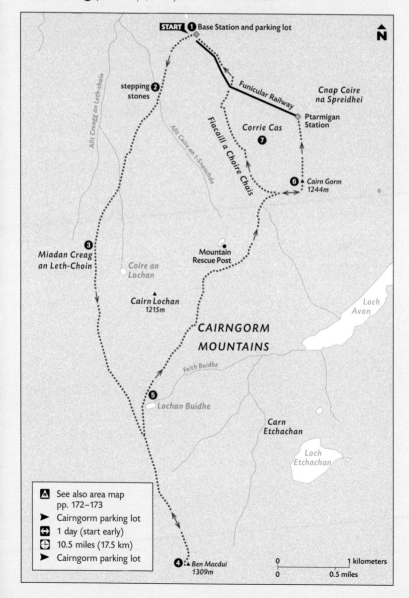

START ❶ Base Station and parking lot

stepping ❷ stones

Allt Creagg an Leth-choin

Allt Coire an t-Sneachda

Fiacaill a Choire Chais

Funicular Railway

Corrie Cas ❼

Cnap Coire na Spreidhei

Ptarmigan Station

❸ Miadan Creag an Leth-Choin

❻ ▲ Cairn Gorm 1244m

Coire an Lochan

Mountain Rescue Post

▲ Cairn Lochan 1215m

CAIRNGORM MOUNTAINS

Loch Avon

Feith Buidhe

❺ Lochan Buidhe

Carn Etchachan

Loch Etchachan

◮ See also area map pp. 172–173
► Cairngorm parking lot
↔ 1 day (start early)
⊞ 10.5 miles (17.5 km)
► Cairngorm parking lot

❹ ▲ Ben Macdui 1309m

0   1 kilometers
0   0.5 miles

Ospreys at Abernethy

In the 1950s the graceful osprey (or fish hawk, as it is also known) was thought extinct in Britain. Then a pair popped up out of nowhere at Loch Garten, just north of Aviemore. Conservationists jumped at this incredible opportunity and set up the **Abernethy Forest RSPB Reserve** (*Aviemore, tel 01479/831 476, www.rspb .org.uk*), which now covers the loch and its attractively forested surrounds. Their efforts have borne fruit, and there are now more than a hundred pairs of ospreys thought to be nesting throughout Scotland. The best time to see them is from April to late August. A visitor center opens during this period, offering telescopes and guided walks to help you make the most of the experience.

BaseCamp Mountain Bikes

- ✉ Laggan Wolftrax, Strathmashie Forest, Laggan
- ☎ (01528) 544 786
- 💲 $$$$
- 🕐 Closed Wed.

www.basecampmtb .com

Loch Insh Watersports and Outdoor Activity Centre

- ✉ Kincraig
- ☎ (01549) 651 272

www.lochinsh.com

Rothiemurchus Estate

- 🗺 173 C2
- ✉ Off the B970 near Aviemore
- ☎ (01479) 812 345
- 💲 $

www.rothiemurchus .net

Hermitage Guest House

- ✉ Spey Street, Kingussie
- ☎ (01540) 662 137
- 💲 $$

www.thehermitage .clara.net

which follows old drovers' roads deep into wild country. Suitable bikes can be hired on-site from **BaseCamp Mountain Bikes,** which also serves as an information center for the trails.

If you don't mind getting wet, head to lovely **Loch Insh,** a 1-mile by 1.5-mile (1.6 km by 2.5 km) stretch of fresh water hemmed in by hills and heather just south of Aviemore, where ospreys roam wild. It is home to the family-run **Loch Insh Watersports and Outdoor Activity Centre,** which supplies canoes (both open and kayaks), sailing dinghies, and mountain bikes. The center is ideal for families as they offer tuition to all ages.

You can paddle down the River Spey all the way from Loch Insh to Aviemore, a lovely adventure that really opens up the beauty of the region and affords some stunning views of the Cairngorms.

Rothiemurchus Estate

The 24,000-acre (9,710 ha) Rothiemurchus Estate is set right on the edge of the remarkable Cairngorms mountain massif, just outside the town of Aviemore.

INSIDER TIP:

Never treat walking in Scotland's hills and mountains lightly or it may be the last thing you do.

—LARRY PORGES
National Geographic editor

Rothiemurchus is one of the best places in Scotland to enjoy indigenous Caledonian woodland, with swaths of Scots pine, birch, and juniper trees draped around a brace of lochs. Wildlife abounds on the route—watch for everything from red squirrels and crossbills to capercaillies (grouse) and pine martens.

The main parking lot has an **information center** with bikes available for rent. If you are short on time, a bike is the best way of getting around the estate. Even if you have a couple of days, it's a good idea to cycle one day, and then walk back to the areas you like best the next. You can also take a pony-trekking ride, which is great fun for older children.

Perhaps the prettiest part of

the estate is **Loch an Eilein.** The "loch of the island" is named for the small islet that nestles in the middle of the silvery blue water, which is topped by a photogenic abandoned castle.

A busier and more fun stretch of water is **Loch Morlich** on the edge of the estate. A popular watersports center borders the loch, which, on a clear day, boasts stunning views of the Cairngorms. Next to the center are a beach and a campsite.

If you prefer what comes out of the water, rather than messing about on it, fishing is also a popular activity on the estate. There are many options, from idly angling for rainbow and brown trout in the lochs to the more adrenaline pumping challenge of catching a wild salmon on the **River Spey.**

Once you've finished sampling the estate's numerous attractions, you can retire to its café-restaurant, which utilizes fresh produce from the estate. You can also stock up on all manner of goodies at their farm shop, including their excellent Highland cattle beef steaks.

Kingussie & Newtonmore

Those in search of a more authentic and relaxed location from which to explore the Cairngorms should head farther south, beyond Aviemore and Rothiemurchus and into the upper reaches of the Spey valley. Here the attractive villages of Kingussie and Newtonmore provide a warm and welcoming atmosphere, largely untouched by the modern

development that dominates Aviemore. Visitors can stay in one of the villages' several excellent family-run guest houses, including the **Hermitage Guest House** in Kingussie, the **Coig na Shee Guest House** in Newtonmore, and **Ruthven Steadings—**located on the opposite bank of the River Spey from Kingussie.

Mountain biking along the banks of Loch an Eilein on Rothiemurchus Estate

These villages are not just great places to stay. The **Highland Folk Museum—**which is divided between sites in Newtonmore and Kingussie—is well worth a visit. Exhibits include a traditional farmhouse, a working waterwheel-powered sawmill, and demonstrations of traditional highland crafts. Looming high above the villages on a hill south of the river is the imposing ruin of **Ruthven Barracks** (on the B970 1 mile/1.6 km S of Kingussie), one of the few remaining examples of the military posts established by the English to subdue the rebellious

Coig na Shee Guest House

✉ Fort William Road, Newtonmore

☎ (01540) 670 109

💲 $$

www.coignashee .co.uk

Ruthven Steadings

✉ Ruthven, Kingussie

☎ (01540) 662 328

💲 $$

www.bedandbreak fastcairngorms.co.uk

Highland Folk Museum

✉ Duke Street, Kingussie and Aultlarie Croft, Kingussie Road, Newtonmore

☎ (01540) 661 307

www.highlandfolk .com

A Grantown bar advertises its wide selection of single malts.

Speyside Way Centre

✉ Old Station Building, Aberlour

☎ (01340) 881 266

$ $

www.speysideway.org

Grantown-on-Spey

◢ 173 D2

Visitor Information

✉ 54 High St.

☎ (01479) 872 773

Walkers Shortbread

✉ Aberlour House, Aberlour

☎ (01340) 871 555

🕐 Closed Sat.–Sun.

www.walkersshortbread.com

Highlanders and suppress their culture after the 1715 uprising.

Speyside

The highest concentration of whisky distilleries in Scotland can be found in Speyside, where the cool, clear waters of the salmon-rich River Spey help conjure up first-rate whiskies at more than 50 distilleries. This scenic region is ideal for touring by car, bike, or even on foot.

There's a particularly appealing route from Aviemore to Speyside on the A95 that passes through graceful **Grantown-on-Spey.** Grand Georgian buildings abound in this relaxed town where you can enjoy a stroll down by the Spey, or explore the busy main street with its cafés and bars. In August the big event is the Grantown-on-Spey Highland Games. Pushing farther northeast, the A95 follows the Spey on its journey to the sea. Numerous distilleries line its banks forming part of the official **"Malt Whisky Trail"** (www.maltwhiskytrail

.com), which covers 70 miles (112 km) and no fewer than nine of the most visitor-friendly distilleries.

One of the trail's most appealing whisky towns is **Charlestown of Aberlour.** Home of Aberlour whisky, Aberlour, as it is more commonly called, is also the birthplace of the world-famous **Walkers Shortbread.** First produced in town in 1898 by Joseph Walker, this delicious treat can be picked up in the factory store. The stately main street is replete with solid granite buildings, and a relaxed park reclines down by the banks of the River Spey.

A railway once ran through Aberlour, and the old station building now houses an information center dedicated to the **Speyside Way,** a hiking trail that runs by the station. This 65-mile (105 km) trail is a great way of exploring whisky country if you can spare the time.

Just a couple of miles along the Speyside Way to the east is **Craigellachie,** a lovely little village that is, of course, home to its own distillery. It also boasts what may just be the nation's finest whisky bar, at the landmark Craigellachie Hotel (*Victoria Street, tel 01340/881 204, www.oxfordhotelsandinns.com*). The **Quaich Bar** (see Travelwise p. 294) is laden floor to ceiling with whiskies of all kinds—a dram from one of the rarest bottles could set you back over $400! Half the fun here is browsing the massive whisky list and chatting to the knowledgeable bar staff.

The village's other attraction is the cast-iron **Craigellachie Bridge,** built by the renowned

INSIDER TIP:

Perhaps the most classic looking distillery in Scotland is Strathisla, with pot stills a couple of centuries old tucked snug into the old wooden stillhouse. The tour is extremely well done.

—JIM RICHARDSON
National Geographic photographer

Scottish engineer Thomas Telford in the early 19th century.

Another 5 miles (7.5 km) south over rugged mountain scenery brings you to **Dufftown,** the self-styled "world capital of whisky." On the way you may want to pop into the **Speyside Cooperage,** which offers intriguing insight into a key part of the industry—the making of the famous barrels. A local saying proudly proclaims, "Rome was built on seven hills, Dufftown stands on seven stills," and this imposing granite-clad town really does seem to almost burst at the

seams with whisky distilleries.

Visiting at least one distillery is practically obligatory in Speyside. Many offer excellent visitor facilities. **Strathisla** *(Seafield Ave., Keith, tel 01542/783 044, www .maltwhiskydistilleries.com, Tour: $)* in nearby Keith is one of the best. In summer a vintage train runs along the **Keith and Dufftown Railway** across the countryside from Dufftown to Keith, a fun way of arriving. Having first opened in 1786, Strathisla claims to be the oldest distillery in the Highlands, and produces many of the whiskies that are used to make the famous blended brand of Chivas Regal.

On the tour, the guide provides a wealth of information peppered with more than a few tall tales. You'll also get the chance to try both the Chivas Regal 12-year-old and the more refined 18-year-old served, of course, with just a splash of water and no ice. At the end of the tour there is the chance to buy a bottle or two in their shop. They will even personalize the label, making it an ideal present or a unique souvenir. ■

Dufftown

🗺 173 D2

Visitor Information

✉ Dufftown Visitor Information Centre, 2 The Square, Dufftown

☎ (01340) 820 501

🕐 Closed Nov.–Easter

Speyside Cooperage

✉ Dufftown Road, Craigellachie, Dufftown

☎ (01340) 871 108

💲 $

🕐 Closed Sat.–Sun.

www.speyside cooperage.co.uk

Keith & Dufftown Railway

✉ Dufftown Station, Dufftown

☎ (01340) 821 181

🕐 Closed Mon.–Thurs., & Jan.–March

💲 $$$

www.keith -dufftown- railway.co.uk

EXPERIENCE: Shinty in Kingussie

High in the Spey valley, away from the distillery tours and ski slopes, it is still possible to catch a glimpse of a Highland tradition that has changed little since the days when it was known as the "perfect exercise for a warrior people." Shinty—a game that resembles a faster moving, rougher version of field hockey—is still played in Newtonmore and Kingussie, whose respective teams dominate the Highland leagues. You can watch matches in either town during the summer, but the highlight of the season comes when the rival towns play each other and both towns turn out to cheer on their side. To find out when the teams are playing, and soak up the atmosphere with partisan onlookers, check www.shinty.com.

The Great Glen

The Great Glen is the mighty geological fault line that cuts around 60 miles (97 km) southwest from the North Sea down to the Atlantic Ocean in a swath of rugged mountains and scenic lochs, connecting two of the Highlands' biggest tourist hubs, Inverness and Fort William.

Urquhart Castle stands high above the famous Loch Ness.

Caledonian Canal

📖 172 C2

Le Boat Laggan

✉ Laggan Locks
☎ (01809) 501 234
🕐 Closed Sun.
💲 $$$$$

www.leboat.co.uk

Caledonian Canal

Four lochs stretch between the North Sea and the Atlantic—Ness, Oich, Lochy, and Linnhe—and these are in turn connected by the **Caledonian Canal,** one of the most remarkable canal systems in the world. Sailing is the best way to really appreciate the canal's grandeur. You can hire boats in Laggan through **Le Boat Laggan.** A week will give you enough time to traverse the entirety of the canal in both directions. The **Great Glen Way** (*tel 01320/366 633, www*

.greatglenway.com) takes walkers on a 73-mile (117 km) route alongside the canal. It is also popular with cyclists, though in the peak season some of the traffic-clogged roads can be off-putting.

Another great way to see the area is by canoe. Although facilities are currently fairly limited, the **Great Glen Canoe Trail** (*Scottish Canoe Assoc., www.canoescotland .org*)—due to be completed in 2012—will provide a network of free campgrounds and canoe-friendly docks along the length of the Caledonian Canal.

The history of the Caledonian Canal dates back to the early 19th century. Striking a waterway from coast to coast was seen as a way of opening up the Highlands, as well as cutting out the arduous sea voyage up around the treacherous northern reaches of Scotland.

Legendary Scot Thomas Telford was the brains behind the plan to link the North Sea at Inverness with the Atlantic at Fort William via a series of canals and locks that would connect the Great Glen's quartet of freshwater lochs. The sheer scale of the engineering involved is staggering. Twenty-nine locks help boats climb from sea level to over 100 feet (30 m) before descending again to sea level.

Loch Ness

The most dramatic section of the canal is Loch Ness. The tourist town of **Fort Augustus** at the southern end of the loch is a relaxed place with a flurry of bars, cafés, and restaurants lining the banks of the canal. There is little to do bar idling by the canal, strolling down to Loch Ness, looking at the beautiful exterior of **Fort Augustus Abbey** (now transformed into luxury holiday apartments and not open to the public), or setting off for a walk in the surrounding hills.

There are many boat tour operators in town, but **Cruise Loch Ness** in Fort Augustus offers one of the best tours. It not only opens up the superb scenery of Scotland's longest inland loch, but

also caters to the monster-spotting set, providing live underwater 3-D imaging as you go, which gives you the chance to search for the submarine lair of the world's most famous monster, Nessie. Loch Ness unfurls for 23 miles (37 km). If you spend long enough scanning every corner of a loch that ripples with large waves and dark shadows, you might start seeing mysterious creatures too.

Castle Urquhart lies just east along Loch Ness from Fort Augustus. A fun way to get here is via the boat tours from Inverness or Fort Augustus, which allow time ashore. This romantic ruin is very much the stereotypical Scottish castle, a ramble of 13th-century

---

In Search of a Legend

Thousands of tourists flock to the banks of Loch Ness (surely the most famous loch in the world) every year hoping to catch a glimpse of Nessie (surely the most famous monster in the world) and snap the unique photo that will make their fortune. Cynics suggest there is no monster at all and it is all a tourist gimmick, but searching for the monster is still a lot of fun. And, even without any mysterious creature, the loch itself is stunning. It's at its most impressive at Castle Urquhart, where the ruined castle watches over the chill waters.

Fort Augustus
🗺 172 B2

Visitor Information
✉ Tourist Information Centre, Fort Augustus Car Park, Fort Augustus
☎ (01320) 366 367
www.fortaugustus .org

Fort Augustus Abbey
✉ St. Benedicts Abbey, Fort Augustus

Cruise Loch Ness
✉ Fort Augustus
☎ (01320) 366 277
🕐 Closed Oct.–March
💲 $$$
www.cruiselochness .com

Castle Urquhart
✉ On the north bank of Loch Ness, on the A82 road from Inverness
☎ (01456) 450 551
💲 $$
www.historic -scotland.gov.uk

BOAT TOURS TO CASTLE URQUHART: Jacobite *(Tomnahurich Bridge, Glenurquhart Rd., tel 01463/233 999, www.jacobite. co.uk)* offers tours from Inverness; and Cruise Loch Ness (see above) offers tours from Fort Augustus.

**Original Loch
Ness Monster
Visitor Centre**

✉ The Village
Centre,
Drumnadrochit

☎ (01456) 450 342

💲 $$

www.lochness
-centre.com

**Loch Ness
Exhibition
Centre**

✉ Loch Ness
Centre,
Drumnadrochit

☎ (01456) 450 573

💲 $$

www.lochness.com

**Glen Nevis
Visitor Centre**

✉ Nevis Bridge,
Fort William

☎ (01397) 705 922

💲 $

www.highland
.gov.uk

**Sierra Club
Visitor Centre**

www.sierraclub.org/
outings/national/
brochure/10618A
.asp

stonework tumbling down the hillside toward the shimmering loch amid a welter of history and myths. It looks its best when floodlit at night, when you almost expect to see Robert the Bruce patrolling the ramparts.

The nearest settlement to the castle is **Drumnadrochit.** Bizarrely there are two competing operations here claiming to be the "official" Nessie visitor center: the **Original Loch Ness Monster Visitor Centre** and the slightly slicker **Loch Ness Exhibition Centre.** They might be a little tacky for some, although Nessie fans will be in tall-tale heaven.

Ben Nevis & the Nevis Range

At 4,406 feet (1,344 m), Ben Nevis is the highest mountain in the British Isles. Known to many Scots simply as "The Ben," this colossal rock giant can be seen from hundreds of other mountain peaks across the nation. It forms the heart of the Nevis Range, a chunky hulk of mountains that have together become one of the United Kingdom's top adventure sports destinations in recent years.

If you were to take a hike up Ben Nevis, you would be tackling the mountain from sea level and would no doubt feel every one of those 4,406 feet (1,344 m) on the ascent. Never treat Ben Nevis lightly, no matter how sunny and warm a day it is at the base in Fort William (see pp. 190–191). Snow can linger on through the summer around the summit, and visibility can drop to zero in

minutes, suddenly turning a nice summer's day out into a life and death struggle to navigate yourself around the lethal gullies to safety. More people die on Ben Nevis every year than on Mount Everest, so beware. If you are in any doubt before you head off, check the conditions at the **Glen Nevis Visitor Centre** in Fort William, where the most popular route starts, or just content yourself with enjoying the views from down below.

INSIDER TIP:

The Sierra Club offers outings retracing young John Muir's meanderings from his birthplace near Edinburgh, through the Highlands, and to the top of Ben Nevis.

—BOB SIPCHEN
National Geographic Traveler
magazine writer

Having said that, if you are properly equipped and fit, you should be able to make it up and down with few problems—more than 100,000 people a year do, although it is a tough slog taking between five and seven hours. More experienced climbers, and particularly those who have no fear of heights, can tackle the alternative descent following the knife-edge ridge of Càrn Mòr Dearg Arête and coming back down to Torlundy.

The Nevis Range breaks east of Ben Nevis and has been really opened up in recent years by a gondola system that whisks anyone who doesn't fancy the 2,000-foot-plus (600 m) hike up from its base in Torlundy to the **Mountain Discovery Centre** on Aonach Mhor. The center has exhibits examining how this rugged land was formed, and you can also garner lots of information about local activities.

Summer & Winter Activities:

Walking is the most popular activity on Aonach Mhor, a stone's throw from Ben Nevis, during the summer. You can go for an easy—but still high level—hike or use the gondola to save energy and time before pushing on to the range's mighty peaks. The easier walks are signposted from the Mountain Discovery Centre.

In the summer the steep and rocky trails that wind down the mountainside make the Nevis Range one of the best mountain-biking venues in Europe. Many trails are not for beginners, but inexperienced riders can hire an instructor from the Mountain Discovery Center to teach them how to handle the terrain. The center also houses **Offbeat Bikes,** where you can rent a bike. Visit *www.ridefortwilliam.co.uk* for more information on biking in the area.

Every year thousands come to watch the world's finest riders tackle the famous **Off Beat Downhill** course—a death-defying hurl down the mountain that sees riders descend 1,800 feet (555 m) in about 5 minutes. Note that during competitions, some trails are closed to the public.

The Nevis Range is not just about serious biking. A variety of longer, and much less steep, trails snake off all around. These gentler forest routes are known as the "Witches' Trails." When the snow batters down, only serious climbers with crampons and ice axes take on the mountains, but the gondola is still busy with skiers and snowboarders, who flock to enjoy the runs at Scotland's highest ski center. When the skiing season has finished elsewhere in Scotland, conditions are still good in the Nevis Range. ■

The snowcapped summit of Ben Nevis looms over the landscape of Loch Linnhe.

Mountain Discovery Centre & Gondola

✉ Nevis Range, Torlundy, Aonach Mhor
☎ (01397) 705 825
💲 Gondola: $$$

www.nevisrange.co.uk

Offbeat Bikes

✉ Nevis Range, Torlundy
☎ (01397) 705 825
🕐 Open mid-May–mid-Sept.
💲 Bike rental: $$$$

www.nevisrange.co.uk

The West

The western portion of the Highlands is a deeply romantic and wildly beautiful oasis laden with history. This is where Bonnie Prince Charlie both raised his standard and fled Scotland forever. It is also a corner that boasts some of the country's finest white-sand beaches, some of its prettiest glens, and a plethora of outdoor activities at all times of year.

Fort William is a popular base for exploring the Nevis Range.

Fort William

 172 B1

Visitor Information

 Fort William
Information
Centre, 15 High
Street, Fort
William

☎ (08452) 255 121

**www.visitfort
william.co.uk**

Fort William

One of largest settlements in the area, Fort William is an oft-derided transport hub blighted with some ill-conceived architecture, a busy two-lane road that dominates its waterfront, and scores of decidedly average places to eat and stay. It does, however, boast handy transport connections, including a direct overnight sleeper train service to London and buses to many points north, south, and east, as well as plenty of tourist facilities, making it a popular base.

In town, Fort William's **High Street** has a swath of tacky tartan

souvenir shops, but it is also a good place to stock up on any outdoor gear needed for a foray up Ben Nevis or out on the Nevis Range. The main sight is the **West Highland Museum.** Its collection delves into the history of the surrounding region and includes the likes of old military medals won by local regiments, preserved wildlife such as golden eagles, and weaponry from through the ages.

The United Kingdom's highest mountain, **Ben Nevis** (see p. 188), looms over Fort William. The long climb from the town to the mountain's base takes you through the idyllic and quintessentially Scottish landscape of **Glen Nevis,** where many scenes from the Hollywood blockbuster *Braveheart* were filmed. Development around Fort William has been kept to a minimum and, reclining in the shadow of "The Ben," the steep forested slopes of Glen Nevis are used for a variety of outdoor activities (see p. 189).

Fort William is also famous as marking the far western end of the mighty **Caledonian Canal** (see pp. 186–187). Just 3 miles (4.5 km) east out of the town, **Neptune's Staircase,** the United Kingdom's largest staircase lock, is the site of the canal's most dramatic set piece. The boats here climb an impressive 64 feet (19 m) from sea level, passing through eight locks. It takes a boat an hour and a half to complete the whole series of locks. You can sit and watch the action, or take a stroll or bike ride along the towpath, while you enjoy the views of Ben Nevis and the Nevis Range.

Sited on the sea loch of Loch Linnhe with a necklace of mountains all around, Fort William's setting could scarcely be more spectacular. A good way to appreciate it in summer is to take one of the boat trips that leave from the pier, where you'll also find the excellent **Crannog Restaurant.** You can enjoy a delicious fresh seafood lunch here before taking to the waters. The trips, run by **Crannog Cruises,** ease along the sea loch, bringing out the best of

West Highland Museum

✉ Cameron Square, Fort William
☎ (01397) 702 169
🕐 Closed Sun., except July–Aug.
💲 $
www.westhighland museum.org.uk

Crannog Restaurant

✉ Town Centre Pier, The Waterfront, Fort William
☎ (01397) 705 589
💲 $
www.crannog.net

EXPERIENCE: Glen Affric

It may only be a short drive from Fort William, but remarkable Glen Affric feels a million miles away from mass tourism and the modern world. A snaking, blood-curdling road takes you into the east end, while on its other three impenetrable flanks is a whole lot of nothing for miles and miles around.

Many Scots consider Glen Affric the finest glen in the land, and it is easy to see why. It is bordered by rugged mountains and split by a loch dotted with picturesque islands. The path that skirts around the shores of the loch is ideal for walkers, while the wider track on the south bank is gaining popularity with adventurous mountain bikers. You may need to ford the burns (if it is safe to do so) to get all the way around. The path itself is surrounded by Scots pines and fringed by swaths of heather, with a treasure trove of the native vegetation that the aftermath of the Highland Clearances destroyed throughout so much of Scotland. Even in summer Glen Affric never overflows with visitors, and in winter you will probably see more stags than people.

One epic hike takes you right along Loch Affric from east to west and then deep into the mountains where you can climb high over the **Five Sisters of Kintail** (see p. 212) before dropping down to finish at the **Shiel Bridge campsite** (*Inverinate, Kyle, 01599/511 221*) on the banks of Loch Duich. A remote youth hostel (*Allt Beithe, Glen Affric, 0845/293 7373, www.syha.org.uk*) makes an ideal base from which to explore the area. More sedentary souls can drive to the eastern fringes of Glen Affric from Cannich and have a picnic to get a little flavor of this unique and wild region.

For more information on the area see *www.glenaffric.org*.

A train steams its way over the Glenfinnan Viaduct, part of the West Highland Line.

Crannog Cruises

✉ Town Pier, Fort William

☎ (01397) 700 714

💲 $$$

www.crannog.net

Jacobite Steam Train

✉ Fort William Railway Station, Station Square, Fort William

☎ (0845) 128 4681

🕐 Closed Nov.–April

💲 $$$$

www.westcoast railways.co.uk

the landscape. You may catch sight of a porpoise or dolphin, and the views are superb of Ben Nevis on one side and the rough terrain of the Ardnamurchan Peninsula on the other.

Fort William's train station used to be the terminus for the West Highland Line from Glasgow and it still welcomes and sends off sleeper trains all the way south to the bright lights of London. The West Highland Line runs on a circuitous route from Glasgow to Mallaig on the west coast, running across mountains and glens at a relaxed pace. From its grand Victorian viaducts and bridges it offers breathtaking views of the Highland landscape and is widely considered the most beautiful railway route in Europe.

In summer, the **Jacobite Steam Train** operates between Fort William and Mallaig on the West Highland Line. The 60-year-old train climbs out of Fort William with a grand puff of steam that takes you right back to the golden age of rail travel. The old-fashioned carriages are part of the attraction and you can wind the windows down to take photographs. This gives you the chance to grab stunning shots of the traverse of the 21-arch **Glenfinnan Viaduct**—though do watch your head!

Glen Coe

Located just a short drive south of Fort William, Glen Coe is one of Scotland's most famous glens. The unassuming village of Glencoe is dwarfed by the huge mountains that rise up toward the glen proper. Descending into the glen from the south is the rural equivalent of walking into St. Peter's Cathedral in the Vatican. Your jaw drops at the sheer scale of it all. It's a

INSIDER TIP:

Take a ride on the Jacobite Steam Train from Fort William to Mallaig. Harry Potter fans: Arrive early to request a seat in the Harry Potter carriage where movie scenes of the Hogwarts Express were filmed.

—JENNIFER SEGAL
National Geographic Development Office

world of deadly crags and killer mountains that appear all but unconquerable. Humans here feel very small indeed.

Glen Coe is extremely popular with both walkers and serious climbers looking to test their skills, and even risk their lives, on its savage peaks and knife-edge ridges. Their hub is the village's legendary **Clachaig Inn** (*Old Village Road, Glen Coe, tel 01855/811 252, www .clachaig.com*), a hearty oasis with its own "boots room" for drying your gear, chunky Scottish food,

and Scots ales on tap. Here all the chatter is of the day's walking adventures and future grand plans. It's a great place to meet other like-minded souls if you are on your own.

A sign at the entrance to the Clachaig Inn harks back to 1692 and the darkest day in the glen's history. It warns "No Hawkers or Campbells." This is a reference to the Campbells, a clan that was then working for the British government, who committed the most horrendous breach of the traditional Highland clan hospitality code imaginable. After having enjoyed a fortnight being fed and watered by the MacDonalds of Glen Coe they—acting on government orders—set upon their hosts as they slept, massacring 38 in cold blood. Another 40 women and children were left to perish in the chill winter snows after their villages had been burned to the ground. The **Glen Coe Visitor Centre** reaches into the darkness of those days and explains how the glen has been shaped since.

Heading back north to Fort William, most people just continue on up the "Road to the

Glen Coe

🔼 172 B1

Visitor Information

✉ Glen Coe Visitor Centre, 1 mile S of Glencoe village off A82

☎ (0844) 493 2222

💲 Exhibition: $$

www.glencoe-nts .org.uk

Bonnie Prince Charlie on the Run

The wildly beautiful western Highlands were the perfect setting for Bonnie Prince Charlie's much romanticized flight from Scotland. He originally landed on the Scottish mainland at Loch Nan Uamh near Arisaig in 1745. After Culloden, with a huge reward on his head, he was saved by the still loyal Highlanders who spirited him from hiding place to hiding place.

After a stint in the Outer Hebrides, and a bizarre boat crossing to the isle of Skye during which he dressed as a woman to evade capture by the English redcoats, the would-be British king left Scotland for the last time from Borrodale. He sailed out through the Sound of Arisaig on a French ship, passing his ghost from a year earlier as he went.

Reenactment of Bonnie Prince Charlie's arrival, Glenfinnan

Road to the Isles

On the "Road to the Isles," which continues from Fort William northwest in search of the sea at Mallaig, **Glenfinnan** is an essential stop. This is the epically beautiful and deeply evocative spot where Bonnie Prince Charlie raised his standard back on August 19, 1745. For much of the day it looked like the prince may have miscalculated, but as the afternoon wore on the skirl of bagpipes over the hills heralded the arrival of more and more soldiers, as the Highland clans rallied in anger for what was to be one last heroic, but ultimately tragic, time.

INSIDER TIP:

Glenfinnan is perhaps my favorite setting for a Highland gathering. Surrounded by mountains, it sits close by the beach where Bonnie Prince Charlie came ashore to rally the Highlanders.

—JIM RICHARDSON
National Geographic photographer

Fittingly, the elevated figure standing atop the **Glenfinnan Monument** that today sits at the heart of all this history is not the prince himself, but just an ordinary Highlander, the kind of man who fought and died for the cause, or perhaps fought, lost, and found his way of life changed forever.

Highland Council Ranger Service

✉ Glen Nevis Visitor Centre, Glen Nevis, Fort William

☎ (01397) 705 922

www.highland.gov.uk

Glenfinnan

🅰 172 A1

Visitor Information

✉ Glenfinnan Monument & Visitor Centre, Glenfinnan, Lochaber

☎ (0844) 493 2221

💲 $

www.nts.org.uk/property/26

Isles," but cast your eyes west across Loch Linnhe and the vision of the **Ardnamurchan Peninsula** soon begins to appear. The most westerly point on the British mainland feels very much like an island and you can catch a ferry over from Corran Ferry, just south of Fort William, or from the Isle of Mull to the south. Ardnamurchan is an impressively wild place. The main population centers of Salen, Kilchoan, Glenborrodale, and Strontian are tiny outposts that function for visitors as little more than bases for setting out on walking or cycling trips. This beautiful oasis of abandoned beaches, ghostly lost villages, and mourning hills has never really recovered from the Highland Clearances (see pp. 206–207). If you find it a bit too wild, try one of the guided walks run by the **Highland Council Ranger Service.** Otherwise, just lose yourself in an area that lies at the heart of what the locals know as the "Rough Bounds."

EXPERIENCE: Exploring Remote Knoydart

This stunning and brutally remote corner of Scotland is one of Europe's last great wildernesses. Even few Scots are lucky enough to ever make it out here. Sandwiched fittingly between what the Gaels called the lochs of Nevis (heaven) and Hourn (hell), this otherworldly retreat has taken on a near-mythic appeal for adventurous Scots.

In many respects this is not a natural wilderness, as most visitors today believe. In fact, it was once home to a thriving crofting and fishing community. Before Culloden, Knoydart was home to more than a thousand clanspeople. Legend has it that Bonnie Prince Charlie sought refuge here after the battle, although there is no proof to back these claims. Whether he did or not, Culloden nonetheless had huge ramifications for the area, with the then thriving local community forced off their land during the Highland Clearances. Today only around a hundred people live in this remote peninsula.

The lonely, isolated settlement of Knoydart

Unless you are keen on the 16-mile (26 km) walk to Knoydart from Kinloch Hourn (staying in a rudimentary shelter on the way) the only way to arrive is on the **Knoydart Ferry** (Harbour Road, Mallaig, tel 01687/462 320, www.knoydart-ferry.co.uk, $$) from the small port of Mallaig, which drops you off by Britain's most remote pub, the **Old Forge** (Inverie, Knoydart, tel 01687/462 267, www.theoldforge.co.uk, $$$), and Knoydart's only hotel-restaurant, the **Pier House** (Inverie, Knoydart, tel 01687/ 462 347, www.thepierhouse knoydart.co.uk).

There are no trains, buses, or planes, and only one tiny and fairly pointless road on the Knoydart Peninsula, which leaves walking the main way of getting around. Knoydart's hiking trails are rewarding with low-level mountain passes for the inexperienced and an impressive trio of Munros (peaks in excess of 3,000 feet/914 m) for more serious adventure types to tackle. Hospitals and friendly mountain rescue services are a long way off in these parts, so take all the usual precautions.

For all the foreboding nature of the history and weather, the Knoydart story has, however, taken on a far more positive note over the last decade. The **Knoydart Foundation** (tel 01687/462 242, www.knoydart-founda tion.com) is a charity that consists of enterprising locals working together.

In 1999 the foundation took over a large area of the peninsula from landowners who previously used it as an exclusive hunting and fishing retreat. They are now trying to develop the economy of the area without decimating the breathtaking landscapes and rich natural resources that attracted people to this peninsula in the first place.

The Lochaline Hotel

✉ Lochaline, Movern

☎ (01967) 421 657

💲 $$

White House

✉ Lochaline, Movern

☎ (01967) 421 777

💲 $$$$

www.thewhitehouse
restaurant.co.uk

Land, Sea & Islands Centre

✉ The Harbour, Arisaig

☎ (01687) 450 263

🕐 Closed winter & Sat. in summer

💲 $

www.road-to-the
-isles.org.uk/centre
.html

Across the road the **Glenfinnan Visitor Centre** depicts the events leading up to the raising of the standard and attempts to conjure up the drama of the day, as well as examining the ensuing events.

To the south of Glenfinnan, away from the well-trodden Road to the Isles, lies the mountainous and empty **Morvern Peninsula.** This area is deserted even by the standards of the Rough Bounds—only around 300 people living in an area the size of Washington, D.C. While the interior of Morvern is bleak, the villages along the Sound of Mull are worth a visit. The largest of the coastal villages, **Lochaline,** has a friendly hotel, an excellent diving center (see sidebar opposite), and the **White House,** one of the finest seafood restaurants

in the United Kingdom.

Beyond Glenfinnan the tarmac and railway Road to the Isles now finally lives up to its billing. Heading north, you catch fleeting glimpses of the Atlantic Ocean before some of Scotland's prettiest beaches appear—white strips of sand set against translucent waters that gaze out dreamily over the Hebrides. **Arisaig** is a trim little village on the water. The beaches aside, there is little to visit here bar the **Land, Sea, and Islands Centre.** This modest but fun museum has displays on the various movies that have been filmed locally, including the Hollywood hit *Local Hero.* It was created largely thanks to the efforts of the local community, whose paintings and artifacts have been on display here in the

Fishing boats crowd the harbor at the west coast port of Mallaig.

old smiddy since 1999. Boat tours are also available from Arisaig in summer, which will take you to see a local seal colony or out to the surrounding islands.

A necklace of white-sand beaches stretches north for some 8 miles (12 km) to the quiet village of **Morar,** which hit the headlines when the beach scenes from *Local Hero* were filmed here. There are campsites right by the sand for adventurous travelers, or hotels and bed and breakfasts available in Arisaig and Morar for those who prefer their comforts.

Inland from Morar is an often ignored loch that many Scots rate as one of the country's prettiest. **Loch Morar** is Scotland's deepest inland loch (indeed, it is the United Kingdom's deepest stretch of fresh water) with parts of it delving down to a chilly 1,017 feet (310 m). This perhaps explains why it is also home to its own monster legend. Morag is said to be Nessie's "sister," but pleasingly here there are no cheesy tours or over-the-top visitor centers, so you'll just have to leave it all up to your imagination—unless, of course, you see her. You can rent a boat, but most people who do so are trying to catch much smaller prey with their rods. Maybe take your camera just in case! Scotland's shortest river, the River Morar, gushes from the loch back out to Morar, and there's a quintet of islands sprinkled around the expansive loch.

The West Highland Railway line and the tarmac Road to the Isles both come to an abrupt halt at **Mallaig,** from where there are views of the isle of Skye (see pp. 232–237). This slightly rough-around-the-edges fishing port is also the departure point for ferries out to the isles. The waterfront is a great place to sit with fish and chips (from one of the town's excellent "chippies") as you watch the busy fishing fleet. Seagulls will be squawking overhead as you look for nosy seals, who like to keep an eye on what you are doing in a part of Scotland where the divisions between man and nature are as thin as anywhere in the country. ■

EXPERIENCE:
Diving in the Sound of Mull

Lochaline's **Dive Centre** (*Lochaline, Morvern, tel 01967 / 421 627, www.lochaline divecentre.co.uk*) is the perfect base from which to explore the mysterious wrecks hidden in the cold, clear waters of the Sound of Mull. Those new to diving can take an introductory course with the center's capable instructors, while experienced divers can charter one of the center's fully equipped dive ships. The exceptionally clear waters around Lochaline are home to a fascinating and diverse range of underwater landscapes and aquatic wildlife, including dolphins and porpoises in the summer. In addition to the natural sights, the Sound of Mull, with its treacherous rocks and fierce winter storms, has more than its share of shipwrecks. The owners of the center, Mark and Annabel Lawrence, are permitted to take groups to protected historic sites, including the cannon-strewn wrecks of the 17th-century warships *Swan* and *Dartmouth*.

Arisaig Boat Tours
✉ The Harbour, Arisaig
☎ (01687) 450 224
$ $$–$$$$
www.arisaig.co.uk

Mallaig
△ 172 A2
Visitor Information
✉ Mallaig Heritage Centre, 15 High St., Fort William
⏱ Closed Nov.–Easter
www.mallaig heritage.org/uk

Dramatic snowcapped peaks, sweeping white-sand beaches, shimmering lochs, and charming centuries-old villages

Northern Highlands

A tumbling burn (stream) just north of Ullapool

Northern Highlands

Many Scots never explore the northern reaches of their country, so it is perhaps unsurprising that comparatively few travelers make it here either. Those who do are rewarded with a magnificent and varied natural landscape, rising from the rolling hills and sea cliffs of the east to the wild and barren mountains of the west.

A land where the people were brutally evicted to make way for sheep farming during the Highland Clearances, Scotland's far north can sometimes seem a quiet and

Good fishing for mackerel and pollack can be had from sea lochs around Guinard Bay.

lonely place. The region's most populated town, Ullapool, and settlements such as Gairloch and postcard-perfect Plockton bring a welcome touch of humanity. They also boast plenty of places to eat and drink, with top-notch seafood often the order of the day.

One of the most accessible parts of the Northern Highlands, the Black Isle Peninsula has a rich Pictish history, as well as a wealth of natural and man-made attractions that can easily be reached from the Highland capital, Inverness.

In the north, the attractive coastal town of Dornoch, with its beautiful beach and grand architecture, is a popular stop, as is John O'Groats, in Scotland's far northeast corner. Considered the most northerly settlement of mainland Great Britain, it marks the start/end point of the United Kingdom's longest trek, the mighty 874-mile (1,407 km) route to Land's End in southwest England.

The Great Outdoors

Nature and the outdoors are the main draw for most visitors to these parts. There are a myriad of opportunities for outdoor activities, ranging from bird-watching and walking along near-deserted beaches to gorge-scrambling and riding the waves at some of the globe's top surfing spots.

There are also plenty of mountains to explore, including the iconic Suilven and Stac Pollaidh on the northwest coast. The vaulting Torridon Mountains, also in the west, are one of Scotland's great wilderness playgrounds. Here visitors can ascend

NOT TO BE MISSED:

Dornoch's elegant Edwardian buildings, cathedral, and beach 202–203

The stunningly scenic and unspoiled beaches of Sandwood Bay   205

Taking the high road of Bealach Na Ba   210–211

The shortbread-tin pretty village of Plockton   213

The spectacular cinematic setting of Eilean Donan Castle   213

the lofty heights of Liathach and Beinn Eighe. The challenging ascent of An Teallach, meanwhile, tempts from Dundonnell. The National Trust for Scotland *(tel 0844/493 2100, www.nts.org.uk)* can put you in touch with knowledgeable local guides to help you tackle the climbs and other outdoor activities.

And if all that sounds far too energetic, this is also a great region for a driving holiday, making your way along winding roads that skirt the windswept coastline, and enjoying spectacular and seemingly endless views of the sea with only an abundance of seabirds for company. ■

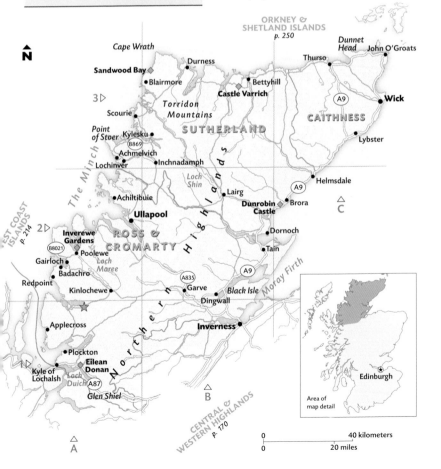

East Coast

Northeast of Inverness (see pp. 174–177), the gentle rolling hills, fertile plains, and low sea cliffs that characterize the landscape in this part of Scotland come as a surprise to many visitors, who often associate the Highlands with the vaulting mountains and sea lochs that dominate the west. As a result, many rush through on their way to Orkney. To skip this part of the country, however, does it a great disservice.

An ornate Victorian fountain frames the medieval façade of Dornoch Cathedral.

Tain Through Time

✉ Tower Street, Tain
☎ (01862) 894 089
💲 $
🕐 Closed Sun. & Nov.–March

www.tainmuseum .org.uk

Glenmorangie

✉ Glen Morangie, Tain
☎ (01862) 892 477
💲 Tour: $$

www.glenmorangie .com

Black Isle & Tain

Leaving Inverness on the A9, visitors find themselves crossing the **Black Isle** (see sidebar opposite), which is not an island but a peninsula sandwiched between the Cromarty, Moray, and Beauly Firths.

Farther north, **Tain** is worth a stop. The **Tain Through Time** exhibition teaches you about this handsome borough's past—it claims to be the oldest Royal Burgh in Scotland. For Scotch whisky aficionados, Tain is also home to one of the country's most prestigious distilleries, **Glenmorangie.** The Fearn Peninsula east of Tain makes a worthwhile diversion. The highlights are the pretty coastal settlement of **Portmahomack** and the Pictish standing stones at **Hilton** and **Shandwick.**

Dornoch

Farther up the A9, Dornoch is the most charming settlement in the northeast Highlands, and it claims to be Scotland's sunniest town. The most architecturally

In Dornoch, book a table at 2 Quail on Castle Street. This charming little restaurant has the best menu in town, and you'll be treated like old friends.

—MARLENE WALKER-GOLDEN
National Geographic Digital Media

striking building in town is **Dornoch Cathedral,** a 13th-century beauty with an unmistakable presence. Dornoch is also home to one of the country's most prestigious golf courses, the **Royal Dornoch,** a links course that is as challenging as it is scenic. Non-golfers can enjoy the epic sweep of golden sand at **Dornoch Beach.**

Another essential stop along the northeast coast is **Dunrobin Castle** *(Golspie, tel 01408/633 177, www.dunrobincastle.co.uk, closed mid-Oct.–March, $$),* home to the Duke of Sutherland. With its towering conical spires, the castle would not be out of place in the pages of a fairy tale. Dating from the 14th century, it is one of the oldest of Scotland's grand houses to be continually inhabited.

Wick

From Dunrobin the A9 continues along the coast to Wick, past the hulking **Sutherland Monument** atop Ben Bhraggie (1,302 feet/397 m), a 100-foot (30 m) memorial to the first Duke of Sutherland. The town's former heyday as a thriving fishing village is retold in the **Wick Heritage Museum,** where you can also learn about the Highland Clearances (see pp. 206–207) that drove crofters from the land to become fishermen. ∎

Dornoch Cathedral
✉ High Street, Dornoch
§ $
www.dornoch-cathedral.com

Royal Dornoch Golf Club
✉ Golf Road, Dornoch
☎ (01862) 810 219
§ $$$$$
www.royaldornoch.com

Wick Heritage Museum
✉ 18–27 Bank Row
☎ (01955) 605 393
⏱ Closed Nov.–Easter
§ $
www.wickheritage.org

EXPERIENCE: Visiting the Black Isle

Gently rolling hills and green pastures are the most striking characteristics of the Black Isle—a hidden corner of the region's east coast where you can stroll through pretty villages, spot dolphins swimming in Cromarty Firth, or visit its prehistoric monuments. Measuring 23 miles (37 km) at its longest point and 9 miles (14.5 km) at its widest, the peninsula is home to a broad array of sights that most people never see as they rush past on the A9.

Stop off at the **Black Isle Wildlife & Country Park** *(The Croft, Drumsmittal, tel 01463/731 656, www.black-isle.info),* where you can get close to myriad farm animals, as well as more exotic creatures.

Alternatively, why not visit the **Black Isle Brewery** *(Old Allangrange, Munlochy, tel 01463/811 871, www.blackislebrewery.com, closed Sun. Oct.–March)* or the **Glen Ord Distillery** *(Glen Ord, tel 01463/872 004, www .discovering-distilleries.com/glenord, closed Sat.–Sun. Oct.–March & Sun. April–June).*

One of the best places to get a feel for the area's Pictish history is at **Groam House Museum** *(High Street, tel 01381/620 961, www.groamhouse.org .uk, closed Jan.–March)* in the appealing coastal village of Rosemarkie. Here you can admire a unique display of 15 carved standing stones and watch a short film about the region's Picts.

Top of Scotland

Many of the visitors who make the journey to the top of Scotland are on a pilgrimage to John O'Groats—a place famous simply for being the "end of the road," the most northeasterly point on mainland Britain's road network. Sadly, once they have reached the small nondescript town, most people turn tail and head back south almost immediately, missing out on the wild and rugged beauty of Scotland's north coast.

Duncansby Head, the epitome of the rugged, sea-battered beauty of Scotland's northern coast

John O'Groats
🅰 201 C3

Last House in Scotland
✉ John O'Groats
☎ (01955) 611 250
💲 $

John O'Groats Ferries
✉ John O'Groats
☎ (01955) 611 353
🕐 Closed Oct.–April
💲 $$$$
www.jogferry.co.uk

Northernmost Points

In truth, there is little to recommend **John O'Groats,** save for the **Last House in Scotland** museum and gift shop—although this may change if a multi-million-dollar improvement plan, aimed at boosting the town's tourist appeal, comes to fruition. A better way to appreciate this far-flung corner of Scotland is to get out on the North Sea—**John O'Groats Ferries** operates wildlife cruises—or enjoy a walk along the rugged coastline of **Duncansby Head.**

Dunnet Head, 11 miles (18 km) west of John O'Groats, is the northernmost point on mainland Britain. A clear day provides dramatic views of the coast, from Duncansby Head in the east all the way to Cape Wrath in the west. When the weather is poor, **Dunnet Head Lighthouse,** the work of world-famous engineer Robert Stevenson (see sidebar opposite), is still worth a visit.

Thurso

Many visitors pass through the unassuming town of Thurso, about 10 miles (16 km) farther west, on their way to catch the Orkney ferry in Scrabster. Those into board-based water sports, however, know **Thurso East** to be one of the best surfing spots in Europe *(www.wannasurf.com/ spot/Europe/UK/North_Scotland/ thurso_east)*. The non-surfing fraternity can pop into **Caithness Horizons,** which is full of exhibits on the area's history, geography, and ecology, and includes an interesting display on the local Dounreay nuclear power station.

Continuing west along the coast takes you past Dounreay and on to **Bettyhill,** site of the pristine white sands of **Torrisdale Beach** and **Farr Beach.** In town, the small **Strathnaver Museum** sheds light on the clan tradition and the Highland Clearances (see pp. 206–207). The ruins of **Castle Varrich,** 12 miles (19 km) farther west in a stunningly scenic location overlooking the hamlet of **Tongue,** is worth a detour.

Durness & Cape Wrath

This wild beauty keeps you company as you travel to Durness *(www.durness.org)*, Scotland's most northwesterly village. With little more than a smattering of houses (some offering rooms with breakfast) and a hostel, Durness is low on facilities but has dramatic scenery in abundance. A visit to the 200-foot (61 m) **Smoo Cave,** 1 mile (1.6 km) east of town, is a must and, from May to September, visitors should consider tackling the 11-mile (18 km) excursion to **Cape Wrath,** reached by a ferry across the Kyle of Durness and then a minibus *(tel 01971/511 343 or 511 287 for minibus details).* Highlights on the route include the steepest cliffs on mainland Britain, the 620-foot (189 m) **Clo Mor,** and another Robert Stevenson creation, **Cape Wrath Lighthouse.**

Heading south through the northwestern Highlands, you could be forgiven for bypassing **Sandwood Bay,** as the trip involves a 4-mile (6.5 km) hike over moorland from Blairmore, a few miles north of Kinlochbervie. Yet those who make the walk are well rewarded. Flanked by cliffs, its impressive sand dunes and sweep of unspoiled pink sand make it a contender for the United Kingdom's best beach. ■

Thurso
🔼 201 C3

Caithness Horizons
✉ Old Town Hall, Thurso
☎ (01847) 896 508
💲 $
www.caithness horizons.co.uk

Strathnaver Museum
✉ Clachan, Bettyhill
☎ (01641) 521 418
🕐 Closed Nov.–March
💲 $
www.strathnaver museum.org.uk

Robert Stevenson's Lighthouses

Traveling around Scotland's coast, you'll quickly become familiar with the name Robert Stevenson (1772–1850). Following in the footsteps of his stepfather, the renowned engineer Thomas Smith (1752–1815), the Glasgow-born Robert was recruited by the Northern Lighthouse Board in 1797. Over the course of the next 47 years he would design 18 lighthouses for Scotland, including those at Dunnet Head and Cape Wrath (both on this spread). Even after his death, the Stevenson family continued to play a pivotal role in the design of Scotland's lighthouses, with no fewer than eight members of the family engineering a grand total of 97 lighthouses over a period of 150 years.

The Highland Clearances

Many visitors are struck by how sparsely populated the northern Highlands are. This is not just a result of their remoteness, nor flagging economies with little industry to employ people, or even the harsh winter climate. Instead, this emptiness is largely a legacy of the brutal Highland Clearances of the 18th and 19th centuries.

A simple cottage of the type used by crofters in the wake of the Highland Clearances

This destruction of the traditional clan system—the allegiance to specific tribes, based loosely on ancestry—and eviction of the people from their land took more than a century to complete. It was done in the name of agricultural progress and as a punishment for Bonnie Prince Charlie's heroic (some would say reckless) attempt to recapture the British throne, which culminated in the fateful 1746 Battle of Culloden (see p. 177).

Brutal Evictions

The early Clearances, which were largely confined to the northern Highlands, are regarded by many historians as the most brutal. They involved forcing Highlanders from their lands to the wind-lashed coast. The landlords then replaced the people with large flocks of sheep, taking advantage of the huge profits that wool then commanded.

Clearing the people from the land and forcing them to live on the coast led to the creation of the crofter. The displaced people were allowed to live on a small piece of land, known as a croft, in return for which they had to pay their landlords rent (often a substantial sum). As a result, these Highlanders cum crofters were forced into collecting kelp (the large iodine-rich seaweed used in the manufacture of soap) or fishing in order to survive.

For visitors today, the idea of relocating the population and giving them somewhere to live and a new trade doesn't sound that bad and the true awfulness of the Clearances can be hard to grasp. One of the most notorious incidents saw more than 400 people mercilessly evicted in just two weeks from Strathnaver in Sutherland. The Marquis of Stafford and the Countess of Sutherland (later to become the Duke and Duchess of Sutherland), who owned the land, didn't politely ask the Highlanders to leave, nor did they serve them with timely eviction notices. Instead, they hired sheep farmers from the Borders and Moray to terrorize the people from their homes. Some of the underhand tactics they employed included ripping roofs off houses or setting them alight to prevent rebuilding. A few elderly tenants, who were unable to escape the blazes, died. This behavior didn't go entirely unnoticed, however.

One of the Duchess of Sutherland's henchmen, Patrick Sellar, was tried for culpable homicide in 1816, but was acquitted. In all, the Sutherlands cleared some 15,000 people from their land in the decade between 1811 and 1821. The Strathnaver Museum (see p. 205) in Bettyhill has exhibits on the event.

Exodus to the Coast

For a people used to an inland, agricultural way of life, starting again on the coast was not easy. Most had no experience fishing or kelping, and earning a living this way proved tough. For many, the money they earned barely paid the rent, forcing them into subsistence farming, growing what food they could on their small plots and keeping limited livestock.

The Highland Clearances are often associated with the mass migration of people to places such as the United States, Canada, New Zealand, and Australia. Although this did take place during the later Clearances, in the early years greedy landlords were keen to keep their tenants on site in order to reap the profits from their labors.

The demise of the kelping industry during the early 19th century made life for the coastal crofters in the northern Highlands even harder. Their income dwindled, while the demand for rent did not. For some crofters, finding the rent wasn't even the hardest part. As kelp revenues fell, landlords began clearing the coastal settlements to graze yet more sheep. This finally forced the crofters to leave for foreign lands. For example, one estimate suggests that 25,000 Gaelic-speaking Scots emigrated to Cape Breton, in Nova Scotia, Canada, between 1775 and 1850, and a large proportion of these were probably refugees from the Highland Clearances. Although their departures were often disguised by landlords as sponsored emigration schemes, with no political representation and no money, the Highlanders really had no choice.

EXPERIENCE: Tracing Your Scottish Roots

The Highland Clearances led to a mass exodus of people to the Americas and even farther afield to Australia and New Zealand. Coupled with earlier and later economic migration, the Scots diaspora around the world now runs into the millions. If you think you might have Scots blood coursing through your veins, then you can trace your ancestry. Many family names hint at Scottish roots, most obviously those starting with "Mac" or "Mc" (in Scottish Gaelic meaning "son of"). Two places you could start searching are at Register House and the National Archives in Edinburgh, where a wealth of official documents are archived. If you are in a hurry, start with a search of your family name at www.ancestral scotland.com before employing a specialized company to do your digging, such as Blue Thistle Genealogy at www .bluethistlegenealogy.com.

The West

This rugged region of snowcapped peaks, looming medieval castles, and gnarled, weather-battered sea cliffs has its more serene side, as represented by great sweeps of white-sand beach, tiny villages perched on the edge of lochs, and even a garden of tropical flowers.

Framed by mountains, the resplendent Eilean Donan Castle guards the chill waters of Loch Duich.

Assynt

Visitor Information

- ✉ The Assynt Visitor Centre, Main Street, Lochinver
- ☎ (01571) 844 654
- 🕐 Closed Sun.

www.assynt.info

Assynt

Scotland boasts a treasure trove of mountains, but there is something special about the peaks of Assynt Parish and those on the neighboring Coigach Peninsula. Unlike the Cairngorms, they are not part of a big massif but stand defiantly alone, each one rising like giant sleeping warriors from miles of inhospitable moorland. For many, a visit to Assynt is all about tackling these mountains, although the area also offers plenty of low, level walks and a clutch of pretty beaches.

South of Blairmore, the curving sweep of white sand at **Scourie**

Bay is a dramatic location for a bracing stroll or a relaxed picnic. On a good day you can make a detour to Tarbet where small boats leave for the offshore island of **Handa,** home to one of the largest colonies of seabirds in northern Europe.

While few venture as far north as Scourie, more visitors find their way to the sleepy village of **Kylesku,** home to a great pub-restaurant, the **Kylesku Hotel** (see p. 298), and a colony of seals. Boat trips (*tel 01971/502 345*) leave from the hotel for Loch Glencoul between March and October, when sightings of seals are nigh on guaranteed. Some boat trips also take in Britain's highest waterfall, **Eas-Coul-Aulin,** nowhere near as impressive as it might sound. This trip is weather dependent, so call ahead.

From Kylesku, the B869 runs west to **Point of Stoer** and its eponymous lighthouse, another Stevenson creation (see sidebar p. 205), which has beamed out across the Minch since 1870. On the head, a rough ramble leads to cliffs overlooking the **Old Man of Stoer,** a distinctive 200-foot-high (61 m) rock plug sitting alone in the surf. You can stare out toward the top of Scotland and Handa, while to the south the distinctive peaks of Assynt rear into view.

Pushing south toward Lochinver, it is worth taking the detour to **Achmelvich.** Its idyllic white beach, backed with impressive dunes, slips down to a lovely little cove, and is a bit of a secret among Scots. It may not be the country's prettiest town, but **Lochinver** is a good place to stock up on supplies in these remote parts. It also boasts the **Culag Woods,** where a series of family-friendly trails take in sea and mountain vistas and lead down to a pretty pebble beach.

There are some great mountain-walking opportunities in this region. **Stac Pollaidh,** or Stac Polly, makes a powerful first impression—a Tolkien-evoking weirdness of crags and pinnacles that looks different from every angle—and presents a few scrambling challenges on the way to its summit. While Stac Pollaidh can be covered in a half day, the most famous peak here, **Suilven,** is a more serious proposition. It's a mighty mountain, 2,398 feet (731 m) high, that makes for a big day out, involving a 4.5-mile (7 km) walk just to get to its base. The epic views over Assynt and out to the Outer Hebrides make it worthwhile, but be sure to take full mountain-walking precautions.

For those heading south to Ullapool (see p. 212), taking a detour along the winding single-track road toward Achiltibuie provides stunning scenery. This dramatic stretch of road, flanked by mountains and running alongside a burn, culminates at a T-junction. Taking the right fork brings you to what is arguably Assynt's most dramatic beach, **Achnahaird,** an epic stretch of cotton-white sand and turquoise waters. To one side lie rocks and

(continued on p. 212)

Lochinver
🔼 201 A3

Inverewe Gardens

His contemporaries may have found the idea of importing exotic plants and flowers from around the globe to Wester Ross bizarre, but it seems Osgood MacKenzie, founder of Inverewe Gardens *(Poolewe, tel 0844/493 2225, www.nts.org.uk, closed Nov.–March, $$; see p. 212),* knew what he was doing. Although the garden lies farther north than Moscow, the warm currents passing through the loch from the Gulf Stream create ideal conditions for Inverewe's foreign blooms. Visitors can join guided ranger walks, amble along the paths that crisscross the extensive woodland (which contain both native and exotic trees), and observe the garden's fauna from the new wildlife hide.

A Drive Around the Applecross Peninsula

The drive from the Torridon Mountains around the Applecross Peninsula to Lochcarron takes in a swath of Europe's most dramatic scenery. The dizzying twists and turns of Scotland's highest road, the Bealach Na Ba, deter some, but stunning loch and mountain views and fine seafood reward those who make the journey.

Take a break from your drive to hike down Liathach Ridge toward Loch Torridon.

This drive can be completed in a day, but to truly appreciate the wild beauty of the peninsula, an overnight stay in Applecross is recommended. This gives travelers opportunities both to get out and about in this stunning natural environment, and to feast on delicious boat-fresh fish and shellfish.

With its myriad walking routes, including an ascent of the mighty Liathach (4,888 feet/1,490 m), the **Torridon Mountains** make an ideal starting point. From the **Loch Torridon Visitor Centre ❶** (*Torridon Mains, tel 01445/791 221*) in Torridon, ease southwest along the A896 through the tiny settlement of Annat and on to **The Torridon ❷** (see p. 297). This grand country house on the banks of Loch Torridon serves good food and an excellent range of single-malt whiskies. It also offers gorge-scrambling and mountain hikes up Beinn Damph (2,960 feet/902 m), just south of the estate, through

NOT TO BE MISSED:

Applecross • Bealach Na Ba
• Kishorn Seafood Bar

Torridon Activities (*tel 01445/791 242, www .thetorridon.com/activities*).

A short hop along the A896 brings you to a **viewpoint ❸** on the right-hand side of the road, which delivers startling elevated vistas over Loch Torridon and the mountains beyond. After passing though Balgy, the road continues onto **Shieldaig ❹**. If you are hungry, turn off the A896 and head to the bar at the **Tigh an Eilean Hotel** (see Travelwise p. 297), which serves wonderful seafood. Leaving Shieldaig, the A896 heads south toward Lochcarron. Take the first road on the right, which skirts the coast of the Applecross Peninsula, winding dizzily along the shore of Loch Torridon, before turning south along the **Inner Sound,** which opens up dramatic vistas over the islands of Rona and Raasay.

You pass through the towns of **Cuaig** ⑤ and **Lonbain,** and as the road sweeps alongside a pretty sandy cove, you will know you have arrived in **Applecross** ⑥. This whitewashed village has an inn and a clutch of quaint cottages. Stop here to take in its stunning location and first-rate seafood served up in the **Applecross Inn** (see Travelwise p. 297). The village is also an ideal base for walking and has a good campsite.

The most exhilarating part of the drive comes next. From Applecross, the **Bealach Na Ba** road winds east, then southeast, as it rises in search of the A896. You will pass several viewpoints on the climb, with the highest located at 2,053 feet (626 m). From here, things get really exciting. If you thought ascending around hairpin bends on a single-lane road was challenging, then wait until

you begin the steep descent to sea level along a snake of stomach-testing turns that feel akin to a roller-coaster ride. At the foot of the Bealach Na Ba, turn right onto the A896; the village of **Ardarroch** ⑦, at the head of Loch Kishorn, is just a short hop away. Reward yourself with mouthwatering shellfish at the **Kishorn Seafood Bar** (see Travelwise p. 298), then head west on the A806 to **Lochcarron** ⑧. This whitewashed village, spread out on the northern shore of Loch Carron, is a great place to unwind, with bicycles and kayaks available for rent, as well as a nine-hole golf course. **Lochcarron Weavers**, 2 miles (3 km) west of the village, boasts a working loom.

> ◩ See also area map p. 201
> ► Torridon Visitor Centre
> ⟳ 50 miles (80 km)
> ⏱ Choice of 1–2 days
> ► Lochcarron

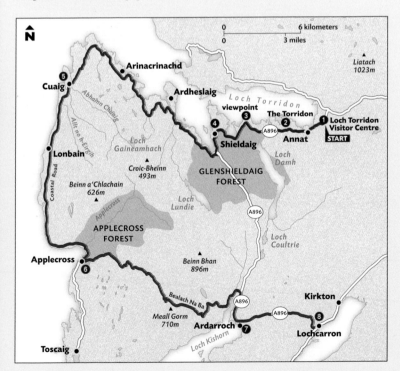

Achiltibuie
🄼 201 A2

Wester Ross
Visitor Information
✉ Ullapool Visitor
Information
Centre, 20
Argyle Street,
Ullapool
☎ (08452) 255 121
www.visitwester
-ross.com

The Ceilidh Place
✉ 12–14 W. Argyle
St., Ullapool
☎ (01854) 612 103
🅂 $
www.theceilidhplace
.com

Gairloch
🄼 201 A2
Visitor Information
✉ Gairloch Tourist
Information,
Auchtercairn
☎ (01445) 712 071

rock pools, while to the other the region's distinctive mountain peaks rear up. Just a few miles away is **Achiltibuie,** a tiny village that is the improbable home to the seriously good **Summer Isles Hotel** (see p. 297), which boasts a Michelin-starred restaurant and a great informal seafood bar. Achiltibuie also provides the opportunity to get out on the water, with **Summer Isles Cruises** (Badentarbet Pier, Achiltibuie, tel 01854/622 200, www .summer-isles-cruises.co.uk, $$$) leaving twice daily in summer.

Wester Ross

When thinking about Scotland, people often conjure up images of dazzling lochs, rugged mountains, quaint villages, and sandy beaches. For many, the region of Wester Ross is perhaps the epitome of this romantic idyll.

Ullapool is Wester Ross's most populous urban settlement. This old fishing port, reclining prettily on the shore of Loch Broom, is integral to Highland history. Many of those exiled during the Clearances set sail for North America, Australia, and New Zealand from here. Today, ferry passengers travel

INSIDER TIP:

Nobody goes by Eilean Donan Castle without stopping to take a picture. It is the quintessential castle.

—JIM RICHARDSON
National Geographic photographer

only as far as Stornoway on the isle of Lewis, and many people quickly pass through. But Ullapool has a lot to recommend, including cozy pubs and the area's premier performance venue, **The Ceilidh Place.** It is also a great base for forays into the Assynt peaks.

Continuing south toward the dramatic Torridon Mountains, the A835 passes **Inverewe Gardens** (see sidebar p. 209) on its way into **Poolewe,** a pretty village with a café and a couple of hotels. From here you can also enjoy a walk to one of Scotland's most attractive lochs, **Loch Maree.**

Gairloch, on the shores of Loch Gairloch, boasts some lovely sandy beaches and makes a good base for a number of local excursions. Following the B8021 on the

Five Sisters of Kintail

Anyone driving on the A87 between Glen Shiel and Loch Duich cannot fail to notice the five steeply pointed peaks blocking the horizon. These are the Five Sisters of Kintail, which together provide one of the most popular ridge walks in Scotland. The walk involves tackling three mountains over 3,000 feet (914 m) high, known as Munros in Scotland: Sgurr na Ciste Duibhe (3,369 feet/1,027 m), Sgurr na

Carnach (3,287 feet/1,002 m), and Sgurr Fhuaran (3,501 feet/1,067 m). As such, it's not recommended for the inexperienced or fainthearted, as you will have to make steep ascents on rocky ground and scramble along narrow ridges. (There are two other slightly lesser peaks.) The best place to start the walk, which takes 8 to 10 hours, is at the pull-in off the A87 between the two sections of forest.

north side of the bay presents drivers, cyclists, and walkers with dramatic coastal scenery. It leads to a headland dominated by the **Rua Reidh** lighthouse, which has a small visitor center and hostel-style accommodation.

To the southwest, a single-track road takes you past pretty loch and glen scenery, through the village of **Badachro,** which is home to a great pub, the **Badachro Inn** *(www.badachroinn .com)* with a waterfront terrace. The next village is **Redpoint,** its expansive pink-sand beach a stunning spot for a walk with views of the Hebrides.

Plockton

Some 60 miles (97 km) south of Gairloch is one of Scotland's most attractive loch-side villages. Wrapped around the shores of Loch Carron with views over the Applecross mountains, chocolate-box-pretty Plockton played a starring role in the BBC Television drama *Hamish MacBeth.*

One of the best ways to view the dramatic arena surrounding Plockton is to take to the sea. A boat trip with the gregarious Calum of **Calum's Plockton Seal Trips** offers fine vistas back over the whitewashed cottages and the haunting Cuillin Hills of Skye beyond. It also guarantees seal sightings (or your money back) and, if you're lucky, dolphin, otter, and porpoise sightings too. If you would prefer to venture out onto the loch alone, you can hire canoes from the gift shop. Land-lubbers, meanwhile, can savor

The lochside village of Plockton, with the silhouette of the Applecross mountains looming beyond

the panorama and boat-fresh "Plockton prawns" (langoustines) from the loch-side garden at the **Plockton Hotel** (see p. 297).

A half-hour drive southeast of Plockton, the A87 opens up to reveal one of Scotland's most postcard-perfect castles, **Eilean Donan.** This photogenic fortress dates from the 13th century, but it was destroyed by 343 exploding barrels of gunpowder in 1719. It lay in ruins for almost 200 years until it was restored in the early 20th century. As striking as the castle is, it's the setting—overlooking Loch Long, Loch Alsh, Loch Duich, and the Five Sisters of Kintail (see sidebar opposite)—that takes your breath away. Film buffs might recognize the castle from *Highlander* and the James Bond movie *The World Is Not Enough,* which were both filmed here. ■

Rua Reidh
✉ Melvaig
☎ (01445) 771 263
$ $

www.ruareidh.co.uk

Calum's Plockton Seal Trips
✉ 32 Harbour St., Plockton
☎ (01599) 544 306
$ $$

www.calums -sealtrips.com

Eilean Donan
🅰 201 A1
✉ Dornie
☎ (01599) 555 202
$ $$

www.eilean donancastle.com

Colorful villages and smoky whiskies on a patchwork of spectacular islands stretching from the Scottish coast to the wild North Atlantic

West Coast Islands

The colorful town of Tobermory, on the island of Mull

West Coast Islands

While many visitors dream of visiting the isle of Skye, a land shrouded in romantic history and misty mountains, few realize that Scotland has more than 800 islands, of which almost 100 are inhabited. Scotland's West Coast islands are diverse both in their geography and landscapes, as well as in their wildlife and cultures.

The most easily accessible of Scotland's islands include the islands of Bute and Arran, whose proximity to Glasgow have made them popular with the vacationing masses since Victorian times. The island today is enjoying something of a renaissance. It is home to boutique hotels, many great places to eat, as well as a number of local businesses that offer outdoor adventures, local produce, and information on the islands' history and wildlife.

For whisky aficionados, the Inner Hebridean isle of Islay needs little introduction. Not only do its eight distilleries produce some of the country's finest whisky, they also enjoy extremely scenic locations, on an island dotted with sandy beaches and whitewashed villages. For most, the isle of Jura provides a dramatic mountainous background to an Islay trip. This

rugged island, whose deer population far outnumbers its human population, offers bountiful rewards for hill walkers, wildlife enthusiasts, and those who are simply looking to get away from it all.

A short ferry trip away from the bustling west coast port of Oban, the island of Mull has long been popular with Scottish and other vacationers, who come to relax in its colorful capital Tobermory and enjoy the picturesque mountains and stunning sandy beaches. Mull is also a good base for forays onto some of the smaller isles, including the deeply religious Iona, a place of pilgrimage for centuries, Eigg, Rhum, Canna, and Muck.

Those who want to travel farther afield can spend time walking, cycling, or just relaxing on the improbably beautiful and empty beaches of the isle of Coll, from where views of the Western Isles (also called the Outer Hebrides) and Inner Hebrides unfold. Neighboring Tiree, meanwhile, enjoys the dual honor of being the sunniest spot in Britain, as well as host to an important global windsurfing event, the Tiree Wave Classic.

To the north, the Inner Hebridean island of Skye is a vast natural playground, complete with challenging hill walks for the experienced mountaineer, attractive whitewashed villages, and miles of breathtaking scenery. Ferries leaving from the port of Uig in the north of the island link Skye to the Outer Hebrides via Lochmaddy on North Uist and Tarbert on the isle of Harris.

A string of causeways links the isles of North Uist, Benbecula, South Uist, and Eriskay, and together these islands offer a rich, scenic web of azure lochs, small lochans, and sprawling

---

NOT TO BE MISSED:

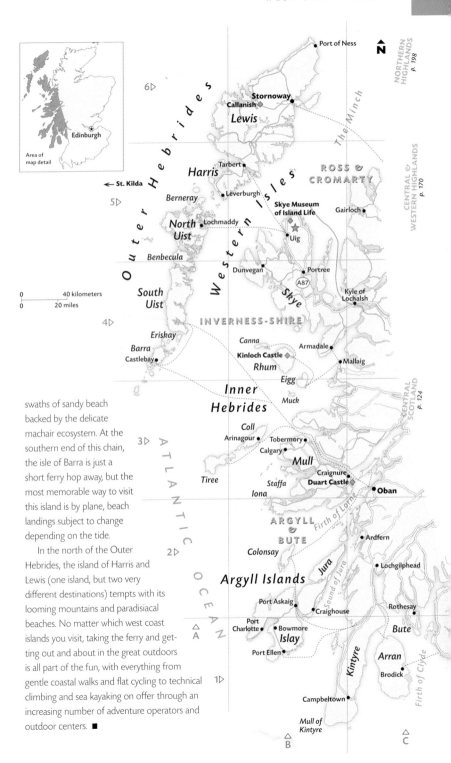

swaths of sandy beach backed by the delicate machair ecosystem. At the southern end of this chain, the isle of Barra is just a short ferry hop away, but the most memorable way to visit this island is by plane, beach landings subject to change depending on the tide.

In the north of the Outer Hebrides, the island of Harris and Lewis (one island, but two very different destinations) tempts with its looming mountains and paradisiacal beaches. No matter which west coast islands you visit, taking the ferry and getting out and about in the great outdoors is all part of the fun, with everything from gentle coastal walks and flat cycling to technical climbing and sea kayaking on offer through an increasing number of adventure operators and outdoor centers. ■

Argyll Islands

Venturing west from the Scottish mainland by ferry brings visitors to the offshore Argyll Islands, part of the archipelago that makes up the Inner Hebrides. There is something for everyone here, from Bute's Victorian charms, Arran's culinary delights, and Jura's unspoiled natural beauty to Islay's whisky distilleries and Mull's dramatic castles and colorful villages.

Car ferry on the Kyles of Bute

GETTING TO THE ARGYLL ISLANDS:
Caledonian MacBrayne (tel 08705/650000, www.calmac.co.uk) and Western Ferries (tel 01369/704 452, www.western-ferries.co.uk) serve the Argyll Islands. You can also fly (Ryanair & British Airlines), drive, or take Scotrail.

Argyll Islands

217 B1–B2, C1

Visitor Information

✉ Tourist Information Centre Argyll Square, Oban

☎ (01631) 563 122

www.visitscottish heartlands.com

Bute

It may measure just 15 miles (24 km) by 5 miles (8 km) at its widest and longest points, but the isle of Bute has much to offer visitors. Located in the Firth of Clyde, Bute celebrated its heyday in the 19th century when it was a popular vacation destination for Glaswegians who came "doon the watter" aboard the traditional paddle steamers (see sidebar opposite).

The main town of **Rothesay** has lost some of its shine, but its lavish Victorian architecture and a pervading sense of faded grandeur still entice. The town also boasts a seafront promenade, **Bute Museum** (*7 Stuart St., tel 01700/505 067, www.bute museum.org, $*), colorful **Arden-craig Gardens** (*Ardencraig Lane, High Craigmore, tel 01700/504 644, www.garden-of-argyll.co.uk, $*) and 14th-century **St. Mary's Chapel** (*High Street*), where Napoleon's niece, Stephanie Hortense Bonaparte, is interred. Its most impressive sight, though, is the 800-year-old ruin of **Rothe-say Castle** (*Castlehill Street, tel 01700/502 691, www .historic-scotland.gov.uk, $$*), the imposing residence of several Scottish kings between the 13th and the 16th centuries.

As you break away from the town, more of the island's heritage unfolds. A short hop south brings you to **Mount Stuart,** a decadent Victorian Gothic mansion, arguably the most impressive in the United Kingdom, and home to the third Marquess of Bute. Mount Stuart alone is reason enough to visit Bute. When the flowers are blooming, in spring and summer, **Ascog Hall Fernery and Garden** are well worth visiting en route.

Like its southwestern neighbor Arran, Bute is an island that is divided into highland and lowland areas by the Highland Boundary Fault. In the north, the seismic activity of millennia past has thrown up peaks, like **Windy Hill** (913 feet/278 m), the island's highest, to tempt visiting hill walkers. The south of the island, in contrast, is characterized by verdant farmland and sandy beaches, among which **Kilchattan Bay** and **Scalpsie Bay** (perfect for viewing the local seals) are highlights.

Located just over 2 miles (3 km) from Bute's southern tip, Kilchattan Bay also marks the beginning of the **West Island Way**—a walk that provides some stunning views. Covering about 30 miles (48 km), the route does a small loop in the south of the island before striking north to Rhubodach and then heading south to Port Bannatyne on the east coast. A highlight of the route is the 12th-century ruin of **St. Blane's Chapel.**

Arran

With seven golf courses, dramatic castles, picturesque villages, a whisky distillery, a first-rate seafood restaurant, and a flurry of local food producers, it is easy to see why the 20-mile-long (32 km) isle of Arran is dubbed "Scotland in miniature."

Bute

🅰 217 C1–C2

Mount Stuart

✉ Mount Stuart Drive, Rothesay, Bute

☎ (01700) 503 877

💲 $$

www.mountstuart .com

Ascog Hall Fernery and Garden

✉ Ascog, Bute

☎ (01700) 504 555

🕐 Closed Mon.–Tues.

💲 $

www.ascoghall fernery.co.uk

EXPERIENCE: Cruise Aboard the *Waverley*

One of the finest ways to visit the isle of Bute is aboard the PS *Waverley (Waverley Terminal, 36 Lancefield Quay, Glasgow, tel 0845/130 4647, www.waverleyexcursions .co.uk).* The last seagoing paddle steamer in the world regularly makes her way down the River Clyde in the summer months from Glasgow to Rothesay on Bute. The original *Waverley* paddle steamer was sunk during the evacuation of Dunkirk in 1940. Her successor, one of the last paddle steamers built after World War II, was launched on June 16, 1947.

The route originally intended for the *Waverley* was the cruise up Loch Goil and Loch Long to Lochgoilhead and Arrochar as part of what then was the "Three Lochs Tour." She spent much of her time, though, cruising from Craigendoran to the Firth of Clyde resorts, whose beaches were as busy in those days as Hawaii's are today.

Taking a trip on the *Waverley* is like delving through a history book. Feel the years peel back as you listen to an accordion performance, nip down to the gleaming engine room, or hear the horn toot "hello." Even if you don't actually take a trip on the *Waverley* (she operates on various routes from June to the end of summer, with some additional sailing in October), watch carefully for this distinctive ship. Today she is bedecked in her signature colors, with a white and black hull topped with eye-catching red, black, and white funnels.

Arran

▲ 217 C1

Visitor Information

✉ Tourist
Information
Centre, The Pier,
Brodick, Arran

☎ (01770) 303 776

**www.visitscottish
heartlands.com**

Isle of Arran
Heritage
Museum

✉ Rosaburn

☎ (01770) 302 636

🕐 Closed late
Oct.–April

$ $

**www.arranmuseum
.co.uk**

Brodick Castle,
Gardens &
Country Park

✉ Brodick, Arran

☎ (0844) 493 2152

🕐 Closed
Thurs.–Fri.

$ $$$

**www.nts.org.uk
Property/13/
Contact**

Then there are Arran's natural attractions—the rugged mountains of the north and the rolling hills of the south, as well as its sandy beaches.

Brodick is the island's main town, with a ferry terminal, hotels, bars, cafés, shops, a sandy beach, and a crazy golf course. Its major attractions, though, are located on its northern fringe. Housed in an early 20th-century cottage, the **Isle of Arran Heritage Museum** delves into the island's social history. A few miles farther on is **Brodick Castle, Gardens and Country Park,** with its stately rooms and expansive landscaped gardens, where 600 years of history unfold. The main path up Arran's highest peak, **Goatfell** (2,688 feet/819 m), whose mighty hulk dominates the island, starts behind the **Isle of Arran Brewery** in Brodrick (see sidebar below). From the summit, on a clear day, you can see a dramatic panorama of craggy mountains and sparkling lochs that stretches to Ireland in the southwest and Ben Lomond on the mainland.

Lochranza, at the northern tip of the island, is home

to **Lochranza Golf Course** (Lochranza, tel 01770/830 273, www.lochranzagolf.com, $$$$) and **Lochranza Distillery** (Lochranza, tel 01770 830/264, www .arranwhisky.com, $$), where you can learn all about this superb single malt in a slick visitor center experience. It is the dramatic 13th-century ruins of **Lochranza Castle,** though, that etches itself most in the memory in these parts. A rich history has seen the castle used by the MacSween family and Oliver Cromwell. There are even reports that Robert the Bruce landed here in 1306 when he returned from Ireland in order to claim the Scottish throne.

As it snakes down Arran's west coast, the coastal road passes through **Catacol,** whose whitewashed cottages have been dubbed the "Twelve Apostles." Although beautiful, they were built in the mid-19th century to house people cleared from the land, whose hardship has earned the cottages the alternative moniker "Hungry Row."

Older history unfurls at **Machrie Moor,** whose chief attraction are its six Neolithic

---

Making the Most of Arran's Food Renaissance

Arran has evolved into a foodie destination. One of the pioneers in the island's renaissance was Arran Fine Foods (www.taste-of-arran.co.uk), which produces preserves, jams, and sauces. The Island Cheese Company (Home Farm, Brodick, tel 01770/302 788, www.islandcheese.co.uk) has, by infusing cheddars with the likes of whisky and chili, created some first-class cheeses. The perfect accompaniment for

these soft, crumbly cheeses is, of course, a Wooleys of Arran oatcake (www.wooleys .co.uk). There is also an ice-cream maker (Arran Dairies, Market Road, Brodick, tel 01770/302 374), a chocolatier (James of Arran, Shore Road, Brodick, tel 01770/302 873, www.jamesofarran.com), a distillery (Isle of Arran Distillers, www.arranwhisky .com), and a brewery (Isle of Arran Brewery, Brodick, tel 01770/302 353).

standing stones. These range from circles with a single stone slab left standing to ambitious double circles that, although they are now reduced to granite boulders, hint at the ambition of this ancient site. The **King's Cave** outside **Blackwaterfoot** also has historic connections, as it claims to be the place where Robert the Bruce, inspired by a spider patiently attempting to rebuild its web, found the courage to avenge his early defeats.

The nearby villages of **Lagg, Kilmory,** and **Torrylin** run into one another, giving the impression that they are all one village. This part of Arran is worth exploring for ancient monuments like the Neolithic **Torrylin Cairn** and **Torr a'Chaisteal Dun** (also known as Corriecravie Dun), a fortified farmstead dating from around A.D. 200.

In recent years, a range of adventure activities has added to Arran's traditional charms. Mountain biking, gorge walking, and sea kayaking are available from **Arran Adventure Company** *(Auchrannie Road, Auchrannie Resort, tel 01770/302 244, www.arranadventure.com, $$$$)* while **Balmichael Visitor Centre** *(Shiskine, tel 01770/860 596, www.balmichael.com, $)* offers helicopter rides, quad biking, and more sedate attractions like a pottery studio and a children's playground.

Jura

One of Scotland's best-kept secrets, Jura is a stunning island spanning some 142 square miles (368 sq km) where nature rules.

The Machrie Moor standing stones on Arran

Its most defining landmark is the Paps of Jura—three majestic mountains that dominate the island and can be seen from Islay and Argyll's west coast.

Pleasantly devoid of roads and traffic (the island has just one road that hugs its southern and eastern shoreline), Jura's wildlife is thriving. Here, ornithologists can spot grouse, snipe, and even golden eagles. Its deer population is reckoned to extend to some 6,000, while only 200 people call this rugged island home. Centuries ago Jura was called Dy Oer (Joora), meaning "deer island."

While Jura does have some attractions, such as the **Isle of Jura Distillery** in **Craighouse,** Jura's only real village, and **Jura House and Gardens** in Ardfin, the main reason to visit is to get out and about in the great outdoors and simply enjoy the tranquility.

For hill walkers and climbers, the **Paps of Jura** are the main attraction. Beinn an Oir, the "mountain of gold," is the highest. Standing 2,576 feet (785 m) above sea level, it is classed as a

(continued on p. 224)

Jura

⬛ 217 B2

Visitor Information

✉ Islay–Jura Tourist Information Centre, The Square, Bowmore, Islay

☎ (01496) 810 254

www.visitscottish heartlands.com

Isle of Jura Distillery

✉ Craighouse, Jura

☎ (01496) 820 240

🕐 Closed Sun.

💲 $$

www.isleofjura.com

Jura House & Gardens

✉ Ardfin, Jura

☎ (01496) 820 315

💲 $$

www.jurahouse andgardens.co.uk

Islay Whisky

People have ventured to the wildly beautiful island of Islay on all kinds of pilgrimages over the centuries and every year life-long devotees still fulfill their dreams and make it out to this remote getaway. They come to pay homage to *Uisge Beatha*, the Gaelic phrase that translates into English as the "water of life." They are in search, of course, of whisky, and more particularly the smoky, richly flavored single malts conjured up by the eight distilleries dotted around this small but scenic isle.

The Bruichladdich distillery is just one of the many distilleries on Islay that delve into the history and culture of whisky-making.

Islay malts are revered around the world by whisky connoisseurs for their unique flavors. The distinctiveness of the Islay malts comes mainly from the influence of the island's peaty soil. The malted barley that whisky is made from is dried over peat fires, which lends the local malts their unique smoky aroma. One sniff of a glass and it is immediately obvious that it is a dram of Islay. Each of the eight distilleries has its own water source, each of which is slightly different, having had greater or lesser contact with the peat. For example, the water used by the southern Islay distilleries is browner and peatier. And individual distilling techniques lead to surprisingly varied tastes and aromas considering the small size of Islay.

Distillation & Distilleries

The guided tours at all of the distilleries take visitors through the whole whisky-making process, from the "malting" to the "mashing." The malting process involves drying the sprouted barley in the smoky heat from the burning peat. The malt that is created is then added to hot water in a mash tun. After mashing, the resultant sugary liquid (wort) is taken off for fermentation using yeast. At this point, the liquid is only weakly alcoholic, but then it is distilled twice in large copper pot stills. Any mistakes at this point will adversely affect the final flavor, and it is the responsibility of the stillman to watch over the distillation process day and night. After the second distillation, the spirit is poured into oak casks, where it remains to mature in a cool warehouse for anything from 8 to 20 years. Over the years in the cask, the whisky loses its initial sharpness and mellows, developing the full flavor of a single malt.

The global demand for Islay whisky has increased considerably in recent years, something that has brought two significant rebirths to the island. The Ardbeg distillery, which stopped production in 1981, was brought back to life in 1997, while Bruichladdich, which was mothballed in 1995, was resurrected in 2001. They now vie for attention with global stars Laphroaig and Lagavulin, as well as Caol Ila, Bunnahabhain, and Bowmore.

In 2005, Islay's eighth distillery, and the first one to be built on the island in 124 years, opened its doors. Housed in former farm buildings, Kilchoman distillery is one of the smallest and most traditional in Scotland. Set up by a farmer, it captures the go-getting spirit that has helped this Hebridean community thrive and conjures up the days before the British exciseman was around to close down the stills that ran in practically every village. The Kilchoman

distillery is one of the few distilleries in Scotland that carries out every stage of the whisky-making process on site. This includes growing the barley in the fields around the distillery, and bottling the whisky once it has finished maturing.

Islay Whisky Festival

Whisky devotees descend on Islay throughout the year, but the best time is undoubtedly in May, when the Islay Whisky Festival bursts into life. Every year this raucously fun event, which starts in the last weekend of May and lasts for a week, bashes through the distilleries in a

The final step in whisky-making: choosing a bottle to take home!

wave of free tastings, parties, open days, and, the wildest night of the year, the celebratory traditional ceilidh (a traditional Celtic celebration with music and dancing). For more information about the festival, visit *www .scotlandwhisky.com/whisky-festivals/Islay-malt -and-Music-festival.*

Every year pilgrims come from all corners of the world to discover where their beloved Islay malts come from, to see the stream (or burn in Scots) where the unique water bubbles into the distillery and to smell the peat that gives the malts their unique flavor. If you have a real love of whisky, or are just interested in an age-old industry that still remains close to its roots in the modern age, then head for Islay, the land of the legendary smoky single malts.

SwimTrek

✉ 63 Landsdowne Place, Brighton

☎ (01273) 739 713

$ $$$$

www.swimtrek.com

Corbett (mountains over 2,500 feet/762 m tall). To the east is Beinn Shiantaidh (2,477 feet/757 m) and to the southwest is Beinn a'Chaolais (2,407 feet/734 m). The former translates as the "sacred mountain" and the latter as the "mountain of sound." The coastline, dotted with beaches, cliffs, and caves stretching out

Islay

With eight whisky distilleries (see pp. 222–223) and a string of stunning beaches on one wildly beautiful island, Islay should be deluged with tourists. Yet such is the remoteness of this Hebridean isle that the hordes have yet to descend on this paradise, leaving the locals

The isle of Jura is home to about 6,000 deer.

more than 115 miles (185 km), provides myriad opportunities for lower level walks, while inland walkers might uncover ancient **standing stones** and ruined **hill forts**, as well as the ruins of **Aros Castle** and **Claig Castle.** If hiking isn't your thing, why not swim the infamous **Gulf of Corryvreckan,** home to a 100-foot (30 m) whirlpool? You can visit it as part of a week-long **SwimTrek** tour of the Inner Hebrides, or visit it by boat with one of the myriad boat operators (see sidebar opposite). Do not under any circumstances try to tackle the dangerous whirlpool on your own.

to get on with the impressively self-sufficient life they have been savoring since the days when the legendary Lords of the Isles ruled whole swaths of the Scottish Highlands and islands from their Islay stronghold.

Covering an area of around 239 square miles (619 sq km), Islay has an airport and two ferry terminals. Beyond the ferry services to the islands of Jura and Colonsay, as well as Kennacraig on the mainland, **Port Askaig** in the northeast of the island has little to offer visitors. Those arriving at **Port Ellen** in the south should keep a lookout for the **Carraig**

Fhada Lighthouse. This striking 19th-century settlement also boasts a long-defunct distillery, which now operates as a malting house for other distilleries, and one of the island's prettiest beaches, the **Singing Sands.** East of the village, the road to Claggin Bay passes by three distilleries, the ruined **Dunyvaig Castle,** and the spectacular **Kildalton Cross**—one of the best examples of an early Christian cross in Scotland—and the ruined **Kildalton Chapel.**

Heading west brings you to the wild and windswept **Oa peninsula** (The Oa), home to the **American Monument,** a monolith that looms out over the Mull of Oa in commemoration of two U.S. ships that were sunk back in 1918. To the north, the road passes the sweep of sandy beach at **Laggan Bay** on its way into Islay's capital, **Bowmore.** Famous for its eponymous **distillery,** the second oldest in Scotland, it also boasts historic churches and picturesque Loch Indaal views.

To the southwest, the **Rhinns of Islay,** once a separate island, has a distinctive Gaelic culture and is dotted with stone crosses, standing stones, and other ancient monuments. Here, you'll also find the island's prettiest village, **Port Charlotte,** its whitewashed houses and a quaint little harbor on the shores of silvery Loch Indaal. The settlement is also home to two attractions: the **Museum of Islay Life,** with a strong emphasis on history; and the **Wildlife Information Centre,** focusing on

the island's animals and birds.

A short hop away are the twin villages of Portnahaven and Port Wemyss. In **Portnahaven** there is little to do but relax on the waterfront and enjoy the world-class view over the tranquil harbor as you ease yourself into the gentle pace of local life. Attractive cottages (whitewashed or in pastel hues) also fringe the **Port Wemyss** seafront, from where your seaward gaze is drawn more to Laggan Bay and the Mull of Oa to the east. Islay has its own woolen mill, a family-run business whose traditionally woven fabrics

Gulf of Corryvreckan

The Gulf of Corryvreckan is a narrow strait separating the isles of Jura and Scarba. It is also home to a 100-foot (30 m) whirlpool, the world's third deepest. The Corryvreckan whirlpool is created by an underwater mountain, whose peak lies close to the surface, and tidal changes. You can look down on the whirlpool, but it is also possible to visit by boat. Operators include Craignish Cruises (tel 07747/023 038, www.craignishcruises.co.uk, $$$$$) in Ardfern, and Farsain Cruises (tel 01852/500 664, $$$$$) in Craob Haven, both near Lochgilphead; and Sealife Adventures (Dunaverty, Easdale, tel 01631/571 010, www.sealife-adventures.com, $$$$$), based in Oban.

Islay
🅰 217 B1–2

Visitor Information
✉ Islay–Jura Tourist Information Centre, The Square, Bowmore, Islay
☎ (01496) 810 254
www.visitscottish heartlands.com

Bowmore Distillery
✉ School Street, Bowmore, Islay
☎ (01496) 810 441
🕐 Closed Sun.
💲 $
www.bowmore.co.uk

Museum of Islay Life
✉ Port Charlotte, Islay
☎ (01496) 850 358
🕐 Closed Nov.–March
💲 $
www.islaymuseum .org

Wildlife Information Centre
✉ Port Charlotte, Islay
☎ (01496) 850 288
💲 $

Islay Woollen Mill
✉ Off the A846, Bridgend, Islay
☎ (01496) 810 563
🕐 Closed Sun.
www.islaywoollen mill.co.uk

A Celtic stone cross on the isle of Islay

Islay Woollen Mill

✉ Bridgend
☎ (01496) 810 563
💲 $

www.islaywoollen
mill.co.uk

Mull

Ⓜ 217 B2–B3

Duart Castle

✉ Isle of Mull
☎ (01680) 812 309
🕐 Closed mid-
   Oct.–March; &
   Fri.–Sat. rest of
   year
💲 $

www.duartcastle
.com

Torosay Castle

✉ Isle of Mull
☎ (01680) 812 421
🕐 Closed
   Nov.–March
💲 $

www.www.torosay
.com

have been used in several films, including *Braveheart* and *Rob Roy*. The north is also dotted with old churches, Celtic crosses, sandy bays, and memorials to shipwreck victims. **Loch Finlaggan** is home to an ancient settlement and was once a power base for the Lord of the Isles all those centuries ago.

One of Islay's biggest charms is how little it has been tainted by tourism. Old industries like fishing, pottery, and weaving remain an important part of local life—a highlight of any visit is to pop into the workshops of local artisans. Islay also has its own **woolen mill, dive center** (*10 Charlotte St., Port Ellen, tel 01496/302 441*), and a golf club (*Port Ellen, tel 01496/302 310, www.machrie.com*) that offers some of the most dramatic scenery of any course in Britain. Visiting during the annual Whisky Festival (see p. 223) or the annual jazz festival in September can help bring out the best of Islay.

Mull

With the Cal Mac ferry from Oban to Craignure taking just 40 minutes, the isle of Mull is one of Scotland's most accessible islands (alternative routes connect Lochaline to Fishnish and Kilchoan to Tobermory). During the summer months, the piers at both ends throng with car, bus, and foot passengers, keen to discover an island that is far from undiscovered. Even at the height of summer, though, the island is big enough never to feel crowded. To get the most out of Mull, spend more than a day on the island.

Easing toward the island from Oban, Mull's appeal is immediately clear, as its looming peaks rear out of the water and the craggy outline of **Duart Castle** hints at the island's alluring history. The area around Craignure is also home to **Torosay Castle—** worth visiting for the ride on the cute narrow-gauge train that rattles people from the ferry port to this grand baronial mansion.

At the north tip of the east coast lies **Tobermory.** Mull's main settlement is familiar to a generation of British children raised on the TV series *Balamory.* It may not be as Technicolor as it appears on TV, but it is still one of the prettiest settlements on Scotland's west coast. Originally fashioned as a fishing port, the main business today is undoubtedly tourism, with plenty of places to stay, eat, shop, and drink, many of which come wrapped in lovely multicolored stone buildings on the waterfront. Local culture

Islay's Great Geese Migration

Even those not into bird-watching cannot fail to be impressed by the huge flocks of migrating geese that descend on Islay in the winter months. Keen ornithologists, however, will know that these magnificent birds come from different places. From late September flocks of barnacle geese arrive from Greenland to the Loch Indaal and Loch Gruinart mudflats, where they stay until April. Dusk is the prime time to see the geese as they head for their roosts. From September to November, you will also see flocks of greylag geese and pink-footed geese. In spring, watch for wading birds, including snipe, redshanks, and curlews.

The best place for geese-watching is Loch Gruinart Nature Reserve in northwest Islay (tel 01496/850 505, www.rspb .org.uk/reserves/guide/l/lochgruinart).

INSIDER TIP:

My favorite golf course is Machrie on Islay. It's right by the sea with waves crashing close to the fairways and grass growing 3 feet high (0.9 m) in the roughs.

—JIM RICHARDSON
National Geographic photographer

is alive and well here with the active **Mull Theatre** and the brilliant **An Tobar** arts center. The latter is a multiuse arts space that is a hotbed of live music, visual arts, and creative learning.

In the south, the Ross of Mull, with its dramatic cliffs and sandy beaches, separates Craignure from Fionnphort, where boats leave for the isle of Iona. In the summer months, Gordon Grant Tours (*Achavaich, Iona, tel 01681/700 388, www .staffatours.com, $$$$$*) organizes boat trips from here to the Treshnish Isles and **Staffa** (see p. 228), with Staffa Trips (*Tigh na Traigh, Iona, tel 01681/700 358, www.staffatrips.f9.co.uk, $$$$$*). It is also possible to catch the Lorn Ferry from Uisken to Colonsay, although the service is sporadic.

For most, a visit to Mull is all about its scenery, with the highlight the coastal road, at its best from Salen to Calgary. As you descend toward the Atlantic from Salen, views of Ben More open up with a whole host of other peaks and ridges. **Calgary** itself is the island's best beach and one of the finest in Scotland. This sweep of white sand is neatly hemmed in by rugged hillsides on three flanks. There is a designated wild camping site where you can pitch a tent by the dunes, with toilets and picnic tables, all for free. Those with more time might also want to hop over to **Ulva** (*on-demand passenger ferry operates from Ulva Ferry June–Aug.*).

For walkers, Mull offers everything from the heights of **Ben More** (3,169 feet/966 m) and challenging coastal walks to easy, low-level strolls.

Machrie Hotel and Golf Links
⊠ Port Ellen, isle of Islay
☎ (01496) 302 310
www.machrie.com

Mull Theatre
⊠ Druimfin, Tobermory
☎ (01688) 302 673
💲 $
www.multheatre .com

An Tobar arts center
⊠ Tobermory
☎ (01688) 302 211
🕐 Closed Sun.
💲 $
www.antobar.co.uk

Iona
⚑ 217 B3

Iona Abbey
✉ Iona
☎ (01681) 700 404
$ $
www.iona.org.uk

Staffa
⚑ 217 B3

Coll
⚑ 217 B3

An Acarsaid
✉ Arinagour Post
   Office , Coll
☎ (01879) 230 329
🕐 Closed Sun.

www.anacarsaid
.co.uk

Breachacha Castle
✉ Arioleod, Coll

Iona

This tiny island, measuring just 3 miles (5 km) by 1 mile (1.6 km), is the island where St. Columba set about trying to convert the Picts to Christianity. The island's main sight is its magnificently restored Benedictine **abbey,** founded in the 12th century. To make the most out of a visit, join one of the free guided tours. For those with more time, the flat island offers a number of easy walks, with the highlights being hikes up to its sandy northern beaches or the pebble-strewn Port a'Churiach, St. Columba's Bay.

Staffa

If you only visit one of Scotland's uninhabited islands, make it Staffa, which has been impressing travelers since the days of the Vikings with its row of black basalt columns. The island entered mainstream culture in 1772 when it was painted by Joseph Mallord William Turner (1775–1851). Felix Mendelssohn's (1809–1847) Hebrides overture ("Die Hebriden"),

also known as Fingal's Cave ("Die Fingalshohle"), really popularized it in the 19th century, when even Queen Victoria visited. In the summer visitors still flock here to visit Fingal's Cave.

Coll

The Cal Mac ferry trip from Oban to the far-flung Inner Hebridean oasis of Coll is all part of the fun. On a journey just shy of three hours, the *Clansman* treats passengers to jaw-dropping views of the Ardnamurchan Peninsula, the isle of Mull, the isle of Skye, the Small Isles, and even the distant Outer Hebrides before berthing at **Arinagour.** From the sea, Coll looks a bit disappointing—flat, rocky, and fairly featureless. First impressions, though, could not be more wrong and with its sandy beaches, this little known Scottish island gives the others a run for their money.

The best base for exploring the island is the **Isle of Coll Hotel** (see Travelwise p. 298) in Arinagour, the only real village on a tiny island that is just 12 miles

---

EXPERIENCE: Windsurfing on Tiree

Stunning sandy beaches, offshore breezes, and Atlantic swells combine to make Tiree Scotland's leading windsports destination. The island has established itself as a world leader within the windsurfing arena, as competitors from around the globe descend for the annual **Tiree Wave Classic** (*www.tireewave classic.com*). Held in October each year, this six-day event is a spectacle to behold.

The instructors at **Wild Diamond** (*www .wilddiamond.co.uk*) will give you expert instruction (whether you are a novice or expert windsurfer) throughout the year. You can also rent equipment from them. If you have more advanced skills, it is better to visit during the island's windiest months (March–June or Sept.–Oct.) when the conditions are more exciting.

(19 km) long and 4 miles (6 km) wide at its broadest points. In laid-back Arinagour a clutch of whitewashed cottages skirt the pretty bay of Loch Eatharna and savor sea views over the Treshnish Isles and the peaks of Mull.

Coll's main attraction is its more than 20 beaches—puffy white strips of sand that are definitely worth seeking out. Hogh Bay and Crossapol are among the best, but whichever stretches of sand you visit you will be unlikely to meet any other people, even at the height of the summer.

Virtually traffic free, Coll is also great for cycling and walking, with bicycle rental *($)* available from the **An Acarsaid** gift shop and post office. The ascent of 341-foot (104 m) Ben Hogh, the island's highest point, is a good option for walkers. The summit commands distant vistas of the Paps of Jura and a panorama that encapsulates whole swaths of the Inner and Outer Hebrides.

Coll doesn't have any slick tourist attractions, but if you have a car it is worth visiting the island's two "castles," although neither is open to the public. Both are in the south of the island. **Breachacha Castle** dates from the 15th century, while nearby the mansion house or "New Castle" from the mid-18th century. Areas of Coll are also protected as nature reserves *(www.rspb.org.uk/reserves/guide/c/coll)*, without tourist facilities, just trails.

Tiree

A 55-minute hop aboard the Cal Mac ferry takes you from Coll

Fresh fish is an isle of Coll specialty.

to the isle of Tiree (the island also has an airport). The most westerly of the Inner Hebrides, this compact island—measuring 12 miles (19 km) by 3 miles (5 km)—is now host to the annual world-class windsurfing competition, the **Tiree Wave Classic,** a contest that hints at the windy conditions on this flat isle (see sidebar opposite).

Tiree also stakes a fair claim to being the sunniest place in the British Isles. Throw in the moderating effects of the Gulf Stream and visitors can often enjoy warm and balmy summer days, with plenty of white-sand beaches on which to unwind.

A haven for birdlife, Tiree also attracts ornithologists, while for keen walkers who don't want to scale the dizzy heights of Scotland's Munros there are plenty of options. Gentle hill walking is possible on the island's three hills: Ben Hynish (463 feet/141 m), Beinn Hough (390 feet/119 m), and Kennavara (338 feet/103 m) ∎

Tiree

🗺 217 A3

The Small Isles

South of Skye is a cluster of islands—Muck, Eigg, Rhum, and Canna. Known collectively as the Small Isles, they are tranquil natural oases where few people live and few tourists venture. As such, they are low on tourist trappings, have limited accommodations, and offer no public transport.

Walking on the An Sgurr, Eigg, with Rhum island in the background

Muck
🅼 217 B3

Eigg
🅼 217 B3–B4

GETTING TO THE SMALL ISLES:
Caledonian MacBrayne Ferries (www.calmac .co.uk) sail from Mallaig to Rhum, Eigg, and Canna. The MV Shearwater (www.ari saig.co.uk) goes from Arisaig to Rhum, Eigg, and Muck.

Muck

Muck, the smallest and most southerly of the Small Isles, is just 2 miles (3 km) long by 1 mile (1.6 km) wide, with little to do but kick back and watch the wildlife or admire the stunning scenery. The island has a craft shop, tearoom, and a hotel *(Port Mor House Hotel, Port Mor, tel 01687/462 365)*, but its population of about 40 is heavily outnumbered by seals. Visitors can try their hand at rug-weaving, using wool from the island's sheep, at **The Green Shed** *(Carn Dearg, Muck, tel 01687/462 363, www.the greenshed.net)*.

Eigg

North of Muck, Eigg is the most distinctive of the Small Isles. A landmass measuring just 5 miles (8 km) by 3 miles (5 km), it is dominated by the hulk of **An Sgurr** (1,289 feet/393 m), pitchstone lava sitting atop the basalt plateau. This striking geological formation dates back some 58 million years, and golden eagles are sometimes seen from its summit. The hike to the top, which begins at the pier where boats arrive from Mallaig on the mainland, is relatively straightforward. It is marked by cairns and takes around two hours. The island also captivates visitors with the beautiful Singing Sands beach.

Rhum

The largest of the Small Isles, Rhum has an area of more than 38 square miles (100 sq km) and is designated as a national nature reserve—one of the largest in Britain. **Rhum National Nature Reserve** (tel 01687/462 026, www.snh.org.uk, $) offers its very own mountain range, the Rhum Cuillin (whose highest peak, Askival, soars at 2,664 feet/812 m high), and low-level walks. It is an ornithologist's paradise where the once extinct white-tailed eagles can now be spotted. Nearby **Kinloch Castle** (see sidebar below) is a red sandstone castle with grand Edwardian interiors dating from the turn of the 19th century. It also has a bistro and offers hostel-style accommodation.

Canna

Birders, walkers, and those seeking solitude visit the tiny island of Canna, which measures just 5 miles (8 km) by 1 mile

INSIDER TIP:

In the waters off Arisaig, between the mainland and the isles of Mull and Eigg, you can often see minke whales and basking sharks. One ferry, the MV *Shearwater*, stops if any are seen.

—RUS HOELZEL
National Geographic grantee

(1.6 km). The entire island is a National Trust for Scotland (tel 0844/493 2100, www.nts.org .uk/Property/76) property run as a farm and bird sanctuary; it is not exactly overrun with tourist facilities, though it does have a tearoom and guesthouse. Those who have permission from the NTS can also wild camp on the island. For travelers with an interest in botany, Canna has a special appeal: It is carpeted with orchids in early summer. ∎

Rhum
⬛ 217 B4

Kinloch Castle
⬛ 217 B4
✉ Rhum
☎ (01687) 462 037
$ $$
www.isleofrum.com/
kinlochcastle-bu
.html

Canna
⬛ 217 B4

The Islands' Newest Castle

Kinloch Castle, on Rhum, was built between 1897 and 1900 by George Bullough, the eccentric son of a British textile magnate. He spared no expense in its construction, importing 250,000 tons (270,000 tonnes) of soil so he could have formal gardens and a private golf course on this windswept island. It was the first home in Scotland to have electricity—provided by a small hydroelectric dam near the castle—which was used for

lighting and powering a giant mechanical music box called the "Orchestrion." The castle went into decline after World War I and eventually, in 1957, Bullough's widow sold the whole island, including the castle, to Scottish Natural Heritage for £1 an acre. You can take a tour of the strange house, which has remained largely unchanged since the 1900s, and even stay the night in one of its grand, but faded, guest rooms.

Skye

Ever since the days when Flora MacDonald spirited Bonnie Prince Charlie away from his English pursuers "over the sea to Skye," the "Isle of Mist" has held a special place in the Scottish imagination. Approaching the island from Kyle of Lochalsh to the east, it is hard not to be impressed by the view that unfolds.

Kyleakin harbor and ruins of Castle Moil, Skye

Skye

⬛ 217 B4–B5

Visitor Information

✉ Tourist Information Centre, Bayfield House, Bayfield Rd., Portree, Skye

☎ (01487) 612 137

www.visithighlands .com

Portree

⬛ 217 B4

Skye is renowned as a paradise for walkers and climbers. There are 12 Munros to choose from (11 of which are on the rugged Cuillin ridge), ranging from easy to very difficult. For many visitors the highlight is the island's highest peak, **Sgurr Alasdair** (3,257 feet/993 m). To tackle the aptly named "inaccessible pinnacle," you will need the right gear including ropes. You don't have to be Sir Edmund Hillary, though, to enjoy yourself on Skye with dozens of great treks dotted all over the island, including forest trails and pretty bay walks. The largest of the Hebridean islands with an area of 639 square miles (1,656 sq km), Skye also boasts a wealth of historic monuments and more modern tourist attractions. In the days when the ferry sailed from Kyle of Lochalsh to **Kyleakin,** the latter was a bustling little tourist village. Today most visitors just skip by after they cross the bridge (see sidebar opposite). In a bid to keep itself alive the village has reinvented itself as a haven for backpackers with cheap hostel accommodation and boisterous bars.

INSIDER TIP:

On the isle of Skye, take time to drive the scenic route along the east coast from Portree to Uig. Prepare to stop often for one stunning photo opportunity after another.

—NICOLE ENGDAHL
National Geographic
Development Office

Portree & the Trotternish Peninsula

As the A87 travels north toward the island's capital, Portree, it passes through **Broadford.** This is a good place to stock up on local crafts; it is also well endowed with tourist amenities like accommodation, grocery stores, adventure tour operators, and gas stations. Those with young children can also pop into what has to be Skye's least likely tourist attraction—the **Skye Serpentarium** *(The Old Mill, Broadford, tel 01471/822 209, www.skyeserpentarium.org.uk, $),* an exhibition and breeding center for reptiles.

Portree is a reasonably charming town, whose harbor—framed by colorful cottages and rugged cliffs—is one of the most attractive in Scotland. Here you will find a Thomas Telford bridge and some decent places to eat, drink, and stay. The rest of the town bustles with bars, cafés, souvenir stores, outdoor specialists and, a real highlight, **Skye Batiks** *(The Green,* Portree, tel 01478/613 331, www.skyebatiks.com, $),* where colorful Celtic batiks are used to make everything from T-shirts to table cloths. The **Aros Centre** *(Viewfield Road, tel 01478/613 649, www.aros.co.uk, $)* on the southern fringe of town is Portree's wet weather attraction, where you can buy souvenirs, grab a coffee, watch films, or see gigs.

From Portree, a visit to the Trotternish Peninsula, just 20 miles (32 km) to the north, is nigh essential. In addition to having some of Skye's most distinctive scenery, it is also bathed in romantic and ancient history. An adventure playground of tumbled boulders, bizarre rock formations, and dramatic cliffs, the **Quiraing** (see pp. 234–235) and the **Old Man of Storr,** a vertical rock pinnacle, should be on every visitor's hit list, even if you are not a keen walker. **Lealt Falls** and **Kilt Rock** carve out their unique shapes by the coast.

(continued on p. 236)

GETTING TO SKYE:
Now that the Skye Bridge is open, there is no need to hop aboard a ferry. For those wanting to take a boat, the main route is via Caledonian Macbrayne (www.calmac.co.uk) between Armadale and Mallaig.

Skye Bridge

The Skye Bridge (actually two bridges that connect on the tiny island of Eilean Ban) opened in 1995, bringing with it 24-hour access to the mainland for islanders and quicker journey times. Rather than celebrating the freedom that it gave them, many islanders felt that it stopped Skye from being an island at all. For most the objections were financial. The bridge toll was based on the old Kyle of Lochalsh to Kyleakin ferry fares, making this 1-mile (1.6 km) structure the most expensive toll bridge in Europe when it opened. The bridge has been toll-free since December 2004.

A Walk on the Trotternish Peninsula: The Quiraing

With most of the high-level walks on Skye demanding technical skills, it can be hard for many walkers to know where to start. Fortunately, the Quiraing (a collection of fantastic rock formations, not a single peak) comes to the rescue in the form of a largely moderate 4-mile (7 km) hill walk that offers breathtaking views, including out to the Western Isles and myriad offshore islets. Note that it does involve some scrambling, and a head for heights is essential, as well as the usual walking gear.

The Needle in the jumble of rock formations in Quiraing, Skye

Organizing a Trip

This circular walk starts and finishes at the parking lot on the Quiraing road about 2 miles (3 km) northwest of Staffin. It is a moderate walk that climbs around 1,115 feet (340 m) and can be accomplished in three to four hours, depending on how much time you spend absorbing this weird and wonderful scenery of crags, rocky pinnacles, and bizarre rock formations. The paths are generally good, but some of the ascent is quite steep. Take full Scottish walking precautions and don't start out if the weather looks poor.

NOT TO BE MISSED:

The Table • The Needle • The Prison

Making the Ascent

From the **parking lot** on the Quiraing road ❶, set out on the footpath sign-posted to Flodigarry. After a few hundred yards, hike up the grassy hillside (take a zigzag line to make this easier) until you reach the high-level path that will lead you northeast across the slope.

Eventually you will reach a **gated fence** ❷. Go through the gate and follow the path that branches off to the right. This path quickly opens up stunning views as you gaze down over the area from the cliff edge above. From here you can see Staffin Bay to the east, the Atlantic Ocean, and the Torridon Mountains back in Wester Ross on the mainland.

The cliffs don't get much higher, so you have done the hard work; although one possible detour, to the west of the path, takes you to the summit of **Meall na Suiramach** ❸ (1,781 feet/543 m). Back on the main path, sticking close to the cliff's edge, walk around a few gullies and then follow the path as it descends into **Fir Bhreugach** ❹, the col (lowest part of the ridge) connecting the peaks of Sron Vourlinn and Meall na Suiramach.

To continue your descent, follow the path as it zigzags down from the eastern side of the col. As you go, take time to enjoy the stunning views north over **Kilmaluag Bay.** Once you have finished the descent, turn right onto the path below the cliffs. This pathway will lead you back to your starting point. From the path you will see a collection of small pinnacles, as well as two of the Quiraing's most iconic rock stacks.

The thin jagged finger of **The Needle** is one of the Quiraing's most easily distinguished landmarks. Nearby, **The Prison** boasts a dramatic triple summit, which the more imaginative can make resemble a castle from the correct angle. To see The Needle from the best vantage point, scramble up to **The Table** ❺. This steep climb over loose scree is best avoided by those lacking experience. Return to the clear path and follow it back to the parking lot. The path is relatively easy to follow, but you will need to use your hands to cross a small gully.

🅰	See also area map p. 217
►	Parking lot on Quiraing road
🕓	4 miles (7 km)
🕓	3–4 hours
►	Parking lot on Quiraing road

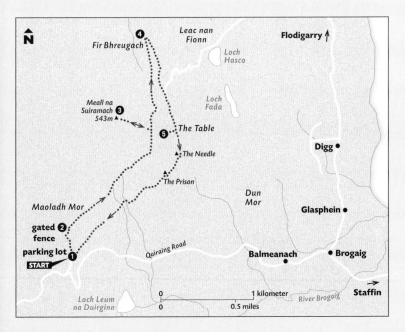

Skye Museum of Island Life
- ✉ Kilmuir
- ☎ (01470) 552 206
- 💲 $

www.skyemuseum
.co.uk

Dunvegan
- ▲ 217 B4

Dunvegan Castle
- ✉ W of Portree in Munegan
- ☎ (01470) 521 206
- 💲 $$

www.dunvegan
castle.com

Colbost Croft Museum
- ✉ Colbost
- ☎ (01470) 521 296
- 💲 $

Talisker Distillery
- ✉ Carbost
- ☎ (01478) 614 308
- 💲 $

www.discovering
-distilleries.com/
talisker

Another attraction worth checking out on the east coast of the peninsula is the **Staffin Museum** (tel 01470/562 321, by appt. only, $), which houses an impressive collection of fossils found in the area. Staffin itself is home to the largest and best-preserved dinosaur tracks—said to be 165 million years old—ever found in Scotland.

On Trotternish's west coast you will find the engaging **Skye Museum of Island Life.** This collection of impressively preserved traditional blackhouses provides a fascinating insight into island life just over a century ago. The views that it commands of the isle of Harris are also magnificent. If you have more than a passing interest in the life of Flora MacDonald and her role in helping Bonnie Prince Charlie flee after his devastating defeat at Culloden, head up to the cemetery behind the museum, where you will find the heroine's grave. It comes as a surprise to some that brave Flora, who was briefly imprisoned in the Tower of London for aiding and abetting the Young Pretender, later married and had a family. She is buried alongside her husband.

Durnish, Vaternish & Minginish Peninsulas

West of Portree **Dunvegan Castle** beckons. The Clan MacLeod have held sway over this historic castle since the 13th century, although much of the fortress that you see today dates from the mid-19th century. Those expecting opulent grandeur might be disappointed; however, the castle is worth visiting for its dramatic lochside setting and attractive gardens. Seal-watching cruises also leave from outside the castle. From Dunvegan, incursions onto the **Durnish Peninsula** to the west or **Waternish** to the north bring their own rewards, not least swaths of dramatic scenery. Highlights include the island's western extremity, **Neist Point,** with its eponymous lighthouse, dramatic sea cliffs, Western Isles views, and

---

EXPERIENCE: Loch Coruisk Cruise

Situated in the jagged Cuillin mountain range, Loch Coruisk is a strong contender for the title of Scotland's most isolated and breathtaking loch. This lake is about 2 miles (3 km) long and a few hundred yards wide. With two operators—**Bella Jane** (tel 01471/866 244, www.bellajane .co.uk, $$$$) and **Misty Isle** (tel 01471/866 288, www.mistyisleboattrips.co.uk, $$$$)—running boat trips to the loch from Elgol, from Easter through September, you can plan the experience you want

once you reach the loch. You can choose a non-landing trip or take advantage of early bird sailings to give you more time ashore and longer to walk in the Cuillins. Most visitors opt for about 90 minutes ashore. The loch's shore is relatively easy terrain for walking (though you should wear walking boots). If you are a seasoned walker or climber with the right gear you can also plan a one-way trip and make your own way through the mountains to Sligachan or back to Elgol.

the pretty village of **Stein,** which gazes out across Loch Bay and the Outer Hebrides.

The **Colbost Croft Museum,** meanwhile, gives insight into crofting on Skye and is home to a restored illicit whisky still. Learn more about illegal whisky making and the production of the island's own legal single malt at the **Talisker Distillery** on the rugged Minginish Peninsula. The peninsula itself is a good base for lower-level walks when the mist settles in on the mighty Cuillin to the east.

Tackling this seemingly impenetrable mountain range may be a no-no for non-climbers and less experienced walkers, but it is possible to immerse yourself in the dramatic scenery without making any effort: Take a boat trip from Elgol out to **Loch Coruisk** (see sidebar opposite), a thin glacial loch flanked by the Cuillin peaks.

Sleat Peninsula

Sleat, the most southern of Skye's many peninsulas, is less affected by tourism than the rest of the island, with few people, bar the passengers arriving on the Cal Mac ferry from Mallaig on the mainland. The ferry docks in **Armadale,** a pleasantly sleepy hamlet with some decent accommodation options. For those seeking adventure, there are also fast-paced rides onboard a speedboat with **Seafari Adventures** *(Armadale Pier, Skye, tel 01471/833 316, www.seafari .co.uk, $$$$).* The west of the peninsula boasts sandy beaches, whitewashed cottages, and great views of Skye's mountains. At

Loch Coruisk on isle of Skye

low tide it is possible to walk out to the **Ornsay Lighthouse** (engineered by David and Thomas Stevenson) from Isle-ornsay, but make sure you check the tide times first. Sleat also has a must-see attraction in the form of **Clan Donald Skye**—a multilayer attraction that includes **Armadale Castle,** its extensive gardens, woodland walks, and the **Museum of the Isles.** The latter, complete with clashing sword sound effects and battle songs drifting through the display rooms, explores the history of the medieval period when the MacDonald family (Clan Donald) were the Lords of the Isles.

Sleat remains the seat of the Clan Donald family today. Those who want to meet the current laird and lady should visit **Kinloch Lodge** *(Sleat, tel 01471/833 333, www.kinloch-lodge.co.uk),* a sumptu-ous old hunting lodge. ■

Clan Donald Skye
- ✉ Armadale, Sleat
- ☎ (01471) 844 305
- 🕐 Closed Nov.–March
- 💲 $$

www.clandonald .com

Armadale
- 🅰 217 B4

Outer Hebrides

Located in the far north, across The Minch from the isle of Skye, Lewis and Harris are often thought of as two islands, but they are in fact one landmass that forms the core of the Outer Hebrides, one of the most remote outposts of Europe. These islands, sometimes referred to as the Western Isles, have played home to Highland clansmen, Jacobite rebels, and even Vikings. The Gaelic language is also alive and well throughout the Outer Hebrides.

Lewis

🗺 217 A6–B6

Visitor Information

✉ 26 Cromwell St., Stornoway

☎ (01851) 703 088

www.visithebrides.com

Lewis

The obvious place to start an exploration of the isle of Lewis is in its main town, and the island's transport hub, **Stornoway.** With a population of more than 6,000 people, Stornoway

Rocky shore and natural arch on a Lewis beach

is the closest that the Western Isles get to a city, so while you are there take the chance to stock up on groceries and gas, and even enjoy a meal out, as tourist facilities are few and far between elsewhere on the twin isles. Stornoway lacks aesthetic appeal, but it does offer a couple of worthwhile sights. The **An Lanntair Art Centre** (Kenneth Street, tel 01851/703 307, www.lanntair.com, $) is a contemporary arts venue whose eclectic role varies from showcasing temporary exhibitions to hosting Celtic music concerts and regular cinema screenings. The nearby **Museum Nan Eilean** sheds light on life for the islanders over the centuries, with diverse exhibits ranging from Viking artifacts to re-created blackhouse interiors. Watching over the town from across the bay is the imposing, but currently vacant, Victorian **Lews Castle.** If you want to learn more about this grand building, then drop into the **Stornoway Trust Woodland Centre** (tel 01851/706 916, $) on the castle grounds; it offers a brief history of the castle and has a tearoom.

Heading west out of Stornoway, the road crosses wild moorland littered with

Stone Circles in Lewis

They may be the most visually impressive and therefore the most visited, but the Calanais stone circles (see above; *www.historic-scotland.gov.uk*) are by no means the only standing stones in Lewis. Many are not that inspiring; eroded over the centuries they can be small with just one or two stones left. There are, of course, exceptions. The largest standing stone in Scotland, Clach an Trushal, lies about 12 miles (20 km) north of Stornoway and is a mighty 20 feet (6 m) tall. The Steinacleit Cairn and Stone Circle, a little farther south, is another site worth seeking out.

INSIDER TIP:

Do not miss the ancient Calanais Standing Stones on Lewis. Visit the site before or after the visitor's center opens for the best light for photographs as well as far fewer crowds.

—JENNIFER SEGAL
National Geographic Development Office

tiny salmon-laden lochans in search of **Callanish** (Calanais in Gaelic), whose awe-inspiring, 5,000-year-old stone circles make up the most visited tourist site in the archipelago, the **Calanais Standing Stones.** A visitor center explains the speculation surrounding this atmospheric site. Lewis also boasts a string of lesser-known stone circles, with the excavations currently under way at **Na Dromannan**—a quarry just a mile (1.6 km) east of the Calanais stones—revealing stones that are believed to be older than the world-famous Stonehenge. The quarry is also thought to have provided some of the standing stones in the Calanais circle.

Slightly to the north, **Carloway** is home to another of Lewis's most important heritage sites, the **Dun Carloway Broch.** With its circular dry-stone walls, this is one of the best preserved of the hundreds of fortified towers that pepper Scotland's Atlantic coastline. The **Doune Broch Centre** sheds light on the mysterious origins of the brochs and tries to recall the days when people sought shelter in them.

Cross north from Calanais onto Bernera, the small island that has been linked to Lewis by a bridge since 1953, and you'll have a chance to learn more about the region's Pictish settlers at the reproduction **Bostadh Iron Age House.** Signs of more recent periods also compel on Lewis. At the **Arnol Blackhouse Museum,** also located on the west coast, you can explore an old croft house, seeing how the local people lived with a roaring peat fire at the heart of their homes. Down the road (even closer to Calanais) in Carloway, a whole hamlet of thatched crofters houses, the **Gearrannan Blackhouse Village,** has been preserved. Here you can amble

Stornoway

🅰 217 B6

Museum Nan Eilean

✉ Francis Street
☎ (01851) 709 266
💲 $
www.cne-siar.gov.uk/museum/stornoway/index.asp

Calanais Standing Stones

✉ Callanish
☎ (01851) 621 422
💲 $

Doune Broch Centre

✉ Carloway
☎ (01851) 643 338

Arnol Blackhouse Museum

✉ Arnol
☎ (01851) 710 395
💲 $

Gearrannan Blackhouse Village

✉ Carloway
☎ (01851) 643 416
💲 $
www.gearrannan.com

Harris

△ 217 A5, B5

between the nine homesteads as they tumble down the hillside to the Atlantic. The adventurous can also stay overnight.

In addition to ancient monuments, Lewis's landscape is one of vast bleak peat bogs, punctuated only by austere settlements that are in keeping with the largely strict Presbyterian way of life on the island. In stark contrast the island's coastline also boasts sandy beaches (most notably **Uig Sands**) and the sheer cliffs and stacks of the **Butt of Lewis.**

All this dramatic scenery lends itself effortlessly to outdoor activities. An increasing number of adventure operators give visitors the chance to try activities as diverse as surfing, sea kayaking, power kiting, and cycling. Lessons are available respectively from **Surf Lewis** (28 Francis St., Stornoway, tel 01851/840 337, www.hebrideansurf.co.uk, $$$$$), **58 Degrees North** (20a Coll, tel 01851/820 726, www.canoehebrides .com, $$$$$), and the **Western Isles Kite Company** (West View, Aird Uig, Timsgarry, tel 01851/672 771, www.powerkitesales.co.uk, $$$$$). Cyclists are also catered to with bike rental offered by both

Bike Hebrides (Macarthurs Yard, Stornoway, tel 07522/121 414, www .bikehebrides.com, $$$$$), which also offers a bicycle delivery service on both Lewis and Harris, and **Alex Dan's Cycle Centre** (67 Kenneth St., Stornoway, tel 01851/704 025, www.hebrideancycles.co.uk, $$$$$).

A raft of sailing adventures are provided by **Sea Trek Hebrides,** whose boat trips range from 12-hour excursions to **St. Kilda** and fishing trips to wildlife tours through to fast-paced rides onboard a rigid inflatable boat.

Harris

South of Lewis, the isle of Harris is one of the most naturally stunning places in the British Isles. The island has it all: vaulting mountains that are among the highest in the islands, sweeping, white-sand beaches, and a smorgasbord of wildlife that encompasses everything from seals to bountiful birdlife. What really crowns the island's appeal, though, is that it is virtually untouched by tourism, even in the middle of the summer.

Like Harris and Lewis themselves, Harris is divided into two distinct geographic halves.

Harris Day Excursion

If you are short on time or traveling without a car, a program of day excursions run by Cal Mac makes visiting the isle of Harris easy. The day excursion from Uig on the isle of Skye whisks you across to Lochmaddy for a bus tour of North Uist before another ferry takes you over to Leverburgh (from Uig on the isle of Berneray). When you arrive in Harris, the bus takes you up the west coast in search of Tarbert and the ferry back to Uig on Skye. Cal Mac also operates a number of other day trips, including a grand tour of the isle of Lewis from Ullapool on the mainland. Details can be found on their website (www.calmac.co.uk).

North of its main settlement, **Tarbert,** the island is impressively mountainous with rugged peaks and lofty ridges everywhere you look—a hill walkers' paradise. Much of the land is now owned by the community as part of the North Harris Trust, which redressed some of the legacies of the Highland Clearances and gave the community more control over its future.

Scooping over to South Harris, the scenery is completely different. Its eastern coast is home to a moonscape of weirdly shaped rocks and a scattering of craggy bays. Astonishingly this seemingly inhospitable land is where most of the residents in the south of the island live, after being relocated there during the Highland Clearances (see pp. 206–207). These disjointed settlements are today linked by a winding road that is known colloquially as the Golden Road, a reference to how much it cost to build—the joke being that it may as well have been made of gold. While it serves some very remote communities, it also provides visitors with access to this strange lunar landscape.

On the west coast the scene is very different. Here there are sweeping beaches, some of the cleanest and most impressive in Europe. The crème de la crème is **Luskentyre Beach,** a seemingly endless sweep of white sand fringed by brooding and translucent water, framed by rolling hills and the distant shadowy mountains of North Harris.

An island relatively untouched by tourism, Harris is also short on sights and wet weather entertainment. The main reason to come to the island is to get out and about in the great outdoors, with hiking, climbing, mountain biking, and watersports all popular activities. Many Scottish holidaymakers also bring their own gear with them. Bikes for all the family are available

Fresh lobster being prepared in a Tarbert restaurant

from **Harris Cycle Hire** *(Sorrel Cottage, 2 Glen Kyles, Leverburgh, tel 01859/520 319, www.sorrelcottage .co.uk, $$$$$)* in Leverburgh, but it is wise to book in advance. For guided hill walks contact **Mike Briggs** *(Bunabhainneadar, tel 01859/ 502 376).*

For days when you don't feel particularly active, though, there are still things that you can do. In

MacGillivray Centre

- ✉ A859, Northton, Harris
- ☎ (01859) 502 011
- 🕐 Closed Sun.

Seallam Visitor Centre

- ✉ Northton, Harris
- ☎ (01859) 520 258
- $ $
- www.seallam.com

North Uist

- 🅰 217 A5

Lochmaddy

- 🅰 217 A5

Northton the **MacGillivray Centre** looks at the work of naturalist William MacGillivray (who once lived there) and the island's nature. Located in the same village, the **Seallam Visitor Centre** delves into the rich history of the island. During the summer **Sea Harris** (East Tarbert, tel 01859/502 007, www.seaharris.co.uk, $$$$$) and **Kilda Cruises** (Heatherlea, West Tarbert, tel 01859/502 060, www.kildacruises.co.uk, $$$$$) offer tourists the chance to visit remote St. Kilda on a full-day boat trip. They also organize shorter trips to the Shiants and some of the other smaller Hebridean islands. These adventurous trips are no ordinary boat cruises and this is reflected in the price.

Sitting just west of Harris you find the island of **Taransay**, which briefly rose to fame in 2000 as the location of the BBC's *Castaway* fly-on-the-wall reality TV show, is an easier day trip. Boat trips to the island (www.visit-taransay.com, $$$$) leave from Horgabost beach. If you want to get closer to Harris's sea mammals and seabirds you should join a wildlife-watching boat tour from Leverburgh with **Strond Wildlife Charters** (Sound of Harris, tel 01859/520 204, $$$$$). When the wet weather sets in you can do worse than pop into the **Skoon Art Café** in Geocrab (4 Geocrab, tel 01859/530 268, www.skoon.com), which dishes up lovely homemade fare and displays paintings by the resident artist, Andrew John Craig. On a clear day the café offers lovely

views over The Minch. It also hosts regular live music gigs.

North Uist

Caledonian MacBrayne ferries (www.calmac.co.uk) travel south around the treacherous rocks from Leverburgh in Harris to Uig on the island of Berneray, itself connected to North Uist via a causeway. Most of the visitors arriving in Uig simply hop across Berneray as they strike out in search of the Uists. This small island, measuring roughly 2 miles (3 km) by 3 miles (5 km), is worth exploring, however, for those who have more time; it is blessed with gorgeous dune-backed beaches and stunning views all around. To really get

INSIDER TIP:

If the tide is low enough, make sure you walk out to North Uist's Scolpaig Tower. This open-to-the-elements folly is worth the effort.

—LEON GRAY
National Geographic contributor

a feel for Berneray follow the marked walk that circles the northern part of the island—the posts are blue and the terrain is relatively easy.

The other main entry point in North Uist is **Lochmaddy** on the east coast, welcoming cars and their passengers from Uig on

Coexisting Religions

While islanders living in the Western Isles peacefully coexist, there is a distinct religious divide with those in the north (North Uist, Harris, and Lewis) following the Protestant church and those in South Uist and Barra largely adhering to the Catholic faith. In addition to the Church of Scotland there are other Protestant denominations in the Outer Hebrides. In their desire to maintain the purity of worship they ensure in these parts that Sunday really is the Lord's Day. Shops, pubs, businesses, and gas stations close. Even children's playgrounds are out of bounds. The Outer Hebrides have the highest level of church attendance in Scotland, and catching a fiery Gaelic sermon is a powerful experience.

the isle of Skye. Lochmaddy has the best amenities on the island including the Uists' only tourist office, bank, a general store, a couple of eateries, and an arts center, so it is a good place to get your bearings. The highlight is **Taigh Chearsabhagh,** an arts center and museum at the heart of the island's cultural scene. Outdoor types can take advantage of the vast range of activities on offer at the residential **Uist Outdoor Centre** (Lochmaddy, tel 01876/500 480, www.uistoutdoorcentre.co.uk, $$$$$), which include scuba diving, sea kayaking, rock climbing, hill walking, wildlife-watching, and coasteering (traveling along a rocky coastline on foot and by swimming).

West of Lochmaddy, the North Uist landscape comes as something of a surprise. Gone are the mountains of Harris and in their place is a haunting landscape of bog and loch where deer and wild salmon outnumber humans. Some small settlements cling to the coastal roads, but the real tragedies are the people who are not here, whose sorrows are played out in derelict crofts and deserted villages. These unfortunate souls were victims of the Highland Clearances (see pp. 206–207). Walking, cycling, or driving around the island is the best way to appreciate its beauty. Keep an eye out for the **Barpa Langais** burial cairn, the three **Na Fir Bhreige** standing stones, and the **Pobull Fhinn** stone circle. These Neolithic sights are remarkable more for the history they tell than their appearance today. In the island's northwestern corner the castlelike folly that is **Scolpaig Tower** enjoys a scenic spot on an islet in the eponymous loch. The RSPB nature reserve at **Balranald,** a short hop south of the tower, is a good place to stretch your legs with lovely coastal views and the chance to see (or at least hear) one of Britain's most rare birds, the corncrake.

South Uist

Unlike Harris and Lewis, the Uists are actually two distinct islands, linked by causeways via the small island of **Benbecula,** dominated by the British military. Most visitors simply pass through, and you would be wise to do the same. South Uist differs from North Uist not

Taigh Chearsabhagh

✉ Lochmaddy, North Uist

☎ (01876) 500 293

$ $

www.museums galleriesscotland.org .uk/member/taigh -chearsabhagh

Balranald

✉ 3 miles (5 km) W of Bayhead; turn for Hougharry off the A865

☎ (01463) 715 000

$ $

www.rspb.org.uk

South Uist

🅰 217 A4

**Loch Druidibeg
Nature Reserve**

✉ Stilligarry, South
Uist

☎ (01870) 620 238

$ $

www.snh.org.uk

**Kildonan
Museum**

✉ Kildonan, South
Uist

☎ (01878) 710 343

$ $

www.kildonan
museum.co.uk

just in its appearance, but also in outlook. The prominence of Catholicism can be keenly felt, with Madonnas popping up by the roadside.

The South Uist landscape is characterized by hills and mountains in the east and golden-sand beaches on its exposed western shore. Tackling the highest peak, **Ben More** (2,034 feet/620 m) is a popular pastime with hill walkers. From its summit views over the Hebridean islands unfold to reward those who have made the steep ascent. This vantage point also allows you to fully appreciate how many lochs and lochans dot

Machair

Machair (a Gaelic word) is a term used to describe a long and low-lying fertile plain. Around half of Scotland's machair is located in the Outer Hebrides. This rare and delicate habitat is difficult to define, but generally speaking it stretches from the sand dunes through to the peaty soil farther inland, has a high shell content, and is characterized by the presence of marram grass. For those visiting South Uist, Barra, and South Harris in July and August this translates as a vivid and colorful carpet of rare wildflowers, including orchids. Myriad birdlife also thrives in the machair, including the ringed plover, the lapwing, and the rare corncrake.

the Uists. **Hecla** (1,988 feet/606 m) yields similar views.

Back at sea level, the island's Atlantic coastline is backed up by machair, sand dunes that in spring explode with a stunning collage of wildflower blossoms. The landscape in between is also dotted with old crofting villages and a wealth of lochans. Keen ornithologists or those who enjoy low-level walks can also visit **Loch Druidibeg Nature Reserve—** this national nature reserve incorporates machair strewn with colorful flowers, moorland, and lochans. The fauna is at its best in July, while the late spring and early summer months also provide the chance to see wading birds, wildfowl, and corncrakes. From Stilligarry a marked trail leads into the reserve. If you plan ahead you can pick up a map of the reserve from the tourist office in **Lochboisdale,** the island's main settlement.

South Uist's indoor attractions are limited, with the **Kildonan Museum,** situated on the main A865, the highlight. Here assorted artifacts shed light on island life over the centuries; the collection's prized possession is the Clanranald Armorial Stone, dating from the 16th century and adorning the coat of arms of the clan that held sway over the island for more than 450 years.

Those moved by the tales of Bonnie Prince Charlie and Flora MacDonald might be interested to know that Flora lived in South Uist as a child, with a cairn marking the spot a short distance south of the Kildonan Museum. The tragic Stuart history is continued

The sea around the Outer Hebrides has many faces, from tranquil blue calm to storm-swept mountainous waves.

on the isle of Eriskay—a causeway runs onto Eriskay from the south of the island—where Charles Edward Stuart reputedly arrived in Scotland in preparation for the 1745 Jacobite rebellion.

South of South Uist, a causeway takes you to **Eriskay,** a beautiful island with sweeping white-sand beaches. Completely unspoiled by tourism, Eriskay is worth exploring; however, many people just pass through on their way to the Barra ferry.

Barra

Located at the southern end of the Outer Hebrides, the isle of Barra is instantly appealing. It may only be 8 miles (13 km) long and 5 miles (8 km) wide,

but what it lacks in size it makes up for in diversity. Here you'll find the vaulting hulks of Ben Tangaval and Heaval giving way to rambling glens, bright machair flowers, moors, rolling hills, and pristine, white-sand beaches.

The capital of **Castlebay** is a good place to start exploring the island. First up should be the **Barra Heritage Centre,** which delves into the local Gaelic culture and stories of the island's people. The town's most unmissable sight, literally, is **Kisimul Castle**—which, as it has its own freshwater spring, is able to stand alone in the water, casting a dramatic presence over the wide bay. The striking fortification is also testimony to the Clan MacNeil family who have ruled

Barra

🄰 217 A4

Barra Heritage Centre

✉ Castlebay, Barra

☎ (01871) 810 413

💲 $

www.barraheritage.com

Kisimul Castle

✉ Barra

☎ (01871) 810 313

🕐 Closed Oct.–March

💲 $$

www.historic-scotland.gov.uk

Two common dolphins skirt through the waters at Barra Head.

Barra for much of the island's history. The 45th Clan Chief Robert MacNeil, who was an American architect, bought the castle back in 1937 and made it his life's work to rebuild one of Europe's oldest castles. In 2000 control passed to Historic Scotland.

The reconstructed fortress houses a museum whose intriguing artifacts include British army weapons that date back to the 1746 Battle of Culloden. One of the best perspectives of the fortification is from the water aboard a kayak; the local company **Clearwater Paddling** (Castelbay, Barra, tel 01871/810 443 www.clearwaterpaddling.com, $$$$$) organizes trips across the bay that culminate by Kisimul. Castlebay is also at the island's cultural heart, regularly hosting folk bands and the island's annual **Barra Fest** in July.

Outside Castlebay, much of the island is easily accessible on foot, though cycling is also a good way of getting around. Barra abounds with spectacular scenery, with highlights including the sandy stretch of Halaman Bay, with its soaring Atlantic surf, and the scattering of beaches that lead north from Halaman.

The island's most unusual attraction is **Barra Golf Club** (Cleat, Isle of Barra, tel 01871/810 240). This unique course would stump the likes of Ernie Els and Tiger Woods. It may only have nine holes, but it contains tricky hazards such as the "largest bunker in the world" (a giant Atlantic beach) and fences built around the greens to keep out the cows that have the same effect on golf balls! Fairways are little more than

INSIDER TIP:

The schedule of flights into the island of Barra is a bit flexible. It needs to be, since the plane lands on the beach at low tide.

—JIM RICHARDSON
National Geographic photographer

rock-strewn hillsides and many players consider themselves lucky to lose only one ball a hole. Still, it has to be one of the most scenic courses in the world. Elsewhere around the island, layers of history reveal themselves through sights like the **standing stones of Brevig Bay** and the **Dun Cuier** complex. Then there is the **Dun Bharpa** cairn, where the dead were laid to rest in Neolithic times. At Craigston, the **Thatched Cottage Museum** (*Craigston, Barra, $*) vividly shows how people lived in the sturdy traditional blackhouses until as recently as the 1970s.

Between Barra and the isle of Eriskay to the north is a stretch of water famous around the world. In 1941 the SS *Politician* ran aground here and her cargo of 24,000 bottles of whisky was "lost." The enterprising locals intervened to lend a hand and by the time customs officials arrived, much of the whisky that had gone down with the ship had mysteriously disappeared. Compton Mackenzie's book *Whisky Galore* vividly recalled the tale and it was made into a movie in 1949 (released as *Tight Little Island* in North America). Soon the locals may no longer have to wait for passing ships to founder before they can get their hands on the "water of life." Rumors are rife that Barra may soon have its first whisky distillery—well, at least the first legal one for generations.

St. Kilda

The remote and mystical islands of St. Kilda lie in the Atlantic 40 miles (66 km) west of the Outer Hebrides. For many Scots St. Kilda has something of the holy grail about it, with many dreaming of one day visiting this World Heritage-listed outpost. Few, though, manage to conquer the Atlantic and land on the islands. Those who do make the stomach-churning journey

St. Kilda
⚠ 217 A5

Flying to Barra

Traveling by boat is the usual form of travel to Barra, but a thrilling alternative is to fly in. Swooping in over the sea Barra "airport" appears amid a rumble of hills overlooking the sweeping sands of Cockle Bay. There is a tiny terminal building, but no runway. The plane tugs around for its final approach, drops down onto the beach, and then bounces along to the terminal. The Barra service must be one of the few in the world whose timetable includes the caveat "subject to tides" and the dramatic beach landing makes an indelible imprint on the memory of anyone who makes it. Flights to Barra airport depart twice daily from Glasgow, and can be booked through Flybe (*www.flybe.com*).

A village house on Hirta, St. Kilda, west of the Outer Hebrides

discover an oasis swirling in myths, legends, and the echoes of a long-lost way of life.

Getting to St. Kilda is all part of the challenge. Not for those who suffer from sea sickness, it is a stomach-testing 16- to 18-hour cruise from Oban, or a 4- to 6-hour trip from the Outer Hebrides. The difficult journey, though, is quickly forgotten as the unique landscapes of this archipelago rear into view, a sight unlike anything else in the British Isles. St. Kilda was never tamed by the smoothing actions of glaciers, and the jagged sheer rock faces and towering *stacs* (Gaelic for "sea stack") that shudder out of the Atlantic to puncture the horizon have more in common with Iceland or the Faroe Islands than Scotland. There are several islands

and stacs in the chain, with the main islands Hirta, Boreray, Soay, and Dun.

In a land where man definitely plays second fiddle to nature, wildlife abounds. With around a million birds nesting in St. Kilda the islands are an ornithologist's dream. Highlights include the tens of thousands of impossibly cute puffins that occupy the cliffs and, on Boreray, the world's largest gannet population, with around 60,000 nesting pairs. On land the scraggy soay sheep are a form of primitive sheep that are unique to the islands.

A Unique Way of Life

For hundreds of years man eked out an existence on St. Kilda. Mother Nature even gave the local men a helping hand, as they had large and rugged feet to help them when they were hunting for bird eggs (vital food) on the cliffs.

The main island of the St. Kilda group is **Hirta,** and this was the only one to have been permanently inhabited. Here you will come across a rather unappealing military installation and an essential research facility for the National Trust for Scotland and Scottish National Heritage. Standing forlornly back from the shore is the island's old residential

The biggest difficulty is avoiding the great skuas, the hulking brown birds that swoop down to buzz walkers in a bid to keep them away from their nests. The rewards, though, far outweigh the effort involved. After all, how many people can say that they have been to the highest point in St. Kilda? On a clear day the views are phenomenal.

Although Hirta is relatively easy to land on and to get around, landing on the other isles is much more problematic. The majority of visitors, therefore, have to content

Evacuation of St. Kilda

The way of life on St. Kilda was rudimentary and some even think Utopian, as there was no money and no government, with the Gaelic-speaking people all just pitching in to help each other and do what work needed to be done. This self-sufficiency became hard to maintain, with the emigration of 36 residents to Australia in 1852, accompanied by a greater reliance on imported food and goods. Acute food shortages in 1912, an influenza outbreak in 1913, the influence of tourism, and the ramifications of World War I sounded the final death knell for island life, with the remaining 36 islanders evacuated in 1930.

street, whose old stone and traditional blackhouses stretch along the hillside. A visit to the small museum on Village Street provides thorough insight into the history of the island and is an essential stop. A fascinating heritage walk weaves through the village, further illuminating how the locals once lived.

Hanging omnipresent above the village is **Conachair,** a 1,411-foot (430 m) peak with Britain's highest sea cliff dropping off, which offers stunning views of the islands and back east toward the Outer Hebrides. The steep hike to the top is pretty arduous, even though a road travels part of the way up.

themselves with the view from the sea. Taking a boat around **Boreray** as 40 percent of the world's gannet population swirls around the hulking rock island and its protective stacs is a stunning experience.

A number of companies organize boat trips out to St. Kilda from the Outer Hebrides, including **Sea Trek Hebrides, Sea Harris,** and **Kilda Cruises** (see p. 242 for details). If you prefer, you can see St. Kilda and spend longer on the islands as a volunteer with the National Trust for Scotland. Details can be found on the St. Kilda World Heritage website (*www.kilda .org.uk.*). ∎

Seabirds soaring over craggy sea stacks and sandstone cliffs on far-flung islands, and ancient secrets emerging from windswept sand

Orkney & Shetland Islands

The prehistoric stone tower of Mousa Broch dominates the island of Mousa in the Shetland archipelago.

Orkney & Shetland Islands

Plowing through the rough seas from the Scottish mainland's northern tip to the remote Orkney and Shetland Islands is no ordinary ferry ride. The journey transports you back to the islands' Norse heritage and then to the prehistoric days of mystical stone circles, mysterious hilltop monuments, and the lost village of Skara Brae, a remarkable netherworld that sheds light on daily life in this area five millennia ago.

Prehistoric Orkney

Skara Brae is just one of the sites dating back to 3000–2000 B.C. that prompted UNESCO to place the Heart of Neolithic Orkney on its World Heritage List in 1999. The archipelago's other must-see sights—valued because of the extraordinary light they shed on Neolithic life and the achievements of these ancient peoples in northern Europe—are Maeshowe, the Stones of Stenness, and the Ring of Brodgar, alongside many as yet unexcavated sites.

NOT TO BE MISSED:

The Ring of Brodgar, Orkney's rival
to Stonehenge **255**

A concert at the magnificent
St. Magnus Cathedral **255**

The Italian Chapel, a testament
of faith built by Italian prisoners
of war **256**

Viewing sunken warships in Scapa
Flow harbor **257–259**

Papa Westray, a wildlife lover's
paradise and one of Europe's top
Neolithic sites **258–259**

The world-famous prehistoric village
of Skara Brae **260–261**

Jarlshof, site of a historic treasure
trove that takes visitors from
Bronze Age to Viking times **266**

Mousa Broch in the "simmer
dim" eternal twilight, when
the storm petrels fly in around
midnight **266**

Orkney's more recent history, centered around the vast natural harbor of Scapa Flow (one of the world's leading scuba dive venues), and its natural environment, are also remarkable. South of Orkney Mainland, the island of Hoy awaits with its rugged, mountain-tossed scenery and the iconic Old Man of Hoy rock stack. The rest of the outlying islands, in common with the Mainland, are blessed with rolling hills rather than hulking mountains. The land is generally smooth and fertile, one of the factors contributing to the prosperous life the islanders have lived, largely unruffled by the machinations of mainland Britain, for thousands of years. Wildlife has thrived here, too, especially in the archipelago's nature reserves.

Green Shetland

Ask many British people to point out the Shetland Islands on a map and they may struggle. Even the BBC weather forecasts have often been a bit reluctant to place this most faraway of northern island archipelagos. In recent years, however, Shetland's green tourism credentials have started to come to the fore, finally placing it on the global map. A fourth annual Destination Scorecard survey—conducted by *National Geographic Traveler* magazine—rated Shetland as one of the most appealing island destinations in the world (it had the fourth highest score).

The island rated highly on criteria such as "environmental and ecological quality," "condition of historic buildings and archaeological sites," and "outlook for the future." An expert panel member described Shetland as having "everything with bells on," which conveys just how special this spectacular northern eco-oasis is, where Mother Nature is firmly in charge.

This protected environment of pristine white beaches, vaulting sea cliffs, and rugged islands also makes for some of the most impressive wildlife-viewing opportunities in Europe. In summer, legions of puffins flutter around the sea cliffs while the mammoth great skuas put humans firmly in their place by dive-bombing anyone foolhardy enough to venture into their territory. Almost all the varieties of seabird found in the United Kingdom grace Shetland. And the water itself is alive with seals (common and gray), porpoises, otters, dolphins, and whales, with orcas one of the most spectacular visitors.

Shetland is also home to some stunning historical sites, where conservation

has been paramount. At Jarlshof, you can ramble among remarkably preserved Iron and Bronze Age houses and conjure up the days when Viking longships patrolled these waters. ■

Orkney Islands

For most visitors, both practicalities and time limit their Orkney island discovery to the Mainland. However, the archipelago is actually made up of 70 or so islands and smaller rock skerries, of which 17 are currently inhabited. Together, the islands cover an area of more than 347 square miles (900 sq km), with the archipelago about 53 miles (85 km) from north to south and 23 miles (37 km) from east to west.

Bird-watching at Yesnaby, in the Orkney Islands

GETTING TO ORKNEY:
Flybe flights *(tel 0871/700 2000, www .flybe.com)* operates flights from major British airports. For ferry information, contact John O'Groats Ferries *(tel 01955/611 353, www.jogferry.co.uk),* Pentland Ferries *(tel 01856/831 226, www. pentlandsferries.co.uk),* or Northlink Ferries *(tel 0845/600 0449, www. northlinkferries.co.uk).*

Mainland

By far the biggest and most populous of the Orkney Islands, the Mainland supports a thriving community of more than 20,000 people who are concentrated around the urban centers of Kirkwall and **Stromness.**

The latter is Orkney's picturesque ferry port, which boasts graceful stone buildings and an attractive setting. Here, the **Pier Arts Centre** *(Victoria St., Stromness, tel 01856/850 209 www.pier artscentre.com, $)* showcases 20th-century British art, as well as some

contemporary pieces by Scandinavian artists. Then learn about the island's natural history at the **Stromness Museum** *(52 Alfred St., tel 01856/850 025, www .orkneycommunities.co.uk/stromness museum, $),* only a short stroll away.

Heading due east, the A965 takes visitors to the Orkney capital, **Kirkwall,** a town that doesn't share the charm of Stromness. A stop here is de rigueur for all visitors, though, as it is home to the magnificent **St. Magnus Cathedral** *(Broad St., Kirkwall, $; see sidebar below).* The **Orkney**

INSIDER TIP:

The St. Magnus Festival in June brings great music to the Orkneys, and the city of Kirkwall is full of performances. Visit a concert in St. Magnus Cathedral and you won't regret it.

—SALLY McFALL
National Geographic contributor

Museum is also worth visiting. On the town's outskirts, a slightly peaty single malt (one of Scotland's finest) is waiting for you at the **Highland Park Distillery.**

You don't need to visit a museum to experience Orkney's history. Signs that man has been living on Orkney for thousands of years emerge at every turn. Spread across the Mainland are upright stones and burial cairns, some of which archaeologists have investigated, but many of which remain a mystery.

In west Mainland, the must-see sights include **Skara Brae** (see pp. 260–261), the Stones of Stenness,

Maeshowe, the Ring of Brodgar, and the ruined **Earl's Palace** at Birsay. The standing **Stones of Stenness** ($), located about 4 miles (6.5 km) east of Stromness, were originally a circle of 12 rock slabs, but today only four continue to defy the elements; the chances are you will be alone at this bleak and romantic spot.

Nearby **Maeshowe** (*tel 01856/761 606, $*) is one of the best-preserved Neolithic burial chambers in Europe, dating back more than 3,000 years. Also nearby is the **Ring of Brodgar** ($), one of Orkney's most dramatic sights. Of all the islands' standing stones, this one is closest in appearance to Stonehenge in England. It is estimated that the circle originally had 60 stones when it was erected over four and a half millennia ago. Today almost 30 remain.

To learn more about Orkney's Viking heritage, head to Orphir, where the **Orkneyinga Saga Centre** brings the violent invasion of the northern isles to life.

On the north coast of the island lie the well-preserved ruins of the **Broch of Gurness,** an ancient fortified settlement

Orkney Islands

▲ 253 A1–A2, B1–B2

Visitor Information

✉ West Castle St., Kirkwall

☎ (01856) 872 856

www.visitorkney.com

Orkney Museum

✉ Tankerness House, Broad Street , Kirkwall

☎ (01856) 873 191

$ $

www.orkney.gov.uk

Highland Park Distillery

✉ Holm Road, Kirkwall

☎ (01856) 874 619

$ Tour: $

www.highlandpark .co.uk

Orkney & Shetland Islands Archaeological sites

www. historic -scotland.co.uk

Orkneyinga Saga Centre

✉ Gyre Rd., Orphir

☎ (01856) 811 319

$ $

St. Magnus Cathedral

Founded in 1137 by the Viking Earl Rognvald, Kirkwall's magnificent St. Magnus Cathedral is also known as the "Light of the North." Over the centuries, erosion has taken its toll on the soft red and yellow sandstone used in the church's construction. The cathedral's ornate exterior is largely medieval in appearance, the work of master stonemasons who are believed to have also worked on England's Durham Cathedral. The best times to visit St. Magnus are during the Sunday morning services at 11:15 a.m. or during one of the regular organ recitals or musical performances that are held here (check *www.stmagnus.org* for listings).

Broch of Gurness

✉ Evie

💲 $

www.historic
-scotland.gov.uk

**Lamb Holm,
Burray, & South
Ronaldsay**

🅰 253 A1

**Orkney Fossil &
Heritage Centre**

✉ Viewforth,
Burray

☎ (01856) 731 255

💲 $

www.orkney
fossilcentre.co.uk

**Orkney Marine-
Life Aquarium**

✉ St. Margaret's
Hope, South
Ronaldsay

☎ (01856) 831 700

💲 $

www.orkney
marinelife.co.uk

**Tomb of the
Eagles**

✉ Liddle, St.
Margaret's
Hope, South
Ronaldsay

🕐 Closed
Nov.–Feb.

💲 $$

www.tombof
theeagles.co.uk

dominated by a circular stone tower. The structure that you see today is believed to date from somewhere around 200–100 B.C., with low walls dotting the site that are actually the remnants of the village that was built around the broch. With a good dose of imagination and a look at the exhibition in the visitor center, you can conjure up a vivid picture of Iron Age life on Orkney.

Italian Chapel

One of Orkney's most remarkable sights is the tiny Italian Chapel on the island of Lamb Holm. This place of worship, constructed of two Nissen huts joined end to end, its interior ornately painted by Domenico Chiocchetti, is an enduring legacy of the hundreds of Italian prisoners of war (who also built the Churchill Barriers) interred at the island's Camp 60 who wished for a place to worship. Watching over the chapel, a concrete statue depicts the patron saint of England, St. George, slaying a dragon.

Lamb Holm, Burray & South Ronaldsay

While Orkney's prehistory is certainly captivating, its more recent history is also worth exploring. Heading south from the Mainland, it is possible to drive on to the uninhabited island of Lamb Holm, home to the fantastic legacy that is the **Italian Chapel** (see sidebar below) and World War II bunkers, to Burray, and then on to South Ronaldsay.

The four causeways connecting the islands are known as the **Churchill Barriers** and were erected on the orders of the British Prime Minister Winston Churchill (1874–1965) between 1940 and 1945, to improve the defenses of the vast natural harbor of **Scapa Flow** (see sidebar p. 259). Close to the causeways, the capsized and rusting ships were deliberately sunk as blockships to protect against attack from German U-boats, a practice that was carried out during both World War I and World War II.

In addition to fascinating military history, these southern islands also have a number of fun family attractions. The **Orkney Fossil and Heritage Centre** on Burray has a UV room that reveals the iridescent colors of the rocks on display, while the **Orkney Marine-Life Aquarium** in St. Margaret's Hope on South Ronaldsay has an interesting array of the native sealife.

For those hankering after more archaeological sites, South Ronaldsay is home to one of Orkney's most impressive, the **Tomb of the Eagles,** or the Isbister chambered burial cairn. The dramatic coastal location of this Bronze Age burial mound just adds to the appeal.

Hoy

The second largest of the Orkney Islands, Hoy also boasts

dramatic scenery, with mountain peaks that rise up to 1,577 feet (479 m) and vertical cliffs. It is also home to one of the archipelago's most iconic sights, the **Old Man of Hoy**—a fabled sea stack that is high on the wish list for many Scottish climbers. The island has as much to offer nature lovers as it does walkers, with its thriving populations of mountain hares and magnificent birds of prey such as hen harriers and peregrine falcons.

Visitors should be aware, however, that the island does not have a public bus service—those who arrive without a car must either walk, cycle, or travel by minibus from the Stromness ferry to Rackwick Bay. Rackwick has a few basic accommodation options and is an ideal base for those wishing to tackle the technically tricky Old Man of Hoy,

3 miles (5 km) to the west.

If scaling a vertical stack cast adrift in the Atlantic isn't for you, then there are a couple of other walking options. You can follow the cliff-top path to **St. John's Head,** where the 1,136-foot (346 m) cliff is dizzyingly high. The path is in poor condition, however, and is not for those who are afraid of heights. Climbing the island's highest peak, **Ward Hill** (1,577 feet/479 m), is not technically difficult and offers panoramic views out over all of the islands.

Orkney's military history comes to the fore once again on Hoy's eastern shore, with the **naval cemetery** in Lyness and its **Scapa Flow Visitor Centre** (also known as the Lyness Interpretation Centre; see sidebar p. 259) both worth a visit. Don't miss the expansive collection of

Hoy & South Walls

🅰 253 A1

Scapa Flow Visitor Centre

✉ Lyness, Hoy
☎ (01856) 791 300
💲 $

www.scapaflow .co.uk

A gray seal pup with its mother on the shores of the Pentland Firth in Hoy

Westray
🅰 253 A2

Westray Heritage Centre
✉ Pierowall
☎ (01857) 677 414
🕐 Closed Oct.–April
💲 $
www.westray heritage.co.uk

Papa Westray
🅰 253 A2

INSIDER TIP:

As you gaze from the cliff top out to the towering sea stack known as the Old Man of Hoy, you'll realize it was well worth negotiating the logistics of the ferry from Orkney's Mainland and the ensuing hike.

—LARRY PORGES
National Geographic editor

photographs that shed light on island life during the two world wars and the assortment of old military vehicles and weapons.

South Walls

Across a narrow causeway from the southern tip of Hoy awaits the island of South Walls. This small island is home to one of Orkney's best hotels and restaurants, the **Stromabank Hotel** (see Travelwise p. 301), as well as the impressive defenses of the **Hackness Battery** and the sandstone **Hackness Martello Tower,** which date from the Napoleonic Wars, another European conflict that still managed to trouble these distant northern shores.

North of the Mainland

Each of the inhabited islands north of the mainland—**Rousay, Wyre, Egilsay, Shapinsay, Stronsay, Sanday,** and **North Ronaldsay**—has something to

recommend it, from prehistoric sights and lighthouses to dramatic sandstone cliffs and nature reserves. Constraints on time, however, mean that many people stick to the larger island of Westray and its smaller Papa Westray sibling.

Westray sustains a thriving community of around 600 people and a visit here is as much about sampling the great local produce as it is viewing its scenic beauty. In the main settlement of Pierowall, you can learn about island life in the **Westray Heritage Centre.** Elsewhere, the ruined 16th-century **Noltland Castle,** the dramatic **Noup Head** sea cliffs, and the **Castle o'Burrian** sea stack, home to myriad nesting puffins, are worth seeking out.

Getting to **Papa Westray,** located in the far northwest of the Orkney archipelago, is all part of the fun, whether you arrive by ferry (*www.orkneyferries.co.uk*) or on board the world's shortest scheduled flight (it takes around two minutes; *www.loganair.co.uk*) from Westray.

Papa Westray is mentioned in the *Orkneyinga Saga*—a semi-mythical history of the Viking Earls of Orkney written in the early 13th century—and it has a strong religious heritage. Legend has it that the "priest isle" (as it literally translates) was so named after it became a pilgrimage center dedicated to Saint Tredwell. Countless pilgrims came here seeking miracle cures for their eyes, although the chapel once dedicated to her is little more than rubble today. Highlights include **Holland House,** a romantic dwelling that was once the seat of the local lairds and the Trails family and is now home to a modest museum; and the sensitively restored **St. Boniface Kirk** church.

Papa Westray's most impressive attraction is **Knap of Howar.** In an atmospheric spot overlooking the sea, this Neolithic farmstead is every bit as evocative as Skara Brae on the Mainland. Experts reckon it dates back to 3500 B.C., making it one of the oldest still existing in Europe, if not the oldest.

Papa Westray also has a lot to offer wildlife enthusiasts, from waters rich in seals and otters to myriad seabirds, with the **North Hill RSPB Nature Reserve** the birding highlight. ■

Holland House
✉ Papa Westray
$ $

North Hill RSPB Nature Reserve
✉ Papa Westray
☎ (01856) 850 176
www.rspb.org.uk

EXPERIENCE: Reliving History at Scapa Flow

During World War I and World War II, Orkney's Scapa Flow was a major naval base, with more than 100 warships moored in the bay at any one time. This military past has left an indelible mark on the harbor; even today, visitors can see the blockships that were sunk to try and protect it from attack by German U-boats while the surrounding hills are dotted with gun batteries.

At the end of World War I, 74 captured German ships were also moored in this vast natural harbor. When the Germans learned that peace terms meant they would have to hand over their ships, the German commander ordered that the fleet be scuttled and all 74 were sunk before the Allies could intervene.

The majority of the vessels didn't stay where they were sunk, and those that were washed ashore were quickly salvaged. In 1920, one of the biggest salvage operations ever attempted by the British began and, in the interwar period, the majority of the wrecks were removed. Some of the vessels, however, including three battleships and a U-boat, are still wedged on the floor of the deep waters of Scapa Flow.

One of the early naval casualties of World War II, the *Royal Oak*, was sunk by a German U-boat in 1939, with more than half of her 1,400-strong crew losing their lives. Today the wreck of the *Royal Oak* is protected as a war grave, with an annual service held on October 13 to commemorate this tragic event. The wreck-strewn harbor—other wrecks lie alongside the scuttled German fleet—is now firmly established as one of Europe's most popular scuba-diving sites. However, divers should note that wetsuits are required and the dangerous nature of the wrecks mean that only experienced divers should delve below the waters. Even then, local advice should be sought beforehand—every year there are casualties in Scapa Flow. **Scapa Scuba** (Lifeboat House, Stromness, tel 01856/851 218, www.scapascuba .co.uk) offers beginner and advanced level PADI courses and guided dives for individuals or small groups.

For non-divers, the good news is that it is possible to experience Scapa Flow without getting in the water. **Roving Eye Enterprises** (Westrow Lodge, Orphir, tel 01856/811 360, www.rovingeye.co.uk) gives you the chance to see the wrecks on a large television screen, with the images beamed back from a remote roving underwater camera. Those venturing to Hoy can visit the **Scapa Flow Visitor Centre** (see pp. 257–258), which delves into the harbor's role in both World Wars.

Prehistoric Orkney

Until 150 years ago, the sparse landscape of Skara Brae on remote Orkney lay as it had for thousands of years. Few people, let alone tourists, ever ventured to this bleak, inhospitable bay that takes the full brunt of the Atlantic breakers and chill winds accompanying them. Yet buried beneath the sand was an ancient secret, uncovered one stormy night, that brought man face-to-face with his prehistoric ancestors.

Skara Brae is a large, stone-built Neolithic settlement on the west coast of Mainland Orkney.

On that night in 1850, the sand miracu-lously cleared away, unearthing the fishing and farming village of Skara Brae, Europe's most complete and best-preserved Neo-lithic village. It soon became clear that this was no normal archaeological dig when it came to light that the remains of Skara Brae dated back as far as 5000 B.C., making them much older than young upstarts like the Colosseum in Rome and even more ancient than the Egyptian Pyramids and England's Stonehenge.

Today "Scotland's Pompeii," as it has been eulogized, has been recognized by UNESCO as part of the Heart of Neolithic Orkney World Heritage site and has become a mecca for historians, archaeologists, and travelers. The location itself is spectacular, as Skara Brae occupies a wide, sandy bay where the chill waters of the Atlantic Ocean tumble onto the unspoiled sands. There have been concessions to the tour bus crowd, like a visitor center and a reconstructed house, but the site really does possess a magical sense of the timeless and speaks for itself.

Visiting Scara Brae

The visitor center is tastefully done and provides some information, or rather specula-tion, on the people who once inhabited the village. We know that they were farmers and fishermen and that they built their homes below the earth to survive the harsh climate, but we are still not certain what forced them to abandon their homes around 4500 B.C., only 500 years after the foundation of the community. Was it a war with a rival village or maybe a savage storm like the one in 1850 that uncovered the village, or was it something more sinister?

The reconstructed house gives a good idea of the conditions that the original people lived in all those millennia ago, but walking around the actual village is the main attraction. It is no longer possible to get right into the houses—they were closed due to fears that they would be damaged by tourists. Today, looking down from the walkways above, there are numerous clues as to how those prehistoric people lived and many recognizable features that you do not need a guide to tell you about. Carved out of stone slabs are dressers, cupboards, shelves, hearths, and even beds, offering a unique insight into a prehistoric life that was not as different from our own as you might have imagined.

Skaill House

In the summer months, the Skara Brae admission ticket also buys access to Skaill House. Once home to the Laird of Skaill, the grand house was built in 1620 and today you can walk around its stately rooms, leafing through the ages as you go.

A fascinating exhibit is the crockery that belonged to the man who stumbled across Australia for the British and set in place the chain of events that led to the founding of modern Australia. Capt. James Cook's dinner service is on view here, a relic left behind after his last fateful voyage (when he was bludgeoned to death in Hawaii) and then given to the Laird of Skaill when the ships *Discovery* and *Resolution* docked in Stromness in 1770.

Visitor Information

The property is located 18 miles (30 km) northwest of Kirkwall, Orkney, on the B9056. Historic Scotland (*www.historic-scotland.gov.uk*) looks after the site ($$). It's open daily year-round, and has an on-site café (though hours may be restricted in winter).

Daily Life in Neolithic Skara Brae

The well-preserved site of Skara Brae gives us many clues as to the daily lives of the people who lived here 7,000 years ago. The signs point to a close-knit farming and fishing community, with its houses arranged in a uniform manner. Some historians believe this architectural uniformity indicates that Skara Brae was an egalitarian society, whereas others think it is simply the result of a tried-and-true homogenous design that dealt successfully with the area's harsh conditions.

Each house consisted of one room with a central hearth and no windows, so that the only interior light would have come through a smoke hole in the roof above the fireplace. Due to the lack of wood

in the area, the furniture was made of stone, including a tank for storing limpets, thought to be used for fishing bait or as emergency food.

Animal bones found on the premises show that the inhabitants kept sheep and cattle—and hunted the nearby red deer and wild boar—for food. They also used the bones to make tools and the skins for clothing and blankets. Shells and seeds were also discovered here, indicating that the residents harvested fish and shellfish, along with wheat and barley as crops.

Houses were linked by a network of sheltered, insulated passageways so that people could travel around the village comfortably during the long, cold winters.

Shetland Islands

If the Orkney Islands seem remote, then the Shetland Islands may as well be, as far as many Scots are concerned, on the moon. They are, in fact, nearer to the Norwegian city of Bergen than they are to Aberdeen on the Scottish mainland. The locals in these far-flung islands know Orkney as the "South," never mind the Scottish mainland or the unimaginable foreign outpost of London.

Norsemen with a model Viking ship at the Up Helly Aa fire festival, Lerwick, Shetland

GETTING TO SHETLAND: Flybe flights *(tel 0871/700 2000, www.flybe.com)* operates flights from major British airports For ferry information, contact Northlink Ferries *(www.northlink ferries.co.uk).*

The Shetland and Orkney Islands may be little explored, but the oil and gas they bring ashore help prop up the U.K. economy. Those who make the considerable effort to travel this far north will be richly rewarded, by dramatic scenery, abundant wildlife, and ancient monuments.

One of the highlights of the year is the **Up Helly Aa** fire festival (www.uphellyaa.org), held on the last Tuesday of January—the main one takes place in Lerwick—when

a Viking longboat is ceremonially burned. This ritual connects the past and the present in a land where reality and myth merge.

If you visit in January, be prepared for cold, short days. These long and gloomy winters are compensated for by glorious summer days when the sun never truly sets. From June to September, when the "simmer dim" sets in, it never really gets dark. This is a magical time to visit this archipelago of a hundred islands and islets and as many beaches.

Mainland

Whether visitors arrive by boat or fly into Sumburgh Airport in the south of the Mainland, it is likely that they will spend some time in the archipelago's capital, **Lerwick.** This attractive waterfront town, with an old harbor, is the center of commercial life in the islands and is often just referred to locally as "the town."

With a few decent accommodation choices and the islands' best dining options, Lerwick makes a good base from which to visit some of the outlying islands, many of which can be tackled as a day trip. It also has a few tourist attractions, including the elevated views from the reconstructed **Fort Charlotte,** an artillery fort that was built in the 18th century, and the 19th-century **Town Hall.** Look at the latter for the stained-glass windows that tell Shetland's story and include many of its most famous faces.

Lerwick's main attraction, though, is the brand-new **Shetland Museum**—the most impressive museum in the archipelago and a shining example of everything a family-friendly, modern museum should be. On its lower level, Shetland's story emerges from deep in the mists of time right up to the 1800s. The upper levels cover the years since, with the open-plan nature of the

INSIDER TIP:

A sprinkling of the old fishing böds have recently been opened up as rudimentary, but deeply romantic and historic, places to spend the night.

—LEON GRAY
National Geographic contributor

museum allowing for a display of boats that have helped shape the island's history. Exhibits include everything from archaeological finds from the Stone and Iron Ages through to the arrival of the oil industry in the 1970s (see sidebar below), which radically changed the islands.

On the fringes of town, the **Clickimin Broch** (*Loch Clickimin, www.historic-scotland.gov.uk*), an (continued on p. 266)

Shetland Islands

🗺 253 B3–B4, C3–C4

Visitor Information

✉ Lerwick Tourist Information Center, Market Cross, Lerwick, Mainland

☎ (01595) 693 434

www.shetland tourism.com

Lerwick

✉ 253 C3

Fort Charlotte

✉ Harbour Street, Lerwick, Mainland

www.historic -scotland.gov.uk

Town Hall

✉ Hill Lane, Lerwick, Mainland

☎ (01595) 693 535

💲 $

Shetland Museum

✉ Hay's Dock, Lerwick, Mainland

☎ (01595) 695 057

💲 $

www.shetland -museum.org.uk

Oil & Gas on Shetland

When vast oil and gas deposits were found in the Brent and Ninian fields in the 1970s, the Shetland Islands Council saw a huge opportunity. They lobbied to get the energy companies to ship it through the islands and also to secure their own cut. The resultant massive Sullom Voe terminal (able to fill up to four 1,312-foot/400 m tankers simultaneously) has shipped billions of dollars of oil. The Shetland Islands Council gets 1 pence (2 cents) for every ton shipped, money it has invested in improving the local infrastructure. Further untapped fields offer the islands the prospect of many more fossil fuel riches to come.

Esha Ness Circular Walk

On these rugged islands, bashed into existence by volcanic forces and then shaped by the mighty Atlantic and battering winds, one of the biggest joys is walking in a land where man plays second fiddle to nature.

Esha Ness Lighthouse beaming out over the basalt cliffs

One of the most geologically diverse and scenic areas in the Shetland Islands—indeed, in all of Great Britain—is the Esha Ness Peninsula, located on the remote northeast coast of the Mainland. Its name, which means "headland of volcanic rock," hints at the scenery to come.

This circular walk begins and ends at the parking lot at Esha Ness Lighthouse. The 4-mile (6.5 km) circuit climbs just 164 feet (50 m), so any reasonably fit adult should be able to complete the walk without difficulty in three to four hours. Dramatic natural scenery that incorporates volcanic cliffs, Atlantic Ocean views, and abundant seabirds make this walk popular with locals and visitors alike. If you begin at the information board in the parking lot, you can also learn more about Esha Ness's remarkable geology.

NOT TO BE MISSED:

Esha Ness Lighthouse • Calder's Geo • Grind o' Da Navir • Loch of Houlland

Views from the Cliff Tops

Before setting out from the Esha Ness parking lot, take time to admire the **Esha Ness Lighthouse ❶**. Engineered by David and Charles Stevenson, the lighthouse itself enjoys a dizzyingly spectacular setting, hovering near the edge of the black volcanic cliffs. Today, the lighthouse keeper's cottage, which accommodates up to six people, can be rented on a self-catering basis for a minimum of three nights (*www.lighthouse-holidays.com/pages/eshaness/eshaness.htm*).

Following the cliff top north, keeping a safe distance from the edge, you quickly reach the head of **Calder's Geo** ②. This narrow and deep cleft in the cliff was gouged out by the Atlantic at a point of weakness in the cliff rock.

Keeping with the line of the cliffs as they continue to wind north, you soon see **Moo Stack** ③. This massive sea stack, seemingly set adrift from the Mainland, has a sheer face and narrow ledge pitted with ridges and caves. It is a great place to see nesting fulmars and kittiwakes—be sure to watch the seabirds as they surf on the air currents above the Atlantic swell. From here, you can also see the Loch of Houlland to the east.

As the cliff-top "path" leads toward the Head of Stanshi, you have to climb over a number of fences. As you look west down onto the Atlantic, you will see the dramatic **Natural Arch** ④, which has been gradually carved out of the rock by marine erosion.

Atlantic storms have also left an indelible mark at the spectacular **Grind o' Da Navir** ⑤. Here the cliffs appear to have an enormous vertical gateway, the result of a raging storm that smashed a huge hole in the cliff and hurled tons of rock inland. In turn, the boulders have trapped a small loch between them.

Just beyond the Grind o' Da Navir, the **Head of Stanshi** ⑥ is a dramatic spot where the waves pound the cliffs and craggy volcanic rocks below. From here this "circular" walk takes you back south along the cliff tops toward the Loch of Houlland. Just before you come to the loch, on the left-hand side, you will pass the **Holes of Scraada**—a subterranean stream that forms an underground passageway from the loch to the sea. Once the **Loch of Houlland** ⑦ comes into view, head over the stile and onto the loch's western shore. Keep to the western side of the water as you continue to make your way south. Looking out over the loch, you will see a small causeway that leads to a small islet. The rocks strewn over the surface of this grassy mound are the remains of an **Iron Age broch.**

After leaving the loch shore behind, you will need to cross a dry-stone wall with a ladder stile. Then continue south until you reach the **cemetery** and the paved road that heads northwest to Esha Ness Lighthouse and the end of the walk.

🗺 See also area map p. 253
► Esha Ness Lighthouse
⟷ 4 miles (6.5 km)
⏱ 3–4 hours
► Esha Ness Lighthouse

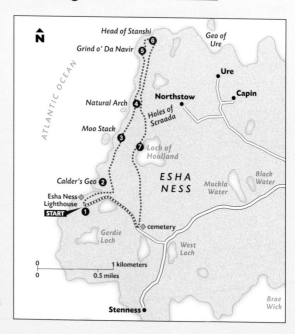

Böd of Gremista

- ✉ Union Street, Lerwick, Mainland
- ☎ (01595) 694 386
- 💲 $

www.shetland-museum.org.uk

Jarlshof

- 🅰 253 C3
- ✉ Sumburgh, Mainland
- ☎ (01950) 460 112
- 🕐 Closed Oct.–March
- 💲 $$

www.historic scotland.gov.uk

Mousa

- 🅰 253 C3

Mousa RSPB Nature Reserve

- ☎ (01950) 460 800
- 💲 $

www.rspb.org.uk

Yell

- 🅰 253 C4

ancient fortified tower that stands adrift on an island in Loch Clickimin, and the **Böd of Gremista** are worth exploring. Along with the diminutive Shetland ponies, the island is also famous for these unique böds. The böds were small storehouses and dwellings located on the coast that were used on a seasonal basis by the islands' fishermen. The Böd of Gremista is a good example of an 18th-century böd. It is renowned as the birthplace of Arthur Anderson, the co-founder of global shipping company P&O. The small exhibition illuminates both his life and the use of the böds and their role in the traditional fishing way of life.

The long, thin strip of land to the south of Lerwick, with its fertile fields, sandy beaches, and great sea views, has what is arguably the Mainland's most dramatic scenery. Heading all the way to the bottom not only brings you to Sumburgh Airport but also the islands' most impressive archaeological attraction, **Jarlshof.** What is remarkable about this site it that it contains remnants of so many different periods, from the Bronze Age stone houses and the Iron Age broch, through to the Pictish art created before the Vikings descended on Shetland, and the most extensive Viking remains left anywhere in the United Kingdom.

Other Islands

Only around 15 of the Shetland Islands are inhabited, with a network of ferries, planes, helicopters, and small boats used to provide transport between them. Shetland can be a bleak place to visit in bad weather and **Yell,** in the north of the archipelago, can be among the bleakest. It is a great place, though, to experience the archetypal Shetland scenery of unremitting peat bogs and brooding *voes* (sea inlets). Its unmistakable dark, earthy beauty gives it a real end-of-the-world feel that helps you recharge your batteries before you batter back into the modern world. It is also one of the finest places in Europe to find otters, which splash around the island's rugged coastline. For those wanting to visit a few islands, Yell is also handy for ferry connections to neighboring **Fetlar,** a much more fertile

---

Mousa, Land of Petrals

It may be tiny and uninhabited, but Mousa—reached from Sandwick on the Shetland Mainland—is one of the most engaging islands in the Shetland archipelago. It is home to Mousa Broch—Scotland's most complete ancient broch (prehistoric circular stone tower), which is over 40 feet (12 m) tall in places.

But the island's wildlife, with its abundance of common seals and birdlife, including arctic terns and black guillemots, is the greatest lure. The island is especially magical during the "simmer dim," when, after midnight, with the imposing bulk of Mousa Broch looming in the twilight, flocks of storm petrels fly noisily home.

Bright-beaked puffins take a break from diving for their favorite meal of sand eels on Fair Isle.

island, and **Unst,** renowned for its cliffs and sandy beaches.

Like **Mousa** (see sidebar opposite), all of the Shetland Islands are alive with wildlife, especially birdlife. To the east of Lerwick, the isle of **Noss** is a real ornithologist's paradise. A skyscraper of rock bursts out of the sea and looms 500 feet (152 m) above the tumbling Atlantic surf. This protected nature reserve can be visited by ferry (*tel 0800/107 7818*) from the neighboring island of Bressay. The cliffs and water are inhabited by many kinds of birds, from diving gannets and puffins to soaring great skuas and surface-skimming shags.

Although administratively part of the Shetland Islands, **Fair Isle** lies 24 miles (38 km) to the south of Sumburgh Head on the Mainland, about halfway between Shetland and Orkney. Decimated by the Clearances in the 19th century (see pp. 206–207), it is now home to a vibrant and,

by necessity, self-sufficient community. This is a walkers' and bird-watchers' haven (hundreds of species migrate through the islands), with little to do except amble around the secluded bays, mighty cliffs, and rolling hills.

The main industry in Fair Isle is the knitting of the famous Fair Isle sweaters, now produced by an island cooperative. They don't come cheap, but they are real quality, with a range of unusual patterns, and make for lifelong souvenirs. The island's modest **George Waterston Museum** (*Ultra, tel 01595/760 244, $*) tells many colorful stories, such as that of the sinking of the *El Gran Grifon*, a waylaid ship that was part of the Spanish Armada fleeing the British fleet in 1588. Hundreds of Spanish seamen were washed ashore here, and the locals fed and looked after them, despite their own meager resources, until relief arrived from the Shetland Mainland. ∎

Fetlar & Unst

253 C4

Visitor Information

✉ Fetlar Interpretation Centre, Beach of Houbie, Fetlar

☎ (01957) 733 206

www.fetlar.com

Isle of Noss Nature Reserve

☎ (01595) 693 345

www.nature -shetland.co.uk/snh/ noss.htm

Fair Isle

253 B2

Fair Isle Bird Observatory Lodge

✉ Fair Isle

☎ (01595) 760 258

www.fairislebirdobs .co.uk

TRAVELWISE

Mountain bikers speed along a woodland track in Mabie Forest, Dumfries & Galloway.

PLANNING YOUR TRIP

When to Go

A raft of events and a varied climate—warm summers and cold Highland winters that have enough snow for skiing—make a visit to Scotland rewarding at any time of year. A busy cultural calendar that sees numerous festivals liven up the country's towns and cities means that July and August are two of the busiest months to visit. August, when the world-famous Edinburgh Summer Festival is in full flow, is peak season in the capital. These months also coincide with school holidays in Scotland and the rest of the United Kingdom, so demand for accommodation is high, as are prices. All across Britain, Easter school holidays (March/April) are also a very popular time to visit, as is the festive period of Christmas and Hogmanay (New Year celebrations) at the end of December.

It is not just Scotland's urban centers that are busy during school breaks. Long sunny days and natural landscapes brimming with opportunities for outdoor activities ensure that rural areas are also busy July through September. Cheaper accommodation and mild weather make the months of May and June a good time to visit.

During the winter months, snow and subzero temperatures draw winter sports enthusiasts to the Highlands for ice-climbing or even skiing. As a general rule, the best time to visit Scotland's five ski resorts—Aviemore, Glenshee, Glencoe, the Nevis Range, and the Lecht—is from mid-January until the end of February. An unexpected cold snap can also see the resorts open in December and March.

October, November, and January to March compose the low season, when accommodation is cheaper. This can be a good time to cozy up in a local hostelry beside a roaring fire, or to make the most of quieter periods in the country's art galleries and museums. Scotland has a temperate climate, with rainfall reasonably evenly distributed throughout the year.

What to Take

Midsummer temperatures hover around a comfortable 68°F (20°C); however, it is important not to underestimate the strength of the sun. Sunscreen is essential for long sunny days. Packing sunglasses, a sunhat, and breathable lightweight clothing (which can be layered if the weather turns cold) is also a good idea during the summer. In the cooler spring and autumn months a sweater and often a jacket are needed. Warm coats, scarves, gloves, and hats help keep the winter chill at bay. An umbrella or waterproof clothing might be needed at any time of year.

Smart or smart casual clothing is generally worn in more expensive restaurants. Elsewhere casual clothing is the norm. Specialist outdoor gear is essential for many activities and is widely available, but can be expensive, so try to bring your own.

It is advisable to carry photocopies of any important documents such as passports and travel insurance in case the originals get lost. For the same reason it is a good idea to make a note of any prescription medicines that you are taking. Travelers who wear contact lenses or glasses should pack spares. Although it is usually possible to buy replacements, it is a good idea to bring spare camera batteries/battery chargers, digital photo memory cards or camera film, and travel plug adapters.

Insurance

It is advisable for all travelers to take out comprehensive travel insurance prior to their departure. This provides medical coverage and compensation for loss, cancellation, and delay. Policy wording should be checked carefully. For example, are medical costs paid by the policyholder and then claimed back or are they paid directly by the insurer? Many policies exclude activities deemed "dangerous" such as skiing, mountaineering, and other adventure sports. Pre-existing health conditions may also be excluded under many policies.

Entry Formalities
Visas

Citizens of the United States, Canada, and many other countries can visit the United Kingdom for up to six months without a visa; the U.K. Border Agency provides details on their website (*www.ukba.home office.gov.uk*). U.K. passport holders and those with passports issued in the EU, European Economic Area, and Switzerland do not need a visa to cross U.K. borders. The U.K. Border Agency lists nationals who need a visa to enter the United Kingdom on their website (*see above*). These countries include South Africa, India, and the U.A.E. Any travelers requiring a visa must apply for and receive it before they arrive in the United Kingdom. The British Foreign and Commonwealth Office (FCO) website (*www.fco .gov.uk*) has a list of embassies and consulates where a visa application can be made.

British Embassies
United States

British Embassy
3100 Massachusetts Ave., NW, Washington, D.C. 20008
Tel (202) 588-6500
Fax (202) 588-7850
E-mail: britishembassy enquiries@gmail.com
http://ukinusa.fco.gov.uk

Canada

British High Commission
80 Elgin Street, Ottawa, Ontario, Canada, K1P 5K7
Tel (613) 237-1530
Fax (613) 237-7980
http://ukincanada.fco.gov.uk

Customs

Travelers are permitted to bring an unlimited amount of most goods from other EU countries. When it comes to alcohol and tobacco the following criteria, however, must

be met: The goods must be for personal use or for a gift, and tax and duty must have been paid in the country where they were purchased. In addition, the owner must transport the goods themselves. (The official individual allowances for these goods are only in metric units, but are shown here with approximate imperial equivalents.)

Customs officials are more likely to question travelers transporting more than 3,200 cigarettes, more than 200 cigars, 400 cigarillos, or 3 kilograms (6.6 pounds) of tobacco. Less than 110 liters (29 gallons) of beer, 90 liters (24 gallons) of wine, 20 liters (5 gallons) of fortified wine, or 10 liters (2.5 gallons) of spirits are also deemed reasonable quantities for personal use. If customs officials think goods are being transported for resale, they have the power to seize them and the vehicle they are carried in.

There are strict limits regarding the importation of duty free goods from non-EU countries. These are set as either 1 liter (1 quart) of spirits/liquor (over 22 percent volume), or 2 liters (2 quarts) of alcohol with less than 22 percent volume (such as fortified wine or sparkling wine). This allowance can be split, for example travelers would be permitted to bring 500 ml (1 pint) of spirits and 1 liter (1 quart) of fortified wine without having to pay duty.

Travelers are also allowed to bring up to 16 liters (4.2 gallons) of beer and 4 liters (1 gallon) of wine. Smokers can bring one of the following: 200 cigarettes, 100 cigarillos, 50 cigars, or 250 g (9 oz) of tobacco. Other goods up to the value of £390 (including perfume) can also be transported without incurring additional tax and/or duty. In order to bring tobacco or alcohol into the United Kingdom travelers must be aged 17 or over. Travelers must also inform customs officials if they are carrying more than 10,000 euros (US$12,500 or its equivalent) in cash.

Items such as stun guns, self-defense sprays, and bladed weapons will be confiscated even if stored in checked baggage. It is prohibited to enter the country with counterfeit goods or obscene materials. Travelers are allowed to bring their own prescription medicine with them, but should make sure they have the relevant paperwork.

FURTHER READING
Nonfiction
Culture & Miscellaneous
Highland Games Made Easy by David Webster and L. Boland Richardson (2010)

Pipers: A Guide to the Players and the Music of the Highland Bagpipe by William Donaldson (2004)

Scotland and Its Whiskies: The Great Whiskies, the Distilleries and Their Landscapes by Michael Jackson (2005)

Tartan: Romancing the Plaid by Jeffrey Banks and Dora De La Chapelle (2007)

History & Archaeology
A History of Scotland by Neil Oliver (2009)

Before Scotland: The Story of Scotland Before History by Alistair Moffat (2009)

Scotland: The Story of a Nation by Magnus Magnusson (2001)

Scotland Archaeology and Early History: A General Introduction by Graham Ritchie and Anna Ritchie (2001)

Nature
RSPB Handbook of Scottish Birds by Peter Holden (2009)

The National Trust for Scotland's Book of Scotland's Wildlife by Niall Benvie (2004)

Outdoors
The Munros: Scotland's Highest Mountains by Cameron McNeish (2006)

101 Best Hill Walks in the Scottish Highlands and Islands by Graeme Cornwallis (2009)

Scotland's Mountain Ridges: Scrambling, Mountaineering and Climbing–The Best Routes for Summer and Winter by Dan Bailey (2008)

Scottish Canoe Classics: Twenty-five Great Canoe and Kayak Trips by Eddie Palmer (2007)

Rivers and Lochs of Scotland: An Angler's Complete Guide by Bruce Sandison (2009)

Scotland: Where Golf Is Great by James W. Finnegan (2010)

Scotland Mountain Biking: The Wild Trails by Phil McKane (2009)

Travel
Caledonian, the Monster Canal by Guthrie Hutton (2009)

Iron Roads to the Isles: A Travellers and Tourists Souvenir Guide to the West Highland Lines by Michael Pearson (2009)

The Southern Upland Way: Official Guide by Roger Smith (2005)

St. Cuthbert's Way: Official Guide by Ron Shaw and Roger Smith (2009)

West Highland Way (British Walking Guides) by Charlie Loram (2008)

Fiction
The Collected Poems of George Mackay Brown by George Mackay Brown, Archie Bevan, and Brian Murray (2006)

Complete Sherlock Holmes by Sir Arthur Conan Doyle (2008)

The Cone Gatherers by Robin Jenkins (1989)

Harry Potter and the Philosopher's Stone by J. K. Rowling (1997)

Kidnapped by Robert Louis Stevenson (1886)

Knots and Crosses by Ian Rankin (1998)

Trainspotting by Irvine Welsh (1994)

The Wasp Factory by Iain Banks (1992)

Waverley by Sir Walter Scott (1814)

Whisky Galore by Sir Compton MacKenzie (1947)

HOW TO GET TO SCOTLAND
By Airplane
From North America it is possible to fly direct to Edinburgh (EDI; *tel 0844/ 4818 989, www.edinburgh airport.com*) from New York's JFK and Newark, as well as Toronto. Glasgow Airport (GLA; *tel 0844/ 481 5555, www.glasgowairport.com*) is served by nonstop flights from Newark, Orlando, Philadelphia, Toronto, and Calgary. Edinburgh Airport, Glasgow Airport, and Glasgow Prestwick Airport (PIK; *tel 0871/223 0700, www.gpia.co.uk*) are also well connected to Europe, with direct flights from Amsterdam, Berlin, Brussels, Copenhagen, Dublin, London, Madrid, Milan, Oslo, Paris, Rome, Vienna, and Zurich, among many others. Low-budget carrier Ryanair (*www.ryanair .com*) is the main airline flying in and out of Prestwick. It is also possible to fly direct to Inverness (INV; *tel 01667/464 000, www.hial.co.uk*), Aberdeen (ABZ; *tel 0844/481 6666, www.aberdeenairport.com*), and Dundee (DND; *tel 01382/662 200, www.hial.co.uk*) from a growing number of U.K. and European cities including Amsterdam, Bergen, Birmingham, Dublin, Leeds, Liverpool, London, Manchester, Oslo, and Paris.

The majority of overseas visitors to Scotland still arrive at Edinburgh or Glasgow airports. Taxis from Edinburgh Airport into the city center cost about £18 and take approximately 20 minutes depending on traffic. The Airlink 100 bus (*tel 0131/555 6363, www.flybus .com*) leaves the terminal every 10 minutes; services take 25 minutes and cost £3.50 for a single journey or £6 return. Bus number 35 (tel 0131/555 6363, www.lothianbuses .com) runs to the city center every 15 to 30 minutes and costs £1.20. It is considerably slower than the Airlink, with journeys of around an hour. The N22 night bus (tel 0131/555 6363, www.lothianbuses.com) also runs to Edinburgh Airport. This leaves every 30 minutes and costs £3.

Taxis from Glasgow Airport into the city cost £20–£22. The Glasgow Airport Flyer Express (tel 08700/404 343, www.glasgow flyer.com) costs £4.20 single or £6.20 return. Journeys take 15 to 25 minutes and buses leave every 10 minutes. Bus 747 or the Airlink City Service (www.firstgroup.com) takes longer and costs £4 single or £5 return.

Both airports are modern and amenities include ATMs, money changing facilities, car rental desks, cafés, restaurants, bars, and shops.

By Boat

Norfolk Line ferries (tel 0844/449 0007, www.norfolkline.com) connect Rosyth (15 miles/24 km north of Edinburgh) to the Belgian port of Zeebrugge. Stena Line (tel 08447/ 707 070, www.stenaline.co.uk) ferries run from Belfast in Northern Ireland to Stranraer. P&O Irish Sea (www.poirishsea.com) ferries run between Troon and Larne and Cairnryan and Larne. Scotland also features on cruise ship itineraries. Royal Caribbean, Princess Cruises, Seabourn, and Silversea all operate cruises that include Edinburgh. Ports at Aberdeen, Lerwick (Shetland), Stornoway (Lewis), Greenock (Glasgow), Portree (Skye), Ullapool, Invergordon, Peterhead, Oban, Scrabster, and Fort William also welcome cruise ships.

By Bus

National Express (tel 08717/818 178, www.nationalexpress.com) operates the United Kingdom's biggest bus network. From London there are direct services to Aberdeen, Dundee, Edinburgh, Glasgow, and Inverness, among others. Megabus (tel 0900/160 0900, www.megabus .com) offers a low-cost bus service between London and Scotland.

By Car

An extensive network of paved and well-maintained motorways (freeways), dual carriageways (divided highways), and single carriageways (highways) make it is easy to drive to Scotland from England and Wales. Those traveling from mainland Europe can travel directly to Scotland by ferry, or cross to ports in England or Wales before driving north. Another way of reaching Scotland from the Continent is to travel via Eurotunnel (tel 08443/353 535, www.euro tunnel.com) from Calais to Folkstone in southeast England and then head north.

By Train

East Coast trains (tel 08457/225 333, www.eastcoast.co.uk) operate services from London to Edinburgh, Glasgow, Aberdeen, and Inverness. CrossCountry Trains (tel 0844/811 0124, www.crosscountry trains.co.uk) connect Edinburgh, Glasgow, Dundee, and Aberdeen to destinations throughout England. Virgin Trains (tel 08457/222 333, www.virgintrains.co.uk) link Birmingham to Edinburgh and Glasgow. An overnight rail service, the Caledonian Sleeper, from London Euston is operated by First ScotRail (tel 08457/550 033, www .scotrail.co.uk). The sleepers stop at more than 20 Scottish stations including Edinburgh, Glasgow, Stirling, Perth, Dundee, Aberdeen, Fort William, and Inverness. For timetable and fare information, contact National Rail Enquiries (tel 08457/484 950, www.national rail.co.uk).

GETTING AROUND
By Airplane

It is often quicker to access some of Scotland's more remote areas via an internal flight. Highlands & Islands Airports (www.hial.co.uk) operate airports in:
Barra (tel 01871/890 212)
Benbecula (tel 01870/602 051)
Campbeltown (tel 01586/553 797)
Islay (tel 01496/302 361)
Kirkwall (tel 01856/872 421)
Stornoway (tel 01851/702 256)
Sumburgh (tel 01950/460 905)
Tiree (tel 01879/220 456)
Wick (tel 01955/602 215)
In the main, flights to these airports leave from Glasgow or Edinburgh, but check the authority's website for full details. Scotland boasts one of the shortest plane journeys in the world—a two-minute hop from Westray to Papa Westray in Orkney. Loganair (tel 01856/872 494, www .loganair.co.uk) operates Orkney's inter-isle services.

By Bus

Local and national bus connections are good in Scotland. The main long distance provider is CityLink (tel 0870/505 050, www.citylink.co.uk). In more remote areas public transport might take the form of the postbus—where you literally pay to ride in the post van (tel 08457/740 740, www.postbus.royalmail.com). Local bus services accept cash (with fares typically ranging between £1.20 and £4) and bus passes. In bigger towns and cities like Edinburgh and Glasgow it is also possible to buy a day ticket that gives you unlimited bus travel in a single 24-hour period. Longer distance coach travel should be paid for in advance, either online or at a ticket office.

By Car

Driving is on the left. A well-maintained and extensive network of paved roads makes Scotland a good driving destination. Outside of city centers and away from main routes the roads can be quiet. Tourists traveling north on the A9 should take extra care. This road switches between single and dual carriageway frequently and is an accident hot spot due to frustrated drivers taking risks in order to overtake slower vehicles. Scotland also has a lot of single-track roads where traffic drives in both directions; here passing places are used to keep traffic flowing.

Visitors from North America in particular may not be familiar with roundabouts. Traffic already on the roundabout has the right of way and cars have to give way to vehicles on their right.

Speed limits are 30 mph (48 kph) in built-up areas, 60 mph (96 kph) on single-carriageways, and 70 mph (112 kph) on motorways and dual carriageways, unless otherwise indicated. Forty mph (64 kph) and 50 mph (80 kph) speed limits are also common. It is illegal to use hand-held cell phones while driving or waiting at traffic lights. Minor speeding offenses and parking violations often incur a fine. The legal blood alcohol limit for driving is 80 mg of alcohol per 100 ml of blood or 0.08 percent, the same as that of the United States. It is much safer for drivers to avoid drinking alcohol altogether.

By Ferry

One of the easiest and cheapest ways to navigate the jagged coastline of western Scotland and its scattered islands is by ferry. Ferries, such as those operated by Caledonian MacBryne (tel 0800/ 066 5000, www.calmac.co.uk) run frequently between and operate vessels capable of carrying cars. In addition to these simple everyday ferries, there are many other companies offering a more exotic experience, such as a trip on a Clyde steamer (see p. 131).

By Subway

Glasgow has a single subway route operated by Strathclyde Partnership for Transport (tel 0141/332 6811, www.spt.co.uk). Many of the city's key attractions are within easy walking distance of a station. Fares are the same regardless of distance traveled, with a single journey costing £1.20. Bulk buying tickets (10 or 20), or purchasing a seven-day pass, can be good value for those staying in Glasgow for several days. Day tickets (Discovery tickets) are also available and cost £3.50.

By Taxi

In larger towns, black cabs can be hailed on the street and journeys are metered. Tariff regulations in black taxis are also clearly displayed. Private hire taxis, more commonly known as minicabs, tend to be cheaper, but must be pre-booked by telephone. Minicabs rarely have meters so it is essential to agree on a price in advance. Minimum charges apply, so short hops cost in the region of £3.50 to £6, with a 20-minute journey coming in at around £20. Longer distance fares should be negotiated, for example Edinburgh to Glasgow would cost in the region of £80–£100.

By Train

First ScotRail (tel 08457/550 033, www.scotrail.co.uk) operate domestic rail services in Scotland. The rail network is extensive reaching Wick in the north, Aberdeen in the northeast, Mallaig in the west, and Stranraer in the south. Rail travel in Scotland can be expensive, particularly if tickets are purchased immediately prior to travel. Advance purchase tickets can be much cheaper, with the Trainline (www.trainline.com) portal being a good place to buy these.

First ScotRail (www.scotrail.co.uk) sells rover passes for those planning to explore Scotland by train (various rates and conditions apply). For full details visit the First ScotRail website.

PRACTICAL ADVICE
Communications

Post Offices: Post offices are located in every city and town; they are also commonly found in rural villages. Services that travelers are most likely to find useful include post, currency exchange, and the purchase of pre-paid international phone cards. Post offices also sell credit for pre-paid cell phones.

Telephone: Public telephones generally accept coins and phone cards. Some phones also take credit card payments. Outside of city centers and busy shopping malls, pay phones can be hard to find. Visitors should consider buying a pay-as-you-go cell phone, or a SIM card to use in an existing phone.

The main phone operator in Scotland and the United Kingdom is BT (www.bt.com). The main cell phone providers are 3 (www.three .co.uk), O2 (www.O2.co.uk), Orange (www.orange.co.uk), T-Mobile (www .T-Mobile.co.uk), Virgin (www.Virgin Mobile.com), and Vodaphone (www .vodaphone.co.uk).

Useful Numbers:
Directory inquiries: 118 500
International directory inquiries: 118 505
Operator: 100
Country code: 44
City codes start: 01
Local rate calls start: 0845
National rate calls start: 0870
Toll-free calls start: 0800

Internet Access: Bigger towns and cities will often have an Internet café. Hotels may provide Internet access through a public computer terminal. Wi-Fi is increasingly available in cafés, bars, hotels, and other public spaces. Wi-Fi is sometimes free of charge.

Conversions

Scotland uses the metric system with two notable exceptions. Road distances are measured in miles and some alcoholic drinks are still served by the pint or half pint. In situations where the imperial system is still used, it should be noted that some British measures are not exact equivalents of U.S. standard measures. For example, an imperial pint (568 ml) is considerably larger than a U.S. pint (473 ml)—something to bear in mind when drinking at a pub or restaurant.

Electricity

Scotland uses 240V, 50HZ. Outlets have three holes and only accept flat pin plugs.

Etiquette & Local Customs

Scots observe normal courtesies such as shaking hands and greeting people with the appropriate good morning, good afternoon, or good evening. In formal meetings smart dress is normally required and business cards are often exchanged. In social situations if someone includes you in a round of drinks it is polite to buy a round in return. The kilt is often worn for formal events like weddings.

Holidays

January 1—New Year's Day
January 2—Additional New Year holiday
March/April—Good Friday
First Monday in May—May Day
Last Monday in May—Spring Bank Holiday
First Monday in August—Summer Bank Holiday
November 30—St. Andrew's Day (not universally observed)
December 25—Christmas Day
December 26—Boxing Day
If a public holiday falls on the weekend, then the following Monday becomes a holiday in lieu of this date.

Liquor Laws

Strict licensing laws mean that it is illegal for anyone under the age of 18 to buy alcohol. It is also illegal to purchase alcohol for minors. New laws introduced in 2009 mean that alcohol can only be sold in shops between 10 a.m. and 10 p.m. The Scottish government is trying to discourage binge drinking and, as a result, many cheap drinks promotions have recently disappeared from bars and clubs.

Media

Newspapers: Scotland has three dedicated national newspapers—The Daily Record (www.dailyrecord.co.uk), The Scotsman (www.scotsman.co.uk), and The Herald (www.heraldscotland.co.uk). Larger towns and cities also frequently have their own local papers. Scottish editions of U.K. papers include The Scottish Daily Mail, The Scottish Daily Express, The Scottish Daily Mirror, and The Scottish Sun. U.K. broadsheets like The Times, The Independent, and The Guardian are also widely available in Scotland. Sunday papers on sale in Scotland include The Sunday Post (www.sundaypost.com), The Sunday Herald (www.herald scotland.co.uk), The Sunday Mail (www.dailyrecord.co.uk), and Scotland on Sunday (www.scotsman .co.uk). Again, Scottish editions of the U.K. Sunday papers and indeed the U.K. editions themselves are also widely available.

Radio: All of the BBC's national radio stations (www.bbc.co.uk/ radio)—BBC Radio 1, BBC Radio 2, BBC Radio 3, BBC Radio 4, and Five Live—are available in Scotland, as are the country specific BBC Radio Scotland (www.bbc.co .uk/radioscotland) and the Gaelic language BBC Radio na Gaidheal (www.bbc.co.uk/radionagaidheal). More stations are available via the Internet and digital radio. There are also dozens of local community radio stations.

TV: Scotland has five analog TV channels—BBC One Scotland (www.bbc.co.uk/scotland), BBC Two Scotland (www.bbc.co.uk/ scotland), STV (www.stv.tv), Channel 4 (www.channel4.com), and Channel Five (www.five.tv). The analog signal in the United Kingdom will be switched off completely by 2012 (in line with most of Europe). As a result, the majority of private houses and hotels pick up a digital or satellite signal. The five main stations listed above are all available via satellite and digital TV, as well as a host of other channels. U.K. residents have to pay an annual TV license fee, which funds BBC programs. These are supposed to reflect the diverse interests of the BBC's audience and are aired without commercial breaks. The majority of programs screened in Scotland are the same as those watched throughout the United Kingdom, although local news broadcasts take a Scottish slant, and country specific issues may also feature on the bill.

Money Matters

Scotland's currency is the British pound (£), divided into 100 pence (p). It comes in bills of £50, £20, £10, and £5, although many places won't accept £50 bills. Coins come in £2, £1, 50p, 20p, 10p, 5p, 2p, and 1p denominations. The best places to exchange money are post offices, banks, or dedicated exchange offices. Larger hotels will also frequently change money, but at a poorer exchange rate or with higher commission charges. The most easily converted currencies are the euro and the U.S. dollar.

ATMs are found inside and outside banks, at transport terminals, in shopping malls, at gas stations, and outside shops. Fees charged for ATM withdrawals will vary depending on the terms and conditions at your own bank and which machine you use. Credit cards carrying the Visa and MasterCard symbols are widely accepted. Larger hotels and retailers (although by no means all) often accept American Express cards. Diners Club cards are less widely accepted.

Opening Times

Banks are generally open 9 a.m. to 5 p.m. from Monday to Friday. Some are also open on Saturday or on Saturday morning. Office hours are also generally 9 a.m. to 5 p.m. Monday to Friday. Shop hours tend to be 9 a.m. to 6 p.m. Monday to Saturday, although this can vary by an hour or two. Many shops in larger towns, cities, and malls open later on Thursdays (usually closing somewhere between 7 p.m. and 9 p.m.) and on Sundays. Typical Sunday opening hours are 11 a.m. to 5 p.m. Supermarkets keep much longer hours (typically 8 a.m. to 10 p.m. daily) and some are open 24 hours. Dentists and doctors tend to keep business hours (roughly 9 a.m. to 5 p.m. Monday to Friday), although many have started opening earlier or closing later. Pharmacies are typically open 8 a.m. to 6 p.m. Monday to Saturday.

Places of Worship/ Religion

The majority of Scots (around two-thirds) identify as Christian, although fewer than 10 percent of the population regularly attends any kind of religious service. That said, in some areas, such as the Outer Hebrides, communities are still firmly religious. The Protestant Church of Scotland is the country's national church, but Catholicism and other Christian faiths also have a significant following. Scotland is a multicultural society so the other major world faiths, Islam, Judaism, Buddhism, Sikhism, and Hinduism, are also practiced. Visitors are welcome to services in churches, mosques, and temples throughout the country.

Time Differences

Scotland is on Greenwich Mean Time. From the last Sunday in March through to the last Sunday in October it operates British Summer Time (GMT+1).

Tipping

Tipping can be a confusing issue in Scotland. Where paying for service is optional some locals simply add a little extra onto the bill, others diligently add an additional 10 percent, while others don't tip at all. As a general guide, add 10 to 15 percent for good service in a café or restaurant. Tipping is not expected in a bar; however, you may hear the bar person being told to buy one for themselves; when this happens they will usually add the price of a drink to the bill and take this as a tip. For taxi fares it is usual to round the fare up to the nearest pound or to add on a couple of pounds.

Travelers with Disabilities

Facilities for travelers with disabilities are reasonable, with many hotels, cafés and restaurants having rooms and rest rooms with wheelchair access. Many buildings also have elevators that can accommodate wheelchairs. Public buses often have drop down ramps to allow wheelchair users to board and trains have wheelchair spaces. This said, the very nature of some of Scotland's historic streets and ancient buildings means that they are not wheelchair friendly.

Visitor Information

Tourist Offices: Scotland's national tourist office is Visit Scotland (tel 0845/225 5121, www.visit scotland.com). It provides a wealth of useful information about accommodation, sightseeing, and activities throughout Scotland via its call center and website. Most cities and towns also have walk-in tourist information offices, where you can pick up brochures, maps, and leaflets; learn about local tours, and book accommodation. Many, but not all, local tourist offices have redirected telephone inquiries to the Visit Scotland call center.

Aberdeen Visitor Information Center, 23 Union Street, tel (01224) 288 288

Dundee Visitor Information Center, Discovery Point, Discovery Quay, tel (01382) 527 527

Edinburgh Visitor Information Center, 3 Princes Street, tel (0845) 225 5121

Glasgow Visitor Information Center, 11 George Square, tel (0141) 204 4400

Inverness Visitor Information Center, Castle Wynd, tel (0845) 225 5121

Stirling Visitor Information Center, 41 Dumbarton Road, tel (0845) 225 5121

Internet Sites:
The List—a guide to what's on in Edinburgh, Glasgow, and farther afield (www.list.co.uk).
The Scottish Government—official website of the Scottish

Government (*www.scotland .gov.uk*).
Traveline Scotland—useful portal for planning journeys throughout Scotland (*www .travelinescotland.com*).

EMERGENCIES
Crime & Police
Scotland is a relatively safe country to visit with low levels of crime reported against tourists. Travelers should take the usual precautions to keep themselves safe, such as carrying handbags slung diagonally across the chest and keeping clasps and openings facing inward; not carrying wallets, cell phones, or other valuables in pockets; keeping cameras inside a bag when they are not in use; and removing valuables from vehicles. Some visitors might also like to consider carrying money beneath their clothing in a money belt, although locals don't do this. Falling prey to a pickpocket is the most serious crime suffered by most tourists. In order to maintain personal safety, visitors shouldn't walk alone in dark places and try to avoid confrontations with anyone who appears high on alcohol or drugs. Scotland suffers from its fair share of poverty and some parts of Glasgow, Edinburgh, and other big cities should be avoided (such as high-rise housing estates). Binge drinking is also a problem in Scotland and alcohol-related violence occasionally spills out onto the streets. The police are usually on hand to deal with this, so there is no need to be unduly concerned.

The police are generally helpful and will take any complaints made seriously. Most insurance policies require proof from victims of crime that the incident has been reported to the police: This involves visiting a police station, where the police will provide a crime reference number to victims if they are going to seek financial compensation.

Embassies/Consulates
U.S. Consulate General
   3 Regent Terrace
   Edinburgh EN7 5BW
   Tel (0131) 556 8315
   Fax (0131) 557 6023
   www.usembassy.org.uk

Canadian Consulate
   By appointment
   Tel 07702 359 916
   E-mail: canada.consul@blue
   yonder.co.uk
   www.unitedkingdom.gc.ca

Emergency Telephone Numbers
Emergency services (police, ambulance, and fire) 999

What to Do in a Car Accident
In the event of a car accident involving another vehicle, a stationary object (such as a street lamp), or an animal, it is imperative to stop and see if anyone/anything is injured or damaged. Once the driver has stopped they must remain near their vehicle to provide anyone else involved (either directly, such as another driver, or indirectly, for example the owner of an injured dog) with their details. The information that needs to be given includes the driver's name and address, the name and address of the vehicle owner (if different) or rental company, the car registration number, and the insurance company. If personal injury hasn't been sustained and details have been exchanged, then nothing further needs to be done.

In the event of causing injury to someone else, the driver must also report the accident to the police and provide their insurance details. Drivers not in possession of their insurance details must provide them to the police within 24 hours. Driving without insurance is a criminal act.

Lost Property
If you lose something, check with any hotel, café, restaurant, bus, train, or taxi company that you have used since you last saw it. If your property isn't relocated, you need to report it at the local police station. Most travel insurance policies require policyholders, if they are going to make a claim, to report any lost property within 24 hours. Travelers who lose their passport should report this to their embassy or consulate, which will help with organizing a replacement. Photocopies of important documents like passports and travel insurance can help in the event of loss.

Health
Scotland has an extensive network of National Health Service (NHS) hospitals, clinics, and doctors. Private health care facilities also exist. The standards of care are generally high. Pharmacies (or chemists) sell over-the-counter medicines such as painkillers, cold remedies, and antihistamines. For prescription medication visitors will need to see a doctor.

EU nationals benefit from free emergency medical care in the United Kingdom if they are in possession of a valid European Health Insurance Card (EHIC). The EHIC does not cover the cost of non-urgent medical attention or emergency repatriation. Some non-EU countries also have reciprocal health care arrangements with the United Kingdom, check if this is the case before your journey. Non-emergency care will normally be charged for, even if the patient is seen by an NHS doctor. Consultation fees are reasonable and can be claimed back by those who have adequate medical travel insurance.

No vaccinations are officially required to enter Scotland and tap water is safe to drink throughout the country.

Hotels & Restaurants

Scotland has a diverse range of places to stay and eat. The selection in this book is limited to some of the best or most interesting choices. Many other places are also excellent and a lack of listing does not mean that you should not eat or stay there.

Hotels

In Scotland you can stay anywhere from a youth hostel or a campsite, to guesthouses offering a bed and breakfast or a luxurious five-star hotel. Inns (pubs with rooms) and restaurants with rooms are also common. More unusual places to stay include country house hotels, castles, and lighthouses. Wild camping is also legal in Scotland, so if you have a tent you can pitch it (as long as you abide by the rules) without spending any money at all.

This variety means that there is something to suit every budget. Even at the lower end of the scale hotels are usually clean if basic. Many hotels and guesthouses have formal accreditation (a star-rating) from Visit Scotland. Five-star accommodation is considered to be of exceptional quality, four-star excellent, three-star very good, two-star good, and one-star acceptable.

Guest rooms are commonly double or twin rooms, the former have one big bed and the latter two single beds. Many places have family rooms, with one double and up to two single beds. Rollaway beds for children and baby cribs are often available. Some places charge extra to accommodate children in their parents' room. Additional charges also depend on age, with a lot of places charging an adult rate for children older than 12. Some hotels have interconnecting rooms.

It is advisable to make advance reservations during the peak holiday season, particularly in July, August, and around Christmas and New Year. In August almost all hotels and guesthouses in the capital increase their prices to coincide with the Edinburgh Summer Festival.

Reservations can be made by phone, fax, e-mail, online, and through travel agents. Internet prices are often much lower than the rack rate.

In the summer some bed-and-breakfast (B&B) establishments will not take bookings for one night. Similarly some hotels may also specify a minimum stay of two nights at busy times or at weekends.

In the summer it can be hard to get a double room in Edinburgh for less than £100, especially during August, with prices in five-star hotels often exceeding £300. Outside Edinburgh double occupancy rooms in a bed-and-breakfast start at around £40 and rise to above £80. Hotels of all grades tend to be cheaper outside the capital.

Restaurants

Edinburgh and Glasgow both have eclectic dining scenes with everything from fine dining restaurants through to pizzerias and chip shops. Ethnic cuisine is also well represented in Scotland's main cities, with Thai, Moroccan, Mexican, North American, Japanese, and French food just some of the varieties on offer. Even outside towns and cities you will come across Indian, Chinese, and Italian restaurants. Hotel restaurants are usually decent, and in more remote areas some bed-and-breakfasts also offer guests dinner. Outside of Scotland's big towns and cities many restaurants are only open for lunch (generally between noon and 2:30 p.m.) and dinner (typically between 6:30 p.m. and 8:30 p.m.). Cafés tend to open from 8 a.m. until 5 p.m. or 6 p.m. and serve breakfast and lunch, with snacks and cakes also available all day. Many pubs serve food throughout the day. Bars tend to stop serving meals at around 10 p.m.

Organization & Abbreviations

Hotels and restaurants are listed by chapter, then by price, then in alphabetical order, with hotels listed first followed by restaurants.

Abbreviations used: AE (American Express), D (Dinner), DC (Diner's Club), L (Lunch), MC (MasterCard), V (Visa).

PRICES

HOTELS

The cost of a double room in peak season is given by $ signs.

$$$$$	over £300
$$$$	£200–£300
$$$	£120–£200
$$	£80–£120
$	Under £80

RESTAURANTS

The average price of a two-course meal for one person, without tip or drinks is given by $ signs.

$$$$$	over £50
$$$$	£40–£50
$$$	£25–£40
$$	£15–£25
$	£15

🏨 Hotel   🍴 Restaurant   ⓘ No. of Guest Rooms   ⬛ No. of Seats   🅿 Parking   🕐 Closed   ⧉ Elevator

■ EDINBURGH & THE LOTHIANS

EDINBURGH

HOTELS

SOMETHING SPECIAL

BALMORAL

🍴 **$$$$$**

1 PRINCES STREET, EH2 2EQ

TEL (0131) 556 2414

This grand old dame offers a slice of Old World luxury with opulent public spaces and elegant guest rooms. Added extras include a top-notch health spa and a Michelin starred restaurant. For a real treat check in to one of their suites, which boast sweeping views out over the city.

ⓘ 188 🅿 🔁 🚭 🔄 🏊 🔅 AE, DC, MC, V

THE BONHAM

$$$$

35 DRUMSHEUGH GARDENS, EH3 7RN

TEL (0131) 226 6050

www.townhouse company.co.uk

This chic design hotel comes complete with funky furnishings. Other neat touches include stand-alone baths in the suites and a good restaurant. Room no. 1, a superior double, houses a fabulous old copper bath, while suite 100, with its four-poster bed, has a funky shower that blasts water from all angles.

ⓘ 48 🅿 🔁 🚭 🔅 AE, DC, MC, V

THE EDINBURGH RESIDENCE

$$$$

7 ROTHESAY TERRACE, EH3 7RV

TEL (0131) 226 3380

www.townhouse company.co.uk

A unique apartment-style setup makes this hotel perfect for anyone spending more than a night or two in the city. The Residence's suites all have their own kitchens.

ⓘ 29 🅿 🔁 🚭 🔄 🔅 AE, DC, MC, V

GLASSHOUSE

$$$$

2 GREENSIDE PLACE, EH1 3AA

TEL (0131) 525 8200

www.theetoncollection.com

If you are looking for a place for a licit or otherwise rendezvous then this is the place, with sultry décor creating the romance, not to mention the private lavender-scented rooftop garden and floor-to-ceiling windows. The Deluxe Suite boasts its own private hot tub and sauna.

ⓘ 65 🅿 🔁 🚭 🚭 🔅 AE, DC, MC, V

MALMAISON

$$$$

1 TOWER PLACE, EH6 7BZ

TEL (0131) 468 5000

www.malmaison -edinburgh.com

This contemporary hotel has resurrected a neglected 19th-century seamen's mission down by Leith docks. Its bright and breezy rooms and public areas are the sort of spaces that make the pages of design magazines. Neat features include full-measure drinks in the minibar.

ⓘ 121 🅿 🔁 🚭 🔅 AE, DC, MC, V

THE HOLYROOD

$$$

81 HOLYROOD ROAD, EH8 8AU

TEL (0844) 879 9028

www.macdonaldhotels .co.uk/holyrood

The Holyrood manages to tread the fine line between tartan tack and modernity with understated "Scottish" décor in guest rooms and public areas, without the national theme ever getting too much. Rooms are comfortable with all mod cons.

ⓘ 156 🅿 🔁 🚭 🚭 🏊 🔅 AE, MC, V

ROXBURGHE HOTEL

$$$

38 CHARLOTTE SQUARE, EH2 4HQ

TEL (0844) 879 9063

www.macdonald hotels.co.uk/roxburghe

A recent multimillion-pound refurbishment has revamped everything at the Roxburghe, from its stylish and elegant guest rooms to its funky revamped bar and a restaurant that makes the most of Scottish ingredients.

ⓘ 198 🔁 🚭 🚭 🏊 🔅 AE, MC, V

THE RUTLAND HOTEL

$$$

1–3 RUTLAND STREET, EH1 2AE

TEL (0131) 229 3402

www.therutlandhotel.com

The rooms at this funky hotel boast lots of character and modern in-room technology. The second-floor restaurant is also excellent, while its buzzing bar serves informal food and is the venue for breakfast.

ⓘ 12 🔁 🚭 🚭 🔅 AE, MC, V

ALBYN TOWNHOUSE

$$

16 HARTINGTON GARDENS, EH10 4LD

TEL (0131) 229 6459

www.albyntownhouse.co.uk

Housed in a Georgian town house, this elegant B&B has been wowing guests with its elegant guest rooms, friendly service, and high standards since Lydie and David opened for business in 2007.

ⓘ 10 🅿 🚭 🔅 MC, V

RESTAURANTS

SOMETHING SPECIAL

🍴 21212
$$$$$
3 ROYAL TERRACE, EH7 5AB
TEL (0845) 222 1212
www.21212restaurant.co.uk
Since opening his creative
restaurant in 2009, chef Paul
Kitching has already earned
a Michelin star. Despite, or
because of, his scientific
approach, all the dishes, with
all their seemingly incongruous ingredients, are allowed
to speak for themselves. The
restaurant also has four lovely
rooms, which are perfect for a
special occasion.
🛏 38 🚫 🚭 AE, MC, V

🍴 NUMBER ONE
$$$$$
THE BALMORAL, 1 PRINCES
STREET, EH2 2EQ
TEL (0131) 557 6727
www.restaurantnumber
one.com
Utilizing fresh Scottish
produce to magnificent
effect, Jeff Bland's Michelin-
starred restaurant blows away
all the old anachronisms about
the quality of Scots cuisine.
Fine food is complemented
by fine wine and first-class
service in a hotel restaurant
that is anything but run of
the mill.
🛏 50 🚫 🚭 AE, DC,
MC, V

🍴 RESTAURANT MARTIN
WISHART
$$$$$
54 THE SHORE, EH6 6RA
TEL (0131) 553 3557
www.martin-wishart.co.uk
For many visitors to Edinburgh
this is the place to dine. Leith's
most established Michelin-
starred restaurant doesn't
disappoint with the likes of
roasted Scottish lobster and

Ross-shire beef gracing the
French-influenced menu.
Tables are at a premium, so
reserve well in advance.
🛏 50 🚫 🚭 AE, MC, V

SOMETHING SPECIAL

🍴 THE KITCHIN
$$$$
78 COMMERCIAL QUAY,
EH6 6LX
TEL (0131) 555 1755
www.thekitchin.com
Celebrity chef Tom Kitchin
lures locals and visitors alike
to his Leith eatery with fresh
and expertly cooked British
produce. Highlights on a
creative menu include
sautéed Devon snails and
Dornoch lamb.
🛏 45 🚫 🚭 AE, MC, V

SOMETHING SPECIAL

🍴 PLUMED HORSE
$$$$
50–54 HENDERSON STREET,
EH6 6DE
TEL (0131) 554 5556
www.plumedhorse.co.uk
Its intimate ambience, personal
service, and mouth-watering
dishes like slow-braised pork
belly and roast halibut make
dining at the Plumed Horse a
must. Then there is chef Tony
Borthwick's Michelin star.
🛏 28 🚫 🚭 AE, MC, V

🍴 ATRIUM
$$$
10 CAMBRIDGE STREET, EH1 2ED
TEL (0131) 228 8882
www.atriumrestaurant.co.uk
This chic oasis has been a firm
favorite with the locals since
it opened back in 1993. The
secret of its success is attentive
service, a relaxed ambience, a
contemporary setting, and the
expert cooking of head chef
Neil Forbes. Monkfish landed
in Peterhead and Perthshire
lamb are just some of the

top-notch Scottish ingredients
on the menu.
🛏 190 🚫 🚭 AE, MC, V

🍴 IGLU BAR & ETHICAL
EATERY
$$
2B JAMAICA STREET, EH3 6HH
TEL (0131) 476 5333
www.theiglu.com
Offering a menu of wild,
organic, and local produce,
Iglu provides one of Edinburgh's most distinctive dining
experiences. In addition to
the main menu, a blackboard
crammed with tantalizing
specials leaves diners spoiled
for choice. Shetland mussels
and pesto-encrusted hake are
just some of the highlights.
🛏 30 🚫 🕐 Closed Mon.–
Tues. 🚭 MC, V

🍴 THE MUSSEL INN
$$
61–65 ROSE STREET, EH2 2NH
TEL (0131) 225 5979
www.mussel-inn.com
Delicately spiced mussels
served by the kilo are the
highlight at this aptly named
restaurant. Fresh oysters and
scallops also tempt from the
menu. The Aberdeen Angus
beef burger and the vegetarian
pasta are a nod to non-fish
eaters.
🛏 52 🚫 🚭 AE, MC, V

🍴 THE VILLAGER
$$
49–50 GEORGE IV BRIDGE,
EH1 1EJ
TEL (0131) 226 2781
www.villager-e.com
This trendy bar-restaurant is
a great place to unwind over
drinks with friends, or to
enjoy tasty treats like chicken
satay, homemade burgers,
and paella. The tempo rises
on Friday and Saturday nights
when DJs play.
🛏 30 🚫 🚭 MC, V

🏨 Hotel 🍴 Restaurant 🛏 No. of Guest Rooms 🛏 No. of Seats 🅿 Parking 🕐 Closed 🛗 Elevator

CHOP CHOP

$

248 MORRISON STREET, EH3 8TD
TEL (0131) 221 1155
www.chop-chop.co.uk
Authentic and affordable
Chinese food and exquisite
boiled and fried dumplings
had the locals flocking to Chop
Chop long before Gordon
Ramsay's Channel 4 program,
The F Word, catapulted it to
fame at the end of 2009.
80 MC, V

THE CRAMOND INN

$

30 CRAMOND GLEBE ROAD,
EH4 6NU
TEL (0131) 336 2035
Feast on the likes of salty
gammon, tender steak pie,
and homemade fish cakes in
this typical village pub. Samuel
Smith ales (only two pubs in
Scotland sell these), a roaring
fire, and dedicated family
room all add to the appeal in
this waterfront suburb.
90 AE, MC, V

THE TASS

$

1 HIGH STREET, EH1 1SR
TEL (0131) 556 6338
If you're seeking a traditional
old-style pub, honest pub
food, or live Scottish music,
this Royal Mile institu-
tion delivers all three. The
Tass is also a good place to
sample Scottish produce like
Stornoway black pudding and
MacSween's haggis.
50 MC, V

HOWGATE

THE HOWGATE

$$–$$$
HOWGATE, MIDLOTHIAN,
EH26 8PY
TEL (01968) 670 000
www.howgate.com
Feast on local food cooked
to perfection in either the

Howgate's informal bistro or
more formal restaurant. The
menu is very similar in both
venues, with the bistro offering
some cheaper options and
more choice. Scotch beef hung
for a minimum of three weeks
is what draws a lot of diners
here, however the menu also
boasts mouthwatering delights
like haggis in a light filo pastry
served with a plum sauce.
68 MC, V

GULLANE

LA POTINIERE

$$$
34 MAIN STREET, GULLANE,
EH31 2AA
TEL (01620) 843 214
www.la-potiniere.co.uk
If you are looking for East
Lothian's best restaurant then
you don't need to look much
further than this relaxed local
eatery. Here the focus is firmly
on food, where the short but
decadent menu features the
likes of braised halibut, fillet
of Scotch beef, and poached
nectarines.
30 MC, V

LINLITHGOW

CHAMPANY INN

$$$$$
LINLITHGOW, WEST LOTHIAN,
EH49 7LU
TEL (01506) 834 532
www.champany.com
This Michelin-starred restau-
rant just outside Linlithgow is
renowned throughout central
Scotland for the quality of its
Aberdeen Angus beef, which
has been hung for a minimum
of three weeks, and its fresh
seafood. For a special treat
book one of the restaurant's
rooms or visit its wine cellar.
Also on site, the Chop and Ale
House is a more informal eatery
serving succulent char-grilled
burgers—it is open seven days
a week.
60 AE, DC, MC, V

TASTE

$

47 HIGH STREET, LINLITHGOW,
EH49 7ED
TEL (01506) 844 445
www.taste-deli-cafe.co.uk
Hearty soups, freshly prepared
sandwiches, and wickedly
calorific homemade cakes
form the bulk of the menu
at this cozy deli and café. For
something more substantial,
try the beef lasagne.
44 MC, V

NORTH BERWICK

MACDONALD MARINE HOTEL & SPA

$$$
CROMWELL ROAD, NORTH
BERWICK, EH39 4LZ
TEL (0844) 879 9130
www.macdonald-hotels.co.uk
Graceful guest rooms, a relaxing
spa, and a restaurant serving
first-rate Scottish and international dishes are all compelling
reasons to check into this
seaside hotel. Then there are
the sea views, the nearby beach,
and the golf course. The views
over Bass Rock and North
Berwick Law from the turret
suites are stunning.
83 AE, MC, V

SOUTH QUEENSFERRY

OROCCO PIER

$$
17 HIGH STREET, EH30 9PP
TEL 0870 118 1664
www.oroccopier.co.uk
Orocco Pier quite simply
boasts one of the most stun-
ning settings in Scotland, over-
looking the Firth of Forth and
its iconic Forth Bridge. Stylish
rooms boast lush fabrics,
Molton Brown toiletries, and
CD/DVD players. The hotel
has an equally chic restaurant
and café-bar that enjoy the
same great views.
17 AE, DC, MC, V

Nonsmoking Air-conditioning Indoor Pool Outdoor Pool Health Club Credit Cards

🍴 THE BOAT HOUSE
$$

22 HIGH STREET, EH30 9PP
TEL (0131) 331 5429
www.theboathouse-sq.co.uk
Panoramic views over the
Firth of Forth would be reason
enough to eat here; however,
it is the first-rate seafood skill-
fully cooked by Paul Steward
that brings diners back again
and again.

🪑 48 🚷 🚭 AE, MC, V

■ GLASGOW & AYRSHIRE

GLASGOW

HOTELS

🏨 ABODE
🍴 $$$

129 BATH STREET, G2 2SZ
TEL (0141) 221 6789
www.abodehotels.co.uk/
glasgow
Its central Glasgow location,
award-wining restaurant (see
Michael Caines @ Abode,
opposite), and chic modern
guest rooms are all compelling
reasons to stay at Abode.
The only downside is that it
can be very hard to leave this
contemporary hotel housed in
a charmingly historic building.
ⓘ 59 🔄 🚷 🚭 🔄 🏊 🚭 AE,
MC, V

SOMETHING SPECIAL

🏨 BLYTHSWOOD SQUARE
$$$

BLYTHSWOOD SQUARE, G2 4AD
TEL (0141) 208 2458
www.blythswoodsquare.com
Opened in autumn 2009,
Blythswood Square delivers
subtle luxury and muted hues
in spacious and comfortable
guest rooms. A contemporary
restaurant, and an opulent
health spa complete with nine
treatment rooms, thermal
suite, rasul mud chamber, and

two pools help ease guests
through their stay.
ⓘ 100 Ⓟ 🔄 🚭 🚷 🚭 AE,
DC MC, V

🏨 CITY INN
$$$

FINNIESTON QUAY, G3 8HN
TEL (0141) 240 1002
www.cityinn.com
Reclining on the banks of the
River Clyde, rooms in this
modern hotel may be a little
on the small side, but they are
impressively well equipped.
The best rooms look out over
the river. The **City Café** is also
worth dining in, especially on
warm spring and summer days
when alfresco tables make the
most of the waterfront locale.
ⓘ 168 Ⓟ 🔄 🚷 🚭
🚭 AE, MC, V

SOMETHING SPECIAL

🏨 HOTEL DU VIN
🍴 $$$

1 DEVONSHIRE GARDENS,
G12 0UX
TEL (0141) 3392 001
www.hotelduvin.com/
glasgow
Glasgow's renowned One
Devonshire Gardens may have
undergone a name and an
ownership change, but as the
Hotel du Vin it is still a strong
contender as Glasgow's best
hotel. Rooms are plush and
spacious and the food in the
bistro (see **Bistro du Vin,** p.
281) is excellent.
ⓘ 49 Ⓟ 🔄 🚷 🚭 🚭
🚭 AE, MC, V

🏨 RADISSON BLU
$$$

301 ARGYLE STREET, G2 8DL
TEL (0141) 204 3333
www.radissonblu.co.uk/
hotel-glasgow
With its cutting-edge design–
it looks like a spaceship
has landed next to Central
Station–appealing lobby,

PRICES

HOTELS
The cost of a double room
in peak season is given by
$ signs.

$$$$$	over £300
$$$$	£200–£300
$$$	£120–£200
$$	£80–£120
$	Under £80

RESTAURANTS
The average price of a two-
course meal for one person,
without tip or drinks is given
by **$** signs.

$$$$$	over £50
$$$$	£40–£50
$$$	£25–£40
$$	£15–£25
$	£15

---

and bar, the Radisson is one
of Glasgow's most desirable
addresses. Then there is its
excellent restaurant, health
club, and spa treatments.
Many of the lovely guest
rooms boast floor-to-ceiling
windows from which to
admire the city skyline.
ⓘ 250 🔄 🚷 🚭 🚭 🚭
🚭 AE, DC, MC, V

🏨 MARKS HOTEL
🍴 $–$$

110 BATH STREET, G2 2EN
TEL (0141) 353 0800
www.markshotels.com
Good-size guest rooms with
slanting cruise ship–style windows that lean out over the
rooftops make this a unique
place to stay. Neat extras
include plasma screen TVs and
free wi-fi. The hotel restaurant
is also worth dining in.
ⓘ 103 🔄 🚷 🚭 AE, DC,
MC, V

RESTAURANTS

🍴 BISTRO DU VIN
🏨 $$$$$

HOTEL DU VIN, 1 DEVONSHIRE
GARDENS, G12 0UX
TEL (0141) 339 2001
Oak paneling, classical music, soft lighting, and candlelit tables set high expectations, expectations that the creative dishes served in this atmospheric hotel restaurant easily exceed. Highlights on a daily changing menu might include veal with snails, roasted lobster, and coffee soufflé. The wine list is suitably indulgent.

🍴 78 🅿 🚭 🚕 AE, MC, V

🍴 MICHAEL CAINES @
🏨 ABODE
$$$–$$$$

ABODE, 129 BATH STREET, G2 2SZ
TEL (0141) 221 6789
www.michaelcaines.com
Attentive service and superb cooking with local ingredients makes this hotel restaurant stand out from the crowd. The seven-course tasting menu is an epicurean treat featuring the likes of poached shellfish and saddle of venison. The Amazing-Grazing menu (served 6–7 p.m. and 9–10 p.m.) is great value.

🍴 45 🚭 🚕 ⏰ Closed Sun.–Mon. 🚕 AE, MC, V

SOMETHING SPECIAL

🍴 TWO FAT LADIES
WEST END
$$$

88 DUMBARTON ROAD, G11 6NX
TEL (0141) 339 1944
www.twofatladies restaurant.com
Since opening in 1989 this cozy restaurant has earned itself a well-deserved reputation as one of Glasgow's best fish restaurants. The likes of king prawns and sea bream are cooked to perfection and the wine list carefully put together to complement the dishes. If you can't decide which of the sumptuous desserts to order then why not go for the waist-expanding sharing platter, with its bowls of crème brulée, pistachio and cherry pavlova, cranachan, and sticky toffee pudding?

🍴 26 🚭 🚕 AE, MC, V

🍴 UBIQUITOUS CHIP
$$$

12 ASHTON LANE, G12 8SJ
TEL (0141) 334 5007
www.ubiquitouschip.co.uk
Whether they're sitting in the lovely courtyard, where plants trail down the trellises, or on the new mezzanine level, diners seldom leave here disappointed. With a Scottish menu delivering delights like venison haggis, organic Orkney salmon, Aberdeen Angus steaks, and Caledonian oatmeal ice cream, the Ubiquitous Chip is a strong contender for the title of Glasgow's best fine dining restaurant.

🍴 150 🚭 🚕 🚕 AE, DC, MC, V

🍴 URBAN BAR &
BRASSERIE
$$$

23–25 SAINT VINCENT PLACE, G1 2DT
TEL (0141) 248 5636
www.urbanbrasserie.co.uk
Fittingly for a restaurant housed in the former headquarters of the Bank of England's Scottish base, this elegant brasserie impresses with its dark woods, subdued lighting and original artwork. The décor, while very striking, is not what brings punters back to the Urban Bar & Brasserie time and time again. Repeat custom is simply due to the excellent quality of the cooking. Highlights on a Scottish-French menu include oysters, beef bourguignon and Buccleuch beefsteak. For a more intimate dining experience sit in one of the booths.

🍴 120 🚭 🚕 MC, V

🍴 CAFÉ GANDOLFI
$$

64 ALBION STREET, G1 1NY
TEL (0141) 552 6813
www.cafegandolfi.com
Lovely carved furniture, ambient mood lighting, and a creative menu have ensconced Café Gandolfi at the top of Glasgow's informal dining scene, with regulars and visitors flocking here for over 30 years. The standard menu features creative sandwiches, pasta, and mains like marinated swordfish.

🍴 66 🚭 🚕 AE, MC, V

🍴 FIFI AND ALLY
$$

80 WELLINGTON STREET, G1 3JX
TEL (0141) 226 2286
www.fifiandally.com
This ultra-modern bistro—with its exposed brickwork and contrasting black and white décor—is one of Glasgow's coolest dining addresses. The eclectic all-day menu features everything from homemade soup to a platter of Italian antipasti and champagne afternoon tea.

🍴 110 🚭 ⏰ Closed Sun. 🚕 MC, V

SOMETHING SPECIAL

🍴 MOTHER INDIA
$$

28 WESTMINSTER TERRACE, G3 7RU
TEL (0141) 221 1663
www.motherindia glasgow.co.uk
Spicy Indian cooking that shies away from an endless list of sauce-laden curries and contemporary décor distinguishes Mother India from the competition. More unusual dishes on the small menu include tandoori roasted haddock and

monkfish kebabs.

🔡 210 Ⓢ 🅰 AE, MC, V

🍴 SCOTIA BAR
$$

112–114 STOCKWELL STREET,
G1 4LW
TEL (0141) 552 8681
www.scotiabar.net

The Scotia Bar is renowned among Glaswegians for its live music. Visit this traditional boozer—apparently the oldest pub in the city—Thursday through Sunday and you have got a good chance of hearing anything from country and folk to blues or jazz (especially later in the evening). A good selection of beer, ales, and spirits are also complemented by a menu that offers good home-cooked pub food.

🔡 40 Ⓢ 🅰 AE, MC, V

🍴 THALI
$$

42 ALBION STREET, G1 1LH
TEL (0141) 552 8332
www.thaliglasgow.com

This stylish restaurant with its ambient lighting, equally chilled music, and spicy cuisine is a firm favorite with Glaswegians and it is easy to see why. Veering away from large creamy curries served up in many Indian restaurants, Thali presents diners with a number of smaller dishes, which they add to a base of rice, naan bread, salad, and either a lentil or raita (yogurt) accompaniment. With numerous vegetarian dishes sitting alongside chicken, lamb, and prawn options, Thali offers plenty of choice.

🔡 60 Ⓢ 🅰 AE, MC, V

LANARK

🏨 NEW LANARK MILL HOTEL
$$

SOUTH LANARKSHIRE, ML11 9DB
TEL (01555) 667 200
www.newlanarkhotel.co.uk

Housed in a former 18th-century cotton mill, this characterful hotel boasts elegant guest rooms, all of which enjoy breathtaking views over the River Clyde or its adjacent conservation area. It also boasts a state-of-the-art leisure center, and a decent restaurant and gives guest-discounted entrance to the New Lanark World Heritage site.

① 38 🅿 🛗 Ⓢ ⛷ Ⓢ 🏊
🅰 AE, DC, MC, V

MILNGAVIE

🏨 TAMBOWIE FARM
$

CRAIGTON VILLAGE, MILNGAVIE,
G62 7HN
TEL (0141) 956 1583
www.tambowiefarm.co.uk

Its rural location, stunning views, and spacious double rooms universally meet the approval of guests. Reasonable prices, an enormous breakfast spread, and the friendly personal welcome extended by Irene Graham are the other winning ingredients at this farmhouse B&B.

① 4 🅿 Ⓢ 🛗 ⛷ 🅰 MC, V

TURNBERRY

🏨 TURNBERRY RESORT
$$$$$

TURNBERRY, KA26 9LT
TEL (01655) 33 1000
www.turnberryresort.co.uk

From one of Scotland's premier golf courses to a sumptuous spa, Turnberry has it all. Guest rooms and refined public spaces make the most of the enchanting sea views. Fine fabrics and rich woods are the hallmark of the classic rooms, while deluxe accommodation delivers elegant luxury and contemporary bathrooms with rolltop baths.

① 198 🅿 🛗 Ⓢ ⛷ Ⓢ 🏊
🅰 AE, DC, MC, V

▪ SOUTHERN SCOTLAND

CASTLE DOUGLAS

🏨 AIRDS FARM
$

CROSSMICHAEL, NEAR CASTLE
DOUGLAS, DG7 3BG
TEL (01556) 670 418
www.airds.com

In addition to large, clean and cozy guest rooms, this lovely B&B also boasts great views over farmland and Loch Ken below. The hearty breakfasts are a taste sensation and guests are welcome to use the TV lounge. A bigger draw for most visitors, though, is the conservatory with its stunning views over the Galloway Hills.

① 4 🅿 Ⓢ 🅰 Cash only

DUMFRIES

🏨 FRIARS CARSE
🍴 COUNTRY HOUSE HOTEL
$$

DUMFRIES, DG2 0SA
TEL (01387) 740 388
www.friarscarse.co.uk

Feel like the lord or lady of the manor at this 19th-century country house hotel. The individually styled guest rooms may vary in size, but the pervading theme is fittingly traditional. Anglers have exclusive access to the stretch of the River Ninth that runs through the hotel grounds, where they can fish sea trout, grayling, and salmon. Alternatively guests can explore the 45 acres (18 ha) of woodland, while a snooker table tempts indoors. The Whistle Restaurant is also worth dining in.

① 21 🅿 Ⓢ 🛗 🅰 AE, MC, V

🍴 AULD ALLIANCE
$$

53 ST. MICHAEL'S STREET,
DUMFRIES, DG1 2QB
TEL (01387) 255 689
www.auldalliance
dumfries.com

This restaurant builds on
the historic alliance between
Scotland and France. Dishes
are classic French–infused
with a contemporary Scottish
twist—for example, scallops
served with black pudding
and fillet of Galloway beef
accompanied by *dauphinois*
potatoes.

🍴 40 🚭 🏧 MC, V

GATEHOUSE OF FLEET

🍴 SHIP INN
$$

11 FLEET STREET, GATEHOUSE OF
FLEET, DG7 2HU
TEL (01557) 814 217
www.theshipinngatehouse
.co.uk

Food that is a cut above your
average pub grub makes the
Ship Inn a favorite with locals
and visitors alike. The menu
makes the most of Scottish
produce and includes the
likes of beef, lamb, pork, and
venison. This inn also offers
overnight accommodation.

🍴 50 🚭 🏧 MC, V

MELROSE

🏨 BURT'S HOTEL
$$$

MARKET SQUARE, TD6 9PN
TEL (01896) 822 285
www.burtshotel.co.uk

This old Melrose institution
is much more than just a
hotel. It also boasts one of the
town's best restaurants (see
Burt's Hotel, below) and a
lively bar well stocked with
single malt whisky. Accom-
modation in this 18th-century
building is fittingly traditional,
but unfussy.

🛏 20 🅿 🚭 🏧 MC, V

🏨 THE TOWNHOUSE
$$

MARKET SQUARE, MELROSE,
TD6 9PQ
TEL (01896) 822 645
www.thetownhouse
melrose.co.uk

It may be owned by the
Henderson family (the same
people behind Burt's Hotel
across the road), but this
funky hotel couldn't be more
different. Here the emphasis
in the individual guest rooms
is on contemporary style with
bold patterns and contrasting
colors. The four-poster room is
a nod to a more classical style.
Both standard and superior
rooms have plenty of space.
The brasserie and restaurant
are both pleasant places to
dine.

🛏 11 🅿 🚭 🏧 MC, V

🍴 BURT'S HOTEL
🏨 **$$$**

BURT'S HOTEL, MARKET SQUARE,
MELROSE, TD6 9PN
TEL (01896) 822 285
www.burtshotel.co.uk

This busy restaurant in the
Burt's Hotel (see left) has
become something of a
Melrose institution and it is
easy to see why. Service is
polite but not too formal
and the food is consistently
good. Venison, duck, halibut,
fillet steak, and Stornoway
black pudding are just some
of the delights you might find
on the menu. The old world
feel of the dining room adds
to the charm.

🍴 50 🅿 🚭 🏧 MC, V

PEEBLES

🏨 CRINGLETIE HOUSE
$$$$

EDINBURGH ROAD, EH45 8PL
TEL (01721) 725 750
www.cringletie.com

Since taking over the 19th-
century property in 2003,
Jacob and Johanna van Houdt

have impressively restored
the baronial mansion and its
ornate grounds. A lift that
allows disabled visitors to
access the upstairs dining
room and the plush Selkirk
Suite are both recent additions
that have further enhanced
the already excellent hotel.
Guests receive the same ten-
der care as Cringletie House
itself, while in the restaurant
head chef Craig Gibb
conjures up an eclectic
menu that marries fine
Scottish ingredients with
French flair.

🛏 13 🅿 🛗 🚭 🏧 AE,
MC, V

🏨 CASTLE VENLAW
HOTEL
$$$

EDINBURGH ROAD, EH45 8QG
TEL (01721) 720 384
www.venlaw.co.uk

This boutique hotel boasts
12 acres (5 ha) of grounds,
a good restaurant, and a
welcoming bar. Some of the
refurbished guest rooms come
complete with oversize baths,
champagne coolers, and starry
ceiling lights.

🛏 12 🅿 🚭 🏧 MC, V

🏨 HORSESHOE INN
🍴 **$$–$$$**

EDDLESTON, EH45 8QP
TEL (01721) 730 225
www.horseshoeinn.co.uk

The cozy rooms at the
Horseshoe Inn are perfect for
guests who want to dine in
the award-winning restaurant
downstairs (see **Bardoulet's
Restaurant** p.284), without
worrying about driving after-
ward. Each of the eight rooms
are individually designed with
feature walls, flat screen TVs,
and luxurious fabrics lending
them a surprisingly contemporary feel. Premier rooms offer
a lot more space.

🛏 8 🚭 🛗 Closed three weeks
in Jan. 🏧 MC, V

🏨 CARDRONA
$$

CARDRONA, EH45 8NE
TEL (0870) 194 2114
www.macdonaldhotels
.co.uk/cardrona

Boasting its own golf course, Cardrona is ideal for golfers or those who want to indulge in a relaxing spa treatment and a first-rate meal. For cyclists the world-class mountain-biking trails of Glentress (see p.117) are just next door. Make the most of its dramatic River Tweed location with a ground-floor room where floor-to-ceiling glass doors open up onto an outdoor terrace.

🛈 99 🅿 🔲 ⬛ 🔃 🔲 ⬛
⬛ AE, MC, V

🏨 THE TONTINE
$$

HIGH STREET, PEEBLES, EH45 8AJ
TEL (01721) 720 892
www.tontinehotel.com

This welcoming family-run establishment is located right in the center of town. The refurbished rooms are chic and modern, with wall-mounted televisions and hospitality trays (complete with tea and coffee) to help make guests even more comfortable. The hotel also serves good food in its bistro and restaurant.

🛈 36 🅿 🔲 ⬛ AE, MC, V

🍴 BARDOULET'S
🏨 RESTAURANT
$$$

EDDLESTON, EH45 8QP
TEL (01721) 730 225
www.horseshoeinn.co.uk

Housed in the **Horseshoe Inn** (see p.283), Bardoulet's restaurant gets its name from Chef Director Patrick Bardoulet and offers a classically French treat in elegant surrounds. Here highlights on an ever changing menu might include halibut and lobster. A seven-course tasting menu is on hand for those who really want to experience the diversity of the French chef's cooking. A second dining venue, the stylish Bistro is a more relaxed space, whose menu offers the likes of Scotch beef, fish soup, and chicken Caesar salad.

🔲 40 🔲 🔃 Closed Mon. & three weeks in Jan. ⬛ MC, V

🍴 OSSO
$$

1 INNERLEITHEN ROAD, PEEBLES, EH45 8AB
TEL (01721) 724 477
www.ossorestaurant.com

This chic café-restaurant with its mirrored walls, polished wood, olive green upholstery, and designer lampshades doesn't just deliver style. Chef Ally McGrath has an excellent cooking pedigree and he brings his expertise to every aspect of the menu, from lighter lunches to the superb dinner dishes like braised hare and hand-dived scallops. In the evenings a tasting menu that makes the most of local seasonal produce is also available.

🔲 40 🔲 🔃 Closed D Sun.–Mon. ⬛ AE, MC, V

🍴 SUNFLOWER RESTAURANT
$$

4 BRIDGEGATE, PEEBLES, EH45 8RZ
TEL (01721) 722 420
www.thesunflower.net

Diners young and old flock to this wonderful little restaurant for light lunches or to savor moist chocolate cakes and a frothy latté. A toy box is on hand to help keep small children entertained. Homemade soups, bruschetta, venison burgers and delicious vegetarian pastas tempt from the menu. On Thursday, Friday, and Saturday nights the restaurant also serves dinner, with a more sophisticated

---

PRICES

HOTELS

The cost of a double room in peak season is given by $ signs.

$$$$$	over £300
$$$$	£200–£300
$$$	£120–£200
$$	£80–£120
$	Under £80

RESTAURANTS

The average price of a two-course meal for one person, without tip or drinks is given by $ signs.

$$$$$	over £50
$$$$	£40–£50
$$$	£25–£40
$$	£15–£25
$	£15

---

menu featuring the likes of lamb curry and wild boar sausages.

🔲 40 🔲 ⬛ MC, V

PORTPATRICK

SOMETHING SPECIAL

🏨 KNOCKINAAM LODGE
🍴 $$$$$

PORTPATRICK, DG9 9AD
TEL (01776) 810 471
www.knockinaamlodge.com

Those looking for a romantic hideaway need look no further. This small and intimate hotel delivers classical luxury in the form of individually styled rooms, a peaceful and welcoming ambience and equally tranquil surroundings. The sea views available from some of the guest rooms and public areas are simply breathtaking. The hotel also has a reputation for serving excellent Scottish food (see opposite). Room rates include dinner, bed and breakfast.

🛈 10 🅿 🔲 ⬛ AE, MC, V

🏨 Hotel 🍴 Restaurant 🛈 No. of Guest Rooms 🔲 No. of Seats 🅿 Parking 🔃 Closed ⬛ Elevator

🏨 THE WATERFRONT
🍴 CORSEWALL
LIGHTHOUSE HOTEL
$$$–$$$$

CORSEWALL POINT, KIRKCOLM,
DG9 0QG

TEL (01776) 853 220

www.lighthousehotel.co.uk

The former living quarters of the lighthouse keeper have been transformed into a unique place to stay. Rooms and suites are all individually styled, with extra space and sea views commanding a small premium. The Lighthouse Suite, with its own private conservatory, and the Firth of Cromarty Room with its private terrace are both popular with guests. The hotel also has a decent restaurant and the tariff includes dinner, bed, and breakfast.

🛏 10 🅿 🆂 AE, DC, MC, V

🏨 THE WATERFRONT
HOTEL & BISTRO
$$

PORTPATRICK, DG 9 9SX

TEL (01776) 810 800

www.waterfronthotel.co.uk

This small and welcoming hotel is located on the harbor of the pretty village of Portpatrick. Guest rooms, like the hotel itself, are cozy. They are also clean and comfortable. Sea view rooms are well worth the extra £5 per person. As you might expect in a fishing village, seafood dominates the menu in the hotel's elegant restaurant.

🛏 8 🅿 🆂 AE, MC, V

🍴 KNOCKINAAM LODGE
🏨 $$$$

PORTPATRICK, DG9 9AD

TEL (01776) 810 471

www.knockinaamlodge.com

The lovely restaurant at this beautiful country house hotel (see above) is open to non-residents. The food on the four-course menu is divine but often only gives a choice of dessert, so advise them about any special dietary requirements in advance. The carefully chosen wine list caters to all wallets, with moderately priced fine wines sitting alongside budget-busting vintages.

🪑 32 🅿 🆂 AE, MC, V

🍴 CAMPBELLS
$$$

1 SOUTH CRESCENT,
PORTPATRICK, DG9 8JR

TEL (01776) 810 314

www.campbells
restaurant.co.uk

This seafront restaurant has been serving Portpatrick locals and visitors first-class Scottish meat and seafood for over a decade now. It is particularly well known for its lobster and seafood platters. The relaxed ambience in the dining room lends itself to a candlelit dinner for two or a celebratory meal. On a warm summer's day diners can sit at the clutch of outdoor tables that overlook the harbor.

🪑 45 🆂 🕐 Closed Mon. & 2 weeks in Jan. –Feb. & 1 week in Nov. 🆂 MC, V

SANQUHAR

🏨 BLACKADDIE COUNTRY
HOUSE HOTEL
$$

SANQUHAR, DUMFRIESSHIRE,
DG4 6JJ

TEL (01659) 50270

www.blackaddiehotel.co.uk

Flat-screen televisions and hospitality trays (with free tea, coffee, shortbread, and mineral water) help guests feel at home. Standard rooms are comfortable enough, but for that added luxury, book a superior room or splash out on a river suite. The two-room suite is particularly good for families or groups of four. A family room that can accom-modate up to five people is also available. The hotel also boasts a fine restaurant.

🛏 9 🅿 🆂 🛎 🆂 MC, V

ROXBURGHE

🏨 ROXBURGHE HOTEL &
GOLF COURSE
$$$

HEITON, ROXBURGHSHIRE,
TD5 8JZ

TEL (01573) 450 331

www.roxburghe-hotel.com

One of Scotland's finest country house hotels impresses guests with its stately guest rooms, first-rate restaurant, spa treatments, and golf course. Sleep like a king and book the Bowmont Suite (originally the master bedroom of the house), with its open log fire, and survey the 500-acre (202 ha) estate from the private balcony.

🛏 22 🅿 🆂 AE, MC, V

■ CENTRAL
SCOTLAND

PERTHSHIRE

HOTELS

SOMETHING SPECIAL

🏨 GLENEAGLES HOTEL
🍴 $$$$$

AUCHTERARDER, PH3 1NF

TEL (01764) 662 231

www.gleneagles.com

For most visitors to Scotland Gleneagles needs little intro-duction, as this oasis of luxury in the heart of Perthshire hosted the 2005 G8 summit. Then of course there is the hotel's championship golf course (one of Scotland's finest), opulent spa, and the wonderful swimming pool that is both indoor and out-door. Graceful public spaces and a range of dining options —including renowned chef

Andrew Fairlie's restaurant (see below)—and activities ranging from shooting to horse riding, offer plenty to keep guests occupied. A playroom and a games/chill out room (the Zone) are also on hand for the kids. The pampering continues in elegant and spacious guest rooms.

[] 232 P 🔄 🅿 📶 🚲 📺 AE, DC, MC, V

🏨 CRIEFF HYDRO
$$$
CRIEFF, PH7 3LQ
TEL (01764) 655 555
www.crieffhydro.com
A firm family favorite, Crieff Hydro offers a wide range of accommodation, from standard double rooms to family rooms and suites in the main hotel and self-catering cottages. Rooms are comfortable rather than luxurious. Crieff's real appeal lies in the diverse raft of activities, including quad biking and an 18-hole golf course, available on site. The hotel has two swimming pools, a games room, and child care facilities. Family-oriented entertainment runs into the evening with ceilidhs and quizzes. The hotel has a number of different dining options.

[] 213 P 🔄 📶 📺 MC, V

🏨 LANDS OF LOYAL HOTEL
$$$
AYLTH, BLAIRGOWRIE, PH11 8JQ
TEL (01828) 633 151
www.landsofloyal.com
This charming Victorian mansion impresses guests with its personal service and elegant rooms where understated luxury prevails. Guests are invited to relax in the pubic areas and the beautiful terraced garden, where they can soak up romantic rural views.

[] 17 P 🅿 AE, MC, V

🏨 ROYAL HOTEL
$$$
MELVILLE SQUARE, COMRIE, PH6 2DN
TEL (017640) 679 200
www.royalhotel.co.uk
This classically luxurious hotel is housed in a historic building, where Queen Victoria was once a guest (hence the name). Individually styled rooms are decorated in muted tones with opulent soft fabrics and dark wood furniture. The Molton Brown toiletries in the modern bathrooms help ease guests through their stay, as do the elegant public rooms, restaurant and lounge bar.

[] 11 P 🅿 AE, MC, V

🏨 PARKLANDS
$$–$$$
2 ST. LEONARD'S BANK, PERTH, PH2 8EB
TEL (01738) 622 451
www.theparklandshotel.com
This charming family-run hotel has to be the best located in Perth, perched prettily on a hill overlooking South Inch Park. Guest accommodation is comfortable and spacious, with wi-fi, flat-screen TVs, DVD players, big bathrooms, and great views over the park and the city beyond bonuses in many rooms. When it comes to food the hotel has two good dining options—the signature **Acanthus Restaurant** and brasserie-style **No. 1 the Bank**—and also offers limited room service.

[] 14 P 🅿 MC, V

RESTAURANTS

SOMETHING SPECIAL

🍴 RESTAURANT ANDREW
🏨 FAIRLIE
$$$$$
GLENEAGLES HOTEL, AUCHTERARDER, PH3 1NF
TEL 0800 704 705

www.andrewfairlie.com
For many visitors to Scotland, dinner in Restaurant Andrew Fairlie is a must. Foodies from around the globe make a pilgrimage to taste the famous Scottish chef's two-Michelin-starred cuisine. The dining room is refined but contemporary, with smooth personal service. Chef Andrew Fairlie, who spent years working in Paris, brings unashamedly French cuisine to the table, but infuses it with a cheeky Scottish flair. Both the à la carte and six-course degustation menus employ the finest Scottish produce like wild venison and Perthshire lamb.

🪑 45 🅿 P 🕐 Closed L & Sun. AE, MC, V

🍴 63 TAY STREET
$$$
PERTH, PH2 8NN
TEL (01738) 441 451
www.63taystreet.co.uk
Everything about this fine dining eatery located down by the river is smooth, from the service to elegant décor complete with muted hues and subtle tartan. This culinary oasis makes the most of Scottish produce, with lamb supplied by the brother of famous chef Andrew Fairlie. Succulent venison is perfectly cooked and the well-selected wines a perfect accompaniment to an epicurean feast that will last all evening.

🪑 35 🅿 🕐 Closed Sun.–Mon. DC, MC, V

🍴 WATERMILL TEA ROOM
$–$$
BLAIR ATHOLL, PH18 5SH
TEL (01796) 481 321
www.blairathollwatermill.co.uk
One of Scotland's few remaining watermills (flour and oatmeal are still milled here) is also the setting for one of Scotland's better cafés. Delicious sandwiches, bagels, soups, and cakes (the carrot

cake is legendary in these parts) feature on the simple menu. Diners can also pick up their own oatmeal and flour, as well as jams, chutneys, eggs, and other Scottish produce.

🛏 24 Ⓢ 🕐 Closed Dec.–March Ⓢ MC, V

ARGYLL

HOTELS

SOMETHING SPECIAL

🏨 ISLE OF ERISKA HOTEL, SPA & ISLAND
$$$$$
THE ISLE OF ERISKA, LEDAIG, PA37 1SD
TEL (01631) 720 371
www.eriska-hotel.co.uk
This luxurious retreat, which reclines on its own 300-acre (121 ha) private island, offers the Old World charm of the country house hotel with contemporary spa suites and two-bedroom cottage suites. Guests staying in the main hotel should consider booking a deluxe room. In the Lismore Suite large bay windows open up on dramatic hill and ocean vistas across the eponymous island. Guests also have access to a first-class restaurant, well-stocked bar, small gym, indoor swimming pool, and spa. If this isn't enough there is also a six-hole golf course, croquet lawn, and tennis court.

ⓘ 21 🅿 Ⓢ 🔇 🎾 Ⓢ AE, MC, V

🏨 ARDANAISEIG
$$$
KILCHREGAN BY TAYNUILT, PA35 1HE
TEL (01866) 833 333
www.ardanaiseig.com
This grand old dame reclining on the shores of Loch Awe has been hailed as one of Scotland's most romantic hotels, and justifiably so. The individu-

ally styled rooms all offer a slice of elegant luxury, with stately public rooms and the good food served in the restaurant its crowning glory. For a really special occasion book the Boat Shed, a deluxe nest for two situated right on the edge of the loch.

ⓘ 18 🅿 Ⓢ AE, DC, MC, V

🏨 STONEFIELD CASTLE
$$$
TARBERT, LOCH FYNE, PA29 6YJ
TEL (01880) 820 836
www.oxfordhotelsandinns.com
The chance to stay in an old castle and a dramatic lochside location are reason enough to stay at Stonefield Castle. Then there is the recent renovation that has treated all the public areas and guest rooms to a tasteful overhaul. For a really memorable stay, book one of the suites, which benefit from big bathrooms, separate sleeping and sitting areas, and truly mesmerizing views over Loch Fyne.

ⓘ 32 🅿 🔇 Ⓢ 🗝 MC, V

🏨 LOCH FYNE HOTEL & SPA
$$–$$$
SHORE STREET, INVERARAY, PA32 8XT
TEL (01499) 302 980
www.crerarhotels.com/lochfyne
Located right on the shores of the eponymous loch, this attractive hotel offers comfortable (if not always luxurious) guest rooms decorated in warm neutral shades, a swimming pool, spa treatments, and a decent restaurant. For a deluxe stay, reserve one of the mini suites with their rolltop baths, DVD players, and stunning loch views. Lagavulin has a charming mezzanine level from which to soak up the lovely water views.

ⓘ 71 🅿 🔇 Ⓢ 🎾 Ⓢ AE, MC, V

🏨 OBAN BAY HOTEL & SPA
$$–$$$
CORRAN ESPLANADE, PA34 5AE
TEL (0870) 950 6273
www.crerarhotels.com
Many of the rooms in the main building of this waterfront hotel enjoy sweeping views over the eponymous bay. For the most part, accommodation is modest but clean and comfortable. For a luxurious stay check into one of the junior suites. Kerrera boasts a four-poster bed and a rolltop bath. The hotel also has a small spa with a steam room, sauna, and massage chair, as well as an outdoor hot tub that enjoys views over the bay to the island of Kerrera.

ⓘ 80 🅿 Ⓢ Ⓢ AE, MC, V

RESTAURANTS

🍴 KILBERRY INN
🏨 **$$$**
KILBERRY, PA29 6YD
TEL (01880) 770 223
www.kilberryinn.com
It may be off the beaten track, but diners who make the effort to find the Kilberry Inn are rewarded with mouthwatering local produce. The likes of plump Loch Fyne scallops seared to perfection and tender Ormsary ribeye steak are hallmarks of cooking that is always delicious and has earned the chef a Bib Gourmand mention. The whitewashed inn with its striking red roof is a fittingly atmospheric place to enjoy this epicurean treat. There are also five cozy rooms.

🛏 40 🅿 Ⓢ 🕐 Closed Jan.–mid-March, Mon. mid–March–Oct., & Mon.–Fri. Nov.–Dec.
Ⓢ MC, V

Ⓢ Nonsmoking 🔇 Air-conditioning 🎾 Indoor Pool 🗝 Outdoor Pool 🎾 Health Club Ⓢ Credit Cards

🍴 LOCH FYNE RESTAURANT

$$$

CLACHAN, CAIRNDOW, PA26 8BL

TEL (01499) 600 236

www.lochfyne.com

This seafood eatery spawned a nationwide chain, but for many the original is by far the best. Sumptuous seafood, which includes the likes of langoustines, oysters, mussels, clams, crab, and lobster, makes its way onto the daily-changing menu. Ingredients are sourced as locally as possible. Quality is also the ethos behind the ingredients and cooking when it comes to the restaurant's meat dishes, with locally sourced Glen Fyne venison and steaks aged for 28 days a real treat.

🪑 56 🚭 🚫 AE, MC, V

🍴 PIERHOUSE SEAFOOD RESTAURANT

$$$

PORT APPIN, PA38 4DE

TEL (01631) 730 302

www.pierhousehotel.co.uk

Soak up the sea views through large picture windows as you enjoy a lovely meal. Oysters plucked from the Lismore oyster beds, Loch Etive langoustine, and fresh lobster are among the highlights on a fish-heavy menu. Meat eaters are well cared for with tender Scotch beef and local game dishes. A children's menu and vegetarian dishes are also available.

🪑 60 🅿 🚭 🚫 MC, V

🍴 COAST

$$–$$$

104 GEORGE STREET, OBAN, PA34 5NT

TEL (01631) 569 900

www.coastoban.co.uk

Housed in a former bank, this contemporary eatery welcomes guests with crisp white table linens, soft hues of brown, and light polished woods. An eclectic menu caters to all tastes with lamb, seafood, beef, and vegetarian options.

🪑 46 🚭 🕐 Closed Sun. 🚫 MC, V

🍴 SEAFOOD CABIN

$–$$

SKIPNESS ESTATE, PA29 6XU

TEL (01880) 760 207

On a warm sunny day enjoy an alfresco seafood meal overlooking Kilbrannan Sound. This wonderful little wooden cabin serves up boat-fresh seafood, including langoustines and crab, accompanied by homegrown salad. Dining outside, though, doesn't mean you have to rough it: Cutlery, plates, and tables are provided. Delicious home-baked goods are available for anyone who is still hungry. In bad weather you can dine in the old kitchen.

🪑 20 🅿 🚭 🕐 Closed Oct.– late May 🚫 MC, V

THE TROSSACHS

SOMETHING SPECIAL

🏨 CAMERON HOUSE
🍴 HOTEL

$$$–$$$$

LOCH LOMOND, G83 8QZ

TEL (01389) 755 565

www.devere.co.uk

The addition of a new golf course, state-of-the-art spa, and an extensive renovation that has enhanced elegant public spaces and guest rooms with plush fabrics has made Cameron House truly world class. Then there is **Martin Wishart**'s fine dining restaurant (see opposite), stylish bars, and the to-die-for location.

ⓘ 128 🅿 🚭 🛏 🍽 📺 🚫 🚫 AE, DC, MC, V

SOMETHING SPECIAL

🏨 MONACHYLE MHOR
🍴

$$–$$$$

BALQUIDDER, FK19 8PQ

TEL (01877) 384 622

www.mhor.net

This chic hotel may be easy to get to from the central belt, but hidden away down a quiet glen it feels a million miles away. Contemporary suites ease guests through their stay, but for many it is the legendary food that lures them here. If a five-course feast isn't enough to show you how seriously chef Tom Lewis takes his food (see **Mhor Fish,** opposite), how about cooking classes and the fact that Monachyle Mhor is also a fully operational farm?

ⓘ 14 🅿 🚭 🕐 Closed Jan. 🚫 MC, V

LAKE OF MENTEITH HOTEL AND WATER-FRONT RESTAURANT $$$

PORT OF MENTEITH, FK8 3RA
TEL (01877) 385 258
www.lake-hotel.com
The hotel has been impressing locals and visitors alike with its pretty lakeside location and good food for a long time now. For overnight guests, it also offers spacious and comfortable rooms, many with great views. Renovated rooms are contemporary, while the rest are classically elegant.
🔢 16 🅿 🔲 🔲 MC, V

ROMAN CAMP $$$

CALLANDER, PERTHSHIRE, FK17 8BG
TEL (01877) 330 003
www.romancamphotel.co.uk
Nestled on the banks of the River Teith, this opulent hideaway is just off Callander's main street, but feels a million miles from anywhere. Its 20-acre (8 ha) grounds, fine dining restaurant, classical rooms, and ornate public spaces are all perfect ingredients for a romantic stay.
🔢 14 🅿 🔲 🔲 AE, DC, MC, V

MARTIN WISHART AT LOCH LOMOND $$$$

CAMERON HOUSE HOTEL, LOCH LOMOND, G83 8QZ
TEL (01389) 722 504
www.martin-wishart.co.uk
Michelin-starred chef, Martin Wishart, has recently brought his innovative brand of cooking to Loch Lomond's premier hotel. Fine-dining French style is complemented by smooth service, an excellent wine list, and a contemporary, yet sophisticated setting.
🔢 40 🅿 🔲 🔲 Closed Mon.–Tues., L Wed.–Fri., & Jan. 20–Feb. 10 🔲 AE, MC, V

MHOR FISH $$

75–77 MAIN STREET, CALLANDER, FK17 8DX
TEL (01877) 330 213
http://mhor.net/fish
Run by the people behind **Monachyle Mhor** (see above) this is a great place for an informal sit-down meal. The fish is fresh and you can even buy some from the fish counter to take away. Fish and chips from the adjacent chippy can be taken away or eaten in the restaurant.
🔢 28 🔲 🔲 MC, V

STIRLING AREA

ADAMO HOTEL, STIRLING $$$

78 UPPER CRAIGS, FK8 2DT
TEL (01786) 430 890
www.adamohotels.com
This gorgeous stone building located right in the center of Stirling is convenient to all the local sights. Large rooms deliver contemporary luxury in the form of oversize beds, plasma TVs, DVD players, and wireless Internet. Ensuite bathrooms are equally spacious and luxurious. The hotel's suitably stylish **Bank Restaurant** (see below) and its buzzing bar are also worth visiting.
🔢 7 🅿 🔲 🔲 MC, V

DOUBLETREE BY HILTON DUNBLANE HYDRO HOTEL $$$

PERTH ROAD, DUNBLANE, FK15 0HG
TEL (01786) 822 551
www.doubletreedunblane.com
Rich colors, relaxing armchairs, and plush fabrics infuse luxury into the contemporary guest rooms. This is heightened by flat-screen televisions, wireless Internet access, and

on-demand movies. Deluxe rooms are even more spacious and can be configured to sleep families of four in a queen and two single beds. Other family-oriented services include interconnecting rooms, children's menus, and a babysitting service (organize this in advance of your stay). Kids will also love the indoor swimming pool. Adults can also use the sauna, steam room, and gym and book spa or beauty treatments.
🔢 200 🅿 🔲 🔲 🔲 🔲 AE, DC, MC, V

THE INN AT KIPPEN $$–$$$

FORDE ROAD, KIPPEN, FK8 3DT
TEL (01786) 870 500
www.theinnatkippen.co.uk
A recent change of ownership has given the Inn at Kippen a new lease on life. The chefs have come up with a menu that offers diners the choice between traditional favorites like fish and chips and more creative dishes like Marseilles-style fish stew. What all the dishes have in common, though, is the use of local ingredients and the fact that they have been well cooked. Sweet treats include clootie dumpling, with a savory course of Scottish cheese also on offer. The inn also has three reasonably priced rooms.
🔢 60 🅿 🔲 🔲 MC, V

BANK RESTAURANT $$

ADAMO HOTEL, 78 UPPER CRAIGS, FK8 2DT
TEL (01786) 430 890
www.adamohotels.com
Good restaurants are hard to find in Stirling. Those looking for more than a simple snack or Scottish dishes by numbers, should make a beeline for the Bank Restaurant. Amid dark woods, rich colors, and atmospheric lighting, diners

can sample well-cooked national favorites like haggis, neeps, and tatties, as well as more innovative dishes like pizza topped with chorizo and Stornoway black pudding. The express menu (12–6 p.m. Sun.–Thurs. & 12–7 p.m. Fri.–Sat.) is a great value.

🛏 56 🅿 🔁 🚭 🚯
🅰 AE, MC, V

▓ EAST COAST

FIFE

SOMETHING SPECIAL

🏨 OLD COURSE HOTEL,
🍴 GOLF RESORT & SPA
$$$$$

ST. ANDREWS, KY16 9SP
TEL (01334) 474 371
www.oldcoursehotel.co.uk
Palatial rooms enjoy views out onto the eponymous golf course and the sea beyond. The hotel's golf stewards can help guests organize a round of golf on one of the local courses (some slots on the world-famous Old Course can be booked in advance, others are entered into a daily ballot). The irresistible allure of this glorious five-star dame embraces such indulgences as the ultimate pampering experience in the opulent Kholer Waters Spa. A handful of decadent restaurants offer everything from good pub food (at the **Jigger Inn**) to champagne and fine dining.

🛈 144 🅿 🔁 🚭 🚯 🛗
🅰 AE, DC, MC, V

🏨 FAIRMONT
🍴 ST. ANDREWS
$$$$

ST. ANDREWS, KY16 8PN
TEL (01334) 837 000
www.fairmont.com/standrews
The welcome and service at the Fairmont St. Andrews is

exemplary. This five-star resort also boasts spacious guest rooms decorated in warm browns and subtle tartan. Many rooms benefit from views across the hotel grounds and golf courses to the sea. Modern in-room amenities that ease guests through their stay include plug sockets compatible with U.S. and U.K. plugs, satellite television, and minibars. The hotel's other big drawcards are its two championship golf courses, indoor swimming pool, and spa.

🛈 209 🅿 🔁 🚭 🚯 🛗
🅰 AE, DC, MC, V

🏨 BEAUMONT LODGE
$

43 PITTENWEEM ROAD,
ANSTRUTHER, KY10 3DT
TEL (01333) 310 315
www.beaumontlodge.co.uk
Spacious and comfortable rooms, hearty breakfasts, and the attractive stone house itself make this one of the East Neuk's most appealing guesthouses. Then, of course, there is the friendly but unobtrusive welcome. For added romance book the four-poster room.

🛈 3 🅿 🚭 🚯 🅰 MC, V

🏨 ROSCOBIE FARMHOUSE
$

DUNFERMLINE, KY12 0SG
TEL (01383) 731 571
www.roscobiefarmhouse.co.uk
For something a bit different, stay on a working sheep and cattle farm. The guest rooms in this traditional farmhouse are surprisingly modern, with flat-screen televisions, heated towel rails, and broadband Internet access. Bed-and-breakfast staples—like the hearty breakfast and hospitality tray, with free tea, coffee, and biscuits—still remain. A high vantage point also affords Roscobie great views over the countryside to

the Pentland Hills beyond.

🛈 2 🅿 🚭 🚯 Cash only

SOMETHING SPECIAL

🍴 THE PEAT INN
🏨 $$$$

BY CUPAR, KY15 5LH
TEL (01334) 840 206
www.thepeatinn.co.uk
This Michelin-starred culinary oasis is run by husband-and-wife team Geoffrey and Katherine Smeddle and styles itself as a restaurant with rooms. The food, which draws heavily on Scottish produce, is superb and the eight luxurious and individually styled suites much more than just rooms.

🛏 46 🅿 🚭 🅰 AE, MC, V

🍴 THE CELLAR
$$$

24 EAST GREEN, ANSTRUTHER, KY10 3AA
TEL (01333) 310 378
www.cellaranstruther.co.uk
Diners have been heaping superlatives on this seafood restaurant for years now, and for good reason. From pre-meal drinks right though to coffee, guests are treated to smooth but unobtrusive service. While fish dishes like halibut, Shetland salmon, and East Neuk fish stew are the undoubted highlights, meat eaters are also catered to. Reservations required.

🛏 36 🚭 🕐 Closed Sun.–Mon. & L Tues.–Thurs.
🅰 MC, V

🍴 THE WEE RESTAURANT
$$$

17 MAIN STREET, NORTH QUEENSFERRY, KY11 1JG
TEL (01383) 616 263
www.theweerestaurant.co.uk
It has only been open since 2006, but already The Wee Restaurant has earned itself a Bib Gourmand nod from Michelin. The secret of its

success are a cozy and inviting ambience and staff that are knowledgeable about food and wine. Then of course there is the food itself, with local produce like Kirriemuir lamb and Anstruther lobster cooked to perfection.

🛏 24 🚭 🕐 Closed Mon. & Sun. D 🏧 MC, V

THE SHIP INN
$$
ELIE, LEVEN, KY9 1DT
TEL (01333) 330 246
www.ship-elie.com
Pop into this cozy seaside watering hole for real ale and food that puts the grub served in many other pubs to shame. The menu delivers traditional dishes like steak-and-ale pie, with daily specials chalked up on the blackboard. On summer weekends the pub often fires up its barbeque and its team plays cricket on the golden sand beach.

🛏 160 🚭 🏧 MC, V

ANSTRUTHER FISH BAR
$–$$
43–44 SHORE ROAD,
ANSTRUTHER, KY10 3AQ
TEL (01333) 319 518
www.anstrutherfishbar.co.uk
In this part of Scotland the East Neuk is well known for the high quality of its fish-and-chip shops. This multi-award-winning chippy has been crowned the best in Scotland on numerous occasions. Here the fish is always fresh and the chips perfectly crisp. The sit-in restaurant and takeaway menu features more than just haddock and cod, with the likes of lemon sole, Pittenweem prawns, and hake, as well as the catch of the day, also on offer.

🛏 52 🚭 🏧 MC, V

CAIRNIE FRUIT FARM TEAROOM
$–$$
CAIRNIE, CUPAR, KY15 4QD
TEL (01334) 655 610
www.cairniefruitfarm.co.uk
If you've got kids in tow this is a great place to head for lunch. The café at this farm dishes up child-friendly staples like soup, sandwiches, and home-baked goods, as well as a handful of hot meals and locally made ice cream. What really wins the children over though is the fun-filled play area that includes trampolines, mini-tractors, and a maize maze.

🛏 50 🅿 🚭 🕐 Closed Jan.– March. & Mon. Sept.–Dec. 🏧 MC, V

PILLARS OF HERCULES
$–$$
PILLARS OF HERCULES FARM,
FALKLAND, KY15 7AD
TEL (01337) 857 749
www.pillars.co.uk
This organic farm shop and café is legendary in these parts, which means steep competition for the outdoor tables during the warmer months. Whatever time of year you visit, the café pleases with wholesome dishes like lentil soup and pasta with homemade pesto. Check the website for details about the monthly restaurant nights, where a mainly vegetarian set price menu is accompanied by live jazz.

🛏 40 🅿 🚭 🏧 MC, V

THE WEE CHIPPY
$
SHORE ROAD, ANSTRUTHER,
KY10 3EA
TEL (01333) 310 106
In 2009 this small waterfront chip shop shot to fame when the *Observer* newspaper magazine voted it as the best tasting fish and chips in the world. The ethos here is simple–good service and high-quality locally sourced fish.

🛏 45 🚭 🏧 Cash only

ABERDEEN

🏨 THE MARCLIFFE AT PITFODELS HOTEL AND SPA
$$$–$$$$
NORTH DEESIDE ROAD,
PITFODELS, AB15 9YA
TEL (01224) 861 000
www.marcliffe.com
Warm colors infuse the comfortable rooms and suites at the Marcliffe with understated luxury. Rooms are all individually designed and seamlessly blend old and new, mixing antique furnishings with more contemporary design. In-room amenities include minibars and 24-hour room service. The hotel's spa and restaurant are on hand to pamper guests through their stay.

🛏 42 🅿 🔁 🚭 🏧 AE, DC, MC, V

🏨 NORWOOD HALL HOTEL
$$$–$$$$
GARTHDEE ROAD, ABERDEEN,
AB15 9FX
TEL (01224) 868 951
www.norwood-hall.co.uk
Nestled amid 7 acres (2.8 ha) of private woodland, this attractive 19th-century Victorian mansion is one of the nicest places to stay in Aberdeen. Decor throughout the hotel is sympathetic to the era in which it was built, with period furnishings and a classical elegance. Guest rooms have flat-screen televisions, ensuite bathrooms with baths, and hospitality trays. Premium accommodations boast additional sleeping and living space. For a really special stay, book a room in the original house. Four-poster suites are also available. The dining restaurant is open every night.

🛏 36 🅿 🔁 🏧 AE, DC, MC, V

🏨 MALMAISON ABERDEEN
$$$

49–53 QUEENS ROAD,
ABERDEEN, AB15 4YP
TEL (01224) 327 370
www.malmaisonaberdeen
.com

The Malmaison chain of
boutique hotels has become
synonymous with affordable
luxury in the United Kingdom.
Its Aberdeen hotel takes this
level of comfort a step further,
with the addition of a spa
and a whisky snug. Spacious
guest rooms have a modern
Scottish theme with rich colors
and sporran curtain tiebacks.
Plasma TVs, DVD players, and
minibars also grace the rooms.
There is a bar and brasserie.

🛈 80 🅿 🔁 🔲 🍸
🔲 AE, DC, MC, V

🏨 MACDONALD PITTODRIE HOUSE
$–$$

CHAPEL OF GAIROCH, BY
INVERURIE, AB51 5HS
TEL (0844) 879 9066
www.macdonaldhotels
.co.uk/pittodrie

This grand country house
hotel is a perennially popular
wedding venue and it is easy
to see why. Comfortable
rooms decorated in warm
hues, turrets, and stone spiral
staircases combine to give it a
romantic feel. Wonderfully the
hotel is also set within a 2,000-
acre (810 ha) private estate
overlooking Mount Bennachie
—perfect for walking or taking
advantage of the outdoor
sports on offer.

🛈 27 🅿 🔁 🔲 🔲 AE, MC, V

🍽 PAVILION CAFÉ
$

5–6 ESPLANADE, SEA BEACH,
ABERDEEN, AB24 5NS
TEL (01224) 587 385
www.thepavilioncafe.com

With a menu featuring simple
sandwiches and salads, more
substantial mains like fish
and chips, a decent children's
menu, and a wonderful selection of ice cream, this bright
and cheerful seafront café has
something for everyone.

🪑 30 🔲 🔲 MC, V

DEESIDE

🏨 DARROCH LEARG HOTEL
$$$

56 BRAEMAR ROAD, BALLATER,
AB35 5UX
TEL (01339) 755 252
www.darrochlearg.co.uk

This family-run hotel is one
of the most charming places
to stay in Deeside. Guests are
accommodated in either the
main hotel building (a late
19th-century Victorian mansion) or its sister property (also
located within the grounds),
Oakhall. All of the guest rooms
are individually styled and
feature period furniture and
opulent soft furnishings. Some
of the rooms have four-poster
or canopied beds. In addition
to its wonderful guest rooms,
Darroch Learg has cozy public
rooms and a good restaurant
that spills out into the conservatory. The hotel's crowning
glory is its attractive
woodland setting and the views
of the Dee Valley that unfold
from its hillside position.

🛈 17 🅿 🔲 🔲 AE, MC, V

🏨 AULD KIRK
🍽 $$

BRAEMAR ROAD, BALLATER,
AB35 5RQ
TEL (01339) 755 762
www.theauldkirk.com

Since 1986 the Auld Kirk has
been offering visitors the rare
chance to stay in a former
Scottish Free church. Renovation and rebranding in 2006
created the **Spirit Restaurant**
(see opposite) with rooms.
The six first-floor guest rooms

PRICES

HOTELS

The cost of a double room
in peak season is given by
$ signs.

$$$$$	over £300
$$$$	£200–£300
$$$	£120–£200
$$	£80–£120
$	Under £80

RESTAURANTS

The average price of a two-
course meal for one person,
without tip or drinks is given
by $ signs.

$$$$$	over £50
$$$$	£40–£50
$$$	£25–£40
$$	£15–£25
$	£15

are comfortable without being
fussy. Superior rooms offer
more space and a higher level
of luxury. Free wi-fi and flat-
screen televisions are some of
the useful in-room amenities.

🛈 6 🅿 🔲 🔲 MC, V

🏨 BURNETT ARMS HOTEL
$–$$

25 HIGH STREET, BANCHORY,
AB31 5TD
TEL (01330) 824 944
www.bw-burnettarms.co.uk

This historic coaching inn
combines character with
modern conveniences. Rooms
are traditionally decorated and
boast flat-screen TVs and free
wi-fi. Guests can also make use
of the public bars and dining
room, with the high tea (an
early dining menu) popular
with both residents and non-
residents.

🛈 18 🅿 🔲 🔲 AE, MC, V

🏨 CLUNIE LODGE GUESTHOUSE
$

CLUNIE BANK ROAD, BRAEMAR,
AB35 5ZP
TEL (01339) 741 330
www.clunielodge.com
Today this former Victorian
manse functions as a charming
guesthouse. Period features
pervade the public spaces and
the classically elegant guest
rooms. The views over Glen
Clunie and the Grampians are
equally appealing

🛈 5 🅿 🚭 🏧 MC, V

🍴 GATHERING PLACE BISTRO
$$$

INVERCAULD ROAD, BRAEMAR,
AB35 5YP
TEL (01339) 741 234
www.the-gathering-place.co.uk
Finding the kind of elegant and
contemporary eatery that dots
the streets of Edinburgh and
Glasgow comes as something
of a surprise for many visitors
to Braemar. Good cooking
with high-quality ingredients.
Game pie, Grampian chicken,
and smoked tiger prawns are
just some of the fine Scottish
dishes on the menu.

🍴 52 🚭 🏧 MC, V

🍴 SPIRIT RESTAURANT
🏨 **$$$**

AULD KIRK, BRAEMAR ROAD,
BALLATER, AB35 5RQ
TEL (01339) 755 762
www.theauldkirk.com
Original features like the
vaulted ceiling and ornate
windows make the fine-dining
restaurant in the old church a
really unique venue. The Spirit
Restaurant also delivers on the
plate with the regularly changing set menu offering the likes
of slow cooked pork belly,
local rabbit, and Aberdeenshire lamb.

🍴 32 🅿 🚭 🕐 Closed L
& Sun. 🏧 MC, V

🍴 STATION RESTAURANT
$$

STATION SQUARE, BALLATER,
AB35 5QB
TEL (01339) 755 050
Station Restaurant offers a
compelling combination of
historic location and solid
home cooking. Enjoy cakes,
snacks, or more substantial
meals throughout the day.

🍴 58 🚭 🏧 MC, V

DUNDEE & ANGUS

🏨 APEX CITY QUAY HOTEL & SPA
$$

WEST VICTORIA DOCK ROAD,
DUNDEE, DD1 3JP
TEL (01382) 202 404
www.apexhotels.co.uk
This chic metropolitan hotel
shows off the impressive new
face of Dundee. The opulent
spa offers a seemingly infinite
number of treatments, while
the fine dining restaurant is a
cut above the average hotel
eatery. The city and river views
from rooms on the top floors
are superb.

🛈 152 🅿 🔄 🚭 🚭 🏊 💈
🏧 MC, V

🍴 OLD BOATYARD RESTAURANT
$$–$$$

FISHMARKET QUAY, ARBROATH,
DD11 1PS
TEL (01241) 879 995
www.oldboatyard.co.uk
Panoramic views over
Arbroath's atmospheric old
harbor are reason enough
to eat at the Old Boatyard
Restaurant. There is more to
this stylish eatery though than
floor-to-ceiling windows. Everything from seared scallops to
whole lobster tempt from the
largely seafood menu. For an
authentic local taste, sample
an Arbroath smokie (locally
smoked haddock). A relaxed
sofa area for pre- or post-

dinner drinks, a decent wine list,
and friendly service complete
the picture.

🍴 100 🚭 🕐 Closed Tues.
🏧 MC, V

🍴 DUNDEE REP CAFÉ BAR RESTAURANT
$–$$

TAY SQUARE, DD1 1PB
TEL (01382) 206 699
www.dundeereptheatre.co.uk
Dundee's cultural hub also
boasts a contemporary café-bar
whose innovative menu make it
a popular food stop. Mediterra-
nean-influenced dishes include
a sharing plate of antipasti and
a mini mezze selection of spicy
olives and Lebanese aubergine
(eggplant) salad. A spicy
spinach, okra and potato curry,
and blackened Cajun chicken,
meanwhile, feature on the list
of creative main dishes.

🍴 60 🚭 🏧 MC, V

🍴 GLASS PAVILION
$–$$

THE ESPLANADE, BROUGHTY
FERRY, DD5 2EP
TEL (01382) 732 738
Enjoy spectacular sea views
through the floor-to-ceiling
windows of this striking
café-restaurant. Satiate the
appetite that you have worked
up walking along the beautiful
expanse of sandy beach outside
on homemade soups, baked
potatoes, filling sandwiches, or
traditional fare like fisherman's
pie.

🍴 60 🚭 🏧 MC, V

EAST COAST

🍴 PENNAN INN
$–$$

PENNAN, AB43 6JB
TEL (01346) 561 201
This historic inn shot to fame
after appearing in the 1983
Hollywood movie *Local Hero*. In
2007 a landslide that engulfed
the attractive seaside village

 Nonsmoking 🔄 Air-conditioning 🏊 Indoor Pool 🏊 Outdoor Pool 💈 Health Club 🏧 Credit Cards

almost destroyed the pub and many feared it would never reopen. Fortunately for visitors it was reincarnated at the end of 2009 when a new owner and landlord, Peter Simpson, took over. Today it serves good pub food with daily specials like Thai curry in one of the east coast's most dramatic settings.

🛏 24 🅂 ⬛ MC, V

🍴 SEAFIELD ARMS HOTEL
$$
17–19 SEAFIELD STREET, CULLEN, AB56 4SG
TEL (01542) 840 791
www.theseafieldarms.co.uk
The portions of food dished up in this family-friendly hotel are generous to say the least. The first-rate cullen skink, perfectly salty and creamy with generous chunks of smoked haddock, is a must-have starter, while the fish and chips are sublime. Those with a sweet tooth might want to leave room for sinful treats like homemade fruit crumble.

🛏 72 🅂 ⬛ AE, MC, V

◾ CENTRAL & WESTERN HIGHLANDS

INVERNESS

🏨 BOATH HOUSE
🍴 $$$$
AULDEARN, IV12 5TE
TEL (01667) 454 896
www.boath-house.com
Get away from it all at this country house hotel set on 20 acres (8 ha) of private land. The décor in the eight guest rooms ranges from contemporary to classically elegant. All rooms are charming with rolltop baths, and canopied and four-poster beds just some of their unique characteristics. The hotel also boasts a Michelin-starred restaurant **Boath House** (see below), on-

site fishing in the ornamental lake, and spa treatments.

ℹ️ 8 🅿 🅂 ⬛ AE, MC, V

🏨 DUNAIN PARK HOTEL
$$$
INVERNESS, IV3 8JN
TEL (01463) 230 512
www.dunainparkhotel.co.uk
This palatial but relaxed hotel is ideally situated between Inverness and Loch Ness. Lovely rural views, a cozy lounge with a roaring fire, a good restaurant, and 6 acres (2.4 ha) of attractive grounds that include a croquet court add to the appeal.

ℹ️ 15 🅿 🅂 ⬛ AE, MC, V

🍴 BOATH HOUSE
🏨 $$$$$
AULDEARN, IV12 5TE
TEL (01667) 454 896
www.boath-house.com
This charming Regency hotel is also home to one of Scotland's best restaurants. Head Chef Charles Lockley's eatery, open to non-residents as well, is the proud holder of a Michelin star and also boasts four AA rosettes. The intimate restaurant enjoys views over the lawn down to the lake, but the pièce de resistance is the six-course fine dining menu, which features game, meat, poultry, and seafood cooked to perfection.

🛏 26 🅿 🅂 ⬛ AE, MC, V

🍴 THE MUSTARD SEED
$$$
16 FRASER STREET, INVERNESS, IV1 1DW
TEL (01463) 220 220
www.themustardseed restaurant.co.uk
Housed in a former 19th-century church, this riverside restaurant has a lot of character. It also has plenty of choice, with a menu that offers the likes of sirloin steak, grilled tuna loin, and lamb chops. Outside balcony tables

have lovely views over the River Ness.

🛏 60 🅂 ⬛ AE, MC, V

🍴 RIVER CAFÉ & RESTAURANT
$$–$$$
10 BANK STREET, INVERNESS, IN1 1QY
TEL (01463) 714 884
www.rivercafeandrestaurant .co.uk
The lunch, high tea (5–6.30 p.m.) and the early evening menus (5–7 p.m.) deliver home-cooked dishes like lasagne and gammon at reasonable prices. Later in the evening the menu becomes more sophisticated, with the likes of venison steak, poached salmon, and seared duck breast.

🛏 40 🅂 ⬛ MC, V

THE CAIRNGORMS

🏨 CRAIGELLACHIE
🍴 $$$
VICTORIA STREET, CRAIGELLACHIE, AB38 9SR
TEL (01340) 881 204
www.oxfordhotelsandinns .com
This whitewashed hotel was built in 1893 and the rooms and public areas, including the lovely drawing room, have been modernized in a way that is sympathetic to the era. In addition to homely and spacious rooms, guests can relax in the **Quaich Bar**, which boasts one of the finest collections of single malt whiskies (more than 650 varieties) on the planet. Craigellachie's restaurant also has a deservedly good reputation.

ℹ️ 26 🅿 🅂 ⬛ AE, MC, V

🏨 CULDEARN HOUSE
$$–$$$
WOODLANDS TERRACE, GRANTOWN-ON-SPEY, PH26 3JU
TEL (01479) 872 106
www.culdearn.com

A warm welcome, inviting public spaces, and good food await guests at this family-run hotel. The six guest rooms seamlessly blend the things that you would expect to find in an old country house—antique furnishings and period features—with modern décor. All rooms have digital TV channels, wi-fi, and feather duvets. In the lounge guests can enjoy a drink in front of a roaring fire, while the intimate dining room offers good Scottish food.

🛈 6 🅿 🆂 🔲 MC, V

🏨 THE BOAT
🍽 **$$**
DESHAR ROAD, BOAT OF GARTEN, PH24 3BH
TEL (01479) 831 258
www.boathotel.co.uk
This welcoming hotel, located at the heart of the Cairngorms National Park, offers comfortable guest accommodation. Free wi-fi access, room service, and fluffy bathrobes are just some of the additional creature comforts. Rooms vary in size and style—those in the main hotel are traditionally elegant, while those in the Garden Wing enjoy more contemporary décor. Dine in the lovely **Capercaille Restaurant** or enjoy a more informal meal in the **Osprey Bar & Bistro.**

🛈 34 🅿 🆂 🔲 AE, MC, V

🏨 THE OLD MINISTER'S HOUSE
$$
ROTHIEMURCHUS, AVIEMORE, PH22 1QH
TEL (01479) 812 181
www.theoldministers house.co.uk
Its enviable position in the heart of Rothiemurchus Estate and the stunning Cairngorm Mountains views on offer from the guest rooms and the shared drawing room would be enough to recommend this welcoming B&B. A stay at the Old Minister's House, though, is about more than location—the contemporary and comfortable guest rooms and the lovely old stone building are other compelling reasons to stay here.

🛈 4 🅿 🆂 🔲 MC, V

🏨 COIG NA SHEE GUEST HOUSE
$
FORT WILLIAM ROAD, NEWTONMORE, PH20 1DG
(01540) 670 109
www.coignashee.co.uk
Set in attractive grounds on the outskirts of Newtonmore, this renovated Highland lodge has tastefully decorated en suite rooms with wi-fi, satellite television, and DVD players. The common spaces are spacious and clean, with excellent views of the grounds and surrounding countryside.

🛈 5 🅿 🆂 🔲 AE, MC, V

🏨 HERMITAGE GUEST HOUSE
$
SPEY STREET, KINGUSSIE, PH21 1HN
(01540) 662 137
www.thehermitage.clara.net
This comfortable bed and breakfast is located in a stout stone town house in the center of Kingussie. All the guest house's rooms are en suite, with wi-fi, and DVD players. In addition to hearty breakfasts, the Hermitage also offers excellent home-cooked dinners for around £22 per person.

🛈 5 🅿 🆂 🔲 Cash only

🏨 RUTHVEN STEADINGS
$
RUTHVEN, KINGUSSIE, PH21 1HN
(01540) 662 328
www.ruthvensteadings.co.uk
This delightful bed and breakfast is located a short walk from Kingussie, close to the ruins of Ruthven Barracks. The well-appointed guest rooms have en suite bathrooms, wi-fi, and excellent views of the area. The friendly owners, Julie and John, can also provide self-catering accommodation in a recently renovated cottage nearby.

🛈 2 🅿 🆂 🔲 Cash only

🍽 THE GLASS HOUSE
$$$
GRANT ROAD, GRANTOWN-ON-SPEY, PH26 3LD
TEL (01479) 872 980
www.theglasshouse-grantown.co.uk
Good food, contemporary décor, and an unusual design that affords diners privacy and also offers lovely views of the landscaped gardens have combined to make this one of the region's most popular restaurants. The weekly changing menu conjures up delights like west coast crab cakes, Cairngorm venison, and tart tatin.

🍴 30 🅿 🆂 🕐 Closed D Sun. & L Mon.–Tues. 🔲 AE, MC, V

🍽 MOUNTAIN CAFÉ
$
111 GRAMPIAN ROAD, AVIEMORE, PH22 1RH
TEL (01479) 812 473
www.mountaincafe-aviemore.co.uk
This lovely café bustles throughout the day. The creative menu features everything from healthy or hearty breakfasts and zucchini pancakes to beef-steak baguettes and mouthwatering home-baked goods. Good coffee and views over the Cairngorms are an added bonus.

🍴 52 🅿 🆂 🔲 MC, V

THE GREAT GLEN

SOMETHING SPECIAL

🏨 INVERLOCHY CASTLE HOTEL
$$$$$
TORLUNDAY, FORT WILLIAM,

PH33 6SN
TEL (01397) 702 177
**www.inverlochycastlehotel
.com**
Follow in the footsteps of
Queen Victoria and enjoy the
palatial public spaces and guest
rooms at one of Scotland's
most luxurious hotels. Dinner
is sublime, too, at a hotel
where you will leave feeling
every bit like royalty.

🛈 17 🅿 Ⓢ ⬳ AE, MC, V

🏨 CORRIECHOILLE LODGE
$
SPEAN BRIDGE, PH34 4EY
TEL (01397) 712 002
www.corriechoille.com
Dramatic mountain views,
bright and spacious guest
rooms, the availability of
home-cooked evening meals,
and a license to serve alcohol
make this 18th-century whitewashed fishing lodge a wonderful place to stay. Guests
have access to free wi-fi and
can use the library/lounge
with its stunning views.

🛈 4 🅿 Ⓢ 🕒 Closed Nov.–
Dec. ⬳ MC, V

🍽 LOCH LEVEN SEAFOOD
CAFÉ
$$$–$$$$
ONICH, PH33 6SA
TEL (01855) 821 048
**www.lochlevenseafoodcafe
.co.uk**
Dining on fresh seafood in this
bright informal eatery is an
enjoyable experience whatever
the weather, but on a warm
sunny day the outdoor terrace
with its views over the epony-
mous loch is hard to beat. The
café's seafood platter is legen-
dary; lobster, langoustines, and
other shellfish also feature on
the changing monthly menu
alongside the daily catch. Call
ahead to check opening times
from November to February.

🍴 50 🅿 Ⓢ 🕒 Closed two
weeks in Nov. & in Jan.
⬳ MC, V

SOMETHING SPECIAL

🍽 CRANNOG
RESTAURANT
$$$
FORT WILLIAM, PH33 6DB
TEL (01397) 705 589
**www.crannog.net/restaurant
.asp**
While their stomachs feast
on fresh west coast seafood,
diners' eyes can feast on the
lovely views over Loch Linnhe.
The menu changes according to
the daily catch, with blackboard
specials offered alongside
the likes of mussels, salmon,
halibut, and hake.

🍴 40–60 🅿 Ⓢ ⬳ MC, V

THE WEST COAST

🏨 GLENFINNAN HOUSE
HOTEL
$$$
GLENFINNAN, PH37 4LT
TEL (01397) 722 235
www.glenfinnanhouse.com
This country house hotel, dat-
ing from 1755, extends a warm
welcome to everyone, including
families and guests traveling
with dogs. Guest rooms and
public spaces are traditionally
decorated and the hotel is
pleasantly homey rather than
luxurious. Its location on the
banks of Loch Shiel is second
to none. The hotel also serves
bar meals and has a fine-dining
restaurant.

🛈 13 🅿 Ⓢ 🕒 Closed mid-
Nov.–mid-March ⬳ AE, MC, V

🏨 CLACHAIG INN
🍽 $$
GLENCOE, PH49 4HX
TEL (01855) 811 252
www.clachaig.com
Catering mainly to walkers and
climbers there are three types
of accommodation. Rooms are
fairly basic, but the location
next to Glen Coe's Three
Sisters is hard to fault. The
inn serves hearty pub grub

PRICES

HOTELS
The cost of a double room
in peak season is given by
$ signs.

$$$$$	over £300
$$$$	£200–£300
$$$	£120–£200
$$	£80–£120
$	Under £80

RESTAURANTS
The average price of a two-
course meal for one person,
without tip or drinks is given
by **$** signs.

$$$$$	over £50
$$$$	£40–£50
$$$	£25–£40
$$	£15–£25
$	£15

(see opposite) and has a large
drying-room, both of which
are great after a day in the
hills. Broadband is available in
its public areas.

🛈 23 🅿 Ⓢ ⬳ MC, V

🏨 KNOYDART LODGE
$–$$
KNOYDART, PH41 4PL
TEL (01687) 460 129
www.knoydartlodge.co.uk
Welcoming hosts, its stunning
natural setting, and its remote
location (you have to take a
boat there) makes Knoydart
Lodge a truly wonderful place
to stay. Creature comforts
are also high on the list, with
oversize beds, DVD players,
a movie library and wi-fi all
easing guests through their
stay. With just four rooms the
lodge is often fully booked, so
book well in advance.

🛈 4 Ⓢ ⬳ Cash only

🍴 CLACHAIG INN
🏨 $$
GLEN COE, PH49 4HX
TEL (01855) 811 252
www.clachaig.com
Busy with walkers and tourists, the Clachaig Inn serves the same varied menu in its three bars. Traditional Scottish favorites like haggis pop up alongside hearty burgers and more unusual dishes like wild boar sausages and burritos.
🛏 70 🅿 🚭 📶 MC, V

▦ NORTHERN HIGHLANDS

THE EAST

🏨 DORNOCH CASTLE HOTEL
$$
CASTLE STREET, DORNOCH, IV25 3SD
TEL (01862) 810 216
www.dornochcastlehotel.com
One of Dornoch's most distinctive buildings is also a great place to stay. Classically themed guest rooms feature soft floral prints, antique furnishings, and some even have four-poster beds. Then there is a cozy bar, a relaxed garden, and tasty food served up in the conservatory-style restaurant for guests to savor.
🛈 24 🅿 🚭 📶 AE, MC, V

THE WEST

HOTELS

SOMETHING SPECIAL

🏨 THE TORRIDON
$$$$
TORRIDON, WESTER ROSS, IV22 2EY
TEL (01445) 791 242
www.thetorridon.com
Opulent guest rooms with enormous stand-alone baths, elegant public spaces, and a first-class restaurant impress guests. It is the magnificent mountain views, though, that are truly unforgettable. The hotel's whisky bar is a good place to learn more about the hallowed spirit. Adventure activities, luxury self-catering accommodation, and basic but much cheaper inn rooms are also available. The inn has a full-service bar.
🛈 19 🅿 🚭 🚭 📶 AE, MC, V

SOMETHING SPECIAL

🏨 TIGH AN EILEAN HOTEL
$$$
SHEILDAIG, IV54 8XN
TEL (01520) 755 251
www.stevecarter.com/hotel/hotel.htm
This whitewashed inn has cozy guest rooms with few modern conveniences (no TVs and no telephones) to allow guests to really enjoy the peace and quiet and the sea views. Tea, coffee, and bathrobes help guests relax even more. Guests also have access to two sitting rooms that look out over Loch Torridon and an honesty bar. They can of course eat in the fine-dining restaurant and the public bar, both of which make the best use of local produce, especially seafood.
🛈 11 🚭 📶 AE, MC, V

🏨 PLOCKTON HOTEL
$$–$$$
41 HARBOUR STREET, PLOCKTON, IV52 8TN
TEL (01599) 544 274
www.plocktonhotel.co.uk
This charming waterfront hotel boasts an award-winning seafood restaurant, as well as a cozy bar. Guest rooms are clean and modern, and the best enjoy views over the bay—one of the prettiest in Scotland.
🛈 15 🚭 📶 AE, MC, V

🏨 THE OLD INN
$$
GAIRLOCH, IV21 2BD
TEL 0800 542 544
www.theoldinn.net
The combination of simple but comfortable rooms and hearty local meat and seafood dishes make the Old Inn a good option for sleeping and eating.
🛈 14 🅿 🚭 📶 MC, V

RESTAURANTS

🍴 SUMMER ISLES HOTEL
$$$–$$$$
ACHILTIBUIE, IV26 2YG
TEL (01854) 622 282
www.summerisleshotel.co.uk
When it comes to food the Summer Isles Hotel has it all—a Michelin-starred restaurant and a relaxed bar which also serves good food. The epicurean treats dished up in the restaurant include the likes of scallop mouse, grilled fillet of Lochinver halibut, and Summer Isles langoustines. The emphasis in the bar is also on boat-fresh seafood.
🛏 50 🅿 🚭 📶 MC, V

🍴 APPLECROSS INN
$$
SHORE STREET, APPLECROSS, IV54 8LR
TEL (01520) 744 262
www.applecross.co.uk/inn
This lovely whitewashed inn is legendary in Scotland, not least for the hair-raising car ride over the Bealach na Ba (Scotland's highest road) to get there. Then there is its stunning waterfront setting. The real reason to make the pilgrimage here, though, is the sumptuous and simply cooked seafood that is dished up every day.
🛏 60 🅿 🚭 📶 MC, V

🍴 KISHORN SEAFOOD BAR
$$
KISHORN, IV54 8XA

TEL (01520) 733 240
www.kishornseafoodbar.co.uk
Langoustines, scallops, mussels, oysters, squat lobsters, crab, and locally smoked salmon are just some of the mouthwatering local fish on the menu. At this modest eatery the seafood is allowed to speak for itself. On sunny days the lochside setting lures diners to the outside tables.
🍴 30 P ⑤ 🕐 Closed Dec.–March ⑤ MC, V

🍴 KYLESKU HOTEL
$$
KYLESKU, IV27 4HW
TEL (01971) 502 231
www.kyleskuhotel.co.uk
Lochinver haddock, west coast mussels, and wild venison are just some of the dishes on the bar menu at the lochside Kylesku Hotel. With its use of local produce, the meals served are superior to those in the average pub.
🍴 40 ⑤ ⑤ MC, V

🍴 LOCHINVER LARDER
$$
MAIN STREET, LOCHINVER, IV27 4JY
TEL (01571) 844 356
www.lochinverlarder.co.uk
There are two reasons to dine at Lochinver Larder—the delicious homemade pies and the views over the River Inver from the dining room. Pies come in savory and sweet varieties, with good vegetarian options. Disappointingly the dining room isn't always open, leaving guests to eat with views of the street.
🍴 50 ⑤ ⑤ MC, V

THE NORTH

🍴 THE CAPTAIN'S GALLEY
$$$$
THE HARBOUR, SCRABSTER, KW14 7UJ
TEL (01847) 894 999
www.captainsgalley.co.uk
Everything about this seafood restaurant is spectacular, from its exposed brickwork walls and barrel-vaulted ceiling to smooth service and a menu that showcases the diversity of Scotland's natural larder. Here the likes of Highland venison and Caithness beef join the medley of shellfish and fish.
🍴 30 ⑤ 🕐 Closed L & Sun.–Mon. ⑤ MC, V

◼ WEST COAST ISLANDS

ARGYLL ISLANDS

HOTELS

🏨 AUCHRANNIE HOUSE HOTEL, SPA RESORT & COUNTRY CLUB
$$$
BRODICK, ISLE OF ARRAN, KA27 8BJ
TEL (01770) 302 234
www.auchrannie.co.uk
Accommodation is classically elegant for those who book a room in the main House Hotel. More contemporary rooms with bright soft furnishings are the order of the day in the newer Spa Resort. Great facilities for all the family include three restaurants, swimming pools, spa treatments, a fitness studio, and a sports hall. All of the hotel rooms are spacious and can comfortably accommodate a family of four.
① 64 P ⊖ ⑤ ⑤ 🌰 📺 ⑤ AE, MC, V

🏨 HIGHLAND COTTAGE
🍴 **$$$**
TOBERMORY, ISLE OF MULL, PA75 6PD
TEL (01688) 302 030
www.highlandcottage.co.uk
Graceful themed rooms, an elegant garden, and relaxing guest lounges (one includes an honesty bar) impress at this boutique hotel. While David Currie tends to the needs of guests, his wife, Jo, affords her culinary masterpieces the same tender loving care. A menu that features the likes of Scottish venison and crab, as well as the islands' famous Mull Cheddar also lures non-residents to the restaurant.
① 6 P ⑤ ⑤ MC, V

SOMETHING SPECIAL

🏨 PORT CHARLOTTE
🍴 HOTEL
$$$
PORT CHARLOTTE, ISLE OF ISLAY, PA48 7TU
TEL (01496) 850 360
www.portcharlottehotel.co.uk
Its location alone is enough to lure guests, however, this lovely old whitewashed hotel offers more than magnificent views across a sea loch and the Atlantic. Rooms are cozy, while the restaurant is a favorite with locals and visitors alike.
① 10 P ⑤ ⑤ MC, V

SOMETHING SPECIAL

🏨 ISLE OF COLL HOTEL
🍴 **$$**
ARINAGOUR, ISLE OF COLL, PA78 6SZ
TEL (01879) 230 334
www.collhotel.com
This remarkable little retreat is the epitome of a family-owned establishment. Run by Kevin and Julie Oliphant for more than 25 years, not only is it a great place to stay but it also is the island's social hub with the fine **Gannet Restaurant** (see below). Room Two boasts an old-fashioned bath and epic sea views.
① 6 P ⑤ ⑤ MC, V

🏨 ISLE OF MULL HOTEL & SPA

$$

CRAIGNURE, ISLE OF MULL, PA65 6BB

TEL (01680) 812 544

www.crerarhotels.com

The hotel may look a bit dated from afar, but the rooms have been impressively renovated. A great new spa (complete with sauna, steam room, and outdoor hot tub with views to die for) and an indoor swimming pool are also fantastic recent additions to the hotel. Many of the comfortable guest rooms and the hotel's public areas enjoy sweeping views, with the Morvern Peninsula and the distant mainland peaks competing for attention across the water.

🛏 86 🅿 🚭 🏊 🏋 🍴 🔇 AE, MC, V

RESTAURANTS

🍴 BRAMBLES SEAFOOD AND GRILL

$$$

AUCHRANNIE RESORT, ISLE OF ARRAN, KA27 8BZ

TEL (01770) 302 234

www.bramblesseafood andgrill.co.uk

Simply cooked food that is allowed to speak for itself, contemporary surrounds, and friendly service combine to make this resort restaurant a good bet for residents and non-residents alike. West coast mussels cooked in Arran ale, Loch Fyne scallops, and cumin-crusted Arran lamb are just some of the highlights on a menu that makes the most of local ingredients. Scotch beef hung for 21 days makes the steaks (which come in rib eye, fillet, or sirloin cuts) a perennial favorite.

🍴 80 🅿 🚭 🕐 Closed Mon.–Tues. & Nov.–March. 🔇 AE, MC, V

🍴 PORT CHARLOTTE HOTEL

$$$

PORT CHARLOTTE, ISLE OF ISLAY, PA48 7TU

TEL (01496) 850 360

www.portcharlottehotel.co.uk

This hotel's elegant restaurant is widely considered to be the best on Islay. A constantly evolving menu offers diners the chance to enjoy fresh local meat and game, as well as seafood caught by the local fishermen. Highlights on a typical menu might include Islay lamb, partridge, or lobster. A refined wine list and a relaxed dining room with exposed brick walls and modern furniture provide the finishing touches. A bar supper menu is also available.

🍴 40 🅿 🚭 🔇 MC, V

🍴 GANNET RESTAURANT

🏨 $$

ISLE OF COLL HOTEL, ARINAGOUR, PA78 6SZ

TEL (01879) 230 334

www.collhotel.com

On a ridiculously good menu in these remote parts are the like of homemade spaghetti with Coll lobster and a seafood platter with yet more local lobster, as well as fresh salmon, plump scallops, local crab, and langoustine cooked thermidor style. The changing daily menu is a real delight and the sort of treat you could spend every day on Coll dreaming of.

🍴 24 🅿 🚭 🔇 MC, V

🍴 WATERFRONT BISTRO

$$

16 EAST PRINCES STREET, ROTHSEAY, ISLE OF BUTE, PA20 9DL

TEL (01700) 505 166

www.thewaterfrontbistro .co.uk

A frequently changing menu, which makes the most of local seasonal produce and tasty home cooking, makes this small restaurant very popular. With over 20 main dishes, the chalkboard menu offers a wide and varied choice, which includes the likes of prawns, monkfish, chicken, venison, and duck. The small size of the restaurant means they don't take groups bigger than six people or bookings between April and October and Saturday evenings.

🍴 24 🚭 🕐 Closed L & Tues.–Wed. 🔇 Cash only

ISLE OF SKYE

🏨 STEIN INN

$–$$

WATERNISH, IV55 8GA

TEL (01470) 592 362

www.steininn.co.uk

Staking claim to being the oldest inn on Skye, this chunky whitewashed hotel, dating from 1790, is a characterful place to stay. The rooms are cozy, the bar food good, and the views sublime. In the spirit of rest and relaxation the guest rooms do not have TVs.

🛏 5 🅿 🚭 🔇 MC, V

🍴 LOCH BAY SEAFOOD RESTAURANT

$$$

STEIN, WATERNISH, IV55 8GA

TEL (01470) 592 235

www.loch-bay-seafood -restaurant.co.uk

Steamed mussels, fresh oysters, local lobster, and prawns harvested in Loch Bay are just some of the tempting dishes on offer in this small restaurant that prides itself on serving fresh seafood. Here the chef eschews fussy sauces and lets diners enjoy the fishy flavor of simply cooked dishes.

🍴 26 🚭 🕐 Closed Sun.–Mon. & Nov.–March 🔇 AE, MC, V

SOMETHING SPECIAL

🍴 THE THREE CHIMNEYS
$$$$$

COLBOST, IV55 8ZT

TEL (01470) 511 258

www.threechimneys.co.uk

Despite its remote location, this intimate restaurant housed in a converted stone croft has won plaudits from around the globe. Fresh local produce, including Lochalsh beef and world-class seafood, like crab sourced in Colbost itself, expertly cooked by Shirley Spear's team, lies at the heart of its success. Reservations are essential.

🔢 38 🅿 🅂 🕀 Closed L Sun., L Nov.–mid-March & 3 weeks in Jan. 🅂 AE, MC, V

OUTER HEBRIDES

🏨 SCARISTA HOUSE
🍴 $$$

SGARASTA BHEAG, ISLE OF HARRIS, HS3 3HX

TEL (01859) 550 238

www.scaristahouse.com

This former Georgian manse oozes character, from its beautiful whitewashed exterior and its cozy drawing room to its library stocked with books and CDs. Three of the guest rooms are in the main house and while they are quite small, they are comfortable and in keeping with the period of the house. Two guest suites are located in the purpose-built Glebe House. All rooms enjoy views out over the lovely bay. The hotel also serves very good food at its restaurant (see right) and is a TV-free zone.

🔢 5 🅿 🅂 🅂 MC, V

SOMETHING SPECIAL

🏨 BAILE NA CILLE
$$

TIMSGARRY, ISLE OF LEWIS, HS2 9JD

TEL (01851) 672 242

www.bailenacille.co.uk

This former whitewashed manse, which nestles in a secluded bay and enjoys panoramic sea and mountain views, not to mention a two-mile (3 km) stretch of pristine white-sand beach, puts the paradisiacal images that grace the pages of tourist brochures to shame. In addition to breakfast, home-cooked evening meals are available and highly recommended.

🔢 6 🅿 🅂 🕀 Closed Oct.–March 🅂 MC, V

🏨 CASTLEBAY HOTEL
$$

CASTLEBAY, ISLE OF BARRA, HS9 5XD

TEL (01871) 810 233

www.castlebay-hotel.co.uk

Accommodation comes in the form of standard or superior rooms. The former are clean, comfortable, and cozy with color televisions to help guests relax and unwind. Superior rooms are more contemporary and benefit from extra space and lovely views.

🔢 15 🅿 🅂 🅂 MC, V

🏨 POLOCHAR INN
$–$$

POLOCHAR, SOUTH UIST, HS8 5TT

TEL (01878) 700 215

www.polocharinn.com

This 18th-century inn on the tip of South Uist was once used by passengers waiting for the ferry to Barra. Today it is a peaceful retreat that stands right on the water's edge and enjoys views to the islands of Eriskay and Barra. Rooms have recently been refurbished to a high standard and boasts televisions with DVD players and tea- and coffee-making facilities; the wow factor, though, comes in the form of

---

PRICES

HOTELS

The cost of a double room in peak season is given by $ signs.

$$$$$	over £300
$$$$	£200–£300
$$$	£120–£200
$$	£80–£120
$	Under £80

RESTAURANTS

The average price of a two-course meal for one person, without tip or drinks is given by $ signs.

$$$$$	over £50
$$$$	£40–£50
$$$	£25–£40
$$	£15–£25
$	£15

---

their sea views. The inn is also renowned for the quality of its food, particularly fish and shellfish.

🔢 11 🅿 🅂 🅂 MC, V

🍴 CASTLEBAY HOTEL
$$

CASTLEBAY, ISLE OF BARRA, HS9 5XD

TEL (01871) 810 233

www.castlebay-hotel.co.uk

The high quality of the food and cooking make this the Isle of Barra's best dining option. A seasonal menu makes the most of the fresh seafood and shellfish that is landed daily in Barra, with the local scallops the highlight. Meat eaters are also well catered for by the likes of island lamb, Scotch beef, venison, hare, and wild boar. These are backed by a number of vegetarian options. Good bar food is also served.

🔢 60 🅿 🅂 🅂 MC, V

🏨 Hotel 🍴 Restaurant 🔢 No. of Guest Rooms 🔢 No. of Seats 🅿 Parking 🕀 Closed 🔗 Elevator

🍴 SCARISTA HOUSE
🏨 RESTAURANT
$$$
SGARASTA BHEAG, ISLE OF
HARRIS, HS3 3HX
TEL (01859) 550 238
www.scaristahouse.com
It may not offer much choice
but the set dinner menu works
wonders with fresh local
produce, much of which is
organic. A typical meal might
include Highland lamb, Sound
of Harris langoustines, and
local Scottish cheeses. A lot
of the vegetables and herbs
come from the hotel's kitchen
garden and the breads, cakes,
jam, yogurt, and ice cream is
all homemade.
🛏 30 🅿 🚭 🏧 MC, V

■ ORKNEY & SHETLAND ISLANDS

ORKNEY ISLANDS

🏨 ALBERT HOTEL
$$$
MOUNTHOOLIE LANE,
KIRKWALL, KW15 1JZ
TEL (01856) 876 000
www.alberthotel.co.uk
Modern and immaculately
clean guest rooms, with large
well-kept bathrooms make
this hotel a good option. Large
beds, flat-screen televisions,
broadband Internet access, and
complimentary tea- and coffee-
making facilities all help make
guests feel at home. The hotel
also has the popular Bothy Bar,
with food options taking the
form of bar or restaurant meals
and room service.
🛏 18 🚭 🚭 🏧 AE, MC, V

🏨 KIRKWALL HOTEL
$$
HARBOUR STREET, KIRKWALL,
KW15 1LF
TEL (01856) 872 232
www.kirkwallhotel.com
Clean and unfussy rooms have

everything that most guests
need for a comfortable stay,
televisions, tea/coffee-making
facilities and direct-dial
telephones. To get the most
out of a stay here, book a
superior room; they look
out over the harbor and
have plenty of space.
ⓘ 37 🚭 🏧 MC, V

🏨 STRONSAY HOTEL
$–$$
STRONSAY, ORKNEY, KW17 2AR
TEL (01857) 616 213
**www.stronsayhotelorkney
.co.uk**
Stronsay's only hotel offers
simple, yet perfectly comfortable, bright and spacious guest
rooms. Home to the island's
only restaurant and bar, guests
will also find themselves at the
heart of the local community.
The hotel does not have any
elevators but the ground-floor
room has been converted for
wheelchair users.
ⓘ 4 🚭 🏧 MC, V

🏨 BANKBURN HOUSE
$
ST. MARGARET'S HOPE, SOUTH
RONALDSAY, KW17 2TG
TEL 0844 414 2310
www.bankburnhouse.co.uk
Dating from the early 18th
century, Bankburn House is a
charming stone property set
in 2 acres (0.8 ha) of private
grounds. Guest rooms are
bright and cheerful, as is the
welcome extended to guests.
In-room facilities include flat-
screen TVs, DVD players, and
tea/coffee-making equipment.
Not all of the guest rooms are
en suite, but the owners hope
to upgrade those that are not
in the future.
ⓘ 4 🅿 🚭 🏧 Cash only

🏨 ORCA HOTEL
$
76 VICTORIA STREET,
STROMNESS, KW16 3BS
TEL (01856) 850 447

http://orcahotel.moonfruit
.com
Situated on Stromness
Harbour, this small guesthouse
offers basic, but clean en suite
accommodation. Family rooms
with one double bed and bunk
beds are available. Rooms have
all the things that guests need
for a comfortable stay, including televisions and hospitality
trays (tea, coffee, and cookies).
ⓘ 6 🚭 🏧 AE, MC, V

🏨 STROMABANK HOTEL
$
LONGHOPE, HOY, KW16 3PA
TEL (01856) 701 494
www.stromabank.co.uk
With just four rooms the
Stromabank is a lovely and
relaxing hotel. Rooms are big
enough to accommodate children on foldaway beds and the
service is friendly and personal.
Highlights of a stay, though,
are the wonderful location and
the delightful conservatory
restaurant.
ⓘ 4 🅿 🚭 🏧 MC, V

RESTAURANTS

🍴 HAMNAVOE
RESTAURANT
$$$
STROMNESS, KW16 3BY
TEL (01856) 850 606
This relaxed and lively restaurant has quite a traditional
menu that makes liberal use of
cream sauces, whisky, haggis,
and Scotch beef. Fish dishes
provide a lighter option with
highlights succulent Orkney
scallops and daily specials like
lemon sole. Consistent cooking and decent service make
this the town's most popular
restaurant, so reserve a table
in advance.
🛏 30 🚭 🏧 MC, V

🍴 THE CREEL RESTAURANT WITH ROOMS

$$–$$$

FRONT ROAD, ST. MARGARET'S HOPE, KW17 2SL

TEL (01856) 831 311

www.thecreel.co.uk

As its name suggests this small waterfront restaurant takes food seriously. The fittingly small menu features imaginative dishes that showcase local produce. Although the emphasis is on boat-fresh seafood, carnivores are catered to with the likes of local beef and lamb. Alongside scallops, mussels, and mackerel diners might find lesser known types of fish on offer like torsk and megrim. Even the vegetables are grown locally. To top it all off the Creel bakes its own bread and makes its own ice cream. Reservations recommended. The restaurant also has three sea view rooms.

🛏 38 🚭 🕒 Closed Jan.–Feb. & Nov. 🚫MC, V

🍴 PIEROWALL HOTEL

$$

WESTRAY, KW17 2BZ

TEL (01857) 677 472

www.pierowallhotel.co.uk

This little waterfront hotel has a dining room for its residents, with non-residents being treated to the same solid home cooking in the lounge bar. Food farmed and fished in Orkney is the order of the day; the shellfish and local beef both excel. Daily specials and home-baked goods also feature on the menu.

🛏 30 🅿 🚭 🚫MC, V

SHETLAND ISLANDS

🏨 BUSTA HOUSE HOTEL

$$

BRAE, SHETLAND, ZE2 9QN

TEL (01806) 522 506

www.bustahouse.com

Individually styled rooms at this 16th-century hotel have fittingly traditional décor, with canopy and four-poster beds nice touches in some. In-room facilities for guests include flat-screen televisions, DVD players, and wi-fi. Guest rooms also benefit from stunning views over the bay or attractive gardens. The hotel's online gallery lets guests choose which of the 22 rooms (all named after Shetland islands) they would like to stay in prior to booking.

ⓘ 22 🅿 🚭 🚫AE, DC, MC, V

🏨 ALDERLODGE

$

6 CLAIRMONT PLACE, LERWICK, ZE1 0BR

TEL (01595) 695 705

www.alder-lodge.co.uk

A pleasant and welcoming B&B located close to the center of town. Good-size rooms and hearty breakfasts are an added bonus. Inject some romance into your stay and book the four-poster room.

ⓘ 6 🚭 🚫MC, V

🏨 BALTASOUND HOTEL

$

BALTASOUND, UNST, ZE2 9DS

TEL (01957) 711 334

www.baltasound-hotel.shetland.co.uk

This remote Shetland bolthole stakes claim to being the most northerly hotel in Britain. There is more to recommend the hotel, though, than its stunning waterside location. Modest but comfortable accommodation is available in the main house or in the garden log cabin-style chalets. Meals are available in the lounge bar.

ⓘ 23 🅿 🚭 🚫MC, V

🏨 QUEENS HOTEL

$

24 COMMERCIAL STREET, LERWICK, ZE1 0AB

TEL (01595) 692 826

www.kgqhotels.co.uk

Housed in an old Victorian stone building right on the waterfront—it is actually in Lerwick Harbour itself—the décor at the Queens Hotel would be described as old world by some and tired by others. Although it could do with modernizing, its stunning location is not in question. Friendly staff and good food (particularly seafood) also make the Queens a good place to stay.

ⓘ 26 🚭 🚫AE, MC, V

🍴 MONTY'S BISTRO

$$

5 MOUNTHOOLY STREET, LERWICK, ZE1 0BJ

TEL (01595) 696 555

This bustling informal bistro is arguably the best place to eat in Lerwick. Seasonal produce, fish, and local meat feature heavily on a menu complemented by home-baked bread. The food is consistent, the service friendly, and the décor a little garish.

🛏 40 🚭 🚫MC, V

Shopping

Both in and outside of its urban centers, traditionally Scottish souvenirs—haggis, Scottish produce, pottery, handicrafts, wool textiles, Celtic jewelry, tartan, and Harris tweed—are widely available. Many visitors to Scotland are keen to take home a bottle of single malt Scotch whisky, which can be purchased in specialty stores and direct from the distilleries.

Fashion

Scotland's largest city, Glasgow, effortlessly lives up to its advertising slogan "Scotland with Style," with designer and boutique clothing stores standing alongside major U.K. chain stores. In fact its retail outlets are so good that Glasgow is widely recognized as the United Kingdom's best shopping city after London.

Not one to be outdone, Edinburgh has also spruced up its shopping credentials in recent years, with stylish stores moving into the old banks and financial institutions and the creation of a new designer shopping street, Multrees Walk, leading the way. The capital also has something that Glaswegians can currently only envy, and that is one of the six Harvey Nichols stores outside of London.

Aberdeen, Dundee, Stirling, and Inverness also have a diverse range of fashion outlets.

Arts & Crafts

Caledonian Craft Connections
115 High Street, Nairn,
IV12 4DB
Tel (01667) 452 423
www.caledoniancraft
connections.com
Selling goods made by over
60 local artisans.

House of Bruar
Perthshire, PH18 5TW
Tel (0845) 136 0111
www.houseofbruar.com
Collection of shops selling country crafts, Scottish knitwear, art, and Scottish food.

Jail Dornoch
Castle Street, Dornoch, IV25 3SD
Tel (01862) 810 500
www.jail-dornoch.com
Department store–style shop selling art, ceramic, toiletries, clothes, and more.

National Trust for Scotland (NTS)
Tel (0844) 493 2100
www.nts.org.uk/shop
The gift shops at NTS properties throughout Scotland often stock a varied selection of local arts and crafts.

Oily Muggie
Hilswick, Shetland, ZE2 9RW
Tel (01806) 503 363
www.designedinshetland.co.uk
Handicrafts from Shetland.

Clothing

Harvey Nichols
32–34 St. Andrew Square,
Edinburgh, EH2 2AD
Tel (0131) 524 8388
www.harveynichols.co.uk
Scotland's only branch of this prestigious department store s ells designer goods from kitchenware to clothing.

Jenners
48 Princes Street, Edinburgh,
EH2 2YJ
Tel 0844 800 3725
www.houseoffraser.co.uk
Jenners may have been taken over by House of Fraser back in 2005, but this formerly independent department store still retains a unique Edinburgh grace and charm.

Slanj Kilts
67 St. Vincent Street, Glasgow,
G2 5TF
Tel (0141) 248 7770
www.slanjkilts.com
In addition to being a good place to buy tartan, this shop is well known for its tongue-in-cheek humor, and is a good place to pick up cheeky souvenirs like T-shirts sporting comic phrases.
Also at:
14 St Mary's Street,
Edinburgh, EH1 1SU, tel (0131) 557 1666.
119 George Street, Aberdeen,
AB25 1HU,
tel (01224) 635 915

Food

House of Bruar
Perthshire, PH18 5TW
Tel (0845) 136 0111
www.houseofbruar.com
Collection of shops selling country crafts, Scottish knitwear, art, and Scottish food.

I. J. Mellis Cheesemonger
30A Victoria Street, Edinburgh,
EH1 2JW
Tel (0131) 226 6215
www.mellischeese.co.uk
This renowned cheesemonger supplies many of Edinburgh's leading restaurants. Great Scottish cheeses are among those on sale.
Also at:
330 Morningside Road, Edinburgh, EH10 4QJ, tel (0131) 447 8889
6 Bakers Place, Edinburgh, EH3 6SY, tel (0131) 225 6566
492 Great Western Road,

Glasgow, G12 8EW, tel (0141)
339 8998
149 South Street, St. Andrews,
KY16 9UN, tel (01334) 471 410
210 Rosemount Place, Aberdeen,
AB25 2XP, tel (01224) 566 530

Taste of Arran
Market Road, Brodick, Isle of
Arran, KA27 8AU
Tel (01770) 302 374
www.taste-of-arran.co.uk
Online retailer of produce from
the Arran Brewery, Arran Dairies
Ltd., Creelers Smokehouse,
Island Cheese Company, Arran
Chocolate Factory, Wooleys
of Arran, Arran Fine Foods,
Robin's Herbs, Torrylin Creamery,
Bellevue Creamery, and Isle
of Arran Distillers. All products
are also available on the Isle
of Arran.

Harris Tweed
Harris Tweed Isle of Harris
4 Plocrapool, Tarbert, HS3 3EB
Tel (01859) 502 040
www.harristweedand
knitwear.co.uk
Harris tweed and knitwear.

The Harris Tweed Shop
Tarbet, Isle of Harris
Tel (01859) 502 493
www.isleofharristweedshop.co.uk
Selling tweed produced on the
island and crafts.

The Harris Tweed Shop
Main Street, Newtonmore,
PH20 1DD
Tel (01540) 670188
www.harristweedshop.com
Harris Tweed and accessories.

21st Century Kilts
48 Thistle Street, Edinburgh,
EH2 1EN
Tel (0131) 220 9450
www.21stcenturykilts.com
Designer Howie Nicholsby's store
sells kilts in a wide variety of
modern styles and fabrics.

Jewelry
Azendi
19 Multrees Walk, Edinburgh,
EH1 3DQ
Tel (0131) 556 9102
www.azendi.com
Scottish outlet for contemporary
designer jewelry.
Also at:
The Atrium, Union Square,
Aberdeen, AB11 5PS,
tel (01224) 210 990

Heathergems Visitor Centre
22 Atholl Road, Pitlochry,
PH16 5BX
Tel (01294) 313 222
www.heathergems.com
Visitors center and factory outlet
of renowned jewelry and silver
crafts specialist made with
natural Scottish heather as part
of the design.

Henderson the Jewellers
217 Sauchiehall Street, Glasgow,
G2 3EX
Tel (0141) 331 2569
www.hendersonjewellers.co.uk
Fantastic selection of Charles
Rennie Mackintosh–inspired
jewelry. Situated above the
seminal architect's Willow
Tearooms. Branches throughout
Scotland.

The Longship
7–15 Broad Street, Kirkwall,
Orkney, KW15 1DH
Tel (01856) 873 251
www.olagoriejewellery.com
The only retail outlet of a leading
British jewelry producer, Ola
Gorie, who is known for her
Celtic and Norse designs.

Skye Silver
The Old School, Colbost,
Isle of Skye, IV55 8ZT
Tel (01470) 511 263
www.skyesilver.com
Beautiful gold and silver Celtic
jewelry in a stunning location.

Markets
Barras Market
Gallowgate, Glasgow, G1 5AX
Tel (0141) 552 4601
www.glasgow-barrowland.com
Selling almost everything
imaginable, but almost nothing
you'd want to take home. Visit
to feel the pulse of the city.
Open Sat.–Sun 10 a.m.–5 p.m.

Edinburgh Farmers Market
Castle Terrace
www.edinburghfarmers
market.com
Saturday market (9 a.m.–2 p.m.),
where more than 65 local grow-
ers and producers sell the fruits
of their labors on Castle Terrace.

Pottery
The Adam Pottery
76 Henderson Row, Edinburgh,
EH3 5BJ
Tel (0131) 557 3978,
www.theadampottery.co.uk
A range of traditional and contemporary ceramics produced by
six artists.

Borgh Pottery
Fivepenny House, Borgh, Lewis,
HS2 0RX
Tel (01851) 850 345
www.borgh-pottery.com
Porcelain and stoneware pottery
made by Alex and Sue Blair.

Crail Pottery
75 Nethergate, Crail, KY10 3TX
Tel (01333) 451 212
www.crailpottery.com
Family-run pottery shop selling
earthenware, ceramics, and
pottery.

Edinbane Pottery
Edinbane, Isle of Skye, IV51 9PW
Tel (01470) 582 234
www.edinbane-pottery.co.uk
Wood-fired and salt-glazed pottery in stunning designs by Stuart
and Julie Whatley.

The Meadows Pottery
11A Summerhall Place, Edinburgh, EH9 1QE
Tel (0131) 662 4064
www.themeadowspottery.com
Lovely hand-thrown stoneware.

Tain Pottery
Aldie, Tain, IV19 1LZ
Tel (01862) 894 112
www.tainpottery.co.uk
See the craftspeople at work and buy stoneware at one of the country's biggest potteries.

Tartan & Kilts
Geoffrey Tailor
57–61 High Street, Edinburgh, EH1 1SR
Tel (0131) 557 0256
www.geoffreykilts.co.uk
One of the Scotland's best kilt makers.
Also at:
309 Sauchiehall Street, Glasgow, G2 3HW, tel (0141) 331 2388
35 Stevenson Street, Oban, PA34 4DJ, tel (01631) 570 557

21st Century Kilts
48 Thistle Street, Edinburgh, EH2 1EN
Tel (0131) 220 9450
www.21stcenturykilts.com
Designer Howie Nicholsby's store sells kilts in a wide variety of modern styles and fabrics.

Slanj Kilts
67 St. Vincent Street, Glasgow, G2 5TF
Tel (0141) 248 7770
www.slanjkilts.com
In addition to being a good place to buy tartan, this shop is well known for its tongue-in-cheek humor, and is a good place to pick up cheeky souvenirs like T-shirts sporting comic phrases.
Also at:
14 St Mary's Street, Edinburgh, EH1 1SU, tel (0131) 557 1666

119 George Street, Aberdeen, AB25 1HU, tel (01224) 635 915

Toiletries & Cosmetics
Arran Aromatics
The Home Farm, Brodick, Isle of Arran, KA27 8DD
Tel (01770) 302 595
www.arranaromatics.com
Brand synonymous with quality and luxury.

Highland Soap Company
Spean Bridge, PH34 4EP
Tel (01397) 713 919
www.highlandsoaps.com
Retailer of handmade soap and other toiletries.
Also at:
48 High Street, Fort William, PH33 6AH

Whisky
Loch Fyne Whiskies
Main Street, Inveraray, PA32 8TU
Tel (01499) 302 219
www.lfw.co.uk
Dedicated to all things whisky related.

Royal Mile Whiskies
379 High Street, Edinburgh
Tel (0131) 524 9380
www.royalmilewhiskies.com
Myriad single malts and other whiskies.

Scotch Whisky Heritage Centre
354 Castlehill, Edinburgh
Tel (0131) 220 0441
www.whisky-heritage.co.uk
Over 300 different single malts on sale.

The Whisky Shop
Buchanan Galleries, 220 Buchanan Street, Glasgow
Tel (0141) 331 0022, www.whiskyshop.com
Largest whisky-only specialist in the United Kingdom, with eight branches in Scotland and seven in England.

Also at:
17 Bridge Street, Inverness, tel (01463) 710 525
93 High Street, Fort William, tel (01397) 706 164
Station Road, Oban, tel (01631) 564 409
11 Main Street, Callendar, tel (01877) 331 936
Princes Mall, Edinburgh, tel (0131) 558 7563
Ocean Terminal, Edinburgh, tel (0131) 554 8211
Gretna Gateway Outlet Village, Gretna, tel (01461) 338 004

The Whisky Shop Dufftown
1 Fife Street, Dufftown.
Tel (01340) 821 097
www.whiskyshopdufftown.co.uk
Over 500 single malts on sale in the "world capital of whisky."

Wool Textiles
Edinburgh Woollen Mill
www.ewm.co.uk
Selling woolen and cashmere knits alongside more contemporary fashion. With almost 50 outlets across Scotland.

Joyce Forsyth
42 Candlemaker Row, Edinburgh
Tel (0131) 220 4112
www.joyce.forsyth.btinternet.co.uk
Designer Scottish knitwear.

Kinross Cashmere
67 George Street, Edinburgh
Tel (0131) 226 1577
www.cashmerestore.com
Lovely cashmere garments.
Also at:
2 St. Giles Street, Royal Mile, Edinburgh.

Spiders Web
51 Commercial Street, Lerwick
Tel (01595) 695 246
www.shetland-knitwear.com
Hand knits including Fair Isle knitwear and hooded tops.

Entertainment

Scotland's main cities are brimming with theaters and music venues, that stage everything from opera and ballet to live music and exciting new plays. Edinburgh's summer festivals (see pp. 68–69) are at the heart of the country's cultural calendar, when everything from stand-up comedy shows to controversial political plays are staged in the city.

High culture is well established in Scotland and the country has its own opera, ballet, and orchestras, as well as myriad theatres staging weighty productions. Scotland also has a burgeoning movie industry, with the highlight of the celluloid calendar the Edinburgh International Film Festival (www.edfilmfest .org.uk). The country also has a strong tradition of folk music and dance. Good places to hear folk musicians are in local pubs, town halls, and community centers. Some venues also host traditional ceilidh dances. Scotland's biggest winter music festival, Celtic Connections (www.celticconnections .com), is a prestigious celebration of Scottish music. The 18-day festival takes place in Glasgow every January. Some of the most popular bands on the U.K. music scene also hail from Scotland.

Ballet
Scottish Ballet
Tramway, 25 Albert Drive, Glasgow, G41 2PE
Tel (0141) 331 2931
www.scottishballet.co.uk
See this touring ballet company perform at the Theatre Royal Glasgow, Edinburgh Festival Theatre, His Majesty's Theatre in Aberdeen, and Eden Court in Inverness (see Theater p. 308).

Ceilidh
These are social gatherings where traditional Scottish music is played. In addition to the following venues, informal ceilidhs are a common occurrence in the inns and pubs of rural Scotland, especially in the Highlands.

The Queens Hall
85–89 Clerk Street, Edinburgh, EH8 9JG
Tel (0131) 668 3456
www.thequeenshall.net
Check the venue's website for details about the regular ceilidh nights.

Lauries Acoustic Music Bar
34 King Street, Glasgow, G1 5QT
Tel (0141) 552 7123
www.lauriesacousticmusicbar.co.uk
Hosting popular Saturday-night ceilidhs.

Cinema
Belmont Picture House
49 Belmont Street, Aberdeen, AB10 1JS
Tel (01224) 343 536
www.picturehouses.co.uk
This independent three-screen cinema shows mainly art-house movies.

Cameo
38 Home Street, Edinburgh, EH3 9LZ
Tel (0870) 704 2052
www.piturehouses.co.uk
Showing a mix of art-house and commercial movies.

DCA Cinema
152 Nethergate, Dundee, DD1 4DY
Tel (01382) 909 9000
www.dca.org.uk
A great venue for watching bigger budget movies.

Dominion
18 Newbattle Terrace, Edinburgh, EH10 4RT
Tel (0131) 447 4771
www.dominioncinemas.net

This independent cinema shows mainstream movies.

Filmhouse
88 Lothian Road, Edinburgh, EH3 9BZ
Tel (0131) 228 2688
www.filmhousecinema.com
This art-house cinema has a busy screening schedule and is at the hub of the city's film festival.

Glasgow Film Theatre
13 Rose Street, Glasgow, G3 6RB
Tel (0141) 332 6535
www.gft.org.uk
This independent cinema shows mainstream and more offbeat movies.

Comedy Clubs
Eden Court (see p. 308)

The Stand
5 York Place, Edinburgh, EH1 3EB
Tel (0131) 558 7272
www.thestand.co.uk
Edinburgh's full-time comedy club hosts everything from breakthrough acts to well-known comics.

The Stand
333 Woodlands Road, Glasgow, G3 6NG
Tel (0870) 600 6055
www.thestand.co.uk
See above listing.

Concert Venues
Aberdeen Music Hall
Union Street, Aberdeen, AB10 1QS
Tel (01224) 641 122
www.musichallaberdeen.com
Aberdeen's premier concert hall

also attracts well-known comics, theater groups, and dancers.

Barrowland Ballroom
244 Gallowgate, Glasgow,
G4 0TT
Tel (0141) 552 4601
www.glasgow-barrowland.com
Widely regarded as the best place to see a live band in Glasgow.

Caird Hall
City Square, Dundee, DD1 3BB
Tel (01382) 434 451
www.cairdhall.co.uk
A large concert hall used by everyone from pop bands to the Royal Scottish Orchestra.

CCA
350 Sauchiehall Street, Glasgow,
G2 3JD
Tel (0141) 352 4900
www.cca-glasgow.com
Host to experimental music, art-house films, and visual art.

City Halls
Candleriggs, Glasgow, G1 1NQ
Tel (0141) 353 8000
www.glasgowconcerthalls.com
A popular venue for classical and world music.

Edinburgh Corn Exchange
11 Newmarket Road, Edinburgh,
EH14 1RJ
Tel (0131) 477 3500
www.ece.uk.com
Multipurpose venue that attracts big-name bands.

Glasgow Royal Concert Hall
2 Sauchiehall Street, Glasgow,
G2 3NY
Tel (0141) 353 8000
www.grch.com
This slick venue, hosting every-thing from comedy to dance, is the hub of the annual Celtic Con-nections (see p. 306) festival.

HMV Picture House
31 Lothian Road, Edinburgh,

EH1 2DJ
Tel (0844) 847 1740
www.mamagroup.co.uk/picturehouse
This former theater is a cozy and atmospheric place to see live bands.

King Tut's Wah Wah Hut
272a St. Vincent Street, Glasgow,
G2 5RL
Tel (0141) 221 5279
www.kingtuts.co.uk
Widely regarded as one of the best places on the globe to see up-and-coming bands.

The Lemon Tree
5 West North Street, Aberdeen,
AB24 5AT
Tel (01224) 642 230
www.lemontree.org
Attracting new talent and cutting-edge bands, as well as hosting dance, comedy, and theater.

Queen's Hall (see opposite)

Royal Scottish Academy of Music and Drama (RSAMD)
100 Renfrew Street, Glasgow,
G2 3DB
Tel (0141) 332 5057
www.rsamd.ac.uk
Music and drama venue.

SECC/Clyde Auditorium
Exhibition Way, Glasgow,
G3 8YW
Tel (0844) 395 4000
www.secc.co.uk
Massive venue played by equally massive bands.

St. Giles Cathedral
Royal Mile, Edinburgh, EH1 1RE
Tel (0131) 226 0673
www.stgilescathedral.org.uk
Regular concerts are staged in the atmospheric interior of this historic cathedral.

Usher Hall
Lothian Road, Edinburgh,
EH1 2EA

Tel (0131) 228 1155
www.usherhall.co.uk
This lovely venue hosts an eclectic array of musical performers.

O2 ABC
330 Sauchiehall Street, Glasgow,
G2 3JA
Tel (0141) 332 2232
www.o2abcglasgow.com
Nightclub and live music venue.

O2 Academy Glasgow
121 Eglinton Street, Glasgow,
G5 9NT
Tel 0844 477 2000
www.o2academyglasgow.co.uk
A great place to hear the bands of the moment and breakthrough artists.

Folk Music

Hootananny
67 Church Street, Inverness,
IV1 1ES
Tel (01463) 233 651
www.hootananny.co.uk
One of the country's best places for traditional Scottish music.

Sandy Bells
25 Forrest Road, Edinburgh,
EH1 2QH
Tel (0131) 225 2751
Live folk music can be enjoyed in this traditional pub every night of the week.

St. Andrew's in the Square
1 St. Andrew's Square, Glasgow,
G1 5PP
Tel (0141) 548 6020
www.standrewsinthesquare.com
See folk performances in this beautifully restored church.

Whistle Binkies
73–75 St. Mary's Wynd, Stirling,
FK8 1BU
Tel (01876) 451 256
This traditional pub is known locally for its regular folk music sessions.

Opera
Scottish Opera
39 Elmbank Crescent, Glasgow,
G2 4PT
Tel (0141) 248 4567
www.scottishopera.org.uk
Scotland's national opera tours
the same grand venues as the
Scottish Ballet (see p. 305), but
also graces smaller stages around
the country.

Theater
The Arches Theatre
253 Argyle Street, Glasgow,
G2 8DL
Tel (0870) 240 7528
www.thearches.co.uk
Hosting everything from
cutting-edge theater to
experimental music.

CCA (see p. 307)

Dundee Rep Theatre
Tay Square, Dundee, DD1 1PB
Tel (01382) 223 530
www.dundeereptheatre.co.uk
Home to the Scottish Dance Theatre and a full-time company of
actors (Rep Ensemble), the Rep
showcases the best of Scottish
performance art.

Eden Court
Bishops Road, Inverness, IV3 5SA
Tel (01463) 239 841
www.eden-court.co.uk
Multipurpose venue for plays,
gigs, stand-up comedy, dance, and
art-house films.

Edinburgh Playhouse
18–22 Greenside Place,
Edinburgh, EH1 3AA
Tel (0870) 606 3424
www.edinburghplayhouse.org.uk
Hosts everything from touring
West End musicals to kids shows.

Festival Theatre
13–29 Nicolson Street,
Edinburgh, EH8 9FT
Tel (0131) 529 6000
www.eft.co.uk
This large and modern venue
stages big-budget dance, musical,
and theatrical productions.

His Majesty's Theatre
Rosemount Viaduct, Aberdeen,
AB25 1GL
Tel (01224) 641 122
www.hmtaberdeen.com
Aberdeen's biggest theater
attracts touring shows and musi-
cals like *Chicago*.

King's Theatre, Edinburgh
2 Leven Street, Edinburgh,
EH3 9LQ
Tel (0131) 529 6000
www.eft.co.uk
Staging popular productions.

King's Theatre
297 Bath Street, Glasgow,
G2 4JN
Tel (0141) 240 1111
www.theambassadortickets.com/
king's-theatre
This large venue hosts touring
theater productions, musicals,
and big-name comics.

MacRobert
University of Stirling, Stirling,
FK9 4LA
Tel (01786) 466 666
www.macrobert.org
Visiting theater, bands, and cinema.

Royal Lyceum Theatre
308 Grindlay Street,
Edinburgh, EH3 9AX
Tel (0131) 248 4848
www.lyceum.org.uk
Known for its quality
mainstream drama.

Theatre Royal
282 Hope Street, Glasgow,
G2 3QA
Tel (0844) 871 7647
www.ambassadortickets.com/
Theatre-Royal-Glasgow
Hosting opera, ballet, and big-
budget theater.

The Tolbooth
Jail Wynd, Stirling, FK8 1DE
Tel (01876) 274 000
www.stirling.gov.uk/tolbooth
Atmospheric venue for theatre,
comedy, and music.

Traverse Theatre
10 Cambridge Street, Edinburgh,
EH1 2ED
Tel (0131) 228 1404
www.traverse.co.uk
Bringing the work of new Scottish
writers to the stage.

Tron Theatre
63 Trongate, Glasgow, G1 5HB
Tel (0141) 552 4267
www.tron.co.uk
A popular venue for theater,
comedy, and music, the Tron also
has its own theater company.

Activities

Scotland's beautiful and varied nature lends itself to outdoor activities, from leisurely walks along forest trails and kayaking on dramatic lochs to mountaineering and skiing. A growing number of accolades have recognized Scotland as one of the best destinations in the world for climbing, diving, kayaking, mountain biking, and surfing. As a result more and more visitors, as well as Scots themselves, are taking part in adventure sports.

Fittingly for a country that yields itself so effortlessly to adventure activities, many of Scotland's facilities are also world class. Many adventure companies are also well-run, slick operations with knowledgeable and highly trained staff. There is also a trend in Scotland for adventure centers that run a mixed bag of adventure sports; some of these are residential.

Climbing & Hill Walking

Venues

Cairngorms
Cairngorms National Park Authority
14 The Square, Grantown-on-Spey
Tel (01479) 873 535
www.cairngorms.co.uk
Brimming with mountains, moorland, forest, rivers, and lochs, Britain's largest national park is a haven for climbers and hill walkers (see pp. 180–181). It also presents plenty of opportunities for mountain biking.

Edinburgh International Climbing Arena
Ratho, South Platt Hill, Newbridge
Tel (0131) 331 6333
www.eica-ratho.com
Hone your climbing skills at this world-class indoor climbing center.

Glencoe
Glencoe Visitor Centre, Glencoe
Tel (0844) 493 2222
www.glencoe-nts.org.uk
Eight Munros, 49 miles (79 km)

of walking trails, and 20 major climbing sites make Glencoe one of Scotland's most popular climbing and hill walking sites.

Isle of Skye
The island is Scotland's most popular walking destination, with climbers and hill walkers drawn to the precipitous Cullin Mountain range that dominates the center. High-level walks can pose serious technical and physical challenges and are not for the inexperienced.

Loch Lomond & the Trossachs National Park
Loch Lomond & the Trossachs National Park Authority
Carrochan Road, Balloch
Tel (01389) 722 600
www.lochlomond-trossachs.org
Loch Lomond, the hulking Ben Lomond, and a stretch of Scotland's most famous long-distance walk, the West Highland Way (*www.west-highland-way .co.uk*) are just some of the things that attract walkers and hill walkers to this national park.

Nevis Range
For many visitors and Scots the ascent of Britain's tallest mountain, Ben Nevis, is the ultimate goal of a climbing or hill walking vacation in Scotland. Other mountains in the range include Aonach Mor and Carn Mor Dearg.

Northwest Highlands
This region offers the chance to walk in and climb some of Scotland's most iconic mountains—

including Stac Pollaidh, Suilven, and Ben Loyal—as well as the formidable peaks of Torridon, Dundonnell, and the Fannichs. Glen Shiel and Glen Affric also number among its attractions.

Pentland Hills Regional Park
Boghall Farm, Biggar Road, Edinburgh
Tel (0131) 445 3003
www.edinburgh.gov.uk/phrp
With trails to suit all abilities the Pentland Hills are popular with everyone from families to serious walkers.

Southern Scotland
Eschewed by those seeking vaulting Highland peaks, southern Scotland still has a lot to recommend it to walkers, with myriad trails dissecting the Lammermuir, Moorfoot, and Cheviot Hills. The south is also home to a number of long-distance walks including the Southern Upland Way (see p. 114) and St. Cuthbert's Way.

Outfitters

Torridon Activities
Torridon
Tel (01445) 791 242
www.thetorridon.com/activities
Offering a multiactivity program in Torridon, including climbing, abseiling, guided walks, and mountain guiding.

North West Frontiers
Strathpeffer
Tel (01997) 421 474
www.nwf.com
Walking and hiking holiday specialists operating in the

northwest Highlands, the Outer Hebrides, Orkney, and Shetland.

Other Resources
Mountaineering Council of Scotland
The Old Granary, West Mill Street, Perth
Tel (01738) 638 227
www.mountaineering-scotland.org.uk
Offering practical and safety advice about hill walking, climbing, and mountaineering in Scotland. Individual membership is available and gives access to the club mountain huts.

Walking Scotland
http://walking.visitscotland.com
Visit Scotland's official walking site with links to walking outfitters and a database of over 1,000 downloadable routes.

Diving
Scotland boasts some excellent diving destinations, including the varied sealife and ancient wrecks in the Sound of Mull (see p. 197) to the fleet of scuttled German ships whose watery graves lie in Orkney's Scapa Flow (see p. 259).

Aqua Stars Dive Centre
Guns Green Basin, Eyemouth,
Tel (018907) 50904
www.aquastars.co.uk
Offering diver training, guided dives, boat dives, and dive trips around Eyemouth and the east coast.

Lochaline Dive Centre
Lochaline, Movern
(01967) 421 627
www.lochalinedivecentre.co.uk
Offering diver training and guided dives on the exciting historic wrecks that lie at the bottom of the Sound of Mull.

Puffin Dive Centre
Port Gallanach, Oban
Tel (01631) 566 088
www.puffin.org.uk
Offering diver training off the west coast.

Scapa Flow Diving Centre
Tel (01856) 751 492
www.scapaflowdivingcentre.com
Wreck diving for suitably accredited divers.

Other Resources
Adventure Scotland
http://adventure.visitscotland.com
Visit Scotland's national portal looking at adventure activities in the country including diving.

Scottish Sub-Aqua Club
Caledonia House, 1 Redheughs Rigg, South Gyle, Edinburgh
Tel (0131) 625 4404
www.scotsac.com
Offering accredited dive training.

Fishing
It is perhaps no surprise that, in a nation awash with lochs, blessed with rushing rivers and a coastline measuring 10,246 miles (16,490 km), angling is a popular pastime. In fact, clean and uncrowded waters make Scotland one of Europe's premier fishing spots. In the Tweed, Dee, and Tay Rivers Scotland arguably boasts the best salmon fishing in the world. Scotland also has a large number of fisheries that permit angling. Many riverside hotels, particularly country house hotels, also have angling activities for guests.

FishPal
Stichill House, Kelso
Tel (01573) 470 612
www.fishpal.com/scotland
Everything you need to know about fishing in Scotland. The website covers the Dee, Tay, and

Tweed Rivers, as well as fishing in lochs or in the sea. Anglers can book angling permits by selecting the relevant beat or fishery and the date through the online reservation system or through the booking office.

Scottish Anglers National Association
National Game Angling Centre
The Pier, Loch Leven
Tel (01577) 861 116
www.sana.org.uk
Scotland's governing body for game angling provides information about how, when, and where to do this type of fishing in Scotland.

Tweedside Tackle
36 Bridge St., Kelso
(01573) 225 306
www.tweedsidetackle.co.uk
Located in the heart of Scottish salmon fishing country, Tweedside Tackle provide permits and equipment rental to anglers.

Horse Riding & Pony Trekking
Swaths of dazzling scenery that incorporate vast sand beaches, gentle rolling hills, and vaulting mountains make Scotland a great destination for horse riding. From children's pony rides to riding lessons, gentle beginners treks, and fast-paced hacks for experienced riders, there is genuinely something for everyone.

Brighouse Bay
Trekking Centre
Borgue, Kirkcudbright
Tel (01557) 870 267
http://brighousebaytrekking.weebly.com
With treks, hacks, children's rides, and riding lessons, this center caters to all ages and abilities. Experienced riders can join a fast hack on the beach.

Isle of Skye Trekking Centre
Skye Riding Centre, Suladale
Tel (01470) 582 419
www.theisleofskyetrekkingcentre
.co.uk
Trek through some of Scotland's
most enchanting scenery. Treks to
suit all abilities

Lettershuna Riding Centre
Appin
Tel 0845 806 0332
www.lettershunaridingcentre.com
Supervised rides, as well as riding and trekking excursions in
the Appin area. Catering for all
abilities and anyone over the age
of four.

North Sannox Pony Trekking
North Glen Sannox
Tel (01770) 810 222
Scenic treks for all abilities including beginners, as long as they
are five years old or over. Short
pony rides available for three- to
five-year-olds.

Other Resources
Riding in Scotland
http://riding.visitscotland.com
Visit Scotland's official horse
riding site with information on
trekking and riding, links to riding
and equestrian centers, and a
map of routes and trails.

Ice Climbing

Thanks to its lofty mountains
Scotland is the United Kingdom's
premier ice climbing destination.
From late December to early
April experienced mountaineers
take to the ice in a test of
their endurance, strength, nerve,
and skill. It may not be a sport
for the novice climber, but it
is possible to learn these skills
in the relative safety of Kinlochleven's Ice Factor, which
is home to the world's largest
indoor ice wall.

Climbmts
Suite 3, Bank House, Bank Street,
Aberfeldy
Tel (01887) 822 699
http://climbmts.co.uk
Offering summer and winter
courses that cover mountaineering, walking, winter skills, naviga-
tion, and more.

Glenmore Lodge
Aviemore
Tel (01479) 861 212
www.glenmorelodge.co.uk
Scotland's national outdoor
training center offers a raft of
skills courses, including winter
mountaineering.

Ice Factor
Leven Road, Kinlochleven
Tel (01855) 831 100
www.ice-factor.co.uk
World-class indoor training
facility for snow skills and ice
climbing.

Other Resources
Adventure Scotland
http://adventure.visitscotland
.com
Visit Scotland's national portal
looking at adventure activities
in the country, including ice
climbing.

Golf

The home of golf has more than
550 golf courses. These range
from public courses where golfers
pay as they play to members-only
courses. Guests staying at some
of Scotland's more prestigious
hotels can often bypass some of
the membership regulations and
secure a round of golf during
their stay. The Visit Scotland
website dedicated to the sport is
a useful resource when it comes
to planning a golfing trip.

Golf Visit Scotland
http://golf.visitscotland.com

This useful Web portal has information about and links to golf
courses and offers advice about
golfing in Scotland and planning
a golfing trip. It also has details
about special offers, events, and
competitions.

Mountain Biking
Cairngorms (see p. 309)

Glentress
Glentress Forest, Peebles
Tel (01721) 721 736
www.thehubintheforest.co.uk
One of the best mountain biking
facilities in the United Kingdom
boasts trails to suit all grades of
mountain biker (see p. 117).

Laggan Wolftrax
Strathmashie Forest, Laggan,
Newtonmore
Tel (01528) 544 786
www.basecampmtb.com
Home to some of Scotland's best
purpose built mountain-bike
tracks. The trail network offers
everything from a beginners
green run and a novice orange
trail to a fast-paced red run and
highly technical black run.

Nevis Range
Torlundy, Fort William
Tel (01397) 705 825
www.nevisrange.co.uk
This first-rate center is Scotland's
most famous mountain-biking
venue. The downhill trail here is
the only World Cup venue in the
United Kingdom and the only
course with gondola access.
With a vertical drop of 1,722
feet (525 m) and a length of
1.65 miles (2.66 km), its rocky
straights, bus stops, tight corners,
exposed hillside, slab rock, tight
gullies, and big jumps mean that
it is not for the fainthearted.

Wheely Good Bike Guides
Tulloch Outdoor Activity Centre,

Tulloch
Tel (0845) 0945 513
www.wheely-good.co.uk
Offering guided mountain biking
in and around Lochaber, including
the Nevis Range. Trails available
to suit all abilities with half-day,
full-day, and longer programs.

Wilderness Scotland
3a St. Vincent Street, Edinburgh
Tel (0131) 625 6635
www.wildernessscotland.com
This adventure company offers a
choice of mountain-biking holidays. Groups are small and the
trips include seven days on the
island of Skye. A lot of distance is
covered each day.

Other Resources
Cycling Scotland
http://cycling.visitscotland.com
Visit Scotland's official cycling
website with links to mountain-
bike centers, events, and a
database of 147 routes. It also has
links to bike rental stores, outfitters offering mountain-biking
vacations and excursions, as well
as a host of other useful weblinks.

Sailing
Stunning coastal scenery, clean
and uncrowded waters, clean
air and good facilities makes
Scotland an excellent sailing destination, particularly on the west
coast with its myriad offshore
islands and islets. Sailing schools
provide tuition for novices,
while more experienced sailors
can organize a bareboat charter.
Skippered cruises, where guests
don't need any experience, are
also available.

Galloway Activity Centre
Loch Ken, Castle Douglas
Tel (01644) 420 626
www.lochken.co.uk
Offering a wide range of residen-
tial and non-residential activities

including sailing, powerboating,
and windsurfing. A host of other
water and land-based activities
are also available.

**Loch Insh Watersports &
Outdoor Activity Centre**
Kincraig
Tel (01540) 651 272
www.lochinsh.com
The wide range of watersports
on offer include sailing, kayaking,
windsurfing, and canoeing. A
wide variety of land-based sports
(winter and summer) are also
available, as are a number of
courses.

Loch Morlich Watersports
Glenmore Forest Park, Aviemore
Tel (01479) 861 221
www.lochmorlich.com
Sailing, waterskiing, canoeing,
and windsurfing in beautiful surrounds. Mountain-bike courses
are also offered. Those with the
necessary know-how can hire
equipment.

National Watersports Centre
Isle of Cumbrae
Tel (01475) 530 757
www.nationalcentrecumbrae
.org.uk
This purpose-built facility runs
RYA accredited residential sailing
courses.

**Port Edgar Marina and Sailing
School**
Shore Road, South Queensferry,
Edinburgh
Tel (0131) 331 3330
www.portedgar.co.uk
An impressive range of sailing
courses cater to everyone from
the novice to the experienced
sailor. The suitably qualified can
also hire Wayfarers.

Other Resources
**Royal Yachting Association
Scotland**
Caledonia House, South Gyle,

Edinburgh
Tel (0131) 317 7388
www.ryascotland.org.uk
Scotland's national body for
sailing provides information on
recreational and competitive
aspects of the sport. It also has
training centers that offer certi-
fied courses.

Sail
http://sail.visitscotland.com
Visit Scotland's official sailing
website with weblinks to boat-
yards, marinas, sailing schools,
and charter companies. It also
has a section on the country's
canals and sailing events, as well
as weblinks into the shipping
forecast and tide information.

Shooting
Scotland has a long association
with game hunting, particularly
among the wealthy. While many
country estates and country
house hotels still organize stalking and shooting of game, there
has been a shift in recent years
toward clay shooting.

Auchterhouse Country Sports
Burnhead Farm, Auchterhouse
Tel (01382) 320 476
www.treemac.co.uk
One of the country's leading
clay-shooting grounds regularly
hosts national and international
competitions. Beginners, though,
are still welcome. Lessons for
all grades of shooter are also
available, alongside quad biking,
archery, falconry, and fishing.

Cluny Clays Activity Centre
Cluny Mains Farm, by Kirkcaldy
Tel (01592) 720 374
www.clunyclays.com
As well as clay pigeon shooting
and air rifle shooting, visitors
can also have a go at archery,
take a golf lesson, or play
a round on the nine-hole golf
course.

ACTIVITIES   **313**

Country Sports
www.countrysports.co.uk
Organizing tailor-made stalking
and hunting trips in Scotland

Dunkeld Park
Hilton Dunkeld House Hotel,
Dunkeld
Tel (01350) 728 370
www.dunkeld-park.co.uk
Air rifle and clay pigeon
shooting are offered alongside
archery, off-road driving and
quad biking on a private 228-
acre (92 ha) estate. Salmon
fishing is also available.

Skiing
The 2009/2010 season was a
bumper year for Scottish skiing,
with a lot of snowfall and conditions ideal for skiing. The country
has five ski centers, as well as a
number of dry ski slopes where
skiers can hone their skills.

Cairngorm Mountain
Aviemore
Tel (01479) 861 261
www.cairngormmountain.org
Runs to suit all grades of skier,
12 ski lifts, ski lessons, and
equipment hire, as well as good
après-ski in Aviemore make the
Cairngorm Mountain resort a
popular choice.

Glencoe Mountain
Glencoe
Tel (01855) 851 226
www.glencoemountain.co.uk
Ski resort boasting 19 runs and
7 lifts. It is also home to the
steepest black-graded run, the
Fly Paper, in Britain. Lift passes,
equipment hire, and tuition
available.

Glenshee Ski Centre
Glenshee
Tel (013397) 41320
www.ski-glenshee.co.uk
Facilities at the UK's largest ski
center include 36 runs, 21 lifts

and tows, equipment hire, lift
passes, and tuition.

Lecht
Strathdon
Tel (01795) 651 440
www.lecht.co.uk
This smaller resort in the eastern
Cairngorms offers 18 runs, equip-
ment hire, instruction, and lift
passes.

Nevis Range (see p. 311)
Skiing and snowboarding on
Aonach Mor is often possible
until late spring. Facilities for skiers include the gondola up to the
snow sports area, equipment hire,
lift passes, and tuition.

Ski Scotland
http://ski.visitscotland.com
Visit Scotland's national skiing and
boarding portal with information
about travel, snow conditions, and
weblinks to ski centers.

Surfing
Scotland's freezing cold coastal
waters might not seem like
an ideal surfing destination,
but thousands of Scottish surfers
and a growing throng of visiting
surfers would disagree with you.
The country is blessed with
a number of great surfing
spots, with decisions about
where to go based around
personal choice and experience.
When it comes to world-class
surfing the clear standout is
Thurso East, which offers some
of the biggest breaks in Europe.
The outermost island of the
Inner Hebrides, Tiree, is also a
popular surfing destination.

Hebridean Surf Holidays
28 Frances Street, Stornoway, Isle
of Lewis
Tel (01851) 840 337
www.hebrideansurf.co.uk
Offering surfing holidays for
everyone from novice to expe-

rienced surfers. Lessons for beginners are given in secluded spots
with manageable waves.
Wild Diamond (see Windsurfing
below)

Other Resources
Adventure Scotland
http://adventure.visitscotland
.com
Visit Scotland's national portal
looking at adventure activities in
the country including surfing.

Windsurfing
Adventure centers located
throughout Scotland offer
windsurfing courses and hire
(see Sailing opposite). The Isle
of Tiree has perfect conditions
for all grades of windsurfer,
with its annual international
windsurfing competition, the
Tiree Wave Classic in October,
putting it firmly on the map.

Wild Diamond
Burnside Cottage, Cornaig,
Isle of Tiree
Tel (01879) 220 399
www.wilddiamond.co.uk
In addition to windsurf hire and
windsurfing tuition Wild Diamond also offer surfboard hire,
instruction in stand up paddle
boarding (and board hire). The
instructors also teach sandyacht-
ing and kitesurfing.

Other Resources
Adventure Scotland
http://adventure.visitscotland
.com
Visit Scotland's national portal
looking at adventure activities
in the country, including windsurfing.

INDEX

Bold page numbers indicate illustrations
CAPS indicates thematic categories

ILLUSTRATIONS CREDITS

National Geographic
TRAVELER
Scotland

Published by the National Geographic Society

John M. Fahey, Jr., *President
and Chief Executive Officer*

Gilbert M. Grosvenor, *Chairman of the Board*

Tim T. Kelly, *President, Global Media Group*

John Q. Griffin, *Executive Vice President;
President, Publishing*

Nina D. Hoffman, *Executive Vice President;
President, Book Publishing Group*

Prepared by the Book Division

Barbara Brownell Grogan, *Vice President
and Editor in Chief*

Marianne R. Koszorus, *Director of Design*

Barbara A. Noe, *Senior Editor*

Carl Mehler, *Director of Maps*

R. Gary Colbert, *Production Director*

Jennifer A. Thornton, *Managing Editor*

Meredith C. Wilcox, *Administrative Director, Illustrations*

Staff for This Book

Barbara A. Noe, *Project Manager & Senior Editor*

Kay Kobor Hankins, *Art Director*

Al Morrow, *Design Assistant*

Michael McNey, *Map Production*

Judith Klein, *Production Editor*

Brittany Brown, Ashley Matthieu, Stephanie Robichaux,
Jane Sunderland, Christine Tanigawa, Sally Younger,
Contributors

Manufacturing and Quality Management

Christopher A. Liedel, *Chief Financial Officer*

Phillip L. Schlosser, *Vice President*

Chris Brown, *Technical Director*

Nicole Elliott, *Manager*

Rachel Faulise, *Manager*

Robert L. Barr, *Manager*

The Brown Reference Group Ltd.

Lindsey Lowe, *Editorial Director*

Tim Harris, *Managing Editor*

David Poole, *Design Manager*

Supriya Sahai, *Senior Designer*

Joan Curtis, *Designer*

Sophie Mortimer, *Picture Manager*

Martin Darlison, *Cartographer*

Clive Carpenter, Joe Fullman, Alastair Gourlay,
Leon Gray, Ben Hollingum, Sally McFall, *Contributors*

National Geographic Traveler: Scotland
ISBN 978-1-4262-0671-9

The National Geographic Society is one of the world's largest nonprofit scientific and educational organizations. Founded in 1888 to "increase and diffuse geographic knowledge," the Society works to inspire people to care about the planet. National Geographic reflects the world through its magazines, television programs, films, music and radio, books, DVDs, maps, exhibitions, live events, school publishing programs, interactive media and merchandise. *National Geographic* magazine, the Society's official journal, published in English and 32 local-language editions, is read by more than 35 million people each month. The National Geographic Channel reaches 320 million households in 34 languages in 166 countries. National Geographic Digital Media receives more than 13 million visitors a month. National Geographic has funded more than 9,200 scientific research, conservation, and exploration projects and supports an education program promoting geography literacy. For more information, visit nationalgeographic.com.

For more information, please call 1-800-NGS LINE (647-5463) or write to the following address:

National Geographic Society
1145 17th Street N.W.
Washington, D.C. 20036-4688 U.S.A.

Visit us online at www.nationalgeographic.com

For information about special discounts for bulk purchases, please contact National Geographic Books Special Sales: ngspecsales@ngs.org

For rights or permissions inquiries, please contact National Geographic Books Subsidiary Rights: ngbookrights@ngs.org

The information in this book has been carefully checked and to the best of our knowledge is accurate. However, details are subject to change, and the National Geographic Society cannot be responsible for such changes, or for errors or omissions. Assessments of sites, hotels, and restaurants are based on the author's subjective opinions, which do not necessarily reflect the publisher's opinion.

Printed in China

10/TS/1

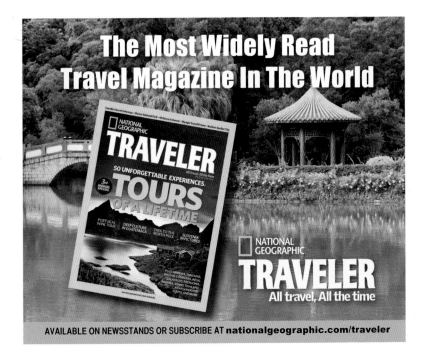